MODERN EUROPE 1870–1945

Christopher Culpin and Ruth Henig

 LONGMAN

Contents

Contents

WITHDRAWN   940.287

Editorial introduction

This aim of this book is to give you as clear a picture as possible of the events and developments in the period you are studying. You may well be using this book to prepare for an examination and the book has several special features, listed below, to help you in this. Most of all, we hope it will help you to develop a critical awareness about, and a continuing interest in, the past.

FOCUS: Each chapter has a main focus, listed in the contents. These are the main issues and 'concepts', like cause and consequence, the evaluation of evidence, the role of the individual, key themes, historical controversies or interpretations and so on. All of these are important in studying and understanding history. Identifying a focus does not mean that the chapter only looks at the past in one way; rather that you are encouraged to find out about topics from a different slant.

TIME CHARTS: Most chapters begin with a time chart. It helps you follow the chronology. Some time charts develop a basic point which is not in the main text. You should also find that the charts provide you with a handy reference point.

KEY TERMS: There are some words or phrases which it is important to know in order to understand a wider topic. These have been highlighted in the text so that you can easily look up what they mean. Sometimes quite simple ideas appear in unfamiliar form or in jargon. Decoding these should help you to make sense of the wider ideas to which the terms relate. Towards the end of the book you will find a separate index of the key terms.

PROFILES: There is not space in a book like this to provide full biographies of the people you will meet. The profiles give you the information you need to understand why an individual is important and what his or her main achievements were. Like the time charts, you might want to use these for reference. As with 'key terms', there is a separate index of people who are the subject of profiles.

TASKS and ACTIVITIES: Nearly all the chapters end with some suggestions for follow-up work and further study. These include:

- guidance on how, and why, to take notes
- suggestions for class discussion and debate

- help on how to use historical evidence of different types
- tips on answering source questions
- hints on planning and writing essays
- specimen examination questions so that you can prepare for assessment.

These tasks are listed in the contents.

FURTHER READING: You will find that you need more help on certain topics than can be provided in a book like this. The further reading guides you to some more detailed or specialist texts. The reading is listed with the most immediately obvious supporting texts placed first, followed by others – some of which may be considerably more detailed – and ending with articles and other shorter pieces, where these are appropriate.

INDEX: Many individuals, issues and themes are mentioned in more than one chapter. The index is designed to help you find what you are looking for quickly and easily by showing you how to collect together information which is spread about. Get practice in using an index; it will save you a lot of time.

The historian's job is to recreate the past. On one level, this is obviously an impossible task. There is far too much of it to put into one book while at the same time much of the information we need has been long since lost. Most of it can never be recovered. It is because there is so much of it that the historian has to impose his or her priorities by selecting. It is because so much more has been lost that he or she has to try to fill in the gaps and supply answers which other people can challenge. The processes of **Selection** and **Interpretation** are the key tasks of the historian and they help to make the subject endlessly fascinating. Every time a historian makes a decision about what to put in and what to leave out that decision implies a judgement which others might challenge. Historians try to get as close to the truth as they can, in the knowledge that others may disagree with what they say. Don't be surprised, then, to find a number of personal views or 'interpretations'. Some of these will make comparisons between the present and the period you are studying. These personal views have not been included in order to persuade you to agree with them. We aim to make you *think* about what you are reading and not always to accept everything at face value. If this book helps you to tell the difference between fact and opinion while keeping up your interest in the past, it will have served its purpose.

Christopher Culpin
Eric Evans
Series Editors

Introduction to modern European history

More A-Level and AS historians study Europe in the late nineteenth and early twentieth centuries than any other period of history. It is easy to see why. Europe in 1870 was overwhelmingly the world's most powerful and developed continent, and it remained so (though under increasing challenge from the United States) until 1945. Europe had already witnessed substantial change in the 80 years before 1870 as a result of the huge impact of the French Revolution and of the rise of new nation states. Our book follows a still more hectic and fascinating period of change, development and, all too frequently, crisis. It covers two world wars of unprecedented ferocity and importance. It also charts the rise and fall of two of the most brutal and evil empires the world has ever seen, Stalin's in Russia and Hitler's in Germany.

Alongside these massive themes, the book tries to make sense of a complex mosaic of other changes. Unless we understand these, it is still difficult for us to make sense of the world in which we live, although more than half a century has passed since the last events discussed in detail in this book. We begin with confident new nation states – a united Germany and a recently united Italy – on the threshold of major, but destabilising, developments and end 75 years later with a war-shattered continent needing to rebuild itself and trying to put in place new structures to ensure peace and stability rather than war and conflict.

You will find that the book deals with six major themes. They feature, to a greater or lesser extent, in all the chapters and it is important to introduce them to you at the outset.

1 The first is Europe's **economic development** which underwent such a dramatic transformation from the middle of the nineteenth century. As countries industrialised, their populations moved *en masse* from small, rural communities to major urban centres. Industrialisation increased a country's power by enhancing its military capacity, and therefore added to international tensions. It also opened up new opportunities and created substantial social and political problems at home.

2 **Political change** on a sweeping scale is another major theme of this period. The French Revolution had spread ideas of liberty and of nationalism around Europe. Old rulers were increasingly challenged, and states adopted a range of constitutional governments. As countries became more unified and more urbanised, mass electorates emerged which demanded a greater say in government. Campaigns for major political changes, and the responses of governments, form an important element of European history in this period.

3 The period also witnessed major **social change**. People's everyday lives were changed out of all recognition, as they moved from a rural to an urban environment, received an elementary education and were able to travel, read daily newspapers and, by the 1920s, listen to radio. Social change generated significant pressures among different groups for more resources and more power. Some groups pressed for more rapid changes; others fought to prevent change. The resulting tensions undermined many governments and brought new types of leaders to power.

4 This period witnessed two great **military conflicts** which totally changed the political and economic face of Europe.

5 Our fifth theme is a very specific one: the role and importance of **individuals** in history. This period of history produced some of the most powerful leaders the world has ever seen. They were hemmed in by economic, social and political pressures, yet they carried through sweeping changes which transformed the world around them. It is always difficult to assess the extent to which individuals alone have the power to challenge their environment and to bring about change. What this book does demonstrate beyond question, however, is the tremendous impact which individual leaders have made on the modern world.

6 **Aspects of continuity and stability**: while much changed in Europe between 1870 and 1945, there were some aspects of life which changed little if at all. Religious beliefs remained strong among large sections of the population. Affinities with particular localities or cultural traditions still shaped people's attitudes and behaviour. Our final theme is to be found in the histories of all countries and of all periods, the interplay between the forces of continuity and the forces of change.

The book is organised in a broadly chronological way, which is to say that it begins in 1870 and works its way through to the end of the Second World War in 1945. Each chapter is a self-contained unit and, to make sense of the book's overall themes, it is not necessary to start at the beginning and work doggedly through to the end.

This period is one of the most exciting and dramatic known to historians. We hope that we can convey to you some of that excitement and drama, and, in doing so, increase your appetite for history itself.

1 How successful was Bismarck in achieving his aims?

Time chart

1815: Establishment of German Confederation. Birth of Bismarck

1834: Formation of German *Zollverein* or customs union

1862: Bismarck appointed prime minister of Prussia

1864: Schleswig-Holstein crisis

1866: War between Prussia and Austria, resulting in Prussian victory

1867: North German Confederation established

1870–71: War between Prussia and France, resulting in a defeat for France

1871: Proclamation of German Empire

1872–3: May laws/Falk laws

1872: League of the Three Emperors (*Dreikaiserbund*) formed between Germany, Austria-Hungary and Russia

1878: Anti-Socialist law passed
Congress of Berlin to settle potential conflicts in Balkans

1879: Alliance with Austria

1881: *Dreikaiserbund* renewed

1882: Triple Alliance formed linking together Germany, Austria-Hungary and Italy

1883: Sickness insurance scheme established

1884: Accident insurance scheme adopted

1887: Mediterranean agreements link Austria-Hungary, Italy and Great Britain. End of *Kulturkampf*. Reinsurance Treaty with Russia

1889: Old age pensions scheme introduced

1890: Kaiser Wilhelm II dismisses **Bismarck**

There can be no doubt about the importance of Bismarck's role as the chief architect of the new German Empire and as one of the outstanding leaders of the nineteenth century. Contemporaries described him as a

1

PROFILE: *Bismarck*

Otto von Bismarck was born in Schönhausen, Germany in 1815, and studied law and agriculture as a young man. He became an ultra-Royalist member of the Prussian parliament in 1847, and served as a Prussian member of the German Diet at Frankfurt between 1851 and 1859, vigorously defending Prussian interests in the face of Austrian domination. He was appointed as ambassador to Russia in 1859, and in 1862 he was recalled to Prussia and offered the position of Prime Minister by the king who was anxious to crush parliamentary opposition to his policies. Bismarck successfully resolved the crisis by dissolving parliament and subsequently masterminding the unification of Germany under Prussian leadership. To this end, three wars were fought by Prussia, over the provinces of Schleswig-Holstein in 1864, against Austria in 1866 and France in 1870–71. Bismarck served as Chancellor of the new German Empire from 1871 until his dismissal in 1890. He died in 1898.

'powerful genius' and a 'great statesman'. Recent historians, while agreeing that he was 'a splendid judge of political opportunities', have also drawn attention to his less desirable attributes such as vindictiveness, a desire to dominate, and the achievement of objectives by the use of threats and bullying.

This chapter seeks to assess the nature of Bismarck's achievements. It will look first at the establishment of the German Empire and at the basis on which it was constructed, and will then consider the ways in which Bismarck sought to protect and to strengthen it between 1871 and 1890.

It is easy to exaggerate the significance of powerful individuals in bringing about decisive change. We should note that Bismarck himself wrote in 1869, 'At least I am not so arrogant as to assume that the likes of us are able to make history. My task is to keep an eye on the currents of the latter and steer my ship in them as best I can.' At the same time, it is clear that Bismarck possessed a remarkable talent for harnessing the prevailing historical currents to serve his political aims. He was quick to identify and to exploit favourable circumstances and to act on his own initiative. One recent historian has pictured him as a 'lone wolf', and another described him as 'a lone hunter who followed no rules but his own'.

Before we go any further, we need to understand the fundamental beliefs which shaped his objectives. Bismarck's father was a Prussian **Junker** and his mother's family had served as state officials. Above all else,

KEY TERM:

Junker

A member of the Prussian aristocracy whose power rested on the ownership of large landed estates, mainly situated to the east of the river Elbe, and on their traditional role as army officers and civil servants. Their position came increasingly under threat after German unification as a result of industrialisation and economic change, but they fought hard to safeguard their existing privileges and power.

Bismarck was concerned to uphold and to extend the power of the Prussian state and the authority of the Prussian king. In this sense, he could be described as a conservative statesman, seeking to maintain and to strengthen the existing political and social structure within the traditional framework of the autocratic Prussian crown and the Lutheran church.

At the same time, Bismarck was acutely aware of the strong currents of change sweeping through mid-nineteenth-century Europe. He witnessed the 1848 revolutions, with their demands for more liberal constitutions and for unity among the German states. He was brought in by the Prussian king in 1862 to combat liberal demands for a greater say in the army reforms which the king and his army officers wished to introduce.

It became Bismarck's aim to defeat the modest demands of the Prussian liberals by turning against them some of their own weapons: the desire for a strong and united Germany, and for a more extensive franchise. In this sense, he could be described as a revolutionary conservative, prepared to use unorthodox means to achieve traditional ends. Such tactics frequently brought him into conflict with his master, the Prussian king, and antagonised the deeply conservative Prussian military and political elites. He was attacked for being unprincipled and opportunistic. But widespread distrust of his methods was combined with grudging respect for his cool judgement and substantial achievements, which made him indispensable to the Prussian monarchy for nearly 30 years.

The establishment of the German Empire

After the Napoleonic wars, the 39 different German states, varying enormously in size and traditions, combined in a loose German Confederation which was in practice dominated by Austria and Prussia. Bismarck's greatest achievement was to transform this Confederation into a German empire centred on Prussia and completely excluding Austria. His avowed aim was the expansion of Prussia and the methods he used were based not on an appeal to German national feeling but on foreign alliances and Prussian military prowess. He is reputed to have told Disraeli as early as 1862, 'I shall declare war on Austria, dissolve the German confederation, subjugate the middle and smaller states, and give Germany national unity under the control of Prussia.' With such a clear vision, and the ability to manipulate diplomatic situations to serve his declared aims, Bismarck made the complex and difficult unification process appear – with hindsight – to run very smoothly in the desired direction. The two major wars

3

Kleindeutsch

In the mid nineteenth century, there were many debates about the form which a united Germany might take. Those who argued for a 'Greater Germany' (*Grossdeutsch*) wanted it to include the 39 states of the German Confederation and the non-Hungarian parts of the Habsburg Empire, which contained many German-speaking areas, but also Czech, Polish and other ethnic communities. The 'Smaller Germany' (*Kleindeutsch*) unification excluded any provinces of Austria-Hungary, and was centred on Prussia.

against Austria in 1866 and against France in 1870 not only confirmed Prussia's military supremacy but secured Bismarck's prime objectives. Austrian influence was removed from Germany, and the 'smaller Germany' or **kleindeutsch** unification inevitably meant the expansion of Prussian power. The Prussian king became the new German ruler, and Prussian conservative institutions and customs were extended to the whole of the new German empire.

The Constitution of the North German Confederation

The constitution of the new empire was modelled on that of the North German Confederation. This was established by Bismarck after the Prussian defeat of Austria in 1866, and covered all German states north of the river Main.

A federal structure   Local rulers retained their powers to regulate the legal and educational system, the police, local forms of taxation and the structure of local government established in their particular state.

The Bundesrat   This was the upper house. It had jurisdiction over the raising of direct taxes, foreign policy, and the federal army. However, since Prussia was by far the largest state in the Confederation, her representatives inevitably dominated this body and determined its policies.

The Reichstag   The lower house. Elected by universal male suffrage – which could be seen as a giant step towards democracy – in fact its powers were extremely limited: neither the king and his advisers nor the Bundesrat, were in any way accountable to it. The reverse was in fact the case. Local rulers wielded authority in their own areas, and the Prussian king, in addition, wielded central powers on their behalf.

The Chancellor   The main driving force in the German Confederation was the federal chancellor, who represented the Prussian king in the federal legislature, and who at the same time filled the posts of prime minister and foreign minister of Prussia. Such a position was obviously tailor-made for Bismarck, who had carefully designed the constitution of the North German Confederation to fit the requirements of Prussian power and his own political position.

The Constitution of the new German Empire

The North German Confederation has been described as 'little more than an extension of Prussia and of Prussian power'. The new German Empire, proclaimed at the end of the Franco-Prussian war, in the Hall of Mirrors

Figure 1.1 *Kaiser Wilhelm I proclaimed Emperor of Germany in the Hall of Mirrors at Versailles, January 1871. Bismarck is in the white uniform, centre.*

of the Palace of Versailles in January 1871 (see Figure 1.1), extended the Confederation to embrace the four southern German states of Bavaria, Baden, Hesse and Württemberg, and the French provinces of Alsace and eastern Lorraine (see Figure 1.2). The king of Prussia was persuaded to become the new German emperor, with Bismarck as his Chancellor.

Position of Prussia   One historian has commented that the establishment of the German Empire represented 'the conquest of Germany by Prussia' and this was to have serious consequences for future German political development. For while Prussia was by far the largest and most economically advanced state in the new empire, it was politically one of the most undemocratic. Bismarck was anxious for political power in the new empire to remain in traditional hands – in those of the Emperor, his army officers, his close advisers and his hand-picked ministers, of whom Bismarck would be the chief. As the historian Lynn Abrams has commented, the German empire was in effect a 'constitutional monarchy governed by a Prussian **oligarchy**'. Karl Marx expressed it more graphically in 1875 when he described the empire as a 'military despotism cloaked in parliamentary forms'.

Federal structure   The new empire remained firmly federal in structure, and the two-chamber legislature of the Confederation was superimposed upon the Prussian assembly and on the local parliaments of the other individual states.

KEY TERM:

Oligarchy

In an **oligarchy**, government is in the hands of a small, privileged, and usually wealthy, group of individuals. They use their wealth to influence electors to support candidates of their own choice.

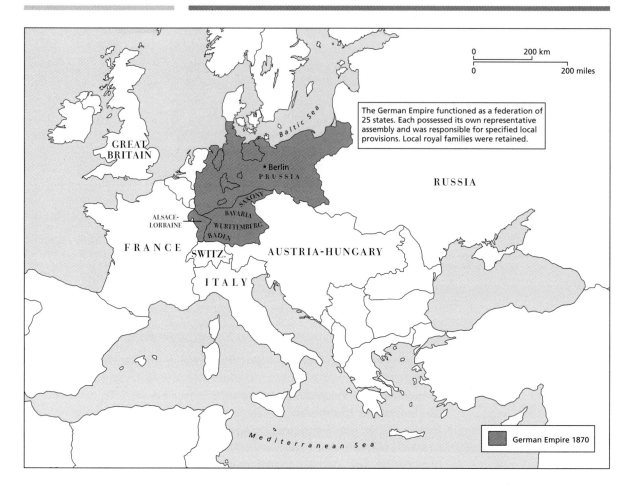

The German Empire functioned as a federation of 25 states. Each possessed its own representative assembly and was responsible for specified local provisions. Local royal families were retained.

Figure 1.2 *The German Empire in 1870*

Bundesrat In the Federal Council, or Bundesrat, Prussia occupied 17 out of the 58 seats, enough to enable her representatives to exercise a dominating influence, since the next largest state, Bavaria, had only six seats.

Reichstag Its 400 deputies were to be elected every three years, subsequently changed to every five years, in nationwide elections based on universal male suffrage. But its powers were extremely limited – in practice, confined to scrutinising the imperial budget and ratifying legislation which could subsequently be vetoed by the Bundesrat or Federal Council. It could be dissolved by the emperor on the recommendation of his chancellor, and neither the imperial government nor the chancellor were in any way answerable to the Reichstag. After 1871, the imperial offices extended their powers and gradually developed into more modern ministries, but they continued to report to the chancellor and to be responsible only to the emperor.

Despite this unpromising outlook, the new German Reichstag managed to secure an increasingly strong foothold in the imperial constitution.

While it had no control over the government, the emperor or the armed forces, it became an important sounding-board for nationwide opinions, expressed through interest groups and political parties which could be mobilised in support of government policies. As the unified German state developed economically, and embarked on a period of intense and rapid industrialisation, the Reichstag was able to perform a useful role in the drafting of new economic and social legislation. But its function remained a limited one, and Bismarck took great care to ensure that no system of responsible, democratically accountable government was allowed to develop. Instead, the principle of rule from above was entrenched in the new German empire.

Conclusion   Not surprisingly, in view of the direction taken by Germany after 1933, many recent German historians have blamed Bismarck for stifling the development of German democracy, and for laying the foundations on which Nazism could later be established. It has been argued that Bismarck's Reich 'deformed the German nation' and that the 'harm' done by the Bismarck era was 'infinitely greater than the good'. There can be no doubt that the manner in which German unification was achieved, and the basis on which the new Empire was established, had fateful political, economic and military consequences, not just for the German people themselves but for Europe as a whole.

Bismarck's domestic policies, 1871–90

While Germany was now established as a new political and geographical state, it remained extremely divided in terms of religion, culture, language and local practice. Ten per cent of its population were non-German minorities – Poles in the eastern provinces of Prussia, Danes in Schleswig and a large French population in Alsace and Lorraine. Sixty per cent of the population were Protestant, but Catholicism was strong in the French provinces, in southern Germany, in the Rhineland and among the Polish communities. The north and west of Germany contained many large cities and much industry; the south and east were predominantly rural and agricultural. The process of unification had unleashed new social and economic forces and had raised expectations of democracy and prosperity. Bismarck's aim was to unify and to consolidate the new empire but under strong and traditional Prussian leadership. Minority groups who might pose a threat to the stability of the new structure were to be severely repressed. They were identified as *Reichsfeinde* or 'enemies of the state' and subjected to continuing harassment and discrimination. Both Catholics and socialists were targeted as 'enemies of the state' between 1871 and 1890, and Bismarck sought to contain and to reduce their political and social influence.

KEY TERM:

Papal Infallibity

Doctrine of the Roman Catholic Church announced at the Vatican Council in 1870 which ruled that papal pronouncements on matters of faith and morals could not be questioned. The basis of this doctrine was that since not all questions were resolved by the Bible, further authoritative guidance needed to be provided by the Pope, God's representative on earth.

Dealing with 'enemies of the state'

1 *The Kulturkampf* Almost 40 per cent of the German population in 1871 were Catholics, and the Catholic Centre Party, formed in 1870, became the second largest party in the new German Reichstag after the National Liberal Party. It was the potential political power which the Catholics could wield throughout Germany which frightened Bismarck, together with their strong links both with the restless Polish minorities in east Prussia and with the Papacy. In 1870 the first Vatican Council issued the doctrine of **Papal Infallibility**; Bismarck's reply was to declare war on the Catholic church in Germany, breaking off diplomatic relations with the Papacy, removing Catholic privileges and expelling the Jesuit order. There followed a lengthy period of struggle between German Catholics and the new state, described by German liberals as a cultural battle or *Kulturkampf*. In Prussia, measures were passed to remove Catholic influence from the administration and inspection of schools. The Prussian Minister of Culture, Falk, aimed to go further and bring about the complete separation of church and state. Between 1872 and 1873 the Reichstag passed a series of far-reaching laws known as the May Laws or Falk Laws, to try to bring the Catholic Church under state regulation as far as possible and to limit the political power of the Catholic Centre Party. In 1874, the articles of the Prussian constitution guaranteeing religious freedom were repealed. Priests could henceforth be fined, imprisoned or even expelled from Germany if they failed to comply with the May Laws. In 1876, civil marriage was made compulsory.

It has been suggested that one of the main motives of Bismarck's campaign against the Catholic Church was a calculated political ploy: to put himself at the head of a popular, national Protestant crusade which would be widely supported by the National Liberal Party and by conservative elites in Prussia. By this means, potential political opponents of Bismarck could be diverted from criticism of the Reichstag's limited role and of Bismarck's considerable powers. The *Kulturkampf* certainly enabled Bismarck and the National Liberal Party to work closely together in the 1870s on a whole range of issues, and in this respect could be seen as successful. However, the power and influence of the Catholic Church in Germany remained considerable. The attempts to repress Catholicism met with considerable opposition, particularly in strong Catholic areas like the Rhineland. Through their own religious and social networks, welfare organisations and political associations, Catholic communities sheltered defiant priests, fought to resist discriminatory measures and fiercely maintained their religious culture and identity. The Catholic Centre Party retained, and indeed increased, its political strength in the Reichstag, and could count on the support of about 80 per cent of Catholic voters. The objective of reducing Catholic power and solidarity

KEY TERM:

KEY TERM:

Socialists

Socialists believe that all economic activity – businesses, banks, transport etc. (and everything else in society) – should be run for the benefit of everybody, not for the profit of the individuals who owned them. These ideas had been put forward in France in the 1830s but were taken up and developed by Karl Marx in *The Communist Manifesto* (1848) and *Das Kapital* (three volumes, 1867, 1884, 1894). In most countries there was disagreement among Socialists about tactics: Revolutionary Socialists believed that a violent revolution was needed to overthrow the old system; Democratic Socialists were prepared to take part in parliamentary democracy in order to use the powers of the state to achieve a more socialist economy and social organisation.

had clearly failed, and Bismarck acknowledged this by the late 1870s. Indeed, typically, he sought to turn failure to advantage, by henceforth harnessing Catholic political power in the Reichstag to the support of conservative and anti-socialist measures.

After the death of Pope Pius IX in 1878, Bismarck worked hard to improve relations with his successor, Leo XIII, and between 1879 and 1882 many of the anti-Catholic measures were repealed. The *Kulturkampf* finally drew to a close in 1887 when most of the remaining May Laws were repealed. However, there can be no doubt that in his campaign against the Catholic Church, Bismarck had gravely misjudged the strength of his opponents and opened up a serious rift between the German state and its Catholic subjects.

2 *The Socialists* Bismarck was equally unsuccessful in his attempts to repress the growing socialist movement in Germany. A Socialist Workers' Party was founded as a political party in 1875 out of two existing socialist groups; by 1878 it had considerably increased its political support, and could spread its message across Germany through the columns of around 75 party newspapers. Rapid industrial development was creating a large and concentrated working class in many German cities which was receptive both to socialist doctrines and to trade union activity. By 1877, the socialist Free Trade Unions could count on about 50,000 members.

Bismarck was extremely alarmed, and in 1875 tried to smuggle into the new criminal code provisions to prevent the stirring up of class hatred and civil disobedience which he could have used to prosecute the new party. On this occasion he was defeated by the National Liberals, but two attempts on the German Emperor's life in 1878 – despite the accused having no connections with the socialist movement on either occasion – gave Bismarck his political opportunity. An anti-Socialist Law was introduced in June 1878, for three years in the first instance, and remained in force for 12 years. Though the Socialist Workers' Party could continue to fight elections and to sit in the Reichstag, its activists at local level could be arrested, imprisoned and expelled, its clubs were closed down and its newspapers were banned.

However, despite constant police harassment and state repression – indeed perhaps because of it – the socialist movement gained in strength and popularity among German workers. Government hostility certainly contributed to its taking on a militant, Marxist policy from the 1880s. By 1890, when the anti-Socialist Law was finally discontinued, the now-renamed Social Democratic Party of Germany held 35 seats in the Reichstag; by 1914, it had more than a million members and nearly a third of the Reichstag seats. Socialism had become an even greater threat to the German empire than Catholicism.

Though Bismarck had clearly failed to curb the growing strength of the socialist movement by direct means, his strategy of attempting to reduce its appeal through a programme of state-sponsored welfare legislation was more successful. He wrote as early as 1871 that 'The action of the state is the only means of arresting the Socialist movement. We must carry out what seems justified in the Socialist programme and can be realised within the present framework of state and society.'

The speech from the throne at the opening of the new Reichstag session in 1879 called for legislation to remedy social evils, and Bismarck then battled with National Liberals and Conservatives in the Reichstag to secure legislation which would provide insurance for every German worker against accidents at work, for sickness and old age. A sickness insurance scheme was introduced in 1883, accident insurance in 1884 and disability insurance, along with a graduated pension for workers when they reached the age of 70, in 1889. Though the schemes were limited, and levels of payment were low, they nonetheless added up to the most comprehensive and far-reaching system of social welfare introduced by any state in the late nineteenth century. Indeed, Bismarck's welfare legislation was regarded as a model of social provision for other countries to aspire to, and subsequent German governments greatly extended its range. Many historians regard his social reforms as his most important and enduring legacy.

The introduction of welfare legislation was accompanied by other social measures designed to produce docile and contented subjects, loyal to the state. Most states in the new German empire had had compulsory elementary education since the beginning of the nineteenth century, and the education system could therefore be used to inculcate not just literacy and obedience but nationalist sentiments and a respect for the new German rulers and empire. Emphasis was placed on the teaching of German language, culture and history, and in 1873 and 1876 laws were passed requiring the use of German language in schools and in official exchanges.

KEY TERM:

Indoctrination

The process of constantly repeating ideas or doctrines so that recipients first understand, and then accept, them without question.

Literacy rates in Germany were extremely high – by the end of the nineteenth century fewer than five Germans in every thousand were unable to read and write – and education therefore served as a powerful weapon of **indoctrination** and of integration into the new state. An education bill introduced in 1890 did not seek to hide its main aim, 'to strengthen the state in its battle against the forces of revolution'.

The army played an extremely important role in the new empire, as it had traditionally done in Prussia; officers owed a special personal loyalty to the emperor, and were concerned to instil into their soldiers qualities such as discipline, obedience, pride in military institutions and love of the German fatherland. The system of conscription ensured that all young German men served for two to three years in the army, and this gave officers ample opportunity to build on the values already inculcated at school. However, no chances were taken – army recruits were not allowed to be members of the Social Democratic Party, and socialism was portrayed as a major threat to the stability of the state, against which the army might some day have to take action.

3 *Industrialisation* In the short term, Bismarck was successful in containing domestic challenges to the structure of the new state. Prussian power was consolidated in Germany, and Prussian values permeated society. Ironically, however, it was economic expansion, in which Bismarck took little interest and played no great part, which was to provide the greatest challenge to the stability of the empire. Unification gave an enormous boost to economic development, and helped to transform Germany in a short space of time into a major industrial state. Whereas in the mid nineteenth century, Germany's economy had been predominantly agrarian, with the majority of the labour force – around 55 per cent – working on the land, by 1907 industry was Germany's greatest employer, providing work for almost 42 per cent of the labour force. Between 1871 and 1890, towns and cities grew rapidly, with landless labourers flocking from rural areas to the new industrial centres. Heavy industry boomed, and the construction of railways encouraged further industrial developments. Dynamic economic growth, centred on the Ruhr valley and the coalfields of the Saar and Upper Silesia, produced new industrial elites and urban-based societies whose values and interests were likely to be in conflict with a traditional political structure based on the landed estates and rural influence of Prussian Junkers. A lengthy economic depression in the 1870s brought about an alliance of landed and industrial interests in favour of protective tariffs in 1879. However, this alliance of 'steel and rye' had serious consequences for German workers and for the social stability and political development of the empire after 1890, as we shall see in chapter 7.

Bismarck's foreign policy, 1871–90

Having achieved German unification through skilful diplomacy allied to military might, Bismarck's major objective was to consolidate Germany's position by stabilising Europe around her. Further conflict and wars could only threaten the security and political structure of the empire.

Patient diplomacy was required to maintain a European equilibrium and to ensure that other major powers did not draw together in alignments hostile to Germany. As far as Bismarck was concerned, Germany was a 'satiated power' after 1871.

Of the five great European powers – Britain, France, Germany, Austria-Hungary and Russia – Bismarck emphasised the importance of Germany being in a grouping of at least three. He was acutely aware of Germany's vulnerability in the heart of Europe, and of the imperative need to avoid getting involved in a war on two fronts. To these ends, he devoted enormous energy and his considerable diplomatic talents. However, the rapid French recovery after the Franco-Prussian war caused great anxiety to Bismarck during the first few years of the German empire. France's inevitable desire for military revenge and for the return of Alsace and Lorraine posed a potentially serious threat to German security. Indeed the speed at which the French paid off the war indemnity which the Prussians had imposed on them and consequently rid themselves of the German army of occupation as early as 1873 alarmed both Bismarck and his military advisers. A further war between Germany and France seemed to be on the horizon in 1875, as Bismarck clumsily tried to warn the French government of the serious consequences that were likely to follow any rapid military expansion on their part. In the event, British and Russian intervention defused the immediate crisis. But France remained a dangerous neighbour who had to be watched constantly. Bismarck worked tirelessly after 1875 to try to keep France diplomatically isolated and to encourage her to salvage her national pride outside Europe by embarking on colonial expansion in Africa and Asia.

In eastern Europe, Bismarck's task was to try to promote stability by binding together the two major rivals for power and influence, Austria-Hungary and Russia, with Germany in some diplomatic alignment. Bismarck secured this objective in 1872 by means of a meeting in Berlin of the emperors of the three monarchies. However the result, the formation of the 'League of the Three Emperors' (*Dreikaiserbund*), did not lead to any significant achievements since the three powers found it very difficult in practice to reach agreement on any concrete objectives.

The major problem facing Bismarck was that his two potential east European allies had conflicting interests, particularly in the Balkans. Each of them sought German assistance, and even the resourceful Bismarck found it impossible to give support to both or to force them to work together to settle their differences. His dilemma was made worse as a result of the Russo-Turkish war of 1877 which further weakened Turkey's hold on her Balkan provinces and brought Russia and Austria-Hungary into sharper conflict in south-east Europe. In 1878 the Congress of Berlin sought to demarcate Balkan spheres of interest between the two eastern European empires, but rivalries and instability continued to threaten south-east Europe in particular and European peace in general.

Bismarck was concerned to bolster up Habsburg power, and to prevent any move on the part of Austria-Hungary to seek French support. Therefore in 1879 he made the fateful decision to conclude a defensive alliance between Germany and Austria-Hungary in a bid to maintain French diplomatic isolation and to force Austrian cooperation with Russia. This second objective was underlined in 1881 when, for the second time, a League of the Three Emperors was constituted, this time in the form of an alliance to preserve the stability of the Near East and to pledge neutrality if one of the three empires came to be involved in war with a fourth power.

Having bound Germany, Austria-Hungary and Russia together, Bismarck now drew in Italy. In 1882, a Triple Alliance was concluded between Austria-Hungary, Germany and Italy and, at the same time, France was encouraged to pursue her colonial ambitions in Africa. Italy's naval interests in the Mediterranean, and her desire to maintain friendly relations with the world's greatest naval power, Britain, brought about a 'Mediterranean agreement' in 1887 between Italy and Britain to maintain the *status quo* in that region. In the same year, the Triple Alliance was renewed, Austria-Hungary and Germany concluded new separate treaties with Italy, and Austria-Hungary associated herself with the Anglo-Italian agreement. Nonetheless, Russia's ambitions in the Near East and attempts to expand her influence over Bulgaria continued to threaten the stability of south-eastern Europe.

Bismarck dealt with this final challenge to his diplomatic system by means of a characteristic double strategy. On the one hand, in June 1887, he concluded the Reinsurance Treaty with Russia, which bound each of the signatories to remain neutral in a war being waged by the other. There were to be two major exceptions, however. The treaty would not apply in a war caused by a German attack on France or in a conflict brought about by a Russian attack on Austria. Nonetheless, the treaty seemed to offer encouragement to Russia in her Balkan ambitions, while removing the threat to Germany of any collaboration between Russia and France.

At the same time, however, Bismarck encouraged the conclusion of a second Mediterranean Agreement, in December 1887, between Britain, Austria-Hungary and Italy. The three powers reaffirmed their intention to maintain peace and the *status quo* in the Near East, to preserve the freedom of the Straits and to uphold Turkish authority in Asia Minor.

This Agreement served as a warning to Russia that any expansionist designs on her part in the Balkans would be firmly countered.

By the time of his departure from office in 1890, Bismarck had therefore secured his diplomatic objectives in Europe. France still remained diplomatically isolated, agreements had been concluded with both Austria-Hungary and Russia, and a Mediterranean compact covered Italy and Great Britain. For the time being at least, European stability had been achieved and this was no mean achievement. But, as with his domestic policies, it is possible to argue that Bismarck's diplomatic strategy and tactics bequeathed to his successors serious long-term problems.

No network of agreements, however elaborate, could extinguish France's resentment over its military defeat and the loss of Alsace and Lorraine. Bismarck was well aware after 1871 that French hostility towards Germany would be enduring, and that French governments would exploit any opportunity to try to overturn the new European power structure. At the same time, Bismarck's alliance with Austria-Hungary inevitably alienated Russia and paved the way for a Franco-Russian understanding which could easily harden into an alliance. Bismarck worked extremely hard to keep Russia aligned to Germany, but the very scale of his efforts is an indication of the difficulties he faced in trying to keep Russia and France apart once he had opted to conclude a binding agreement with Austria-Hungary in 1879.

The Austro-German agreement itself was a dubious asset to Germany. Bismarck had hoped to use it to try to keep Austro-Russian rivalry in check and to prevent Austria-Hungary from concluding destabilising agreements with other powers. It was to be a mechanism through which Germany could control Austrian foreign policy. But it could equally be used by a declining Austria-Hungary to drag Germany into the south-east European minefield and to force it to agree to military assistance against Russia. It limited German diplomatic options and the short-term stability it yielded turned very quickly into long-term inflexibility and the tense situation of two European alliance systems confronting each other menacingly.

Conclusion

In his own day, and more recently, Bismarck has been portrayed as a national hero, as a man of action, a great statesman, architect of German unification and of Prussian and German power. He has also been attacked as a man obsessed by power for its own sake, an arch-manipulator, and the prime cause of Germany's failure after 1871 to develop a mass-based, liberal-democratic parliamentary system. As we have seen, his overriding objective was to perpetuate and to expand Prussian power within Germany, and to consolidate Germany's position in Europe. The means he employed were elaborate, exploiting fragile balances between new and old forces, between the monarchy and parliament, between competing great powers. His diplomatic prowess and negotiating skills were formidable, and he achieved his major objectives. But the systems he created, both at home and abroad, relied upon his unique blend of talents to make them work; after 1890, less skilful operators were unable to deal with the pitfalls which he had sought so hard to avoid.

Task

The class sets up a mock interview with Bismarck. Like political interviews nowadays, you pose hostile questions which 'Bismarck' has to answer. One group devises the questions and another prepares answers as Bismarck might have made them. You could change roles when the questioning shifts from domestic to foreign policy. Here are a few ideas for questions. You will think of others.

■ Autocracy and democracy: 'Didn't your cynical attitude to democracy, your strong preference for autocracy, lead your new country to mistrust democracy?'

■ 'You were always living in the past, a Prussian past – you failed to recognise the strength and legitimacy of both Roman Catholicism and Socialism, and you failed to wipe them out. You also failed to recognise that Germany's future lay as an industrial power.'

■ 'You gained your main aim in 1871 – the creation of a German Reich. However, through war and conquest, you left a legacy of resentment in France, while you taught Germany to regard war as a legitimate means of achieving diplomatic ends. These were bound to lead to major wars sooner or later. The system of rival military alliances which you created only ensured that this would be a war which ranged over most of Europe.'

Further reading

L. Abrams, *Bismarck and the German Empire, 1871–1918,* Lancaster Pamphlet (Routledge, 1995) – a good introduction to social and economic issues, though less useful for foreign policy.

William Carr, *A History of Germany, 1815–1990* (Arnold, 1991, 4th ed.) – good standard text.

Gordon Craig, *Germany, 1866–1945* (Clarendon Press, 1978) – very informative for all periods of modern German history.

Stephen Lee, *Aspects of European History, 1789–1980* (Methuen, 1982) – see chapter 13: Bismarck and the German Political Parties, 1871–9.

W. O. Simpson, *The Second Reich,* Cambridge Topics in History (CUP, 1995) – a useful introductory survey for the period 1870–1914.

A. J. P. Taylor, *Bismarck: The Man and the Statesman* (Hamish Hamilton, 1955) – still an excellent read, despite its age.

2 Was the Third Republic more than just 'The government which divided Frenchmen least'?

Time chart

1870: Third Republic proclaimed following defeat and capture of Napoleon III by Prussian army at Sedan. Gambetta flies out of Paris by balloon to lead a 'Government of National Defence'

1871: Armistice with Prussia. National Assembly elected, with monarchist majority. **Thiers** becomes 'Head of executive power', later first president
March–May Paris Commune

1873: MacMahon elected President

1874: Monet's 'Impressionist' paintings first exhibited

1877: Crisis of 16 Mai

1878: Start of the Freycinet Plan

1886: Boulanger becomes Minister for War

1889: Boulanger flees to Belgium

1892: Panama Scandal. Franco-Russian military agreement

1894: Dreyfus convicted of spying for Germany and sentenced for life to Devil's Island

1898: Esterhazy tried and acquitted. Zola writes 'J'Accuse'

1899: Dreyfus re-tried and re-convicted. Georges Méliès produces first film drama

1901: First congress of Radical and Radical-Socialist party

1902: CGT (Confédération Générale du Travail) formed

1904: Entente Cordiale

1905: Cézanne finishes 'Les Grandes Baigneuses'. Formation of SFIO

1906: Dreyfus pardoned. Clemenceau ministry

1907: Picasso's 'Les Demoiselles d'Avignon'

1909: Briand ministry. Blériot flies the Channel. Matisse paints 'La Danse'. Diaghilev and Russian ballet in Paris

1914: Jaurès assassinated. Outbreak of First World War

PROFILE: *Thiers*

Louis Adolphe Thiers was born in 1797. He served as minister to Louis Phillippe (King of France, 1830–48) several times. He opposed the Second Republic of 1848 and was a scathing critic of Napoleon III's Second Empire. He accepted the post of President of the Third Republic in 1871, negotiated peace with Prussia at the Treaty of Frankfurt and suppressed the Paris Commune. He resigned in 1873 and died four years later.

The Third Republic was born in the defeat and national humiliation of the successful Prussian invasion of France in 1870. It was periodically racked by crises and scandals which, if the newspapers were to be believed, meant that it was on the point of collapse and replacement by some other form of government. There were always groups of people who favoured other forms of government. The shifting ministries – there were 60 governments between 1871 and 1914 – gave an impression of weakness.

Thiers's famous judgement, quoted at the head of this chapter, was that the Third Republic was 'the government which divided Frenchmen least', and history has tended to confirm this downbeat assessment.

With the benefit of hindsight, we know that the Third Republic in fact lasted for 70 years. But Thiers's comment was no less than the truth as he saw it. He himself was a lifelong supporter of monarchy and opponent of **Republicanism**. He was also aware that the elections of 1871 had returned an Assembly of about 400 **monarchists** out of 645 members. On the other hand, there was a powerful left-wing tradition in France and the Commune was in control of Paris. Between these two extremes, the Third Republic seemed to have only negative and grudging support. Was this the situation throughout its life?

French society

France is not only much larger than Britain; it is a country of regions, of very different landscapes, traditions and economies. Many French historians have spent their careers working on local studies, seeing these as more useful than trying to find national patterns which may not exist. Nevertheless, we can make some broad statements about French society in the late nineteenth century.

KEY TERMS:

Republicanism

A republic is a state without a monarch or emperor. A Republican is someone who supports this form of democratic government. The beliefs of the Republican Party in France in the Third Republic are discussed on pages 20–21.

Monarchist

A supporter of rule by one person, a king/queen or emperor/empress. One-person rule, it was believed, gave strong, authoritative government. **Monarchists** opposed democracy on a universal franchise as they feared that it gave power to the masses who were easily swayed and in France smacked of the horrors of the Reign of Terror in the 1790s. Unfortunately, monarchists in France were divided between those who wanted to restore the old, pre-Revolutionary line of monarchs, those who supported the heirs of the so-called 'bourgeois monarchy' of 1830–48, and those who supported the heirs of Napoleon Bonaparte.

The 'notables'

Despite the French Revolution, France still had its wealthy aristocracy. They were mainly landowners, as they always had been, used to running the local areas where they lived. Most of them were monarchists, suspicious of the **universal suffrage** on which the Third Republic was based. The irony of being monarchists operating a republican government was not lost on them and they expected to restore some form of monarchy as soon as possible. They saw themselves as offering an old-fashioned, moral, paternalistic sort of rule to the people. They worked closely with the Roman Catholic Church, which still retained enormous power and influence in France. The Church was particularly strong in rural areas rather than in towns and played a large part at all levels of education.

These were the men to whom the French turned, in the crisis of the humiliating defeat of 1870. Most of this group had been out of power for most of the previous 40 years – only 27 per cent of those elected in 1871 had ever been involved in national politics. They represented an old, provincial, rural France.

The peasants

France was far less urbanised than Britain in 1870: 67.5 per cent of French people lived in rural areas (an urban area was defined as any place with over 2,000 people). Most of these rural French were **peasants**: 53 per cent of the land was worked by its owner-occupier. There were many local variations in livelihood, but the stereotypical peasant was hard-working, thrifty, with limited, local horizons. Figure 2.1 shows a market in rural France. Note the local costume, almost a uniform, worn especially by the women. Social contact seems as important as doing business, which looks very small scale anyway. But note the wholesaler and distillery in the background: larger-scale commerce was penetrating even into the depths of the countryside. Politically the peasants of France were regarded as inert and conservative, manipulated by others.

Workers

Of the 36.1 million people in France in 1872, less than 4 million could be called working class. There were areas of the north which were like industrialised Britain or Germany, with large factories and mines and a largely unskilled working population. Elsewhere in France there were isolated pockets of heavy industry.

There were also old-established manufacturing industries in Paris and Lyon, but here workers were skilled, often in small workshops, or self-employed. They were the heirs to the left-wing traditions of the French

Figure 2.1 *Peasants at a market in France, 1905*

Revolution and quite different from the mass of 'hands' in an industrialised factory.

The middle classes

The very rich, the upper **middle classes**, had helped to initiate the early stages of French industrialisation, from the 1830s, although more as investors than as entrepreneurs. Left-wing critics claimed that there were '200 families' who controlled all economic life in France and Republican critics called them 'a barony of bankers'. Napoleon III had certainly preferred to deal with the small group of bankers who, for example, controlled the railway companies.

Below them came a much larger group of the middle and lower middle class. This group was growing through this period: from 1876 to 1896 the percentage of the population employed in industry rose from 27.6 to 29.2 per cent but the number employed in the tertiary sector rose from 23.1 to 25.5 per cent. This sector included doctors, lawyers, shopkeepers, civil servants, local merchants, small-town bankers and, towards the bottom, clerks and schoolteachers. These were people who kept accounts, always dressed carefully, wanted their children to be educated and to get on.

KEY TERM:

Middle classes

The **middle classes** cover a very wide group of people, which is why we often subdivide them by using terms like 'lower middle class' etc. The middle classes included anyone who was not a manual worker, a peasant or an aristocrat. At the top came those who lived by investing in banks or commerce. In France these are often called the 'bourgeoisie'. Below these came business managers, shopkeepers and the professions (doctors, lawyers, civil servants, teachers). At the bottom, often earning less than a skilled manual worker, came clerks and minor officials.

PROFILE: *Léon Gambetta*

Léon Gambetta, born in 1838, joined in proclaiming the Third Republic in 1870. As a Minister in the government of National Defence, aged only 32, he escaped from the siege of Paris and for the next five months ran the French war effort. He opposed the negotiated peace. He toured France giving speeches and helped to build up support for the Third Republic among peasants and middle classes. He later formed a government from 1881 to 1882. He died in office.

The Republicans

Thiers may have thought that the Third Republic only made the best of a bad job, but others saw it more positively. From the elections of 1869 onwards, leading Republican politicians, notably **Gambetta**, put forward certain beliefs – they can hardly be called policies. Around these they began to create their support. What were these beliefs?

1 Radical rhetoric

Republicans proclaimed their support for the Revolution of 1789, which gave everyone the same rights as citizens, and the Revolution of 1848, which gave all men the vote. This made the Republicans sound radical, the heirs of the great French Revolutionary tradition.

2 Property rights

The citizen's right they emphasised most was the right to own property. They especially supported the rights of peasants to retain the land they had gained in 1789 and of business people to run their businesses freely. They liked to put themselves forward as the party of order, based on property rights.

3 Individuals not classes

Republicans rejected the Socialist doctrine of class and class conflict. They emphasised the rights of individual workers and opposed the collective solidarity of trade unions. If they spoke of social groups they called them *'couches'* (layers or strata) not classes.

4 Anti-clericalism

For the Republicans, as for many other groups, defining who they were against was as important as defining what they were for. Their

Figure 2.2 *Cover of a Republican magazine*

democratic ideals made them anti-monarchist but they also criticised the monarchists' allies, the Church. This was the late nineteenth century – an age of science, rationalism, belief in progress and popular education. Many Republicans wanted the state, and particularly the state education system, to be free of all religious influences. The Church was seen as sinister, superstitious and malevolent – the antithesis of nineteenth-century rationalism.

This fear and hostility can be seen in Figure 2.2. In this illustration a priest is portrayed as a supernatural, menacing figure over the caption 'There is the enemy!' The church he is clutching is Sacré Coeur, in Montmartre, Paris, built in the 'moral order' period of the 1870s (see page 22).

In 1871, the French people had turned to traditional, paternalistic forces and elected a right-wing Assembly with a majority of monarchists – a monarchist republic, an apparent contradiction in terms. How soon would it be before Gambetta's new Republican coalition of interests would begin to pay electoral dividends?

The defeat of the monarchists: 1871–9

Before Thiers and the new government could begin to govern France, they had first to deal with the huge problems facing the country: German troops on French soil and the Paris Commune.

An armistice was arranged in January 1871. Thiers negotiated the terms of the Treaty of Frankfurt: France had to pay 5,000 million francs to the newly united Germany, which also gained the provinces of Alsace and Lorraine. The recovery of the lost provinces was the prime aim of French foreign policy for the next 48 years.

During the siege of Paris by the Germans, from September 1870 to January 1871, most Parisian men had joined the National Guard. The Committee of the National Guard in Paris was virtually the government of Paris and displayed left-wing views. Thiers and the government were suspicious of Paris, where revolutions had caused changes in government in 1789, 1814, 1830, 1848 and 1870. In March 1871 they ordered the stopping of payments to National Guardsmen and sent troops to seize guns in Paris. They were prevented by an angry mob and two generals were killed. Thiers ordered the withdrawal of all forces and government officials from Paris. The Committee of the National Guard held elections and set up the Paris Commune – an independent, revolutionary commune.

After laying siege to Paris for two months, Thiers's government sent in troops to crush the Commune in May 1871. Soldiers had orders to shoot on sight anyone who resisted and the Communards retaliated. Class hatred was rampant and 20,000 people were executed or massacred. Life in Paris returned to normal surprisingly quickly after the destruction of much of the city, but the 'left' in France was in disarray, and discredited with the electorate, for a whole generation.

MacMahon and 'moral order'

The deputies now began to discuss ways of restoring the monarchy. Thiers was forced to resign in 1873, as too committed to Republicanism, and Marshal MacMahon was elected President in his place. He promised a 'moral order', a phrase reflecting the strong Catholic influence on him and his ministers. However, the tide of feeling that had elected them in early 1871 was now ebbing away fast, leaving the monarchists in an increasingly untenable position.

Their leader, the Duc de Broglie, was aloof and a poor speaker. The restoration of the monarchy grew more and more unlikely as different groups of monarchists squabbled among themselves. When they finally agreed on a candidate, he refused to accept the tricolor as his flag. This 'fiasco of the flags' made the Republicans look like the party of order and stability, while, curiously, the monarchists looked like the party of change. The Republicans were gaining support in **by-elections**, winning 99 of the first 114 seats contested.

The monarchists also openly supported the religious revival taking place in France. However, this religious revival did not have widespread support, and the monarchists were seen to be aligned with one, unrepresentative, faction in the country.

In 1875 the new constitution was agreed. There was violent disagreement over whether it should be called a republic, even though it clearly wasn't anything else. There was to be:

- a strong President, a role that some hoped could in the future be taken by a monarch or emperor
- a Senate, including life members, which over-represented rural areas.

These two were intended to counter-balance the Chamber, elected on universal suffrage.

The crisis of 16 Mai

After the 1876 elections about two-thirds of the representatives were Republicans. This led to a struggle for power between MacMahon and the Republicans culminating in the crisis of 16 Mai 1877.

KEY TERM:

By-election

In a general election all the seats in an assembly are contested. In between general elections a **by-election** is held when a seat becomes vacant, through death or retirement of the elected member, in order to fill that seat. They are therefore one-off events.

MacMahon dismissed his Republican ministers and asked the Duc de Broglie to form a government: it was within the President's power to choose whom he liked. However, in order to govern, that person had to be able to get their measures through the Assembly. The Republican majority refused. MacMahon called for new elections. The government used all its influence to promote its own candidates. Gambetta used all his oratorical and organisational skills. A Republican majority was returned.

MacMahon balked at the idea of a coup and possible civil war and decided he had to accept the verdict of the election. The last straw for him was the Senate elections of 1879. A Republican majority was returned and he resigned. The Third Republic was safe.

The Republican triumph, 1879–99

The Republicans seemed to have found a stance (see above) which united peasants and middle classes to bring electoral success. Now they set about giving expression to the kind of France their supporters wanted. There were some symbolic changes: the Parliament moved back to Paris; the 'Marseillaise' became the national anthem and 14 July a national holiday. But there were also more serious programmes:

1 *Democratisation* Some of the more repressive measures of the 'moral order' period were removed: in 1881 freedom of the press was declared, along with the right to hold public meetings. From 1882 and 1884 mayors and local councils were to be elected. These elections helped to break the control of the 'notables' over local affairs and established the Republicans in power. In 1884 trade unions were legalised and in the same year life membership of the Senate was abolished.

2 *Railways* One of the complaints of provincial business people was that the French railway system was inadequate and its rates more expensive than those in other countries. They blamed the elite of bankers, many of them monarchists, who controlled them. They wanted good communications to break up local monopolies and make France into a real national market for the first time.

The Freycinet Plan, beginning in 1878, set about a huge construction programme of ports, canals and 16,000 kilometres of railway. The Republicans resisted calls from their more radical members for state control of the railways.

3 *Education* The importance of education was a central Republican belief. By spending their childhood years sitting together on the

---

> **PROFILE:** *Jules Ferry*
>
> **B**orn in 1832, **Jules Ferry** was, like many Republicans, trained as a lawyer. He was Mayor of Paris during the siege of 1870–71 and always a rival to Gambetta within the Republicans. He masterminded the anti-clerical educational reforms and supported French Imperial expansion. He died at the age of 71.

school bench, children of all classes would learn to respect each other and have Republican patriotism instilled in them. A rational, scientific curriculum would be the best defence against clericalism and socialism. Many local Republicans had, in fact, already begun educational schemes, setting up schools, libraries and adult classes. Yet in 1876 the church controlled 40 per cent of all primary schools, taught over half of all schoolgirls, and many boys, and ran colleges and universities. **Ferry's** education reforms changed all this:

▇ primary education was made free for all between the ages of 6 and 13 in 1881, and compulsory in 1882

▇ by a law of 1886 religious orders were to be completely phased out of teaching in state schools

▇ state secondary schools for girls were set up and universities freed from religious intervention in their affairs.

4 *Tariffs* The Republicans, however much they might have in common with British liberals, were not free-traders. French producers wanted protection from competition from British or German industrial goods. French peasant farmers were only slowly moving from farming for subsistence to farming for the market. They also wanted protection from cheap food imports. In 1881 protective tariffs were introduced and these were extended by the Méline tariff of 1892.

5 *Colonies* There were also economic motives behind French imperialism, encouraged by Ferry. New possessions in Indo-China, Tunisia, Madagascar and West Africa were taken over and land seized from native Algerians to give to settlers. However, imperialism was regarded by many as suspect, a distraction from the only lands which really mattered: the two provinces lost in 1871.

Boulanger

The Republican enjoyment of power was shaken by the man they appointed as Minister of War in 1886, General Boulanger. His sympathy with the common soldier, his veiled threats to Bismarck, heightened by his press coverage, made him enormously popular. He brought together opponents of the Republicans from the right and the left. Republicans were paranoid over the dangerous appeal of the 'strong man' in French politics and sent him away from Paris. Then, in 1887, Daniel Wilson, President Grévy's son-in-law, was accused of selling honours. With Republican politicians tainted with corruption, there was much talk of a *coup d'état*. Boulanger threw in his lot with the monarchist Right following his dismissal from the army in 1888. This allowed him to stand in by-elections: he won seven out of eight in 1888 and another in Paris in 1889, winning votes from Radical Republicans as well as from the traditional Right. Accused of treason in 1889, he lost his nerve and fled to Brussels.

The Republicans' opponents

The Right   The old, monarchist right had shot their bolt in the crisis of 16 Mai 1877. They were permanently out of office, locally and nationally. Some moved into cooperation with the right of the Republicans. In the 1890s there was even a Roman Catholic 'Ralliement', a move to work with the Republicans to form a broad conservative group.

The Left   Left-wing opposition to the Third Republic was weak and disunited until after 1900. France had several revolutionary and socialist groups, each with heroes and traditions of their own, many of them pre-dating Karl Marx. Each group was convinced they were right. It also took 20 years for working-class politics to recover from the defeat of the Commune. Meanwhile, the Republicans had stolen some of the revolutionary rhetoric for themselves.

Far fewer French workers were in trade unions than in Britain or Germany. In 1895 the Confédération Générale du Travail (CGT) was formed, a national federation of trade unions of skilled craftspeople. The French anarchist tradition led many trade unionists towards **syndicalism**, and contempt for reform through Parliamentary socialism.

The largest socialist party was the Parti Ouvrier Français, led by Guesde, but they had to compete for working-class votes with Radical Republicans, Boulangists and independent Socialists like Jaurès. Only 12 Socialists were returned in the 1889 elections, although this rose to about 50 in 1893.

The Republicans in the 1890s were thus secure, shaken only by the Panama Scandal and the anarchist's bomb which killed President Carnot in 1894. Concern at the growth of Socialism led to a drift towards right-Republican administrations. Then came the Dreyfus Affair.

KEY TERM:

Syndicalism

A 'syndicat' is the French term for a trade union. Syndicalists despised political action. They believed that the state could be overthrown by strikes of important workers, or a general strike. **Syndicalism** is a combination of the ideas of Karl Marx and the French anarchist Proudhon. It was developed in the 1890s by Fernand Pelloutier and took strong hold in the CGT as well as in trade unions in other countries, notably amongst Welsh miners.

> ### *The Panama scandal*
>
> In 1881, Ferdinand de Lesseps, successful builder of the Suez Canal, proposed to build a canal across Panama, linking the Caribbean and the Pacific. Lots of small investors put their savings into the scheme. However, building the canal was much more difficult than de Lesseps had realised. His company went bankrupt in 1889 and investors lost almost everything. When full details of the bankruptcy were revealed in 1892, several politicians were found to have received money not to reveal how great de Lesseps' difficulties were until it was too late. However, their opponents were too weak to use the scandal to bring down the Republicans.

Dreyfus

In 1894 a cleaner who was working for French counter-espionage handed over a document she had recovered from the wastepaper basket of the German military attaché in Paris. It seemed to come from a spy in the French army. A Jewish officer, Alfred Dreyfus, was arrested and tried for treason. There seemed to be no motive: Dreyfus was well-off and patriotic. The evidence was slim but the army was under pressure to convict someone so they supplied the judges, but not the defence, with a secret file which further incriminated Dreyfus. He was found guilty, humiliatingly stripped of his military insignia in a public ceremony and sent for life to Devil's Island, in the Caribbean.

That was not the end of it, however. Dreyfus's wife and his brother, Mathieu, were convinced of his innocence. They campaigned ceaselessly. In 1896 another note came to light, written by a French officer, Major Esterhazy, to the German military attaché. Colonel Picquart, now in charge of counter-espionage, became convinced Dreyfus was innocent but was removed from his post. The army dared not re-open the case because of the secret file and the Republican government supported them to avoid another scandal. As part of the army 'cover-up', Major Henry faked other documents to add to Dreyfus's file, 'proving' his guilt. The matter rumbled on in the newspapers and in 1898, in an effort to settle the matter, Esterhazy was tried and acquitted.

Two days later the writer Émile Zola published an article about the case under a headline provided by the Radical politician, Clemenceau, 'J'Accuse':

> *'I accuse the first court-martial [of Dreyfus] of having violated the law in convicting an accused person on the evidence of a document that was kept secret and I accuse the second court-martial [of Esterhazy] of having covered up this illegality by committing in its turn the political crime of knowingly acquitting a guilty person.'*

From then on the Dreyfus Case became the Dreyfus Affair, with forces on both sides using the issues it raised to attack the government and promote their own advantage. Some historians have argued that the violent passions the Affair stirred up were confined to newspapers, politicians, intellectuals and what we would now call 'the chattering classes'. Certainly feelings did not run so high in the village bars and provincial town cafés, but the Affair did alter French politics permanently.

KEY TERM:

Democracy

Democracy is a system in which all citizens choose the government, usually by voting in elections.

The Right claimed that the army could not have made a mistake and it was unpatriotic to criticise it. Extreme Catholic and anti-semitic newspapers blamed the whole Dreyfus campaign on an 'international Jewish conspiracy'. To the Right, the nation, the army and its prestige and morale were more important than justice to one individual, more important than **democracy**. The roots of twentieth-century French Fascism emerged: anti-democratic, nationalist and anti-semitic.

The Left also had its conspiracy theory: an alliance of '*le sabre et le goupillon*' ['the sabre and the holy water sprinkler' *i.e.* the Army and the Church]. There was a resurgence of militant anti-clericalism. Socialists had to consider their position: many, including Jaurès, could see that justice for an individual was an important principle and supported Dreyfus. The Affair strengthened the hand of those who wanted Socialists to participate in the democratic process, even to take part in government.

The Republicans split. Right Republicans, who had been in power through the 1890s, had resisted giving justice to Dreyfus and now joined with other groups on the Right. They shared nationalist priorities and hostility to Socialism. The Left had supported Dreyfus and now gained strength. They made links with the Radicals and the Socialists and in 1899 a left Republican, Waldeck-Rousseau, formed a government which included a Socialist minister, Millerand. A move further left took place in 1902: Combes led a ministry supported by the 'Bloc', an alliance of left Republicans, Radicals, Radical-Socialists and Socialists.

The Dreyfus Affair soon unravelled: the forgeries were discovered and Henry committed suicide in 1898. Dreyfus was recalled and re-tried in 1899. The army judges could not bring themselves to acquit him. Instead they found him guilty 'with extenuating circumstances' (whatever that might mean). He was pardoned but not formally cleared until 1906.

The Radical Republic, 1899–1914

The one issue which could keep the 'Bloc' together was anti-clericalism. We have already seen this in action in Ferry's educational reforms of the 1880s and it was certainly a popular cause. In 1901 Combes's government dissolved all religious orders and confiscated their property, and in 1904 clergy were forbidden to teach in any school. In 1905 the Roman Catholic Church in France was disestablished.

What else might the Radicals achieve? In France, as in Britain and else-where in industrialised Europe, the key issue of the day was what was called 'The Social Question'. This was a shorthand for all the problems of industrialisation and urbanisation: health, housing, welfare, working conditions, workers' rights and so on. The Left was pressing these issues hard. The trade unions joined together in the CGT (Confédération Générale du Travail) in 1895 and made their strength felt through a number of serious strikes: electricians blacked out Paris in 1907 and seamen, dockers, postmen and railwaymen all caused havoc through industrial action. In 1905 the various Socialist groups joined together in the SFIO (Section Française de l'Internationale Ouvrière). They gradually increased their parliamentary strength, gaining 103 seats in 1914.

The Radicals' response was minimal and far from radical. Clemenceau's government (1906–9), for example, came to power with a programme of 17 pieces of legislation. In fact Clemenceau gained the nickname '*le premier flic de France*' (France's top cop) for using troops to break strikes. He arrested leaders of the CGT and used troops to break up wine-growers' demonstrations in 1907. Only one plank of his programme was carried out: the nationalisation of the Western Railway. Some items did become law later: old age pensions, in 1910, and income tax, in 1914.

Conclusion

What of the lives of ordinary Frenchmen and women during these years? Some have called them years of stagnation. The population rose to 39.6 million in 1911, a rise of only 9.7 per cent since 1871 (Germany's rose by 57.8 per cent in the same period). The French birth rate was only 19.5 per 1,000 people (Germany: 29.1). Thirteen per cent of the French were over 59 in 1911 and only 35 per cent under 21 (Germany: 8 per cent over 59 and 44 per cent under 21). Do these figures reflect a happy and successful society? Are they anything to do with the Third Republic? If so, are they a cause or a result of the Third Republic?

Industrial growth was slow during the 1870s and 1880s but increased after about 1896; 5 per cent growth was achieved per year in the period 1906–13. Much of this growth was in new industries: chemicals, electrics, cars (both Renault and Citröen started in these years). But France was still 56 per cent rural, and agriculture was certainly almost stagnant, with its peasant, mainly subsistence, economy largely unchanged. French society was still very conservative. Women did not have the right to vote; they were treated as minors in law. Only 0.3 per cent of lawyers and 3 per cent of doctors were women.

Nevertheless, the years 1870–1914 were regarded by many French people, afterwards, as a glorious period – the '*Belle Epoque*'. Certainly painting, sculpture, music, literature, science and philosophy all flourished. Paris was not only the cultural and artistic capital of Europe, it also gained its reputation for fun and entertainment. Is there any link at all between the achievements of the '*Belle Epoque*' and the Third Republic?

Let us end with two more judgements of the Third Republic to set alongside that of Thiers:

> '*It doesn't govern very much and I'm tempted to praise it for this more than anything else.*'
>
> Anatole France, contemporary novelist.

> '*The system was adapted to the needs, inclinations, even the failings of the French people.*'
>
> André Siegfried, historian son of a leading Republican politician.

Task

You will have probably learned, during your earlier history lessons, that historians find out about the past by using historical sources. You will also have learned some of the basic techniques for evaluating and making use of historical sources: looking at who wrote it, when, why, in what context and so on. This skill (or rather, group of skills) continues to be important in A and AS study and examinations. As you would expect, source analysis at A Level is demanding. It might involve using more sources and/or longer sources. It could require wider and deeper knowledge of the historical context that gave rise to the source. Throughout this book there are examples of the kind of source analysis work you might be asked to do in one of your A or AS papers. Here is the first:

Below are six extracts from the speeches of Léon Gambetta, made during the period when he was defining what the Republicans stood for and who they were seeking to win over as their supporters. Read them and answer the questions which follow.

A

'I am a candidate of democracy, which, precisely because it is radical, is that much more devoted to order, the fundamental basis of all societies, and to liberty, which provides the indispensable guarantee necessary to protect the dignity and rights of all.' (1869)

B

'What we want is a rural Assembly in the broadest and truest sense of the word, for a true rural Assembly is not a collection of backward country gentry, but a body composed of free and enlightened peasants.' (1870)

C

'I do not want the new Frenchman only to be able to think, read and reason: I want him to act and to fight. At the side of the teacher the physical instructor and the soldier must stand; so that our children, who will be our soldiers as well as our future citizens, can handle a sword, shoot a rifle, carry out long marches, sleep under the stars, endure bravely all conceivable hardships for the fatherland.' (1870)

D

'France cannot be governed in opposition to the bourgeoisie; at the same time, their interests cannot be allowed to predominate to the total exclusion of labouring people. Only the Republic can effect the harmonious reconciliation between the legitimate demands of workers and respect for the sacred rights of property ... To attain this goal, two things are necessary: to dissolve the fears of one and to calm the passions of the other; to teach the bourgeoisie to cherish democratic government and to teach the people to have confidence in their elder brothers.' (1870)

E

'[The Republican Party is] a conservative party ... which assures the peaceful and legal working out of the legitimate consequences of the French Revolution.' (1872)

F

*'All these elements [small businesses and peasants] have attained a degree of prosperity and they comprise the "*nouvelles couches sociales*" [new social strata] of which I have spoken before. Remember, gentlemen, I said* couches *not* classes: *that is a distasteful word I never use.'* (1874)

1 Use all six of these sources to make a list of those things or people the Republicans were for and those they were against.

2 On the evidence of these sources which groups in society did Gambetta seek to cultivate and how did he intend to do this?

3 'Radical', 'democracy', 'liberty' (Source A); 'conservative' (Source E). How did Gambetta seek to reconcile these apparently opposite ideas?

4 Why did Gambetta claim to find the use of the word 'classes' (Source F) 'distasteful'?

5 Use the information in this chapter, and the sources A–F, to explain how the Republicans tried to put their views of society and the reconciliation of classes into practice, up to 1899.

Further reading

R. D. Anderson, *France 1870–1914* (Routledge and Kegan Paul, 1977) – chapter 1 gives a good account of the whole period, useful for revision. The rest of the book has detailed accounts of important aspects of France in the Third Republic.

Keith Randell, *France: The Third Republic 1870–1914* (Hodder and Stoughton, 1986). This volume in the 'Access to History' series gives plenty of detail in the readable form associated with this series.

Alfred Cobban, *A History of Modern France*, vol. 2 (Penguin, 1961) and J. P. T. Bury, *France 1814–1940* (Methuen, 1969) are both quite old now but give full and readable accounts.

Guy Chapman, *The Third Republic of France: the first phase, 1871–1894* (Macmillan, 1962) is more detailed than you will strictly need for A Level, but is good to read if you want to follow up a particular event or person.

It would also be interesting to read some of J. M. Mayeur and M. Reberioux, *The Third Republic from its Origins to the Great War*, published in France in 1973 and translated for Cambridge University Press in 1984.

3 Austria-Hungary 1867–1914: the Nationalist challenge

The Habsburg Empire in the nineteenth century was a diverse collection of dukedoms, crown lands and provinces which had been amassed by successive Habsburg rulers over several centuries. It extended from the Polish region of Galicia in the north-east, and the Czech and German-populated crown lands of Bohemia and Moravia in the north-west, down through the Austrian Alps, Hungary, Slovenia and Croatia, to the coastal provinces of Istria and Dalmatia on the Adriatic. The map in Figure 3.1 shows the mix of regions and of peoples contained in the empire. After 1878, the Habsburgs also administered the former Turkish possessions of Bosnia and Herzegovina in the Balkans. In territorial size, the Habsburg Empire was second only to Russia among the European powers. Like Russia, it contained many different ethnic groups. However, unlike Russia, there was no single dominating nationality.

The 1910 census revealed that German-speaking subjects numbered just under a quarter of the population, approaching some 50 million people. Twenty per cent were Magyar-speaking Hungarians, 12.5 per cent were Czechs and the Poles constituted a further 10 per cent. The remaining one-third of the population encompassed Ruthenians, Romanians, Slovaks, Slovenes, Croats, Serbs and Italians. As Professor Paul Kennedy has observed, 'Vienna controlled the most ethnically diverse cluster of peoples in Europe – when war came in 1914...the mobilisation order was given in 15 different languages'. An empire containing such a diverse mix of territories and peoples would inevitably face serious challenges in an age of modernisation, industrialisation and growing nationalism.

The 1867 'Compromise'

The Habsburg Empire's humiliating expulsion from the Italian peninsula, followed by defeat at the hands of Germany in 1866, underlined its growing weakness. The Hungarians were not slow to exploit this situation, and the Habsburgs were therefore forced to conclude the Compromise of 1867. The Empire was divided into two parts, and the price of continuing Habsburg rule in the Austrian half was to agree to Hungarian dominance in the other half (see Figure 3.1).

Figure 3.1 *Peoples of the Habsburg Empire, 1867–1918*

Thus from 1867 the Habsburg Empire became the Austro-Hungarian empire, a dual monarchy of two separate states, each with its own parliament and prime minister. The Germans in Austria agreed to this division of power only out of bitter necessity, in order to preserve their remaining political authority. The Magyars in Hungary, however, viewed it as a step on the way to ultimate independence. Hence from 1867 onwards, political divisions made the task of ruling the empire even more difficult.

There were to be joint ministries of foreign affairs, defence and finance and the respective prime ministers of the two halves were to participate in a joint Council of Ministers. There was a single army and navy, a common set of tariffs, one foreign policy and the strong unifying influence of the Roman Catholic Church. Above all, unity was symbolised by the Emperor, **Franz Josef** (see Figure 3.2). He came to the throne in 1848, and reigned for a remarkable 68 years.

PROFILE: *Franz Josef*

Francis Joseph I (German: Franz Josef) was born near Vienna in 1830 and became Emperor of Austria in 1848. He ruled the Habsburg Empire for 68 years, until his death in 1916. He favoured government by a strong central administration, and was hostile to the development of party politics. He allied the monarchy strongly to the Catholic Church.

Figure 3.2 *Emperor Franz Josef meets Kaiser Wilhelm II and German princes, towards the end of his long reign*

Despite his best efforts, the two halves of the empire developed as separate units. In the Austrian half, the Emperor's ministers found themselves trying to run an increasingly fractious federation of eight nationalities; while in Hungary the nobles and landowners concentrated their energies on constructing a national Magyar state in which the Hungarian nobility would be the dominant ruling class.

Economic and social change

Industrialisation: a mixed picture

Though Austria-Hungary contained some valuable mineral deposits and areas of rapidly advancing industrialisation, up to two-thirds of the population in Hungary and over a half in Austria continued to earn a precarious living from subsistence agriculture. Substantial economic development took place in the empire in the 50 years after 1867, but it was unevenly spread and heavily concentrated in certain areas such as the provinces of Bohemia and Moravia. Mining industries expanded, as did the production of pig iron. There was also a substantial growth in the sugar, petroleum, chemical, electricity and textile industries. Indeed, in this period the Austro-Hungarian economy enjoyed growth rates which were among the highest in Europe, recording an increase in output of some 5 per cent a year between 1873 and 1913.

However, growth rates per head of population were much more modest, illustrating the enormous variation in economic activity between the advanced regions of the empire, and rural backwaters such as Galicia and Dalmatia. The government in Austria tried hard to promote a modern infrastructure which would encourage economic development, and invested heavily in the development of railway networks and in a modern education system. The Viennese banks also played an important role in financing industrial development. But as Robin Okey has noted, 'Galicia, with more than a quarter of the population, had only 6 per cent of the industrial workforce and a per capita income one-third of that of the Alpine provinces'.

Economic development also took place in Hungary. There was a six-fold rise in the Hungarian national product between 1850 and 1913, but at the same time industrial development remained closely tied to agriculture, via trades such as brewing, sugar distilling, flour milling and the production of agricultural machinery. On the eve of the war, over 60 per cent of the population remained dependent on agriculture for their livelihood, and only 18 per cent were employed in industry. But rates of economic growth were accelerating, and the Hungarian economy was developing faster than that of Austria by 1914.

Most of the wealth, however – whether from the land or from industry – remained in the hands of the Hungarian landowning aristocracy, who increased their power between 1867 and 1914. At the turn of the century, Magyars owned nearly all of the large estates over 1,400 acres, and some 3,000 aristocrats, landowners and ecclesiastical bodies between them owned about half the arable land.

Social change

Social change to a large extent mirrored the pattern of economic development. In some parts of the empire, there was considerable evidence of increasing freedom, of substantial movement of individuals from rural areas to urban centres, and of steadily growing emancipation.

Vienna was one of the great capital cities of Europe, offering a wide range of opportunities to professional men, to artists and writers, and to members of minority groups, especially Jews who by 1890 made up 12 per cent of its population. In the decades before 1914, hundreds of thousands of people flocked to Vienna, including the young aspiring art student, Adolf Hitler. The population rose from half a million in 1840 to over 2 million in 1910. Viennese culture flourished, along with new ideas and political developments. Budapest, while not as cosmopolitan in character as Vienna, also developed in this period into a thriving cultural and political capital city, and in 1910 almost 25 per cent of its population was Jewish.

At the same time, society remained dominated by the aristocracy and landowners. There were parts of the empire where traditional rural life continued virtually unchanged, and where grinding daily poverty was the lot of the local inhabitants. For some families, emigration seemed to provide the only promise of an improvement in circumstances, and nearly 5 million people left Austria-Hungary between 1876 and 1914 (2 million of them after 1900), many hoping for a better life in the United States of America. The influence of the Church remained strong, particularly in rural areas. Many minority groups, such as Ruthenes in Galicia and the Croats and Serbs in Dalmatia, continued to live in primitive conditions in isolated village communities.

Education

Undoubtedly the most significant social development after 1867 was the spread of primary and secondary education across the empire. Levels of literacy rose sharply, especially in the Austrian half of the empire, where Czechs and Poles seized the opportunity to establish networks of schools in which their own language and cultural traditions could be taught. It is estimated that literacy levels in the Czech lands reached 98 per cent just before 1914, and by this date most Poles in the Habsburg Empire were also receiving basic education. The expansion of educational facilities for girls as well as for boys opened up new horizons and opportunities, as did an increase in more specialised secondary education and in the numbers of universities.

Educational achievements in Galicia, however, and in the Hungarian half of the empire were more modest, though equally important. Literacy levels in Hungary rose from one-third to two-thirds of the population, but the vast majority of state schools – 91 per cent after 1900 – instructed their pupils in the Hungarian language. This clearly handicapped children from minority groups. With the spread of education came the rise of a popular press, and the growth of local libraries, reading rooms and social clubs. Many of these developments stimulated, and were in turn reinforced by, a strong increase in national consciousness. Thus economic and particularly social development intensified the problems posed to the empire by the conflicting demands of the different national groups.

Nationality conflicts

Nationality issues in the Austro-Hungarian Empire presented a dual threat to the government. In the first place, quarrels between different national groups paralysed the political system in Austria and caused growing tension and resentment throughout the empire. Secondly, they involved neighbouring states and therefore acquired a dangerous international dimension. Oppressed Ruthenians in Galicia looked for support to their fellow Ukrainians in Russia; Serbs in Dalmatia and Bosnia looked to the Serbian government to free them; while Romanians in Transylvania increasingly agitated to join with their fellow nationals in independent Romania.

Nationality issues in Austria

The three main national groupings in the Austrian half of the empire were the Germans, the Czechs and the Poles. While not constituting a majority – they comprised just under 10 million of Austria's 28 million population in 1910 – the *Germans* were the largest group, exercising a dominant influence. The Habsburg dynasty was German in origin; German was its official language; and the civil service was composed largely of German officials.

The Czechs   The 6.5 million Czechs mounted an increasingly powerful challenge to German domination after 1870. They were outraged by the compromise of 1867, which so increased and entrenched Magyar power in the Hungarian part of the empire. They resolved to secure for their own people as much autonomy as possible. Their power base was in Bohemia, which was 60 per cent Czech-speaking and 40 per cent German, and in Moravia, where they constituted over 70 per cent of the population. Here they pressed for the local administration to be in Czech hands, and for an expansion of Czech schools and universities. Prague became an increasingly important Czech city, only 9 per cent German by 1910. By 1914, a powerful Czech middle class had emerged, along with a Czech bank and a network of nationalist groups and societies. Its aim at this stage was not to agitate for independence, but to increase Czech power and influence within the multinational Habsburg empire.

The Poles   To the east of Bohemia and Moravia was the province of Galicia, where most of the empire's nearly 5 million Poles lived. Like the Czechs, their aim was to secure increased autonomy in terms of control over the local administration and the school network. They also worked to maintain their dominant position in Galicia over the Ruthenians who made up 40 per cent of its population, and constituted a majority in eastern Galicia. While a Polish national identity remained strong, there seemed little prospect before 1914 of a reconstituted, independent Polish state incorporating the Poles of the German empire and of Russia as well as those of Galicia. The Poles in the Austrian Empire were therefore content to safeguard and to extend their existing rights, and to ensure that Czech and German power did not encroach on their own area of influence.

Ruthenes and Slovenes   The Ruthenes consisted mainly of poor peasant communities, many of them very remote geographically from Vienna. As their national aspirations developed, many saw their future as lying in some sort of union with the 30 million Ukrainians in Russia rather than within the Habsburg Empire. However, they exerted little political or economic influence on the Austrian government and continued until 1914 to be ruthlessly exploited by the Poles. In a slightly better position economically were the one and a quarter million Catholic Slovenes scattered around the Austrian half of the empire. They were also mainly peasants, but secured some benefits from the economic and social developments which took place after 1900.

Italians   The last national group worthy of mention were the three-quarters of a million Italians in the south Tyrol, in Trieste and Istria. Increasingly after 1900, Italian nationalists demanded their incorporation into the state of Italy. Though this was not a demand likely to be conceded by the Austrian government, the compact Italian-speaking areas of the empire constituted yet another centre of nationalist discontent and agitation.

Political attempts to resolve nationality conflicts

Taafe, Austrian Prime Minister between 1879 and 1893, commented that the best way to govern Austria was to keep all the national groups in a moderate state of dissatisfaction and to do nothing drastic to change existing conditions. However, economic and social change intensified nationalist ambitions, and challenged the prevailing policy of 'muddling through'. The Austrian parliament became increasingly paralysed as competing groups vied for power, and attempts to satisfy one group alienated the others. In 1897 the Austrian Prime Minister Badeni introduced proposals which would have had the effect of giving the Czech language equal status with German in Bohemia. The resulting German backlash led to vehement protests in parliament, to the resignation of Badeni and to the withdrawal of the decrees. The Czechs now threatened to obstruct parliamentary proceedings, and the government increasingly resorted to rule by emergency decree.

While there was some support for an attempt to recast the Austrian empire as a federation of different national groupings, there was little agreement on how, if at all, this could be achieved.

An alternative way of trying to resolve the nationality deadlock was adopted in 1907 with the granting of universal male suffrage. This move merely compounded the problems facing the Austrian government, by adding a number of class-based, but still nationalist, parties to the traditional groupings. In the first parliament to be elected on the basis of universal male suffrage, there were 17 groupings with 10 or more deputies. Of these, only one, the Social Democrats, tried to represent workers of different nationalities. Alongside them were five different German parties, four Polish ones, three Czech groups, a Croat group, a group of Italian Clericals, one of Slovene Clericals and a party of Ruthenian National Democrats. Only strong ministerial rule was able to overcome the resulting parliamentary deadlock.

Nationality issues in Hungary

The position of the Hungarians in their half of the empire was much stronger than that of the Germans in Austria. They constituted nearly half of the population, while non-Magyar groups were relatively small, rural based and divided against each other. The Hungarian government worked hard to increase Magyar influence after 1867. By 1900, 95 per cent of state officials were Hungarian, as were over 92 per cent of high school and university teachers and 87 per cent of lawyers. Hungarians also dominated industry and commerce, and comprised the bulk of the professional classes. Three-quarters of Budapest's population by 1910 were Hungarian, and this reflected the determination of the Hungarian government to transform the Hungarian half of the empire into a strong national state.

Not surprisingly, therefore, it was in Hungary that nationalist tensions rose most sharply. Increasingly, the three and a quarter million Romanians in Transylvania looked to their fellow Romanians across the border for assistance against discriminatory Magyar policies. Nearly two million Slovaks in the north of Hungary began to make common cause with Czech nationalists in a desperate attempt to counter oppressive Hungarian influence. Even Catholic Croats in the south, who were more leniently treated than other minority groups, overcame decades of suspicion of Orthodox Serbs in Dalmatia to try to form a southern Slav bloc against Hungarian power. Because the Hungarians were totally unwilling to devolve political power or to contemplate any reforms which might threaten their political and economic domination, they were able to block change in the whole empire. They fiercely resisted the introduction of

KEY TERM:

Annexation

Taking possession of territory, and adding it on to the existing state. The annexed areas are then integrated into the rest of the state, and ruled as a part of the state.

universal male suffrage, and up to 1914 only about a quarter of the population in the Hungarian half of the empire were entitled to vote under the existing property qualifications. In Hungary proper, excluding Croatia and Slavonia, in the last elections before 1918, the Magyars secured 450 parliamentary seats, while the other national groups – covering some 45 per cent of the population – gained between them only 8 seats!

Tensions in the Hungarian half of the empire were sharpened when the provinces of Bosnia and Herzegovina, administered by the Habsburgs since 1878, were formally annexed in 1908. Almost half of the population of the two provinces consisted of Orthodox Serbs, a further 30 per cent were Moslems and a quarter were Catholic Croats. The **annexation** of the provinces inflamed southern Slav passions, and the existence of 7.3 million southern Slavs now resident in the Habsburg Empire, as against only 3.3 million in an increasingly nationalist independent Serbia, raised the threatening prospect of a campaign for a united Greater Serbia. The Balkan wars of 1912–13, which saw Serbia emerge victorious and territorially and militarily stronger, increased the challenge facing the Habsburg Empire.

Behind the Serbs, and to a lesser extent behind the Ruthenes in Galicia as well, the Habsburg government perceived the greater menace of Russian expansionism. Hardly surprisingly, therefore, Austria-Hungary saw in the Sarajevo assassinations of June 1914 overwhelming evidence of the Serb government's determination to destroy the empire. It seized on them as possibly the last opportunity to crush the Serb threat once and for all, at the same time disposing of the southern Slav problem. Alas, as Samuel Williamson has commented, the ensuing war 'brought not victory or a solution to the Slav problem, but rather defeat and dissolution'.

Assessments of the state of Empire in 1914

After four years of gruelling involvement in the First World War, the Habsburg Empire collapsed suddenly in the final stages of the conflict. How strong had the Austro-Hungarian Empire been in 1914? Historians disagree about this. Some have argued that its ability to survive as a united empire for so long in the face of the enormous pressures exerted by the war demonstrates the resilience of the empire; they point out that it took four years of fierce fighting to bring about its dissolution. Others believe that the empire was already on the brink of disintegration by 1914, and that the First World War merely hastened the inevitable process.

Task: interpretation and historiography

One of the central ideas you will have to think about during your A-Level history course is that different historians reach different conclusions about the same topic. Obviously they agree on basic factual matters: no one is going to insist suddenly that Franz Josef died in 1910! But as you move on to handling bigger topics and attempting to answer more serious questions at A Level, you will encounter different interpretations and will have to reach your own judgements about them. There are several possible reasons for these differences: sometimes it is because historians have found new evidence; sometimes it is because they interpret old evidence in new ways; sometimes it is because they put different priorities on existing and known facts.

This chapter has been written in such a way as to point up three different interpretations about the state of the Habsburg Empire in 1914. The questions which follow the three views below will help you to begin to analyse these interpretations.

Read the three passages carefully.

View 1

In his book *The Habsburg Monarchy* published in 1948, A. J. P. Taylor argued that by 1914, the Habsburg empire was on its knees:

'*By 1914 the constitutional mission of the Habsburg Monarchy had everywhere ended in barren failure . . . Though* rigor mortis *was setting in, there was no lack of schemes to revivify the derelict corpse . . . All recognised the feebleness, the dead weight of bureaucracy, the conflict of national claims; yet all, without exception, looked forward to a "solution" . . . The ossified carcase of the Habsburg Monarchy kept a balance from its own dead weight. The impulse which brought the gigantic structure down had to come from without; though it could never have achieved its tremendous effect had not all been rotten within . . . Italian nationalism had been the David which brought down the old Austria; Serb nationalism was the David of Austria-Hungary.*'

View 2

In *The Habsburg Empire* by the American historian Robert Kann, published in 1957, the dilemma facing Austria-Hungary by 1914 is clearly summarised:

'The empire's attitude in foreign affairs from the time of the Bosnian crisis in 1908–9 to the outbreak of the World War . . . strongly suggests the actions of a man committing suicide from fear of death or staking his entire fortune on a gambling party. The difference between this policy and the cautious and generally passive conduct of foreign affairs during the years after 1866 was marked. The change was unquestionably connected with the accentuation of the domestic political crisis after the 1890s. The immobilisation of parliament in . . . Austria, Czech intransigence, Serb leadership in Southern Slav affairs within and outside the monarchy, the Magyar demands for revision of the Compromise . . . – all these factors played their part . . . the feeling spread "that something must be done . . . action of almost any kind offered at least a chance of survival".'

View 3

A rather different view is offered by American Bruce Pauley in *The Habsburg Legacy 1867–1939* (published in 1972).

'The picture of Austria-Hungary on the eve of the First World War is obviously complex. Those observers who have looked only at the darker side have had no trouble in persuading themselves that Austria-Hungary was doomed . . . In their view the lesser nationalities were all determined to free themselves . . . and were merely biding their time until the proper moment arrived to establish complete independence. Pro-Habsburg writers insist that the Monarchy was basically sound and was endangered only by a handful of traitors and greedy neighbours . . . Many Bohemian Czechs and Serbs, some Croats, extreme Magyar nationalists, Transylvanian Romanians, and a good many Austro-Italians were unappeased. The German Austrians, Poles, Ruthenes, Slovaks and most Magyars, Slovenes and Romanians were reasonably content. Only a smattering of radicals . . . strove for complete dismemberment of the Dual Monarchy . . .

'. . . In Austria the principle of national equality was carried further than in any other European country except Switzerland. Every nationality enjoyed full civil and cultural rights and had political influence corresponding roughly to its relative size . . .

'Only one domestic issue existed which could prove a mortal danger to the integrity of the Monarchy in the foreseeable future: Magyar nationalism. Other national ambitions might have become deadly at some later date, but dissatisfied nationalities in 1914 were still too weak and divided seriously to challenge the Habsburgs. Furthermore, the two most vital elements in the preservation of the state – the civil and military services . . . remained trustworthy.'

1 Make a list of all the points on which the historians agree.

2 Use the evidence in the chapter to provide support for each of the points of agreement.

3 Now make a summary of the points of disagreement. Use the formula: 'Historian 1 says ... but historian 2 says ... (and, possibly, historian 3 says ...)'.

4 Use the chapter to find evidence to support one, or both, sides of the points of disagreement.

5 *EITHER* Which of the passages do you think best sums up the situation facing Austria-Hungary by 1914? Write a paragraph explaining the reasons why you think so.
OR Write your own paragraph summing up your view of the situation in the Habsburg Empire in 1914.

Further reading

R. A. Kann, *The Habsburg Empire* (Octagon Books, 1973) – an interesting study of the strengths and weaknesses of the Empire.

J. W. Mason, *The Dissolution of the Austro-Hungarian Empire* (Addison Wesley Longman, 1985) – a good introduction to the problems facing the Empire in this period.

R. Okey, *Eastern Europe 1740–1985* (Hutchinson, 1982).

B. F. Pauley, *The Habsburg Legacy 1867–1939* (Holt, Rinehart, Winston, New York, 1972).

S. Williamson, *Austria-Hungary and the Origins of the First World War* (Macmillan, 1991) – a detailed account of why the Habsburg government provoked war against Serbia in 1914.

A. J. P. Taylor, *The Habsburg Monarchy* (Hamish Hamilton, 1948) – rather dated, but contains characteristically forthright Taylor judgements!

4 The industrialisation of Russia, 1870–1903

Time chart

1861: Emancipation of the Russian serfs

1864: Local government reforms, including introduction of local assemblies or *zemstva*

1881: Alexander II assassinated; succeeded by his son, Alexander III

1892: Appointment of Witte as Minister of Finance: rapid industrialisation programme

1894: Alexander III dies; succeeded by his son Nicholas II

1903: Witte is dismissed

1904: War breaks out between Russia and Japan over Korea and Northern Manchuria

1905: Russia agrees to a peace treaty with Japan, signed in Portsmouth, USA. Outbreak of revolution in Russia

While Russia was by far Europe's largest state in terms of both population and geographical size, most of its territory lay in Asia rather than in Europe. It spread over an entire continent, covering approximately one-sixth of the globe's surface and spanning ten different time zones. Its very size, northern latitude (over two-thirds lying north of the 50th parallel), and generally cold climate placed great strains on its social and economic development and posed problems far greater than those faced by any other European country. At the same time, it possessed vast natural resources of timber, coal, oil, gold and other precious metals, but these were often to be found in remote and inaccessible locations.

The Russian empire had expanded over the centuries through a process of military conquest and colonisation of a huge land area spreading first west and south of the Duchy of Muscovy, and later pushing relentlessly east towards the Pacific. As a result, by 1870 the empire encompassed an enormous range of nationalities, cultures and languages. According to the government census of 1897, only 43 per cent of the population of just over 120 million were ethnic Russians; the rest were divided between over 100 different nationalities. It is worth noting that the Russian empire also contained about 5.5 million Jews – almost half of the world's total at that time.

Thus Russia's government and social structure reflected both its military origins, and the need to maintain control over a wide variety of ethnic groups and land areas. As one of Europe's greatest powers possessing – in size if not in quality – a formidable army, it inevitably played a central role in European diplomacy. However, the industrialisation and modernisation of its European rivals, and in particular the emergence of a strong German empire after 1870, posed a great threat to the security of Russia's western provinces and to her claims to be a great power. Could Russia match the other great European powers in terms of economic and social modernisation and industrial development without weakening the powerful autocratic political structure which held the empire together?

Political structure

The sole ruler of Russia was the Tsar. Under the Fundamental Laws governing the empire, he was an 'autocratic and unlimited monarch; God himself ordains and all must bow to his supreme power'. Thus the Tsar not only had the support of the Russian nobility, a loyal and extensive network of officials and a large standing army, but he also embodied the full authority of the Russian Orthodox Church.

Armed with such vast powers, the ability of individual tsars to pursue coherent policies and to rule effectively was crucial to Russia's survival as a great power. Under a strong and determined ruler, such as Alexander III (1881–94), there was enough direction from the top, coordinated through a State Council, both to initiate some economic reforms and to retain firm control of the political structure. The accession of his son Nicholas II brought to the helm a young man who was both weak and irresolute. He confessed to his uncle in the year of his coronation, 'I always give in, and in the end am made the fool, without will and without character'. A member of Nicholas's State Council wrote in his diary in 1899 that the new Tsar lacked any independent judgement. 'Everyone can convince him and change his mind.' In a system where the ruler enjoyed absolute authority, this was a dangerous weakness.

Clearly no Tsar could rule alone; he had to work in partnership with other members of the royal family, the Russian nobility and the Orthodox Church and through his appointed Ministers. This made reform extremely difficult, as Alexander II (1855–81) found to his cost.

The failure of reform

Alexander made a determined effort to bring about substantial changes. The **emancipation of the serfs** took place in 1861, a measure of local

KEY TERM:

Emancipation of the serfs

All peasants in Russia were legally freed from their previous masters, but had to purchase their freedom and a share in the village land by paying taxes to the government. They became members of their village commune, which allocated land on a collective basis and was responsible for paying taxes and redemption dues to the government on behalf of individual peasants.

government was introduced in 1864 with the introduction of assemblies or *zemstva*, and reforms of the judicial system and of the army took place.

Such a sweeping programme of change aroused great opposition, as well as raising expectations of further reform and a greater degree of political freedom. After an unsuccessful attempt on his life in 1866, Alexander's rule became more repressive. This in turn stimulated more determined revolutionary opposition among a handful of young Russian activists opposed to the autocratic system. They succeeded in assassinating Alexander in 1881. The perils of reform were graphically illustrated, and the fears of conservatives who had opposed any tampering with Russia's traditional institutions were fully realised. Yet by the 1880s Russian government, its social structure and the economy were all desperately in need of reform. Without change, Russia was facing stagnation and relegation to the status of a second-class power.

Social structure

Russian society in the second half of the nineteenth century – and indeed well into the twentieth – was overwhelmingly rural. Only just over 10 per cent of the population lived in urban areas and drew their living from trade, industry or government service. The vast majority – whether nobility or peasant – depended on agriculture for a livelihood. Russian subjects were classified according to their social category, such as landed nobility, merchants, peasants or the church, or a military category such as the Cossacks. They were liable to the obligations specified for that category, and could not easily change their status.

The nobility   The Russian nobility, while occupying a prominent position in society, faced a decline in their influence as the century progressed, largely owing to increasing economic difficulties. Many found it difficult to make their large estates pay, and emancipation of the serfs, and the consequent loss of serf labour, compounded their problems. Geographical isolation, harsh climates and poor communications made it difficult to attract migrant labour, and great landowners largely lacked the technology and the interest to develop their estates. As a result, the amount of land owned by the nobility fell by over a third between 1861 and 1905. They remained staunch supporters of the government's efforts to keep peasant communities isolated and under strict local controls, yet ironically it was the resulting ignorance and traditional farming methods of the peasants which contributed so markedly to their own economic decline.

The peasantry The overwhelming majority of the Russian population, about 85 per cent, were peasants – feared, exploited and strictly controlled by local officials and by government regulations. Until the 1880s they paid a poll tax, from which the nobility were exempt, in addition to local taxes and indirect taxes on household goods and on vodka. They were liable to long periods of military service, were subject to corporal punishment, and could not travel to another part of the country without first obtaining a passport. Emancipation, on which so many hopes rested, turned out to be a bitter disappointment. Not only did peasants have to purchase their freedom – by paying heavy redemption dues stretching over 49 years – but most found themselves in the years after 1861, as the rural population steadily increased, with considerably less land than they had supported themselves on before emancipation. Decisions formerly taken by owners – relating to marriage, to allocation and to division of plots of land – were now taken by the village commune.

The village commune or 'mir' regulated the life of the peasant community (see Figure 4.1). It divided the fields up into strips and allocated them according to size and need of families, paid taxes on behalf of the

Figure 4.1 *A village council in Russia in about 1900*

47

entire community, and decided which individuals would be allowed to seek seasonal work in cities. Peasants owned few animals, and most labour was carried out by hand with the help of primitive implements such as the sickle, the scythe and the wooden plough. Not surprisingly, given the scattered location of their strips of land, the prospect of periodic redistribution and the difficult climate, productivity was very low. Agricultural yields were between a third and a half of those of western Europe, and there was no action taken locally or nationally to improve this low level of output.

Indeed, the government did its best to keep peasant communities isolated and ignorant. Little in the way of educational facilities were available to them, other than rote learning of Orthodox prayers through the good offices of the local priest. Travel was difficult, and therefore new ideas were slow to percolate through to the village. The 'dark masses' remained resentful and for the most part cowed, anxiously watched by local officials who were fearful of a sudden uprising or outburst of violence.

Townspeople Life in the towns was somewhat quicker in pace, and offered greater opportunities for employment and for education. Merchants and artisans plied their trades alongside government officials, nobles and peasants working as migrant labour on a temporary basis. However, what was lacking in Russia in the second half of the nineteenth century was a sizeable professional and commercial class of the sort which had developed in western Europe. Furthermore, the census of 1897 showed that only 21.1 per cent of the population could read and write, and employers in St Petersburg in the 1890s commented that 'the illiteracy of workers constitutes . . . the main cause of unproductive work'.

The drive to industrialise

By the 1890s, there was a growing recognition in government circles and among the educated classes that Russia needed to modernise and to industrialise in order to keep pace with the other great powers of Europe. The following two quotations summarise the concerns which were increasingly felt.

In regard to social conditions, a publicist and Russian traditionalist Vorontsov lamented as late as 1906:

'We want to eat, dress, entertain ourselves and construct our homes, streets and urban buildings on the model of what is being done in these areas by modern Europe, not by the Europe of the middle ages.'

PROFILE: *Count Sergei Witte*

Sergei Witte (1849–1915) was a Russian statesman and Minister of Finance from 1892 to 1903. He recognised the importance of expanding Russia's railway network, and one of his great achievements was the construction of the Trans-Siberian railway (see Figure 4.3). He also urged the rapid industrialisation of Russia, and took measures to stabilise the rouble and to attract foreign loans into Russia to provide the necessary finance. He was removed from office in 1903 as a result of criticism of the results of his policies, but recalled in summer 1905 to help to negotiate a peace with Japan and to quell revolution at home. After a six-month spell as prime minister, he was once again dismissed from office.

More seriously, the outstandingly able Director of Railways, **Count Witte**, who became Minister of Finance in 1892, pointed out to Nicholas II in 1900 the economic dangers facing Russia:

'If we do not take energetic and decisive measures so that in the course of the next decades our industry will be able to satisfy the needs of Russia . . . then the rapidly growing foreign industries will break through our tariff barriers and establish themselves in our fatherland . . . and drive their roots into the depths of our economy. This may gradually clear the way also for the triumphant political penetration by foreign powers . . . Our economic backwardness may lead to political and cultural backwardness as well.'

There had already been a drive by the government in the 1880s to extend Russia's railway network. Because Russia lacked the domestic capital to invest in extensive modernisation schemes, it needed to attract foreign capital, and this required a stable Russian currency to gain the confidence of investors abroad. As Minister of Finance, Witte sought to create a stable financial climate in Russia which would draw in the large amounts of investment capital the country so desperately needed. In 1897 Russia was brought onto the gold standard and paper roubles became convertible into gold. In the following years, large amounts of money flowed into Russia principally from her new ally France and from Belgium, but also from Germany and Britain. It is estimated that by 1900 nearly half of company capital came from abroad, and in some industries – such as mining and oil extraction – it was considerably more. There were 269 foreign companies operating in Russia at the turn of the century, all but 12 founded since 1888.

Clearly foreign investment played a major role in the expansion of railways and the growth of industry, but the policies pursued by the Russian state were also crucial to success. Both direct and indirect taxes were increased, and substantial funds were used to subsidise railway construction and to promote industrial development. To protect the growing Russian industries, Witte imposed high tariffs and tried to reduce the numbers of items imported into Russia. At the same time, the government sought to keep a favourable balance of trade by forcing the peasants to sell large amounts of grain which was then exported.

The economic effects of these policies were impressive. In the 1890s the annual industrial growth rate was just over 8 per cent per year. The value of output of all industry more than doubled in ten years, and by 1900 the industrial labour force was approaching 3 million. Russia's railway network was by this time second only to that of the United States, and the construction of the Trans-Siberian railway (Figure 4.3) – not completed until 1907 – underlined the scale and determination of the government's efforts to link up the different regions of Russia and thereby to stimulate economic activity.

Figure 4.3 *The Trans-Siberian railway, 1891–1917*

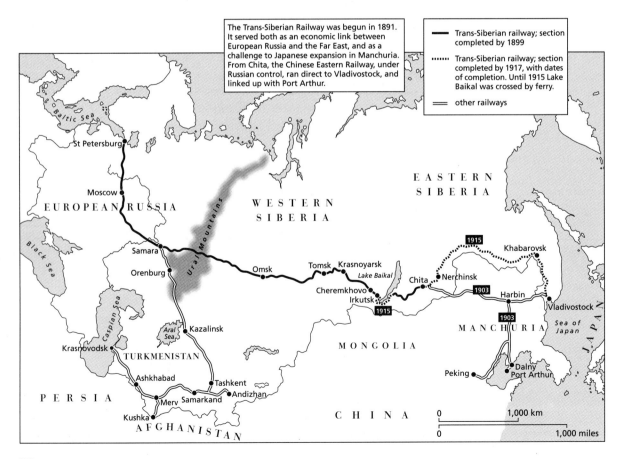

Figure 4.4 *Main industrial regions in Russia to 1917*

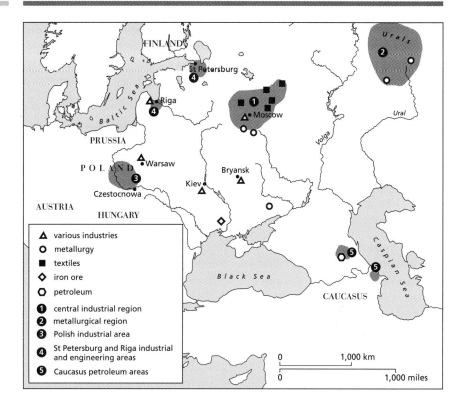

Eight main industrial areas emerged during this period, which you can see on the map in Figure 4.4:

■ the Moscow region, specialising in textiles;

■ St Petersburg and Riga, where a large number of metal-processing and machine-building factories were established;

■ the Polish region, producing textiles, coal and chemicals;

■ the Donets basin, centre for coal, iron ore and chemicals;

■ the mining region of the Ural mountains;

■ Baku and the Caspian Sea, which became one of the world's leading centres of oil production;

■ south-west Russia producing considerable crops of sugar beet;

■ the Caucasus region which specialised in the production of oil and manganese.

The output of steel, pig iron, coal, oil and textiles increased substantially in the 1890s. Coal production more than doubled between 1892 and 1902 and in the Donets basin it trebled. Pig iron output in European Russia grew almost threefold, and fivefold in the Ukraine. Oil production from Baku increased by 243 per cent, and Russia became the world's second largest supplier of oil. While it is true that Russia was starting from

51

a low base, and consequently growth figures can give a misleading impression, there is no doubt that in the 1890s Russia became a major industrial producer, rapidly catching up with Britain, Germany and the United States in the volume of output of coal, iron and steel.

Social and political consequences

Industrial development on such a scale inevitably brought with it social and political change which increasingly posed challenges to the autocratic Russian government.

Peasants

Peasant communes found it increasingly difficult to cope with rising prices and heavy burdens of tax. Peasants were forced to sell more and more grain, often leaving themselves hungry. As the rural population rose – by some 25 per cent between 1877 and 1905 – peasant distress and frustration grew. Arrears on direct taxes and on redemption dues grew; the number of horses owned by peasants fell dramatically in the 1890s, and the rate of infant mortality was the highest in Europe. Frequent epidemics and increasing signs of malnutrition all testified to the growing plight of the Russian peasantry. A fifth of army recruits were rejected as physically unfit in the 1890s. A run of below-average harvests between 1897 and 1901 hit hard, particularly in the most productive grain-producing areas. One consequence was a rapid rise in emigration to Siberia. But for the most part peasant families stayed put and turned their frustrations and growing hostility against local landowners who continued to own land they felt should be rightfully theirs.

In 1902 peasants rose up against their landlords in two provinces; nobles throughout Russia shivered apprehensively.

Industrial workers

In the new industrial areas, large numbers of former peasants were recruited to fill the factories and to work in the mines and on the railways. They were expected to work for long hours at very low rates of pay, in insanitary and often dangerous conditions. Outside the workplace, their situation was no better; there was little housing available and single workers shared rooms and often beds. Water supplies were frequently polluted, and epidemics of **cholera** and **typhus** were a regular occurrence. Medical provision and other amenities were sadly lacking, and food and drink took up a large proportion of weekly earnings. Inevitably, feelings of solidarity developed among workers concentrated in large factories, but attempts to secure improvements in conditions by

KEY TERMS:

Cholera and **typhus**

These two killer diseases are associated with overcrowded living conditions and poor hygiene. **Cholera** is spread by drinking polluted water; **typhus** is spread by lice.

forming unions or organising strikes were met with savage reprisals by the government which would brook no challenge to its authority. Inevitably, therefore, workers were drawn into increasingly sharp conflict with the Tsar and with the police.

The government also tried to keep strict control over factory-owners and budding entrepreneurs, and became increasingly alarmed as Poles, Finns, Ukrainians and particularly Jews proved more adept at running capitalist enterprises than Russians. Along with greater opportunities for minority groups, came an influx of foreign businessmen and new ideas, which encouraged existing institutions such as the local *zemstvas* and city guilds to press for more powers and influence. While their demands were relatively modest, more radical and even revolutionary parties emerged, pressing for sweeping changes in the political structure.

Nicholas II and reaction

While Nicholas II was willing to allow Witte to promote economic and industrial growth, he was not prepared to agree to any political or social changes. He saw himself as a divinely appointed monarch who had a duty to uphold the Fundamental Laws as laid down by his predecessors. The tensions and resentments generated by rapid economic development were met by increasing repression on the part of the government. As industrial growth slowed down at the turn of the century, and economic recession led to closures and lay-offs, pressures on the government grew.

Witte, widely blamed for these misfortunes, was relieved of his post. The more reactionary Minister of the Interior, Plehve, was of the view that only 'a short, victorious war' would 'stem the tide of revolution' or, failing that, the tactic of 'drowning the revolution in Jewish blood'. To this end, a number of **pogroms** were unleashed against Jewish areas of settlement, to stimulate nationalist sentiment and feelings of solidarity with the government. However, they failed to have the desired effect.

KEY TERM:

Pogrom

A Russian term used to describe the physical persecution of Jews in Tsarist Russia. Anti-semitic violence was especially marked in the Polish provinces and in the Ukraine, and was on occasions unofficially encouraged by government officials to provide an outlet for popular discontent.

Instead, the government blundered into a war in the Far East against Japan which it could have avoided, and which it was ill-equipped to fight. Mobilisation for such a distant war aroused much antagonism, and a string of defeats made the situation worse. By early 1905 the government's fears had turned into reality – they were facing a serious revolutionary situation in many parts of Russia.

Thus Russia achieved significant economic progress and, in particular, the rapid development of heavy industry, at the end of the nineteenth century. It was beginning to catch up with the more modernised countries of western Europe. But with industrialisation came severe social unrest, generating increasing tensions and revolutionary sentiments which threatened to tear the empire apart.

Task

Read the following sources and then answer the questions which follow.

Source A

An extract from the memoirs of Count Witte, written before the First World War, and published in an English translation in 1921:

'*Owing to the confidence of foreign capital in Russia's credit, which I built up, our country obtained several billion roubles of foreign capital. There are people, and their number is not small, who hold this against me ... Throughout my administration I have defended the idea of the usefulness of foreign capital ... Nicholas, as usual, favoured now one, now the other viewpoint. He went as far as calling a special session to discuss the advisability of importing foreign capital ...*

'*A great many people, including the Emperor, opposed the importation of foreign capital to Russia for purely nationalistic considerations. They argued that Russian national resources should be exploited by "true" Russians and with the aid of Russian money. They overlooked the fact that the amount of available capital in Russia was very small ...*

'*The development of our national labour was another great problem. The productivity of Russian labour is exceedingly low, this being due to the climate, among other reasons. For the latter reason, tens of millions are idle several months during the year. The scarcity of ways of communication is another factor lowering the productivity of labour ... Thus I strained every effort to develop a railroad net.*'

Source B

Russian workers in the late nineteenth century pulling a barge loaded with timber on a tributary of the river Volga

Source C

Commodity	Value of production ('000 roubles)		Employment	
	1887	1897	1887	1897
Textiles	463,044	946,296	399,178	642,520
Food products	375,286	648,116	205,223	255,357
Animal products	79,495	132,058	38,876	64,418
Wood products	25,688	102,897	30,703	86,273
Paper	21,030	45,490	19,491	46,190
Chemicals	21,509	59,555	21,134	35,320
Ceramics	28,965	82,590	67,346	143,291
Mining and metallurgy	156,012	393,746	390,915	544,333
Metal products	112,618	310,626	103,300	214,311
Others	50,852	117,767	41,882	66,249
Total	1,334,499	2,839,144	1,318,048	2,098,262

Figure 4.6 A table showing the value of Russian industrial output and the numbers of people employed in 1887 and 1897

Look carefully at all three sources. They are very different.

1 What does Source A reveal about the nature of the problems facing Count Witte as he tried to promote policies of industrialisation? *(4 marks)*

2 In what ways could you use Source B to support Witte's analysis of the problems he faced? *(5 marks)*

3 Which problem was more serious: Russia's backwardness or the Tsar's lack of understanding? Explain the reasons for your opinion, using the evidence of these three sources. *(6 marks)*

4 What are the advantages, and the limitations, of using these three sources as evidence about the industrialisation of Russia in the late nineteenth and early twentieth centuries? *(7 marks)*

5 Using the evidence of Source C and the material in the rest of this chapter, how successful were Russian attempts to industrialise in the period 1887–1903? *(8 marks)*

Further reading

Edward Acton, *Russia* (Addison Wesley Longman, 1986) – a good textbook covering modern Russian history.

Alan Wood, *The Origins of the Russian Revolution 1861–1917,* Lancaster Pamphlet (Routledge, 1994) – good starting-point for further reading.

M. E. Falkus, *The Industrialisation of Russia 1700–1914* (Macmillan, 1972) – very useful economic analysis.

Lionel Kochan, *The Making of Modern Russia* (Penguin, 1963).

Robert Service, *The Russian Revolution 1900–1927* (Macmillan, 1986) – pages 1–14 outline the problems of the period 1900–1904 very succinctly.

5 What were the reasons for imperial expansion 1870–1900?

In the 40 years after 1870 European countries expanded their existing colonial empires by over 10 million square miles and acquired in the process up to 150 million new subjects, about a tenth of the world's population at that time. They also established spheres of influence in China and in Latin America, and were joined in their search for concessions and economic privileges by the newly unified states of Germany and Italy, and by the United States and Japan. In the 36 years after 1878, Europe and the United States acquired about 17.4 per cent of the world's land surface at an average rate of some 240,000 square miles a year. The two maps of Africa (Figures 5.1 and 5.2) illustrate vividly the speed at which the vast land areas of that continent were claimed and then carved up by the European powers.

The issue historians have debated ever since is: what factor, or combination of factors, triggered off such a massive and rapid expansion?

■ Was this another, more modern, phase of imperialist expansion – the age-old phenomenon of stronger powers wanting to dominate weaker ones? Or was there something new about it, connected with industrialisation and the development of capitalist economies?

■ Some commentators at the time, and others since, have called it 'economic' imperialism and sought to explain it in terms of a search by industrialising powers for raw materials, for new markets, and for lucrative investment opportunities.

■ More recent historians have stressed political rather than economic causes, and the importance of the spread of mass nationalism and a popular press.

■ Other historians argue that one set of factors cannot satisfactorily explain such a complex phenomenon, and that different combinations of factors were at work in different parts of the globe.

KEY TERM:

Imperialism

The idea that one nation should take over other areas as colonies or dependent territories.

■ In recent years, a considerable amount of research has focused on the societies and peoples of Africa and Asia themselves, and has argued

Figure 5.1 *Africa circa 1880*

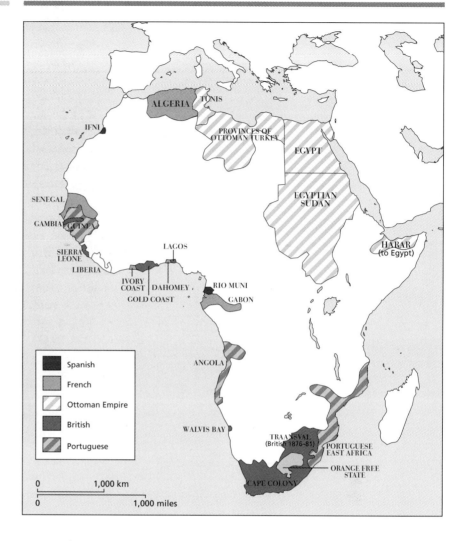

that their different responses to European expansion were significant in shaping the process.

Clearly this new and explosive phase of European imperialism was a complex phenomenon which cannot be explained in simple terms. Many different factors were involved, and this chapter will attempt to consider the main issues and explanations.

1 Scientific and technological advances

It was the rapid march of scientific and technological progress in the second half of the nineteenth century which made such extensive European expansion overland and overseas possible after 1870. The construction of railways and of steamships made long journeys more feasible;

Figure 5.2 *Africa circa 1914*

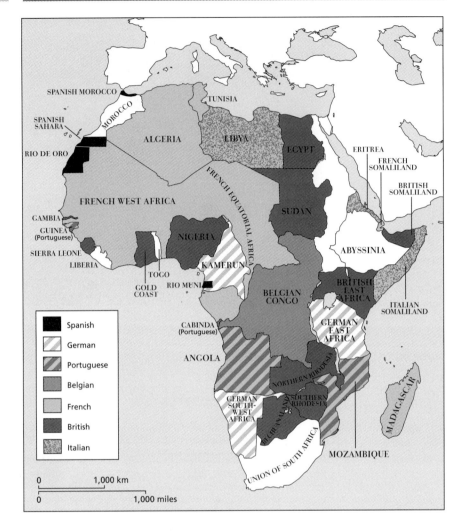

the spread of the electric telegraph enabled contact to be maintained over greater distances; and important medical breakthroughs – such as the use of quinine to treat malaria – enabled explorers and missionaries to survive for longer periods in the tropical climes of Africa and Asia. By the 1870s and 1880s, therefore, the pace of exploration and of economic and humanitarian activity quickened. Accounts of the exploits of earlier travellers such as David Livingstone (1813–73) and Henry Morton Stanley (1841–1904) reached a wide and interested audience. Pioneers such as **Cecil Rhodes** and the German Karl Peters, who were searching for economic and mineral wealth in south and east Africa, single-handedly acquired treaty rights to vast expanses of land which they looked to their home governments to annex.

More and more missionaries flocked to Africa and to Asia to combat the slave trade at source and to 'convert the heathen' (see Figure 5.3). The

Figure 5.3 Church missionaries

construction of the Trans-Siberian railway (see page 50) and the possession of superior weapons and military strength enabled Russian explorers, adventurers and soldiers to expand and tighten their hold on the vast expanses of territory east of the Ural mountains and to the north of India and China.

2 Social Darwinist beliefs

Hand in hand with these advances went the belief that European peoples were the most advanced and civilised in the world, and therefore had a duty to try to civilise and to educate the non-European natives. Charles Darwin's scientific researches were popularised and distorted to demonstrate that the laws of evolution applied to races and to nations as well as to plants and animals. The notion of the 'survival of the fittest' appeared

---

PROFILE: *Cecil Rhodes*

Born in England in 1853, **Cecil Rhodes** travelled to South Africa at the age of 17. He amassed a fortune through the mining of diamonds. After a period of study at Oxford University, he returned to South Africa and secured for Britain a protectorate over the territory of Bechuanaland in 1884 and a charter allowing his British South Africa Company to operate to the north of South Africa. After his death in 1902, this area was named Rhodesia in his memory (see Figure 5.2).

to explain why the white races had evolved to a higher level of civilisation than the yellow races, and why the brown and black races lagged far behind. Many Europeans genuinely felt that they had a 'calling' to help the less fortunate peoples of the world, and to teach them Christian values and European skills (Figure 5.3). Other more cynical individuals simply wanted to wield their powers for economic or political advantage.

If life was indeed a perpetual struggle for existence, nations needed to continue on their expansionist course or they would inexorably fall from the ranks of the great powers. The French political leader Jules Ferry warned his countrymen in 1885 that unless France expanded her colonial possessions, 'we shall take the broad road leading to decadence'. The British Prime Minister Lord Salisbury in a speech in 1898 distinguished the 'living nations from the "dying" nations', and his Conservative colleague Lord Curzon believed passionately that as long as Britain ruled over India, she would be 'the greatest power in the world' but that the loss of India would reduce her to the status of a third-rate power. As it became more and more feasible to weld together great land-masses and to control extensive empires, being a first-rate power required a large territorial base or sizeable colonial possessions.

3 Popular Nationalism

As states modernised and industrialised in the mid and late nineteenth century, their populations became more concentrated in urban areas and were increasingly likely to receive four or five years of elementary education. With the spread of mass literacy came the rise of a popular press and a growth in the market for adventure stories and travel books. Tales of tropical adventure provided a welcome escape from lives increasingly spent in oppressive factories and crowded lodgings. Colonial expansion was increasingly advocated by groups such as the Colonial League in Germany, the *Union Coloniale* and *Comité de l'Afrique Française* and the British Empire League. Their ideas proved popular among the new mass electorates. As governments sought to foster and to increase nationalist sentiments, colonial exploits provided one means of cementing and of intensifying them. The popular press avidly dramatised rivalries and incidents, to the point at which Lord Salisbury commented in 1901 that 'the diplomacy of nations is now conducted quite as much in the letters of special correspondents, as in the despatches of the foreign office'. Many historians have argued that well before the turn of the century, imperial expansion had 'become a projection of nationalism beyond the boundaries of Europe' or even 'the product of a national mass hysteria'. Such popular pressures exerted a considerable influence on governments and increasingly shaped their expansionist colonial and trade policies.

4 Political factors: prestige and national pride

France's defeat by Germany in the Franco-Prussian war in 1871 saw the emergence of both a united Germany and an Italian state with Rome as its new capital. Many historians have emphasised the significance of these events in the subsequent colonial expansion. An American historian, Professor Hayes, argued in *A Generation of Materialism, 1871–1900*, published in 1941, that:

'Basically the new imperialism was a nationalistic phenomenon. It followed hard upon the national wars which created an all-powerful Germany and a united Italy, which carried Russia within sight of Constantinople, and which left England fearful and France eclipsed. It expressed a resulting psychological reaction, an ardent desire to maintain or recover national prestige. France sought compensation for European loss in overseas gain. England would offset her European isolation by enlarging and glorifying the British Empire. Russia, halted in the Balkans, would turn anew to Asia, and before long Germany and Italy would show the world that the prestige they had won by might inside Europe they were entitled to enhance by imperial exploits outside.'

When the French government, encouraged by Bismarck, thwarted Italian expansion in the area by occupying Tunis in 1882, Prime Minister Gambetta declared that 'France is recovering her position as a great power'. Richard Langhorne, in *The Collapse of the Concert of Europe* (1981), put forward another possible explanation as to why the French government might want to encourage colonial expansion in north and west Africa in the 1870s and 1880s:

'... it was difficult for the republican government to forbid advances made by the army in North Africa, even if it did not want desert for an empire, since the defeated officers of 1870 were more safely occupied in the rear of Algeria than they might be supporting generals such as Boulanger who wanted revenge against Germany in Europe.'

France's bitter resentment after 1871 over the German seizure of Alsace and Lorraine, and Bismarck's attempts to lessen it by encouraging French colonial expansion in Africa and Asia, have been put forward by A. J. P. Taylor as a reason to explain Bismarck's sudden bid for colonial possessions in 1884. Many of the areas in which the German government expressed an interest – south-west Africa, Togo and the Kameruns, East Africa, New Guinea – were adjacent to territories in which the British Government had a particular concern or enjoyed long-standing trading rights. Taylor's theory was that Bismarck was using such colonial claims, and other colonial disputes such as Britain's occupation of Egypt in 1882, to increase Anglo-French rivalry and at the same time to promote the possibility of a Franco-German entente on colonial issues. Other historians, however, have seen Bismarck's bid for colonies as a response to a variety of domestic pressures. They have drawn attention to Germany's increasingly aggressive *weltpolitik* in the 1890s which, they suggest, stemmed from a variety of domestic, economic and political factors.

5 Political factors: the challenge of Germany

There can be no doubt that the sudden entry of Germany into the colonial arena in the period 1884–5 injected a new element of rivalry and intensified the scramble to claim concessions and territories. It led to the West African Congress which met in Berlin in 1884–5 to adjudicate on conflicting claims in that area and around the mouth of the river Congo, and set off 'the race for Africa' in which, as the British Prime Minister Lord Rosebery later remarked, it was vital to peg out 'claims for the future' by a policy of pre-emptive annexations. Historians have put forward a number of different explanations for Bismarck's change of heart in suddenly launching a bid for colonies in 1884, having stated bluntly in 1881 that 'as long as I am Imperial Chancellor we shall not pursue a colonial policy'. Many have shared A. J. P. Taylor's views that Bismarck was seeking to protect Germany's position in Europe and his increasingly complex alliance system. They cite his subsequent remark to Karl Peters when declining to adopt a more aggressive stance to British claims in East Africa: 'My map of Africa lies in Europe' as clear evidence of this. Langhorne has argued that 'the laying down of smoke-screens became a common tactic of Bismarck and among the many means that he employed, for a time Africa became foremost'. He points out that the French occupation of Tunis, 'very much at Bismarck's suggestion, unexpectedly produced a serious crisis in Italian domestic affairs', as a result of which she was 'admitted to the Austro-German alliance'. The occupation of Tunis was therefore 'one of the causes of the Triple Alliance – albeit indirectly – (and) was also a foretaste of European activity in northern Africa which was to provide Bismarck with further means for creating smoke-screens to conceal German insecurity...the occupation of Egypt in 1882 by Britain made it possible to use consequent Anglo-French hostility to achieve three objects: to issue warnings to Britain; to extend the isolation of France; and to further Franco-German accord'.

Other historians argue that domestic pressures rather than foreign policy concerns explain Bismarck's entry into the colonial field. They point out that in Germany Reichstag elections were approaching, and that claims to colonial spoils in Africa and Asia were electorally popular. Once the elections were over, it is alleged that Bismarck's interest quickly waned, as he had no intention of allowing Germany to be drawn into adopting expensive colonial obligations. A German historian, Wehler, has argued that Bismarck adopted a colonial policy in 1884 as 'the alternative to the stagnation of economic life which would have entailed severe class conflict'. He called this a policy of 'social imperialism', since the aim was to preserve the supremacy of the traditional ruling elites in Germany and their authoritarian power structure.

Yet another factor arising from domestic concerns is Bismarck's alleged concern to minimise the influence in German ruling circles of the pro-British Crown Prince Frederick. Some historians quote Bismarck's son Herbert, German Foreign Secretary in 1890, who said, 'When we started colonial policy, we had to face a long reign by the Crown Prince during which English influence would predominate. In order to forestall this, we had to launch colonial policy which is popular, and can produce conflicts with England at any moment.' Whatever the motives, Bismarck's actions bequeathed to Germany the foundations for an overseas empire, and after his fall from power in 1890, there was a growing desire in Germany to build on them.

Germany's spectacular economic expansion and industrial and scientific achievements after 1870 inevitably made her a strong commercial competitor across the globe, and the governments of the 1890s were keen to turn this to more concrete advantage. Chancellor Caprivi commented that many Germans believed that 'once we come into possession of colonies . . . we would become a great people'. And a future Chancellor, von Bülow, explained in the Reichstag in 1897 that while 'We do not by any means feel the need to stick our fingers in every pie . . . we don't want to put anyone else in the shade, but we too demand a place in the sun'. Thus the pursuit of German *weltpolitick* after 1890 and demands for spheres of influence and railway concessions greatly increased colonial rivalries and imperialist tensions in Africa and Asia.

6 The decline of British imperial power

Some historians view the scrambles for Africa and for Asia as the result of a marked decline in Britain's ability to protect the informal economic relationships which she had established in earlier decades. As a powerful supporter of free-trade policies, she had used her naval and military strength to open up new commercial opportunities and to safeguard trade routes. Her strength as the world's greatest power ensured that she had no need to incur expenditure on costly annexations of territory. However, by the 1880s Britain's worldwide supremacy was being challenged in a number of ways – navally, commercially, technologically – and 'evidence of British military weakness, coinciding with a decline in its naval strength relative to other maritime states, suggested to Bismarck that Britain's ill-defined claims to influence over sub-Saharan Africa were vulnerable to concerted pressure. Britain's acceptance of Franco-German demands for an international conference in 1884 marked the end of British "paramountcy", but its sudden collapse left a void which was quickly filled by rival claims to African territory.' The resulting Congress of Berlin attempted to demarcate respective spheres of influence, but when the colonial powers began to define these on the ground, 'partition stimulated the territorial rivalries it was intended to prevent'.

In China, too, Britain was unable to prevent an informal partition in terms of spheres of influence in the 1890s. Though she controlled about 70 per cent of China's external trade, and had taken the lead in opening up 'treaty ports' – of which there were over 30 by the turn of the century – she was increasingly thrown on the defensive by the activities of France and Germany, and the increasing challenges of Russia and Japan. In both Africa and China, Britain was forced to define her particular areas of interest, and to allow areas where she had formerly traded to be claimed and then annexed by other powers, with the likelihood that tariffs would then be imposed to protect the territory in question against British commercial penetration.

7 Strategic motives

Some historians have stressed the importance of strategic motives, particularly in explaining Britain's role in the scramble for Africa. In a celebrated study of partition, *Africa and the Victorians* (1961), Robinson and Gallagher stressed the crucial importance of the concern of successive governments for the security of the routes to India via Suez and the Cape. The construction of the Suez Canal intensified Britain's interest in a stable regime in Egypt, and led to the occupation of that country in 1882 to quell a nationalist rising. This in turn led to French resentment and to a 'chain reaction' of rivalries and of annexations which spread to west Africa and then further south. Britain was determined to defend the 'imperial' factor in South Africa, to safeguard the naval base and sea routes there, and her concern to annex territories in east Africa was also for strategic and not for economic reasons.

Strategic factors were also important in explaining Japan's colonial expansion in North China in the 1890s which triggered off a very intensive period of competition in China. The Sino-Japanese war of 1894–5 over rights in Korea, and subsequent Japanese victory, led to demands by Japan for the Liaotung peninsula which contained Port Arthur. This was opposed by Russia, Germany and France in the 'Triple Intervention' of 1895 and, in a bid to check growing Japanese influence in northern China, Russia then seized Port Arthur, Germany demanded the cession of the port of Kiaochow on the Shantung peninsula and Britain and France felt the need to claim further bases in their turn. Japan continued to expand its sphere of influence in Korea and into Manchuria, prompting the other powers trading in China to wrest further concessions from the Manchus and to define more clearly their own spheres of economic influence. China came close to partition itself after 1900; one of the main factors preventing this outcome was the realisation by Britain, France and Germany that in any formal division of the spoils, Russia and Japan would be the great gainers because of their strong strategic position in northern China.

8 Peripheral factors

The weakness of China in the late nineteenth century and the expansion of Japan clearly illustrate the importance of wider world reactions to European imperialist policies. Both China and Japan faced European demands for trading concessions and for treaty ports in the mid nineteenth century. The Chinese government was unable to respond constructively. Continued European pressure weakened, and finally caused the collapse of, a regime which was already in decline. In Japan, however, European pretensions aroused enormous hostility and nationwide anger. The existing regime was overthrown, and a new Emperor and government installed. A period of dramatic reforms followed, which saw the beginnings of Japanese industrialisation and the creation of a strong national army and navy. Chinese weakness was both a concern to Japan, because of the openings it gave for increased European influence, and an opportunity for economic and political gain which it grasped firmly. One outcome – which challenged the notion of European superiority early in the twentieth century – was Japanese victory in the Russo-Japanese war.

Native regimes, and their reactions to European demands, could therefore decisively shape the course of imperialist advances. It was the Egyptian Khedive's weakness and mismanagement of the country's finances which precipitated a major crisis and brought the British into occupation. Some rulers, however, profited from European rivalries to build up their own strength and systems of defence. A notable result was the Ethiopian success over the Italians at the Battle of Adowa in 1896.

As Richard Langhorne has argued, it was largely the collapse of native regimes which brought European powers into action in the first place.

> '... the last thing that western governments wanted was local collapse; but ironically everything that they did to shore up the existing regimes contributed to their eventual disappearance, by further undermining the spiritual and practical bases of their existence. This development was by no means confined to Africa, or to North Africa. It had already occurred across India, and was beginning to be felt in central Asia as the Russians advanced eastwards. Before long it would destroy the ancient society of Persia ... Assistance became military support against nationalist movements which had resented their assistance; military support finally rendered incompetent governments unacceptable; and the price of permanent support had to be the end to incompetence. So support slid into control, and control into colonial government.'
>
> R. Langhorne, *The Collapse of the Concert of Europe* (1981).

Thus weak native regimes and the imbalance of power between the European and non-European peoples drew the Europeans into conflict and helped to precipitate the scrambles for territories and economic concessions. What was true for north and south Africa applied also in central Asia. One historian has noted that 'Like the British in India, the frontiers of the Russian Empire in Central Asia moved steadily forward because the vacuum in power that existed in the Trans-Caspian regions left her with little alternative'. One must therefore view late nineteenth-century imperialism not only in terms of the motives of the expansionist powers, but also in terms of the situation on the ground which the Europeans had to contend with, and the local reactions which their demands sparked off.

9 The search for markets and for raw materials

Economic factors such as these clearly played an important part in the scrambles for colonial concessions and territories in the later nineteenth century. However, a range of economic issues are involved, and we must therefore separate them out and consider each one separately.

There is no doubt that the industrialisation of the major European powers greatly increased levels of interest in the commercial potential of the wider world after 1870. As the historian Moon explained in the 1920s:

> '...during the last quarter of the century the industries of Germany, United States, France, and other powers...suddenly waxed mighty...This situation meant cut-throat competition. Each of the great industrial nations was making more cloth, more iron and steel, or more of some other manufacture, than its own inhabitants could possibly consume. Each had a surplus which had to be sold abroad. "Surplus manufactures" called for foreign markets. But none of the great industrial nations was willing to be a market for the others' surplus...All except Great Britain built around themselves forbidding tariff walls...There appeared, however, one bright ray of hope, one solution – colonies ...whose markets could be monopolised by the mother country's industries... "Surplus manufactures", then, provided the chief economic cause of the imperialistic expansion of Europe in the last quarter of the nineteenth century.'

The attraction of China, with its vast population of over 400 million potential customers, was certainly a strong one for the European powers, and there were other countries which also offered possible outlets for European manufactures. The fear that she would be excluded from possible markets by tariffs certainly strengthened Britain's determination to stake out claims to particular territories. French Prime Minister Jules Ferry wrote in the 1880s that 'Europe's consumption is saturated. It is essential to discover new...consumers in other parts of the world.'

However, there was another demand generated by industrialisation – the demand for more raw materials. Cotton factories in Lancashire devoured enormous and increasing amounts of raw cotton from India and Egypt. Tyres for bicycles and wagons, and later for cars, required rubber from the Congo and the Amazon. When these areas failed to provide enough, huge rubber plantations were established in the Malay peninsula, Ceylon and the Dutch East Indies. The demand for coffee, cocoa, tea and sugar led companies to negotiate with native peoples and stake claims for concessions, which could pave the way for later conquest of territories. The prospect of gold lured hundreds of explorers into the African hinterlands – the possibility of discovering raw materials was often as strong a factor in creating interest in territories as their actual existence.

Thus a search for raw materials, and a desire to exploit them for the sole benefit of one's own nation, undoubtedly intensified the scramble for colonial spoils after 1870. King Leopold of Belgium was in no doubt whatever that Britain and Holland had derived enormous economic advantage from their respective colonies of India and the Dutch East Indies, and that Belgium needed to stake out her own claim. He wrote in 1863 that 'India and Java are inexhaustible mines of wealth...overseas provinces have brought back to the mother country far more in hard cash than they have cost' and that it would be in the interests of Belgium 'that it should have its own overseas possessions'. Accordingly, Leopold worked out a strategy to acquire territory in west Africa inland from the mouth of the river Congo on behalf of Belgium. His interest in this area sparked off a rush of claims by other powers, and the subsequent Congress of Berlin in 1884–5 to deal with them.

Thus an intense search for markets and for raw materials after 1870 undoubtedly played a major part in European expansion and colonisation. However, such economic factors on their own did not bring about the partition of Africa or the division of China into spheres of influence. They operated in tandem with many of the other factors mentioned, and varied in their importance from one continent to another, and from one great power to another. While Latin America and Asia provided possible lucrative markets for European manufactures and investment projects, Africa was of interest more for its raw materials, those which were already available, and the ones which were waiting to be discovered.

10 Surplus capital, and imperialism as the highest stage of capitalism

In addition to the search for raw materials and for markets, many historians have drawn attention to the importance of surplus capital in fuelling expansion and imperialist policies. They argue that the profits generated by nineteenth-century industrialisation could produce higher rates of return if they were re-invested overseas rather than at home. The world's leading powers were therefore drawn into an increasingly competitive struggle to find lucrative outlets for their investments. It was the British radical and journalist J. A. Hobson, in his book *Imperialism: A*

Study, written in 1902, who first pointed out the strong connection between surplus capital and late nineteenth-century imperialism:

> *'By far the most important factor in Imperialism is the influence relating to investments. The growing cosmopolitanism of capital is the greatest economic change of this generation. Every advanced industrial nation is tending to place a larger share of its capital outside the limits of its own political area, in foreign countries, or in colonies, and to draw a growing income from this source ... Aggressive imperialism, which costs the taxpayer so dear, which is of so little value to the manufacturer and trader ... is a source of great gain to the investor who cannot find at home the profitable use he seeks for his capital, and insists that his Government should help him to profitable and secure investments abroad.'*

It is certainly the case that the leading European powers competed vigorously across the globe for economic concessions. However, there is little connection between the investment of surplus capital and the formal annexation of territories. European powers invested only a small part of their capital in their newly-acquired colonies; in the case of France, the figure was about 10 per cent, and in the case of Germany it was a puny 2 per cent. Britain's surplus capital went to the United States, to Latin America or to her older colonies. Little went to the newly-acquired possessions. Russia was chronically short of investment capital, and much of it came from France, Germany, Britain and Belgium. Germany re-invested a large part of its surplus capital into domestic industrial development.

Nonetheless, Hobson's arguments persuaded many of his contemporaries that late nineteenth-century imperialism was a new phenomenon: 'economic' imperialism driven by the development of capitalism in Europe and North America. The Russian Marxist leader, Lenin, while still in exile in Switzerland, wrote a critique in 1916, *Imperialism*, in which he defined economic imperialism as the highest stage of capitalism, the stage at which 'big monopolist combines' concentrated financial domination in a few hands. A small number of financially 'powerful' states were thus able to exercise a 'virtual monopoly' across the globe and to divide the world among themselves. Lenin followed Hobson in attributing the main motive for such expansion to 'the necessity for exporting capital' arising from the fact that in a few countries capitalism has become 'over-ripe and ... capital cannot find "profitable" investment' at home. However, it was the consequences of such policies that Lenin was more concerned about. As the great powers came into increasing imperialist competition for territories, the result was bound to be war. Therefore the outbreak of war in 1914 came as no surprise to Lenin. It was the inevitable outcome of capitalism in its highest phase, and was therefore 'an imperialist war'.

Many historians have pointed to the weak points in Lenin's correlation between great powers dominated by financial monopolies and the outbreak of war in 1914. Russia, Austria-Hungary and Serbia – all centrally involved in the crises following the assassinations at Sarajevo – were by no stretch of the imagination powers in the higher stages of capitalist development. And the United States, which arguably was, was not involved in the conflict at this stage. Nonetheless, many historians have argued that economic imperialism, of the type described by Lenin, did increase competition after 1870 and inflame international rivalries. They cite the growing commercial competition between Britain and Germany, which intensified after 1900, and the frequent conflicts in Africa and Asia as evidence of developments which increased tensions and fuelled antagonisms. In this interpretation, economic imperialism, broadly defined, was one cause of war in 1914.

However, this interpretation has been strongly challenged. The opposing view has been put forward that colonial disputes acted as a 'safety valve' for European rivalries, rather than intensifying them, and that while powers played out their ambitions in Africa or in Asia, the likelihood of a serious war was diminished. It was only when Russia's Far Eastern ambitions were checked by Japan in 1905, and when German leaders turned away from the pursuit of *weltpolitik*, that the European situation became fraught with danger. Furthermore, historians point out that most individual colonial disputes were resolved by 1900, and that the most bitter rivalries had arisen between Britain and France and between Britain and Russia. These were settled by negotiations in the early twentieth century, and indeed it was the consequent emergence of the Triple Entente between Russia, France and Britain which so alarmed German leaders after 1907, and not imperial rivalries. One historian has pointed out that:

> *'Though on more than one occasion colonial rivalries brought the Great Powers within sight of war, it is not for that reason to be concluded that colonial rivalry was a fundamental cause of war. On the contrary the colonial policies of the Continental states were formulated in the light of the European balance of power and designed to serve European ends. When they no longer served those ends the colonial scene slips unobtrusively into the background. From 1900 onwards there were no important colonial disputes between Germany and England ...'*
>
> Nicholas Mansergh, *The Coming of the First World War* (1949).

Clearly economic factors played a part in late nineteenth-century imperialism, but there are many conflicting assessments of their importance in bringing about territorial annexations and promoting conflict.

Conclusion

This chapter has tried to show the many different elements which were involved in European expansion after 1870. A variety of factors were involved, and it is important not to generalise too much – different sets of factors applied in different parts of the world, and affected European powers in different ways. But there were undoubtedly major forces at work which enabled a handful of powers to divide up so much of the globe by 1900. The results of this late nineteenth-century imperialism profoundly influenced international relations in the twentieth century.

Task: writing essays

As essay-writing is a major form of assessment at A and AS Level, it is important to understand what is expected of you and what the examiners are looking for. Ideas for developing your essay-writing skills are given in several of the tasks in this book. Here we will consider the first and most important: an essay title is *not* an invitation to write all you know about the topic mentioned. This may seem hard. You have learned all this stuff and want to show it off. The fact is that you can, but it needs to be shaped to the demands of the title of the essay. **You must make a plan**.

This is made clear in the approaches given below to the two essay titles. In both cases you would need to know the same material – the substance of this chapter – but it would be organised in a different way in each case. The essence of a successful approach to essay-writing is organisation: you go into the examination knowing as much about the period you have studied as possible, and with your own ideas, but prepared to respond to what the examiner asks, organising your carefully-revised information to fit.

1 Read through the different factors listed under points 1–10, which contributed to European expansion after 1870 (on pages 56–71). Rearrange them in the order which you think indicates their relative importance. At number 1, place the factor which you think was of greatest importance in precipitating the scramble for territories and concessions; at number 2 the second most important, and so on. Give reasons for your order.

You should now have the outline for an essay entitled 'What factors were most important in explaining late nineteenth-century "new" imperialism?'. Your opening paragraph should explain the logic behind your order – for example, whether you have put political factors high up and economic ones lower down, or economic ones first and local and cultural factors next, and more importantly, why. The main part of your essay will then consist of five main paragraphs, each one examining a different reason for the expansion, with a concluding paragraph at the end which draws together what you have said.

2 You might be faced with a different question – 'What was "new" about late nineteenth-century imperialism?' Go through the five points, and extract a list of elements which distinguished late nineteenth-century imperialism from earlier periods of expansion. Alternatively, the emphasis might be on the economic side – 'How valid is it to label late nineteenth-century imperialism "economic"?'

Having been through task 1, you should have a clear idea of whether you think economic factors were of central importance or not. If you think they were, you can agree with the proposition to some, or to a great, extent, but then bring in non-economic factors you think were also of significance. If you are not convinced of the importance of economic factors, you can argue that it is not really valid to take this approach. You can then list all the factors which you think were more relevant in accounting for late nineteenth-century imperialism.

Further reading

D. K. Fieldhouse, *The Theory of Capitalist Imperialism* (Addison Wesley Longman, 1967) – very useful introduction to economic arguments and debates.

Richard Langhorne, *The Collapse of the Concert of Europe* (Macmillan, 1981) – accessible survey of the international diplomacy of the period.

John Lowe, *The Great Powers, Imperialism and the German Problem* (Routledge, 1994) – up-to-date and informative study which covers many aspects of imperialism in an accessible way.

Harrison M, Wright, *The 'New' Imperialism* (D. C. Heath, Boston, USA 1961).

6 Russia, 1903–14: reform or revolution?

Time chart

1905: **January** Revolutionary upheavals in Russia, following 'Bloody Sunday' massacre
August Tsar promises constitution
October St Petersburg Soviet formed. Tsar authorises elections to State Duma

1906: First Duma meets and is dissolved after 72 days. Stolypin becomes Prime Minister

1906–11: Stolypin introduces a series of agrarian reforms

1907: Second Duma meets, and is dissolved after four months. Stolypin alters electoral laws

1908–12: Third Duma lasts out its full four-year term

1911: **November** Stolypin assassinated

1912: Lena goldfields massacre sparks off renewed industrial unrest

1912–17: Fourth Duma in session

1914: Germany declares war on Russia

We saw in chapter 4 that rapid industrialisation in Russia in the 1890s brought about political and social unrest. By 1903, the Tsar and his ministers were facing mounting protests from all parts of the empire.

- Peasants were demanding more land;
- workers wanted a shorter working week, higher wages and an improvement in their living and working conditions;
- many nobles and professional men wanted to see the formation of a national assembly which might be given consultative powers or even a part to play in drafting new laws;
- minority groups, particularly the Poles, Finns and the Jews, wanted greater freedom and an end to persecution and to harassment by the state police.

Because of the wide gulf which separated the different social classes and ethnic groups in Russia, the government tried to deal with unrest by clamping down firmly on each outbreak of violence, by inciting Russians to violence against non-Russians, and by segregating workers from other townspeople and peasants from nobles. But the rising tide of protest in the early twentieth century, and the formation of new political parties which aimed to unite the opposition, posed new threats to the Tsar.

Opposition

Popular protest

In 1902 there were major peasant uprisings in the Ukraine, the Volga area and in Georgia. In early 1905, over 3,000 peasant disturbances had to be put down by government troops. Although the number of industrial workers in Russia was still small – around 2 million – many were concentrated in factories with a workforce of a thousand and more, especially in the metallurgical and textile industries in St Petersburg and Moscow. Such concentration, and the harsh working conditions, fostered militant attitudes which resulted in mass strikes in 1902. By 1903, 138,000 workers had taken part in 550 work stoppages, and many employers were questioning the wisdom of the government's hard-line tactics of police repression rather than treating some of the causes of unrest by improving working conditions. Indeed, one police officer, Zubatov, was given permission in 1901 to organise educational activities for workers and to help them to frame their demands to the authorities in a moderate way. By 1902, 'police unions' had spread from St Petersburg to Minsk, Vilna and Odessa, and the scale of their activities was causing alarm to the authorities. The following year one of the new police labour organisations was alleged to have taken a leading role in bringing about a general strike in Odessa, and the experiment was hastily brought to an end. Once again, repression was to be the order of the day. But this quelled neither worker unrest nor the growing mood of revolt among the minority peoples of Russia. In the Baltic provinces, in the Ukraine, in Poland, Armenia and Georgia unrest was spreading, and national parties of opposition were being formed.

Liberal opposition

Among educated Russians, challenges to the government took a different but equally dangerous form. Nobles who had gained a limited experience of local government through membership of *zemstvo* councils, liberal intellectuals and professional men were increasingly alienated by the government's refusal to allow them any real participation in the running of the country. Many of them began to support the Union of Liberation, a movement which aimed to draw together as wide a section of opposition groups as possible on a platform of overthrowing the tsarist regime and establishing in its place a democratic government. In late 1904, the Union organised a very successful 'banquet campaign'. On the pretext of celebrating the fortieth anniversary of the judicial reform carried out by Alexander II, banquets were held in most major cities, at which resolutions were passed calling for the formation of a constituent assembly to prepare the way for democracy.

The Social Revolutionaries

More radical opposition groups resorted to direct action. The Social Revolutionary Party, founded in 1901, wanted to see a change not just in the form of government, but in society itself. It wanted new rights and improved conditions for workers, self-determination for minority groups and land being given directly to those who worked it, principally the peasants. To speed up change, some members of the party were prepared to resort to the use of terror as a 'necessary evil'. Between 1902 and 1904 they were responsible for the assassinations of two Ministers of the Interior, a Minister of Education and a Grand Duke.

The Social Democrats

In opposition to the Social Revolutionary Party was the All-Russian Social Democratic Workers' Party, founded in Minsk in 1898. While the Social Revolutionary Party concentrated their efforts on the peasantry, and saw the village commune as the stepping stone to the establishment of a socialist society in Russia, the Social Democrats were a Marxist party who looked to the industrial worker to bring about social change. They believed that the industrialisation of Russia which Witte was promoting so vigorously would lay the essential economic base on which socialism would be built.

Industrial development would inevitably create a bourgeois class of entrepreneurs whose economic interests would drive them to overthrow the Tsar and the remnants of feudalism in Russia, and establish a capitalist regime. Increasing numbers of workers would be employed, and in due course they would rise up against their employers and establish a socialist state. An increasing number of Russian intellectuals after 1900 were attracted to this Marxist model of development, and started to direct their aspirations and their organisational efforts at the 2 million Russian factory workers. Although the Social Democratic Party did not become fully organised until 1903, and had to hold its congresses abroad since so many of its members were in exile, its influence grew steadily, as did the amount of underground literature it was able to smuggle into Russia. By 1904, its 10,000 supporters made it the largest anti-monarchist party in Russia, and in **Lenin** and **Trotsky** it had two of the most dedicated and gifted revolutionary leaders of the twentieth century.

PROFILE: *Lenin*

Vladimir Ilyich Lenin, originally V. I. Ulyanov, was born in Simbirsk province in 1870, the son of an education official. He gained a law degree after study at the Universities of Kazan and St Petersburg. His older brother was executed in 1887 for plotting to assassinate the Tsar, and his influence drew Lenin into revolutionary activities from an early age. He soon developed a strong interest in Marxism, and vowed to devote the rest of his life to the promotion of a Marxist revolution in Russia. At the second Congress of the Russian Social Democratic Party in 1903, he brought about a split in the party between the 'men of the majority' (Bolsheviks) who supported his views on the need for a strong, disciplined and tight-knit party of professional revolutionaries, and the 'men of the minority' (Mensheviks – on most issues a much larger number than Lenin's supporters) who argued for a looser party of members which would embrace both workers and intellectuals. Lenin spent much of his life before 1917 in exile in western Europe. Following the February 1917 revolution, he returned to Petrograd from Zurich with the assistance of the German military authorities and urged an immediate seizure of power by the proletariat. In October 1917 he led the Bolshevik revolution, and became the head of the first Soviet government until his death in 1924.

Russia's disastrous involvement in a war with Japan in the Far East brought all these strands of opposition together and set them alight. As news spread of humiliating defeats, of the destruction of over half of the Russian ships in the Yellow Sea, of the surrender of Port Arthur and of retreat at Mukden, a mood of frustration and of anger at the government's handling of the war grew. A liberal and local government activist, Astrov, wrote:

> *'Impatience, feelings of resentment, indignation – these grew everywhere and became stronger. With each new defeat, with each new retreat to "previously prepared positions" in "accordance with prior plans", indignation grew more intense and there took shape a mood of protest. There was no malicious joy. Oh no! There was a feeling of burning shame and undeserved injury.'*

Leon Trotsky was born Lev Davidovitch Bronstein at Yanovka in the Ukraine in 1879 to a Jewish family. He was educated in Odessa, and became involved in revolutionary activities as a teenager. He was soon arrested as a Marxist and exiled to Siberia, from where he escaped in 1902 and joined the Social Democratic Party at its 1903 Congress in London. He opposed Lenin's call for a tight-knit party of dedicated revolutionary leaders, and warned prophetically in 1904 that such a party would substitute itself for the working class, the party organisation would substitute itself for the party, the Central Committee would substitute itself for the organisation, and finally a 'dictator' would substitute himself for the Central Committee. Between 1905 and 1917 Trotsky worked abroad, earning his living as a left-wing journalist. He returned to Russia in 1917, joined the Bolshevik Party and played a major role in the October Revolution. In the civil war which followed, he was Commissar for War, and his creation of the Red Army was an important factor in the Bolshevik victory. After Lenin's death in 1924, he became involved in a power struggle with Stalin for the party leadership which he lost. He was ousted from the Communist Party, and expelled from Russia in 1929. Trotsky was assassinated at his home in Mexico in 1940 by one of Stalin's agents.

The 1905 Revolution

The war disrupted communications and the transport of commodities around Russia, and greatly increased government expenditure. As the long, hard winter of 1904–5 unfolded, as prices rose and food became scarce, workers in St Petersburg were the first to protest. They were assisted by a priest, Father Gapon, who had been enlisted by the police in 1903 to help with the organisation of the ill-fated 'police unions'. He had continued to expand his activities amongst the workers of St Petersburg, and in January 1905 he helped to organise a massive strike which closed down virtually all the factories in the city. On 22 January, he marched at the head of a huge column of workers and their families, possibly as many as 200,000, dressed in their best clothes, to seek redress of their grievances from the Tsar. The head of the St Petersburg secret police, Kremenetsky, in his report of the event, noted that the crowd had at its head 'banners and icons stolen from a Narva chapel as well as portraits of Their Majesties'. The Tsar, forewarned of trouble, had fled to another of his palaces. Instead, the procession was met by Cossacks who charged into the crowds with drawn sabres, and soldiers who also fired on the peaceful protesters. 'In all', reported Kremenetsky, 'some 75 people were killed and 200 wounded. It appears that among the dead are numbered women and children.' Unofficial estimates of the death toll ranged much higher, from 200 to over 1,000. But more important than the actual numbers killed was the psychological impact of the slaughter of innocent marchers. 'Bloody Sunday', as it came to be known, irreparably damaged the Tsar's image as the father of his people for millions of his subjects, and set off a year of revolutionary activity.

As revolutionary activity grew, the government grudgingly promised concessions which only served to inflame the situation. In February the Tsar promised to summon a consultative national assembly, but the response was a spate of more radical demands, the spread of strikes and of student agitation, and uprisings of Poles, Finns and Georgians. While liberals and intellectuals demanded a constitutional assembly elected by universal, secret, direct and equal male franchise, peasants resorted to illegal pasturing and wood felling on gentry estates, and some violent seizures of land and an increased number of cases of arson were reported. The announcement of the cancellation of all **redemption dues** owing from emancipation failed to quieten the peasants. Instead, the All-Russian Peasants' Union was formed, which demanded the abolition of private property in land and the convening of a Constituent Assembly. Anger and demoralisation spread to the armed forces and in June 1905 sailors on the battleship *Potemkin*, stationed in Odessa harbour, mutinied. This was followed at the end of the year by further mutinies at the Kronstadt naval base near St Petersburg, and in the ranks of the Far Eastern Army. They were crushed by loyal troops, but the authorities were severely shaken by such a demonstration of disaffection.

KEY TERM:

Redemption dues

These were the sums of money which peasants paid every year to the government to purchase the freedom they had been granted in 1861.

The revolutionary tide gathered momentum as the year progressed. There was a further wave of strikes in September, paralysing Moscow and St Petersburg, and the Union of Railwaymen brought the railways to a standstill. Workers' councils or soviets began to appear in many Russian cities, and in October the St Petersburg soviet appeared. Five hundred and sixty-two deputies elected from factories all over the district formed an executive committee to coordinate revolutionary activities in the city, and for a brief period Trotsky was its chairman. For 50 days, the soviet played a leading role as a centre of authority in conflict with the government. Workers gained a taste of power as they organised further strikes, published their own newspaper and worked to establish contact with soviets elsewhere. Not until December was the government able to arrest the Executive Committee and over 200 deputies, and close down the Soviet. Further uprisings, notably in Moscow, were ruthlessly crushed.

It was Witte who finally managed to restore calm at the end of the year.

Recalled by a desperate Nicholas II to head a unified cabinet of ministers, Witte offered the Tsar a choice of two strategies for ending the revolution: the granting of a constitution or the establishment of a military dictatorship. The Tsar reluctantly chose the first option, and on 17 October issued a manifesto, guaranteeing full civil liberty and promising a national assembly with legislative powers which would be elected on a broad franchise. This historic concession gained the support of millions of Russians who had waged an increasingly united struggle to secure it. They were now prepared to become loyal subjects once more, to work with the Government and to await the elections. Those who had hoped to replace Tsarist autocracy by a more full-blooded constitutional monarchy or even by a democratic republic, revolutionary parties campaigning on a socialist platform, and workers seeking higher pay and better conditions battled on. But as mass support for their efforts waned, they were gradually crushed by loyal troops brought home from the Far East and by police activity. By the end of December, the revolution was over, and the Tsarist government had survived the onslaught.

1906–14: evolution or revolution?

The nine years between the 1905 revolution and the outbreak of the First World War are the subject of some of the fiercest historical debates in Russian history. Historians in the West are broadly divided between 'optimists' and 'pessimists'.

The 'optimists' believe that in these years Russia evolved slowly but surely into a more modernised and more broadly-based state, a process halted only by involvement in the First World War. They point to the achievements of the four Dumas, to significant changes in the pattern of land tenure and to impressive industrial and educational advances.

The 'pessimists', on the other hand, argue that the Tsar had no intention of permanently relinquishing any of his powers, that repressive policies continued, particularly towards Russia's minority peoples, and that standards of living and levels of productivity, particularly among Russia's vast peasant population, remained low. They point to the growing isolation of the Tsar and his family, to the rise in the number of strikes after 1910 and to the pessimism of state officials about Russia's future as evidence of an impending revolution which was delayed by the outbreak of war.

Soviet and Marxist historians have no doubt that Russia was heading towards revolution by 1914 and that 1905 was a 'dress rehearsal'. Their interpretation of this period is coloured by the view that a revolution was inevitable, brought about by the growing impoverishment of workers and poor peasants who were being mercilessly exploited by an expanding capitalist system and by foreign investors looking for handsome profits.

How can we reconcile such conflicting interpretations? How strong is the evidence on which they are based? How much are they coloured by the knowledge of what happened after 1914? To try to obtain a clearer picture, this section will focus on four major issues:

- the impact of the constitutional changes
- the attempt by Stolypin to change the basis of peasant agriculture
- conditions facing workers and minority groups
- the extent of industrial and social modernisation by 1914.

Was Russia evolving towards a system of parliamentary democracy by 1914?

1 *The role of the Tsar*   The first area to consider here is the role of the Tsar himself. He had only issued the October Manifesto to save the monarchy. Once the crisis passed, his inclination was to try to whittle down the reforms which had been promised. Even before the first Duma met he issued the Fundamental Laws of April 1906 which declared that 'Supreme Autocratic Power belongs to the emperor' and that he 'possesses the initiative in all legislative matters...no law can come into force without his approval'. The Tsar 'determines the direction of Russia's foreign policy' and 'is the Commander-in-Chief of the Russian army and navy'. He could also publish exceptional decrees that had the force of law, and could replace existing laws in a given area. By 1912 the great majority of Russians lived under some form of 'exceptional measures'.

2 *The Duma*   This was to be the lower chamber of a legislature that had above it a State Council, half of whose members were appointed by the Tsar, and half of whom were chosen from among the members of the Holy Synod, provincial noble assemblies, *zemstva* and city dumas. The State Council could veto any Duma bill. Furthermore, the Duma's financial powers were extremely limited. It had oversight of only just over half of government expenditure, and if they failed to approve the budget, the previous year's allocations would continue. Ministers remained accountable to the Tsar alone, and the Tsar continued to rule according to the dictates of his conscience and the will of God.

There were charges at the time, and since, that the system operating in Russia after 1905 was 'sham constitutionalism' or 'constitutional monarchy under an autocratic Tsar'. The historian Richard Charques in *The Twilight of Imperial Russia* called it 'demi-semi constitutional monarchy'. Others, however, have seen it more positively as 'an important turning-point in the development of Russian constitutional law. It transformed the Russian empire from an absolute and unlimited monarchy into a constitutional monarchy', albeit one in which the Tsar 'continued to enjoy very considerable rights and prerogatives'.

How important a role did the Dumas play after 1906? Here again opinion is sharply divided. Historians of the 'pessimistic' school cite the fact that the first Duma lasted for only 72 days before being dissolved, and the second for only slightly longer – four months – as clear evidence that the Tsar had no intention of allowing the Duma to play any meaningful role in the government of Russia. They point out that the franchise was shamefully manipulated in 1907, in defiance of the Fundamental Laws, to produce a more docile, Russian, aristocratic and landowning Third Duma which managed to last out its full four-year term from 1908 to 1912. However, the even more conservative Fourth Duma once again came into fierce conflict with the Tsar's government in May 1914.

3 *Political repression* The 'pessimists' also point out that though membership of political parties and trade unions was allowed after 1906, 600 were shut down by 1911. There were only three parties registered in 1906: the extreme right-wing Union of Russian People of which Nicholas himself was an enthusiastic member; the Octobrists, a party of nobles and of professional men who were happy to work within the framework of the Manifesto of October 1905; and the tiny Party of Peaceful Reconstruction. Other parties – such as the Social Revolutionaries and the Social Democrats – had their applications for registration turned down. Deputies representing the Kadet Party, who wanted more extensive constitutional reform, and issued a manifesto from Vyborg in 1906 urging passive resistance in protest against the dissolution of the First Duma, found themselves deprived of their political rights. Jails in St Petersburg in the same year remained full of political prisoners, and right up to 1914 police retained special powers and could, under 'exceptional measures', interfere extensively with political liberties. In the rural areas, between 1906 and 1909, the Tsar's chief minister, Stolypin, ordered more than two and a half thousand peasant ring leaders of the 1905 uprisings to their deaths after field courts martial.

So was Russia becoming more democratic?

Despite such evidence, historians of the 'optimistic' school find signs of evolution and of significant political change. They point out that peasants born as serfs in the mid nineteenth century could now vote in national elections. Given the lack of powers of local and municipal bodies before 1905, and the high hopes placed in the Duma, there was bound to be a period of adjustment before newly-elected deputies could wield their limited powers effectively and work to extend the constitutional framework. Not only could the Tsar not dispense with elected Dumas despite confrontations with the first two, but the Third Duma played a very constructive role in promoting educational expansion and improving on Stolypin's land reforms.

> *'There was no immediate prospect of an expansion of the franchise; but years or even decades are very short periods in the life of a nation, and it was perhaps not unreasonable to expect that in due course democratic institutions would develop along the same lines as in other countries. The door for these changes was now open.'*
>
> Michael Florinsky, *The End of the Russian Empire* (1961).

The one serious flaw in this analysis is the attitude of the Tsar himself. He never became reconciled to the notion of meaningful constitutional reform, and in May 1914 consulted his ministers as to whether the State Duma could be changed from a legislative to a merely consultative body. They unanimously counselled against such a change, and the matter was allowed to drop. But Nicholas had no intention of adapting to the role of a constitutional monarch and of relinquishing any of his autocratic powers. Instead, the royal household became more and more isolated, and increasingly wrapped up in its own preoccupations, particularly centred on the haemophilia inherited by the young heir to the throne. Only an unorthodox 'holy man' of peasant origins and dubious morals, **Rasputin**, seemed to be able to staunch the Tsarevich's bleeding attacks. 'Our friend', as the Empress referred to him, came to exert an increasing influence over the Royal couple, much to the dismay and displeasure of

PROFILE: *Rasputin*

Born into a Russian peasant family in Siberia in 1871, **Gregory Rasputin** proclaimed himself to be a mystic with hypnotic powers. In the years before the First World War, he gained great influence at court as a result of his ability through hypnosis to stop the bleeding of the Tsar's haemophiliac son, Alexei. There were damaging rumours in the capital of a sexual relationship between Tsarina Alexandra and Rasputin, though they were never proved. Rasputin's extravagant lifestyle and frequent public displays of drunkenness and lewd behaviour scandalised the upper levels of Russian society, and he was finally murdered in November 1916 by a young Russian noble.

Figure 6.4 The Tsarina, the Tsar and their haemophiliac son, Alexei, aged 8, carried by a Cossack soldier on tour in 1913: the Tsar was not enthusiastically received.

the rest of Russia's leading families. By 1914, a wide gulf was opening up between Nicholas, dominated by his German-born wife, and most of the Russian nobility. The far from radical Guchkov, leader of the Octobrist Party, spoke in late 1913 of a 'grave crisis through which we are now passing' and prophesied that government policy, or rather lack of it, was carrying Russia towards an 'inevitable and grave catastrophe' in which Russia would be 'plunged into a period of protracted, chronic anarchy which will lead to the dissolution of the empire'. The reason was because 'faith in the government is steadily waning and with it ... faith in the possibility of a peaceful issue from the crisis'. The irony was that Nicholas, unreconciled to becoming a constitutional monarch, was completely unfitted by nature to play the role of an unfettered, autocratic ruler. He was utterly incapable of giving his country the leadership it so desperately needed as it faced the stresses and strains of modernisation, and the question marks over his son's future made the situation worse. It is true that up to 1914 Nicholas retained the loyalty of his armed forces, Tsarist officials and the police. But what he was losing was the confidence of the nation (see Figure 6.4). This factor alone was bound to bring into question the long-term future of the Tsarist regime.

How successful were Stolypin's agrarian reforms?

Stolypin's agrarian reforms have been the subject of great debate since 1917. Would they, given a period of peaceful development, have transformed the face of rural Russia? Or would they simply have set poor peasants against their richer neighbours and increased rural tensions to breaking-point?

There were three main elements in Stolypin's 'wager on the strong':

1 A decree of November 1906 permitting all peasants to apply to hold their strips of land as private property, and to ask their commune to exchange the scattered strips for a consolidated holding as far as possible.

2 An increase in resources for the Peasant Land Bank so that peasants could borrow money to purchase extra land, particularly from gentry estates.

3 The launching of a resettlement programme with government aid to enable peasants to move from overcrowded regions to the empty spaces of Siberia and Central Asia.

Such a comprehensive package of agrarian reform was aimed at the break-up of the commune and its replacement by a new class of prosperous peasants who would both promote economic modernisation and ensure social stability. In the years before 1914 there was an initial rush to register lands in individual ownership, and some movement towards consolidation. At the same time, there was a reverse trend of some families opting back into the commune, to escape from the harsh realities of independent farming. In some areas, the conversion of the peasantry into independent farmers proceeded rapidly; in others, very slowly. Statistics are not always easy to interpret, given the size of Russia and the variety of agricultural soils and regions. However, most historians agree that substantial progress had been made by 1916. Edward Acton has calculated that 'about half the peasant households in the Empire had private ownership' by this date.

Contemporaries believed that such changes paved the way for a greater use of machinery, increased yields and an improvement in animal husbandry, and that they corresponded 'to the interests of a considerable mass of peasants'. Cancellation of redemption dues, promised in 1905 and put into effect in 1907, increased levels of well-being.

On the other hand, the impetus for change was slowing down by 1914. Applications to leave the commune declined. Acton points out that:

> *'few peasants had the means to set up viable independent farms, and many of those who did contract out of the commune did so only to sell their land . . . it was only in the more commercially developed areas . . . that the rate of consolidation was high. In the more overpopulated areas, where land-hunger and peasant unrest were most acute, the response was minimal. Among the peasants of Great Russia, very few indeed went so far as to move their households out of the village, and there was a steady counterflow back towards communal tenure.'*
>
> Edward Acton, *Russia* (1981).

The period did witness substantial purchase or leasing by the peasantry of noble lands, to the point where in 1916 nearly nine-tenths of European Russia's sown area was under cultivation by peasants. There was also a significant increase in the numbers of peasants embarking for a new life in Siberia – one and a half million arrived there between 1907 and 1909. Furthermore, a series of good harvests in the years before 1914 kept rural protest to a minimum.

Peasant land-hunger still persisted, and old resentments were now reinforced by new strains arising from changes in the patterns of rural ownership. Divisions grew between rich and poor peasants, between the successful and enterprising outside the commune and the slothful or unlucky left behind. Cereal yields rose, and Russia became the largest cereal exporter in the world between 1908 and 1913, exporting 11.5 million tons annually. At the same time, peasants remained isolated and superstitious, following the time-honoured ritual of centuries. More than half could not read or write their own names, and as one historian observed, 'not nature but primitive husbandry condemned Russia to yields one-half or one-third as large as those obtained in western Europe'. The government did little in this period to promote more effective agricultural methods or to provide more modern farming implements.

Were Stolypin's reforms a 'painful but hopeful new beginning' cut short by the war, or was his valiant effort to 'solve the almost insoluble' agrarian problem, launched too late to be effective? Martin McCauley suggests that they were 'likely to have only moderate success in Russia in the short term' though they might have been more successful in the longer term. However, he adds a cautionary note that 'it is very doubtful if 20 years would have been sufficient' as the reforms 'required fast growth in the rest of the economy to siphon off surplus rural labour as well as changed attitudes and a higher cultural level among the peasantry'. The problem remained that, however land was distributed, there were too many peasants trying to earn their living from the soil. Russia remained overwhelmingly rural in 1914, with nearly 80 per cent of its population still dependent on the land. As one historian has observed, 'in Russia, as in all underdeveloped countries with a swollen rural population, the costs and hardships of modernisation would fall mainly on the peasant'. That fact alone would be bound to slow down the pace of change, cause widespread peasant resentment and undermine Stolypin's reforms. Stolypin himself was assassinated in 1911, a sad but revealing testimony to the tensions and the fears aroused by his policies.

Did industrial workers and minority groups become less revolutionary after 1905?

The reforms promised in 1905 offered least to industrial workers and to minority groups. Though workers won limited rights to form trade unions and political parties, their working and living conditions did not improve. Belatedly, in 1912, the government introduced some labour legislation to create sickness benefit funds and to introduce accident insurance for workers, but as in other areas of reform, the measures were half-hearted and inadequate to deal with the real problems facing the growing Russian proletariat. They remained crowded and badly housed in factory barracks and in cramped rooms, and their wages scarcely increased (see Figure 6.5). Acton tells us that the real wages of workers in 1914 were below those of 1903; Robert Service in *The Russian Revolution 1900–27* points to a slight rise in average real wages between 1900 and 1913. Strikes to secure higher wages were still regarded as illegal forms of protest; in 1912, in the Lena goldfields in eastern Siberia, 270 striking workers were killed by government troops.

Not surprisingly, therefore, worker unrest grew once again as Russia after 1909 entered a new phase of industrial expansion. While the degree of militancy varied from region to region and from one industry to another, the number of strikes rose inexorably. Their aim was not just an improvement in economic conditions, but greater political change as well. Factory inspectors listed over half a million workers as 'political' strikers in 1912,

Figure 6.5 Soup kitchen for
unemployed workers in
St Petersburg

and nearly one million in 1914, and these figures are likely to be conservative estimates. In all, there were over 2,000 strikes in Russia in 1912
and over 3,000 in the first half of 1914. On the eve of Russia's entry into
the war, St Petersburg again witnessed massive anti-government demonstrations, as workers and peasants agitated for an eight-hour working
day, for a democratic republic and for the expropriation of gentry land.

Leaders of more progressive political parties were pessimistic about the
future. On the one hand, they feared the growing militancy and
radicalism of workers which was increasing the gulf between them and

'educated Russia'; on the other hand, the government would contemplate no reforms to enable the workers to engage in legal protest or to work constructively with government officials. Not surprisingly, on this evidence, there are many historians who share Trotsky's view that Russia's declaration of war in late July of 1914, which aroused a wave of popular patriotism, temporarily held back the revolutionary forces which were gathering in many parts of Russia.

The period after 1906 was a lean time for professional revolutionaries and for socialist parties. The major revolutionary leaders were hunted down and exiled. Less active members were constantly harassed by the police, and some were embarrassingly exposed as secret police agents. The membership of the Social Democratic Party plummeted from 150,000 in 1906 to a mere 10,000 in 1910. Desperately short of money, the party resorted to terrorist activities or 'expropriations' such as the robbing of banks and holding-up of trains. Lenin, contemplating the revolutionary prospects for Russia as late as the spring of 1914, believed that 'only war' could crack open the country, and that 'Franz Josef won't give us this pleasure'. Clearly, revolutionary groups were finding it difficult to spread their message around Russia, though the Social Democrats did make headway in some large factories, especially among younger, more militant, workers. But stories abound of strike meetings in which, while workers' hostility was directed at employers, they reaffirmed their loyalty to the Tsar. Many workers were newly-recruited simple peasants, quick to express anger, and to react spontaneously, but difficult to organise in more systematic and long-term activity.

Anti-Semitic agitation   One strategy employed by the government to deflect social and industrial tensions was to encourage attacks on minority groups and especially on Jewish settlements. The Union of the Russian People, with its fighting organisation the Black Hundreds, led a number of pogroms after 1906 resulting in thousands of Jewish deaths and extensive loss of property. The childhood recollections of Nikita Khrushchev, later Soviet Prime Minister between 1958 and 1964, hint at the tactics employed:

> *'Some of the miners were telling about how the "yids" marched around calling the Russians abusive names, carrying banners ... a rumour started that there had been a decree that for three days you could do whatever you wanted to the Jews. For three days there was no check on the looting. After the three days were up, the police ... started to restore order. But nothing was done about all the looting and rampage ... and all the pillage and murder went unpunished.'*

National minorities Fierce Russian nationalism was promoted by the principle of Russia 'one and indivisible' proclaimed in the preamble to the Fundamental Laws of 1906. There could be no question of a move to a federal state, or the granting of autonomy to minority groups. Instead, non-Russians were to be 'Russified', subject to Russian language and culture and the Orthodox religion, and persecuted for preferring Roman Catholicism or Judaism. Thus minority resentments remained strong and some areas were in a state of virtual war with the Russian authorities, particularly the Finnish provinces. Such policies did little to remove the resentments of Russian workers and peasants, but instead ensured that any future explosions of violence and revolution would be fully supported by large numbers of non-Russian subjects. Thus 'pessimist' historians point to the radicalism of growing numbers of workers by 1914 and to the hostility of minority groups as evidence that the Tsarist government was signally failing to solve the growing antagonisms caused by industrialisation and by programmes of modernisation, and that this failure was imperilling Russia's very existence on the eve of war.

How successful was Russian industrial and social development after 1905?

There is no doubt that Russia underwent considerable industrial expansion between 1909 and 1913. Its rate of industrial growth in these years was a hefty 8 per cent per annum, and accelerating. Bumper harvests gave a boost to the development of a more dynamic consumer market, and along with the growth of heavy industry went the spread of light industry and of rural handicrafts. But it is in the field of heavy industry that the most spectacular advances were recorded. Given a boost by heavy government spending to replace the naval losses suffered in the Russo-Japanese war and to re-equip the army, coal and steel production rose by nearly 50 per cent, and Russia became the world's fourth biggest producer of coal, pig iron and steel. As an oil producer, the Russian oil-wells at Baku were rivalled only by the Texan oilfields. By 1913, Russia ranked as the fifth greatest industrial power, behind Britain, the United States, France and Germany. It is true that her population was by far the biggest of any European country, and that per head her industrial output looked much less impressive. Per capita income in Russia in 1910 was only about a third of the West European average, and escalating industrial growth in Germany and in the United States was widening the gap. Nonetheless, Russia was beginning to harness its vast industrial potential, and the success of her efforts was seriously alarming the Germans, to the point where many German leaders believed by 1913 that a war with Russia was necessary sooner rather than later, when the progress of Russian industrialisation would have advanced far enough to put the outcome in some doubt.

Along with industrial advances went considerable social change. There was a determined effort to expand educational facilities, and the Third Duma took the lead in pushing government spending on elementary schools from 1.8 per cent of the budget to 4.2 per cent. Russia was still nowhere near to providing universal primary education by 1914, but the period since 1905 saw a 77 per cent growth in the number of pupils and an 85 per cent growth in the numbers of schools. The literacy rate rose from under 30 per cent at the turn of the century to over 40 per cent in 1914.

The period also saw an expansion in the numbers of professionally qualified people, particularly doctors, veterinary surgeons and teachers. Local *zemstva* worked hard to improve facilities in their areas, and the great bulk of their spending was devoted to education and to health. Historians of the 'optimistic' school point to such developments as clear evidence that Russia was experiencing significant economic and social modernisation between 1905 and 1914 and that such developments were underpinning political evolution to a more constitutional and broadly-based state.

'Pessimists', however, argue that such changes were too late and only affected part of the population. Even in 1914 only a small percentage of Russian children went to school, and much of what they learned was very basic. There were still woefully small numbers of doctors and teachers in rural areas, and the social gap between the educated and peasant families was as wide as ever. There was significant industrial growth, but this had the effect of increasing the number of industrial workers – to over 3 million – without improving their conditions or dealing with their grievances.

Was Russia on the brink of revolution in 1914?

There is no agreement on this issue among historians. There is evidence which points to considerable potential for a revolutionary uprising by 1914; but how widespread it was, and how serious a threat it posed to the government, is much disputed. Let us give two contrasting views.

Martin McCauley points to the widening gulf between the autocracy and the educated classes, and between the latter and the working class, and concludes that:

> '... the support base of the autocratic regime was very narrow in 1914. Had war not intervened the confrontation between the authorities and the rest of the population would possibly have come sooner than 1917... If revolution is taken to mean that the Tsar would have to concede much of his power to an elected parliament and educated society then revolution was inevitable by 1914. If revolution means the Bolshevik seizure of power then revolution was not inevitable by 1914.'

Michael Florinsky agrees that the imperial regime had numerous weaknesses, that its harsh and aggressive policy towards national minorities was fraught with danger and that the aloofness of the educated classes from the masses was 'ominous'. Nonetheless, he presents positive developments, too.

> 'The venerable structure of the autocratic State had gone through a very remarkable transformation. The Tsar of All the Russias was now limited in the exercise of his legislative powers by the Duma, where the sons of the serfs of yesterday were rubbing shoulders with their former masters. The bureaucracy succeeded in reaching a considerable degree of efficiency... Institutions of local government... were working with remarkable devotion to raise the economic and educational standards of the masses. A real movement had been made, at last, to put an end to illiteracy by introducing the compulsory education of children. A no less drastic step had been taken in the direction of advancing the prosperity of the farmer by freeing him from the bondage of the land commune. The general economic progress of the country could not be seriously questioned. In spite of all the imperfections and drawbacks of the new departures, it seems safe to say that they contained the elements for the future progress of the nation along the road that had been followed by other countries.'
>
> Michael Florinsky, *The End of the Russian Empire* (1961).

Each of us must come to our own conclusions about how close to revolution Russia was by 1914, and what sort of a revolution it was likely to be. As we know, three years of war from 1914 to early 1917 put the whole political, economic and social framework to a test so severe that it brought the country to its knees. By 1917 the Russian empire had fallen. But whether the revolutionary parties, and in particular the Bolsheviks, would have been given such an opportunity to promote their kind of revolution without Russian involvement in the First World War remains a much debated issue.

Task: interpretations in history

Look back at the two quotations from Martin McCauley and Michael Florinsky (page 91). Read them through carefully.

1 Summarise in your own words what each is saying.

2 Do they contradict each other? Or do they differ in emphasis?

Further reading

Edward Acton, *Russia* (Addison Wesley Longman, 1981) – excellent textbook for nineteenth-century and twentieth-century Russian history.

Michael Florinsky, *The End of the Russian Empire* (Collier-Macmillan, New York, 1961) – a lively account of the last years of the Russian empire.

Robert Service, *The Russian Revolution 1900–27* (Macmillan, 1986) – very useful, succinct introduction.

Theodore von Laue, *Why Lenin Why Stalin: A Reappraisal of the Russian Revolution 1900–30* (Lippincott, USA 1971).

Alan Wood, *The Origins of the Russian Revolution 1861–1917*, Lancaster Pamphlet (Routledge, 1987) – another good introductory survey.

7 Germany, 1890–1914: grasping at world power?

Time chart

1888: Accession to throne of Wilhelm II

1890: Fall of Bismarck. Replaced as Chancellor by Caprivi

1893: Pan-German League founded

1894: Caprivi resigns as Chancellor and is replaced by Höhenlöhe

1898: First Navy Law passed to lay basis for German battle fleet
Navy League founded

1900: Second Navy Law passed. Von Bülow becomes Chancellor

1905: First Moroccan crisis

1909: Von Bülow resigns as Chancellor and is succeeded by Bethmann-Hollweg

1911: Second Moroccan crisis

1914: Germany declares war on Russia and France, and invades Belgium

In chapter 1 we looked at the ways in which Bismarck had carefully constructed the constitution of the new German Empire. When he was finally dismissed from office by Wilhelm II in 1890 Bismarck left behind a political system designed to give maximum power to the Kaiser and his Chancellor, to government ministers, state officials and military advisers. Though there was a limited role in the new constitution for the Reichstag at a national level and for local councils at regional level, there were no popularly elected governments, no ministers answerable to the Reichstag or cabinets exercising collective responsibility on behalf of the government of the day. Instead, power rested with the state and with those who were born to exercise it on behalf of the German nation. These men, drawn from the traditional landed and professional elites, were determined to maintain their privileges and their power and to resist any challenge to their political predominance.

However, in the 24 years from 1890 to 1914, the German economy expanded on a massive scale, and as a result German society underwent a dramatic transformation. Millions of people migrated to the expanding industrial centres in the Ruhr, in the Saar valley and in Upper Silesia. As economic output soared, Germany became a dynamic modern state, leading Europe in the production of steel, and in the new industrial fields of electrics, optics and chemicals. The rapidly changing economic and social structure was bound to raise new challenges and to bring considerable pressures to bear on the static political structure. Could these pressures – in the form of the largest socialist party in Europe, massive urbanisation, and demands for more participation in government and for better working conditions – be accommodated by political compromise, or would they be bitterly resisted?

The main focus of this chapter is on the attempts of the Kaiser, his ministers and advisers to resolve the succession of internal and external crises which faced them without making any political concessions whatsoever. As we shall see, this stubborn determination to resist political change led them to ever more desperate stratagems both at home and abroad, until finally, in 1914, war seemed to offer the only alternative to what were perceived as cowardly and utterly unthinkable political and diplomatic concessions.

The Kaiser and his advisers

The key relationship in the new German Empire between 1871 and 1888 had been that between Kaiser Wilhelm I and his Chancellor, Bismarck. The latter had exercised far-reaching powers on behalf of the Kaiser, had operated as chief minister both in the Prussian state and in the German empire, had coordinated the work of the many different ministers and royal advisers and had worked reasonably effectively, though at times disdainfully, with the Reichstag. However, in 1888 the Kaiser died, and his son, who was married to Queen Victoria's eldest daughter, Victoria, did not long survive him. It was Wilhelm's grandson, Wilhelm II, who now became the new ruler of Germany just before his thirtieth birthday. Within two years, he had brought about Bismarck's resignation and made it abundantly clear that he intended to take a much more active part in government than his grandfather had done.

Much has been written about Kaiser Wilhelm II. All accounts agree that he was hyperactive, enthusiastic and able, but lacking in self-discipline or the ability to focus his energies constructively. He had a very strong sense of the importance of his position, but could not command the respect of his ministers and advisers who increasingly became irritated by his violent and impetuous outbursts and intemperate views. There has been much speculation about the effect upon him of a difficult birth which for a brief time left him without oxygen. A withered left arm was one obvious result, but the extent of brain damage, if any, is less easy to assess. It is clear, however, that his parents were worried about his progress and about his violent outbursts of temper from an early age. While his mother tried to nurture in him English ways, he developed a strong interest in military manoeuvres and in his Prussian heritage. As she wrote sadly to Queen Victoria in 1880, 'Willy is chauvinistic and ultra Prussian to a degree and with a violence which is very painful to me'. Seven years later, she confided to her mother that 'he is so headstrong' and 'so impatient of any control except the Emperor's'. Such was the young man who now became ruler of the powerful German empire.

Like his cousin, Tsar Nicholas II of Russia, Wilhelm II had a strong sense of a divine mission, making him answerable for his actions only to God. He wrote to his Chancellor Caprivi in 1892: 'What do I care about popularity! For, as the guiding principles of my actions, I have only the dictates of my duty and the responsibility of my clear conscience towards God.'

Wilhelm's ministers

What Wilhelm II wanted was a Chancellor who would take his orders meekly from the Kaiser, and who would both bully the Reichstag into submission and combat the threat of socialism. Chancellors found themselves in an impossible position, fighting against the Kaiser's favourites on the one hand, and incurring the wrath of Reichstag deputies on the other. Wilhelm's first Chancellor, Caprivi, resigned after four years. His second, Höhenlöhe, highlighted the difficulties facing him after three years in office:

> 'If I cannot get the Kaiser's consent for measures I regard as necessary, then I have no authority . . . I cannot stay if the Kaiser appoints Ministers without consulting me . . . I cannot govern against public opinion as well as against the Kaiser. To govern against the Kaiser and the public is to hang in mid-air. That is impossible.'

Höhenlöhe lasted until 1900, and was then replaced by a diplomat, Bernhard von Bülow, who saw himself as the Kaiser's 'chief of staff'. The Kaiser was confident that at last he had found a Chancellor through whom he could govern, and exulted, 'Bülow shall be my Bismarck and . . . we two will clean up the filth of parliamentary and party machinery internally'.

Bülow survived for nine years, but gradually lost the confidence of the Kaiser as he tried to work with the Reichstag to solve mounting financial problems caused by the expansion of the German navy. He resigned in

---

PROFILE: *Bethmann-Hollweg*

Theobald von Bethmann-Hollweg was born in 1856. He started his career as a civil servant in Brandenburg, served in the Prussian Ministry of the Interior, and became Secretary of State in the Imperial Office of Internal Affairs in 1907. He was appointed Chancellor in 1909 and served until 1917. He was an extremely competent administrator, but lacked detailed knowledge and experience of foreign and military affairs. He was opposed to political reform and therefore became increasingly dependent on non-Parliamentary centres of influence such as the court, army and bureaucracy. Some historians argue that he tried hard to avert a military conflict in 1914; others believe that in the last resort he was willing to run the risk of the outbreak of a European war (see next chapter). He died in 1921.

1909 and was succeeded by a Prussian bureaucrat, **Bethmann-Hollweg** who the Kaiser was confident would 'straighten out the Reichstag for me'.

Instead, the elections of 1912 saw the German Social Democrat Party secure one-third of the votes and emerge as the largest party in the Reichstag, in spite of – perhaps because of – Wilhelm's increasingly frenzied attempts to outlaw and destroy it.

No Chancellor could work effectively caught between the unrealistic demands of the Kaiser, the intransigence of both right and left-wing parties in the Reichstag, court favourites manoeuvring for royal support for their pet schemes, and the expansionist ambitions of the military and naval authorities. Wilhelm's contempt for the Reichstag was unconcealed and frequently expressed; on one occasion he referred to the deputies as a 'troop of monkeys and a collection of blockheads and sleep-walkers'.

He preferred to surround himself with young military attachés, and to spend his time on matters of elaborate military etiquette and detail, which his army and navy chiefs tolerated so long as it kept him out of areas of serious decision-making. He spent much of his time in military dress, inspecting troops, conducting imperial military reviews (see Figure 7.2) or cruising in the Baltic on board the imperial yacht.

Thus there was no clear decision-making structure or centre of authority in Wilhelmine Germany. Frequently the Kaiser cut across the work of his ministers by launching his own personal initiatives or authorising some alternative approach. But on one issue the Kaiser and his chief advisers

Figure 7.2 *Wilhelm II instructing a group of generals during military manoeuvres*

were in full agreement. The Reichstag was to be granted no increased powers, and no concessions at all were to be made to the hated socialists, who were still seen in the first decade of the twentieth century as enemies of the state.

The expansion of the German economy

No other European country expanded as rapidly or as successfully as Germany in this period. By 1914 it had overtaken Great Britain to become Europe's leading industrial and commercial power. In addition, it possessed formidable military and naval strength. Historians estimate that by the eve of the First World War, its national power was about three or four times that of Italy, well ahead of France and Russia, and probably just ahead of Britain as well.

Already in 1890, there were more Germans working in industry, transport, trade, banking and insurance than in agriculture; industry's share of the national product was rapidly overtaking that of agriculture. Between 1890 and 1914 Germany's population soared from 49 million to 66 million, and most of this increase was to be found in urban centres which expanded dramatically. As well as possessing abundant supplies of coal and other raw materials, Germany also had an extremely able work-force, as a result of the high standards of literacy and numeracy which a century of compulsory state elementary education and a good network of technical institutes and universities had brought about. Not surprisingly, therefore, in the later 1890s industrial output increased by a third, and it accelerated further in the 1900s (see Figure 7.3).

Historian Paul Kennedy gives a good summary of German economic development in this period in *The Rise and Fall of the Great Powers*:

> '*Its coal production grew from 89 million tons in 1890 to 277 million tons in 1914, just behind Britain's 292 million and far ahead of Austria-Hungary's 47 million, France's 40 million, and Russia's 36 million. In steel, the increases had been even more spectacular, and the 1914 German output of 17.6 million tons was larger than that of Britain, France and Russia combined. More impressive still was the German performance in the newer, twentieth-century industries of electrics, optics, and chemicals. German chemical firms . . . produced 90 per cent of the world's industrial dyes. This success story was naturally reflected in Germany's foreign trade figures, with exports tripling between 1890 and 1913, bringing the country close to Britain as the leading world exporter; not surprisingly, its merchant marine also expanded, to be the second-largest in the world by the eve of the war. By then, its share of world manufacturing production (14.8 per cent) was higher than Britain's (13.6 per cent) and two and a half times that of France (6.1 per cent).*'
>
> Paul Kennedy, *The Rise and Fall of the Great Powers* (1989).

The 'cluster of insignificant states under insignificant princelings' in the 1850s had become welded together by 1914 into a powerful industrial giant right in the heart of Europe. Yet though this was a cause for great national rejoicing, it also posed tremendous challenges to Germany's rulers. In the first place, economic expansion on such a massive scale had profound social and political implications within Germany. Secondly, could Germany exploit its economic strength to establish itself as a leading European and world power without frightening other powers into a defensive alliance against it? In both domestic and foreign policy areas, the Kaiser, his advisers and ministers failed to meet the challenges thrown up by the scale of Germany's economic and industrial expansion, with fateful results both for the second German Reich and for Europe.

Figure 7.3 *Steam-engine wheels at the huge Krupp factory at Essen in the Ruhr, about 1900*

Challenges at home

Socialism

The movement of millions of people from rural areas to cities and towns in search of jobs and new opportunities had profound social consequences. Some found a new freedom and began to question the existing social and political order; others found wretched living and working conditions and were driven to protest and to strike. These years saw the growth of organisations campaigning for greater equality for women – by 1900, more than 850 organisations, with a combined membership of almost a million, were pressing to extend the educational and vocational opportunities open to women. At the same time, in workshops and factories, employees toiled for long hours and low rates of pay, and were frequently moved to protest. In 1900, there were nearly 1,500 strikes involving 321,000 workers. By 1912, nearly 3,000 strikes brought out over a million protesting workers. By the eve of the First World War, 2.6 million German workers were members of trade unions, and over a million had joined the Social Democratic Party (SPD) making it the largest socialist party in Europe.

All these developments frightened the Kaiser, his advisers and the traditional landed elites of Prussia. The Kaiser tried – and failed – to get the Reichstag to pass a bill which would send to prison anyone who 'tries to prevent a working man who is willing to work from doing so or who encourages him to strike'. He attempted to cripple the SPD by legal action or by State coercion; some of his ministers preferred to combat the rise of socialism by extending Bismarck's social insurance schemes, and introducing industrial arbitration courts. Yet others at court were attracted by the notion of a suspension of the whole constitution, and a royal *coup d'état* to impose dictatorial rule on the population. What was never seriously considered was any accommodation with socialist leaders or working-class bodies.

While many men of the left were equally intransigent, and were committed to a revolutionary struggle to overturn the existing system, growing numbers of workers and socialist leaders sought changes within the political and social structure. But their attempts to promote modest social and political reform were resisted, and they continued to be seen as a major threat to the regime, especially after the 1912 elections when the SPD became the largest party in the Reichstag, having secured the support of a third of the electorate. To refuse to make any political concessions to a party of this size was bound to provoke serious domestic conflicts.

Protectionism and Nationalism

While refusing to countenance working-class demands, the German government was only too receptive to the pleas of landowners and of certain industrialists for protection against cheap imports of food and of manufactured goods. Cheap Russian and New World grain was therefore kept out of Germany by tariffs, which secured the livelihood of the agricultural elites, but resulted in high food prices for workers. And while there were extensive indirect taxes on a range of everyday items, the landed elites bitterly resisted the introduction and extension of an inheritance tax or taxes on property.

Such glaring inequalities were justified on the grounds of loyalty and patriotism. The landed elites, industrial combines and naval and military authorities saw their privileged position as a just reward for their strong support for the imperial state. At the same time, they portrayed groups who wanted to bring about social or political change as unpatriotic and disloyal, and tried to weaken their appeal by encouraging the forces of nationalism and of imperialism within Germany.

Through the schools, through the army, and by a variety of other means, the German authorities after 1890 fostered a strong sense of nationalism and of Germany's imperial mission. Pressure groups were encouraged, such as the Colonial Society, the Pan-German League, and the Society for the Eastern Marches. The most popular by far proved to be the Navy League, which by 1914 boasted nearly a million members. There were also radical peasant leagues, and anti-Semitic organisations, dedicated to the expansion of German influence and to a battle against the nation's enemies at home and abroad. While the government found it relatively easy to arouse strong nationalist passions, it was not always able to control them, and frequently in their turn they then put further pressure back on to the government.

National pride and imperial ambitions increasingly centred on an active foreign policy and on the German Navy. Chancellor von Bülow wrote in 1897 that 'only a successful foreign policy can help to reconcile, pacify, rally, unite'. Admiral Alfred von Tirpitz, who had the Kaiser's strong support for his programme of naval expansion, cited as one of the main benefits that 'in the national purpose and economic gains consequent upon it lies a strong palliative against trained and potential Social Democrats'.

Thus Germany looked to imperial and naval expansion and to a vigorous foreign policy to overcome domestic opposition and calls for political change. But difficulties and serious challenges arose abroad as well as at home. Foreign powers were even less willing than German workers to agree to German demands or to submit to German threats. By 1914, Germany found herself dangerously encircled, as a result of a series of ill-conceived expansionist policies.

Challenges abroad

There has been considerable debate among historians as to the precise aims of German foreign policy after 1890. Part of the problem arises directly out of the unstructured way in which decisions were taken and policies were formulated and then changed by the Kaiser and his advisers. But there was also a lack of clarity over aims. While some leaders wanted to see more vigorous German action to gain colonial possessions in Africa and the Far East, others agitated for the extension of economic influence into areas such as the Balkans, China and South America. Military leaders and some industrialists were more interested in the possibilities of acquiring land in Eastern Europe or creating a huge trading bloc – *Mitteleuropa* – under German leadership. Thus the term *Weltpolitik* covered a range of possible options, as the following three extracts, taken from W. O. Simpson's *The Second Reich* (1995) show:

Admiral Müller to Prince Henry, 1896:

'*...our motto must be all or nothing.* Either *we harness the total strength of the nation, ruthlessly, even if it means accepting the risk of a major war,* or *we limit ourselves to continental power alone. The middle way of contenting ourselves with a few left-over pieces of East Africa and the South Sea Islands...; of maintaining a fleet too strong for the mere defence of our coastline yet too weak for the pursuance of* Weltpolitik – *all this implies a dispersal of our strength and a squandering of personal wealth...*'

Speech by Bülow (later Chancellor) to the Reichstag, December 1897:

'*...We regard it as one of our foremost duties, specifically in East Asia, to further and cultivate our shipping, our trade and our industry... We must demand that the German missionary and the German trader, German goods, the German flag and German ships in China are just as much respected as those of other powers... we don't want to put anyone in the shade, but we demand our place in the sun too...*'

Chancellor Bethmann-Hollweg, 1909:

'*On all fronts we must drive forward quietly and patiently in order to regain that trust and confidence without which we cannot consolidate politically or economically. Then we shall be able to realise our greater aims in colonies and world trade without having to risk our existence.*'

As we have seen, the Kaiser was a man of strong opinions who was determined to see Germany play a major world role under his dynamic leadership. The major obstacle to his ambitions seemed to be Great Britain, who possessed by far the greatest empire of any power and whose strong navy protected imperial communications and British trade. Despite – or perhaps because of – his upbringing, which included frequent visits to his English relatives, the Kaiser and his court displayed considerable jealousy and hostility, tinged with a grudging admiration, for Britain. They desperately wanted Germany to be a world power on the same scale as Britain, but to achieve this they believed that British naval mastery would first have to be challenged. At the same time, they hoped that the prospect of a strong German navy would induce Britain to come to some sort of accommodation or diplomatic alliance with Germany, further enhancing Germany's position in the world.

Germany's naval challenge

Admiral Alfred von Tirpitz shared the Kaiser's belief that Germany should mount a naval challenge to Britain, particularly by the creation of a fleet of battleships. Establishing such a fleet would fulfil many objectives. It would guarantee a steady market for the expanding iron and steel works of the Ruhr and of Upper Silesia. It would provide tangible evidence of growing German power, which would in turn satisfy the patriotism of the German population, fostered by the schools, the army and the popular press. It would serve as a unifying force to resolve social tensions, and would symbolise the nation's firm intent to become a leading world power, taking a full part in world affairs and receiving a fair share of colonial spoils and imperial concessions. Two Navy Laws of 1898 and 1900 laid the basis for a powerful German battle fleet, to be constructed 'so that it can unfold its greatest military potential between Heligoland and the Thames...'.

As Gordon Craig concluded in *Germany 1866–1945* (1981):

> 'The new naval programme was, in short, from its very inception directed against Great Britain... the Risk Theory... envisaged a German fleet stationed in home waters that was so strong that in the event of a war with Great Britain it could take offensive action against the British home fleet... As the German fleet grew in size, the British would... be inclined to avoid conflict with Germany or... seek an accommodation with it on terms that would strengthen Germany's continental position...'

In fact, Tirpitz's naval strategy proved totally misconceived both as an instrument for securing increased world power and as a weapon with which to bludgeon Britain into diplomatic negotiations (see chapter 8). Germany's blundering attempts to exert influence on the world stage merely strengthened the forces of opposition to German ambitions in Europe. Britain responded to the direct German challenge in two ways: firstly by increasing the size of its own navy and introducing the revolutionary new battleship, the *Dreadnought*; and secondly by making agreements with other powers. An alliance with Japan in 1902 was followed by an entente with France, which was mainly conceived as an agreement over colonial issues, but was also designed to ensure that Britain and France did not come to blows in the conflict in which their respective allies, Japan and Russia, became involved in 1904.

German rulers after 1890 had indirectly helped France to secure Russia as an ally when they failed to renew Bismarck's Reinsurance Treaty of 1887 with Russia. They had watched in the 1890s as the new allies threatened British power in Asia and in the Mediterranean region. By the first decade of the twentieth century, German naval expansion was driving Britain to seek an agreement with her former colonial rivals – a development which was bound to cause alarm to the German government.

The Moroccan crises

The German government felt menaced by the new Anglo-French entente of 1904 and resolved to challenge it as soon as possible in an effort to drive the two powers apart and at the same time to try to secure from Britain a pledge of neutrality in the event of a European war. In March 1905 the Kaiser, who was en route for a cruise in the Mediterranean, agreed to the suggestion that he should stop off at Tangiers to pay his respects to the Sultan of Morocco. This he did with a theatrical flourish intended to underline the fact that the Sultan could count on German help against further French expansion in the area. At the same time he pointedly told the French consul that 'he knew how to defend German interests in Morocco'.

The visit sparked off an international crisis, and the French were convinced that war was close. In the end, nothing further happened – but the crisis did not succeed in driving Britain and France apart. Quite the opposite happened; relations became closer, as the British government became seriously alarmed at Germany's bullying tactics and at the continuing German naval build-up. Furthermore, in 1907, Britain concluded a historic understanding with her great imperial rival for Asian influence, Russia. By the end of 1907, a Triple Entente had come into being, largely as a result of Tirpitz's naval strategy.

In 1911, Germany made a second attempt to exploit the situation in Morocco, sending the German gunboat *Panther* to Agadir. This gesture was as unsuccessful as the first, but nonetheless, as Winston Churchill (serving at the time as First Lord of the Admiralty in the Liberal government of 1905–14) observed, it set 'all alarm bells throughout Europe' ringing. It also drove British and French military and naval advisers to serious planning to coordinate their naval defence and military strategies to combat any further German challenges. Thus by 1912, Germany's leaders felt that their world ambitions had been thwarted, and at the same time that their position in Europe was being menaced by the growing power of the Entente. More dangerously, the German public had been expecting a series of diplomatic and naval triumphs, and had been disappointed. German leaders felt only too keenly the humiliation of the second Moroccan climb-down. The Chief of Staff, von Moltke, commented bitterly to his wife, 'If we creep out of this affair with our tails between our legs, if we cannot be aroused to an energetic set of demands which we are prepared to enforce by the sword, then I am doubtful about the future of the German Empire. And I will resign.'

From this point onwards, historians have detected a growing desperation among German leaders, and a growing sense that war in Europe was inevitable. Disorders in the Balkans were threatening to weaken their Habsburg ally. Britain would not guarantee to remain neutral in the event of a European conflict. Most menacingly of all, Russia was industrialising, and was increasing both the quality of armaments she could produce, and the speed at which she could mobilise her armies. Given Russia's alliance with France, and the prospect of a two-pronged attack on Germany, German army chiefs had adopted the principles of the Schlieffen Plan (see chapter 8) to combat this threat. Growing Russian power threatened the whole basis of the Schlieffen Plan, and made von Moltke and other military leaders impatient for a war sooner rather than later, while Germany still had the military capacity to defeat her European enemies.

Thus German leaders found their world ambitions thwarted, their European domination increasingly under threat and the situation at home full of revolutionary menace. Their immediate response was to increase the size of the German army, and in 1912 the Reichstag agreed to fund the biggest ever peacetime increase – of more than 30 per cent – to a total of 665,000, with plans for further increases in numbers to over three-quarters of a million in 1914. This move prompted France and Russia to increase their own military strength, and the four-year programme introduced by the Russian government to expand its army by 40 per cent by 1917 threatened to leave Germany even more vulnerable than before. German leaders became ever more frustrated as every move they made to consolidate their own position provoked responses from other powers which seemed to put Germany in a worse position.

Conclusion

Germany's industrial expansion and naval and military power had seemingly failed to deliver world power or European domination. Instead, it had provoked radicalism at home and encirclement abroad. As we shall see in chapter 8, historians are now generally agreed that it was a growing sense of desperation mixed with frustration which led German leaders in 1914 to exploit the crisis caused by the assassination of the Austrian Archduke Franz Ferdinand in Sarajevo in June 1914. A short, sharp, victorious war offered an escape from what seemed to German leaders to be an intolerable situation facing them both at home and abroad. It had worked for Bismarck in the 1860s and again in 1870, and now it could work again, serving to smash the pretensions of the Reichstag and to break the stranglehold of France and Russia.

Alas, once again Germany was proved to have miscalculated. The war which broke out in August 1914 was not short and sharp, but long and bloody. It temporarily drained away German wealth, and it finally brought about not just the abdication of the Kaiser but the collapse of the German empire itself.

Further reading

G. A. Craig, *Germany 1866–1945* (Oxford University Press, 1978) – an excellent textbook for modern German history.

Paul Kennedy, *The Rise and Fall of the Great Powers* (Fontana, 1989) chapter 5 – extremely useful for economic and military statistics.

J. C. G. Rohl and N. Sombart (eds), *Kaiser Wilhelm II, New Interpretations* (Cambridge University Press, 1982).

William Simpson, *The Second Reich*, Cambridge Topics in History (Cambridge University Press, 1995) – contains a lot of useful primary source material.

Hans-Ulrich Wehler, *The German Empire 1871–1918* (Berg, 1985) – a controversial re-assessment by a German historian.

8 The debate about the origins of the First World War

> 'The Allied and Associated Governments affirm, and Germany accepts, the responsibility of Germany and her allies for causing all the loss and damage to which Allied and Associated governments and their nationals have been subjected as a consequence of the war imposed on them by the aggression of Germany and her allies.'
>
> Article 231, Treaty of Versailles, June 1919.

> '... German policy in the crisis of July 1914 must rank as one of the great disasters of world history. The leaders of arguably the most successful country in Europe ... took decisions which plunged it and the other powers into a ghastly war in which almost ten million men lost their lives ... any German with inside information on how the war had really begun knew that the responsibility for the catastrophe lay principally not with France, or Russia, or Britain, but with a small handful of men in Vienna and Berlin.'
>
> Professor John Rohl, *Decisions for War* (1995).

More than 75 years separates these two extracts, yet their findings are remarkably similar. Both lay the blame for the outbreak of the First World War on Germany and on her principal ally, Austria-Hungary. However, in the intervening period, a vigorous historical debate has been raging over the origins of the war, and over the wide range of contentious issues which helped to provoke it. Both general and particular factors have been cited as possible causes of war in 1914.

This chapter will first list the most commonly cited causes of war in 1914, and then review the debate which has raged since 1919 about why war broke out in the summer of 1914. As you follow the course of the various arguments, you will notice that the debate has turned full circle in the past 20 years; it is now back to a firm assertion of German guilt.

Time chart

1882: Germany, Austria-Hungary and Italy form the Triple Alliance

1894: France and Russia sign defensive alliance

1904: France and Great Britain sign agreement on colonial disputes, which becomes known as the Entente Cordiale

1905: First Moroccan crisis. Wilhelm II intervenes in Moroccan affairs, hoping to drive a wedge between Britain and France, but fails

1906: **January** Algeciras Conference settles crisis. Britain and France hold military talks, including possibility of a British expeditionary force being sent to France in the event of a military conflict

February Britain launches the *Dreadnought*, a big-gun battleship which makes existing naval vessels obsolete. Naval rivalry between Britain and Germany is intensified

1907: Britain and Russia sign a convention; Britain, France and Russia now referred to as the Triple Entente powers

1908: Austria-Hungary annexes Bosnia and Herzegovina

1911: Second Moroccan crisis when German gunboat, *Panther*, arrives at Agadir. Crisis is resolved by the autumn in talks between Germany and France.
Italy declares war on Turkey, and annexes Tripoli in Libya

1912: First Balkan war breaks out with Serbia, Greece, Bulgaria and Montenegro fighting against Turkey. Turkey is defeated

1913: Second Balkan war breaks out when Greece and Serbia fight against their former ally Bulgaria

1914: **28 June** Archduke Franz Ferdinand assassinated at Sarajevo by a Bosnian extremist trained and equipped in Serbia
23 July Austria-Hungary sends Serbia a ten-point ultimatum
24 July Russia declares support for Serbia in the event of attack by Austria-Hungary
25 July Serbia accepts most, but not all, points of the ultimatum. Austria-Hungary begins mobilisation
28 July Austria-Hungary declares war on Serbia
30 July Russia begins general mobilisation
1 August Germany declares war on Russia. France mobilises
3 August Germany declares war on France and invades Belgium
4 August Germany declares war on Belgium; Britain declares war on Germany
5 August Austria-Hungary declares war on Russia
10 August France declares war on Austria-Hungary
12 August Britain declares war on Austria-Hungary

General factors

The following factors could be considered to have heightened international tensions in the first two decades of the twentieth century:

1 The mood of the period: the development of Social Darwinism led to a belief that a competitive environment was natural, and that nations were bound to compete with each other for resources and for power.

2 The growth of popular nationalism: the spread of primary education and the growth of a popular press led to the intensification of a sense of national identity and of awareness of rivalries with other nations.

3 The growth of economic and colonial rivalries, and the development of capitalism led to the spread of 'economic imperialism' as well as to the clash of more traditional imperialist rivalries.

4 The development of European alliance systems, especially the Triple Alliance between Germany, Austria-Hungary and Italy, and the Triple Entente of France, Russia and Britain, intensified the production by individual nations of offensive military plans. Germany claimed it was being 'encircled' by the Triple Entente.

5 Arms races – both military and naval, but in particular the Anglo-German competition in naval armaments – increased international tensions between 1900 and 1914.

Specific rivalries

1 The decline of Turkey and the rise of Balkan nationalism.

2 Rivalry between Austria-Hungary and Russia in eastern and south-eastern Europe.

3 Franco-German hostility, and in particular, French bitterness at the loss of Alsace and Lorraine in 1871.

4 Germany's ambitions as a world power, and its challenge to British and French global political and economic interests.

5 The growth of Russian economic and military power, and the challenge this posed to Germany.

The debate in the interwar period

Reparations

Reparations were the payments Germany was supposed to make to the victorious Allies to compensate them for their losses and expenditure during the First World War. Article 231 of the Treaty of Versailles declared that Germany was to blame for the war, so was liable to make these payments. The amount was fixed in 1921 at £6,600 million, but Germany never paid more than a fraction of them. Reparations were a source of much resentment in postwar Germany.

Hardly surprisingly, Article 231 of the Treaty of Versailles caused a storm of protest in Germany. The German delegates, representing the new republican regime which had emerged since the abdication of the Kaiser in November 1918, signed the Treaty only under duress. The German interpretation of the situation which had faced the country before 1914 was that Germany was encircled by an aggressive ring of great powers – Russia, France and Britain – and had no alternative but to try to break out of it. This was widely believed, not just in 1914 or in 1918, but as late as the 1930s. A popular German textbook of the 1920s, used in secondary schools, explained the situation thus:

> 'In the so-called peace treaty, the unheard of demand for **reparations** and the unexampled exploitation of Germany was founded on the lie regarding Germany's war guilt. Did Germany desire the war, did she prepare it maliciously and begin it wantonly? Today every informed person inside and outside Germany knows that Germany is absolutely innocent with regard to the outbreak of war. Russia, France and England wanted war and unleashed it.'

Weimar Germany never accepted the findings of Article 231. Leaders of successive governments believed that if they could show that the detested 'war guilt clause' was a lie, then the legal basis for the repayment of reparations would disappear, and the way would be open for wholesale revision of the entire treaty. A special branch of the German Foreign Office was set up, the War Guilt Section. This section organised, financed and directed two main units: a Working Committee of German Associations for Combating Lies Concerning War Responsibility, which circulated literature to trade unions, clubs and employers' associations, and a Centre for the Study of the Causes of War. This recruited scholars, journalists and teachers to demonstrate the inaccuracy of Article 231, and by extension, the whole treaty. Forty volumes of material were published between 1922 and 1927, based mainly on German Foreign Office archives, and excluding material from General Staff records, Navy Office files or from the Ministry of War. Some documents have since been found to have been falsified, and crucial episodes were ignored – such as the Potsdam meetings between the Austrian envoy, the Kaiser and Chancellor Bethmann-Hollweg on 5–6 July 1914, at which the so-called 'blank cheque' was issued to the Austrians.

German interpretations of events in 1914 centred on the aggression of the Serbian government, which, they alleged, had close connections with the Black Hand group to which the Archduke's assassin belonged. Austria had to meet this challenge, and Germany had no option but to support her ally. Britain should have helped Germany to localise the conflict, but in any event this would have been virtually impossible because of full Russian mobilisation in support of Serbia. The German conclusion was that no single nation was responsible for the events of 1914, and certainly not Germany. Some German historians acknowledged that there might have been miscalculations on the part of German leaders, such as the Kaiser's belief that, because a royal heir to the throne had been murdered at Sarajevo, Tsar Nicholas II would not support Serbia and condone such an act, or a mistaken belief that Britain might stay neutral in the face of an unfolding European war. However, they argued, these errors of judgement did not in any way lead to unwarranted aggressive action on the part of Germany.

Germany's massive output of documents and publications in the 1920s provoked other governments into publishing their prewar diplomatic records to show that they, too, had nothing to hide. The British Government published 11 volumes between 1926 and 1938, the Austrian Government eight in 1930, and France started on a complicated project divided into three series. Some Russian documents were published in Berlin between 1931 and 1934; no Serbian documents, however, were published by the Yugoslav government until 1980. Because most of the primary sources produced were diplomatic documents, and because the destructive impact of four years of war had discredited the 'old' diplomacy, increasing emphasis was laid by historians on prewar 'secret diplomacy'. They blamed the increasingly rigid alliance systems, and what appeared to be the total bankruptcy of the entire European diplomatic system. This view of a general European breakdown was shared by two very different world leaders after 1918, the United States President, Woodrow Wilson, and leader of the new Bolshevik regime, Lenin.

Shared guilt: Woodrow Wilson's views

Woodrow Wilson believed very firmly that secret diplomacy and the selfish greed of the prewar European great powers had brought them into collision in 1914. Only a transformation of the way in which the international system operated would prevent wars in future; hence he saw his great mission as the establishment of a League of Nations. Many League enthusiasts in Britain in the interwar period shared Wilson's distrust of secret diplomacy and his view of a general European diplomatic breakdown in 1914. So did two United States academics, Harry Barnes and

Sidney Fay. In 1925, Barnes wrote a book called *The Genesis of World War*, largely to express his anger at war in general and at the authors of the Great War in particular, who he deemed to be the Serbian and Russian governments. Three years later, Fay produced a two-volume *Origins of the World War*. He exonerated the Serbian government, and believed that Germany should not have promised her Austrian ally a free hand against Serbia. However, he blamed this on the Kaiser's short-sighted diplomacy, not on a general German attitude of aggression. Fay's conclusion was that it was Russian mobilisation which precipitated the final catastrophe leading to German mobilisation, but that it was the reckless policy of Austria-Hungary which was more responsible than any other power for the immediate origin of the war. As for Germany, it never planned for war in 1914 and did not want war.

Fay's assessment was extremely influential both in the United States and in Britain for the next 30 years, though it was immediately challenged by Renouvin in France and by Schmitt in the United States. Both these historians placed their emphasis on the dangerous gamble which Germany took in 1914 by giving full support to Austria and counting on the willingness of Russia to accept diplomatic defeat. Schmitt argued that the two Central Powers were out to alter the balance of power in the Balkans, and that this was bound to provoke Russia into a military response. Therefore German policy was belligerent and dangerously aggressive.

Shared guilt: Lenin's views

The perspective of Lenin was somewhat different; he saw the policies of all the great powers before 1914 as being inherently aggressive, as a direct result of their development as advanced capitalist states. As we saw in chapter 4, Lenin viewed the First World War as an imperialist struggle among the great capitalist powers for the reallocation of world resources and markets. He argued that the war in 1914 was caused by economic rivalries generated by cliques of highly-organised financiers putting pressure on their governments. There was enough plausibility in this approach to cause a lasting impact, particularly among those of a left-wing or radical persuasion. Armaments manufacturers, whether French or German, had clearly exerted a powerful influence before 1914; there had been strong Anglo-German commercial and naval rivalry; there had been imperial scrambles for territory and concessions in Africa, in the Near East and in China.

However, colonial and trading disputes, while they may have contributed to a more inflamed international atmosphere, were largely resolved by the end of the first decade of the twentieth century. Far more of a threat to international stability was posed by more traditional rivalries, involving struggles for power in areas regarded as strategically and militarily important. These rivalries provoked the most serious clashes – Austria-Hungary's attempt to impose its will on Serbia, Russia's hopes to spread its influence in the Near East, the dreams of the pan-German nationalists to secure German mastery of the Russian steppes. It was not the capitalist system as such which was giving rise to ambition, but traditional desires for prestige and influence and great power status. These may well have been sharpened directly or indirectly by economic competition and the development of industry, but were not primarily caused by such factors.

Thus one could query whether Serbia was an industrialised power in 1914. Was monopoly capitalism exercising such a considerable influence on the Russian court and on the Habsburgs? Why did not that most advanced of capitalist nations in 1914, the United States, become embroiled in the imperialist rivalries which triggered off the war? One can show that Lenin's theories do not fit the facts of 1914 very closely, but nonetheless his interpretation exercised a powerful influence during the interwar period. It became the orthodox Marxist 'explanation' of the outbreak of war in 1914 adopted by east European governments after 1945. As late as 1968, East German historians were arguing that the First World War constituted 'a quarrel among the imperialists for a new division of the world'. Monopoly capitalists and Junker agrarians, assisted by the military, unleashed the war which was inevitable owing to the 'conflicts inherent to the capitalist social order'.

The essential point which was common to both the United States and Soviet interpretations of 1914 was that no one single nation or alliance was responsible for war. If guilt was appropriate, it should be shared. If the breakdown of the entire European diplomatic system or the development of an advanced stage of capitalism was at fault, then this was beyond the control of a single nation. By the late 1930s, the view which prevailed most strongly about the origins of the war was the one put forward by the former British Prime Minister David Lloyd George in his *War Memoirs*, that 'the nations in 1914 slithered over the brink into the boiling cauldron of war'. There was no general 'will to war'; the crisis escalated, nations were carried away despite themselves, and a war broke out which no single country really wanted.

Shared guilt: the generals' fault

More recent historical work offered a variant on this theme. L. C. F. Turner, in his *Origins of the First World War* (1970), drew attention to the miscalculations made by leading statesmen in the various European countries, especially in Germany, and to the failure of civilian leaders throughout Europe to appreciate until too late the military implications of their decisions. Other historians have drawn attention to the predominance of military decision-making in 1914, and to the eclipse in the great European capitals of the power and influence of civilian leaders by high-ranking and power-hungry military and naval leaders.

This line of analysis, which seeks to suggest that the outbreak of war in 1914 was really an accident arising out of a crisis in which events careered out of control, is not supported by the full weight of historical evidence now available. There was no equivocation on the part of Austria-Hungary after 28 June, as work by recent historians has shown. Austria-Hungary was determined to exact military revenge on Serbia. Equally, the Russian government was resolved to support Serbia if it was attacked. The German government was well aware that Russia might be drawn into the Austro-Serbian conflict, but nonetheless gave full support to its Austrian ally and prepared itself for any military consequences which might arise. The French government was prepared to honour the terms of its alliance with Russia, even if this meant war. Certainly there came a point, in late July, when military considerations took precedence over diplomatic ones, but these stemmed from political decisions which had been taken by the various governments concerned as early as the end of June.

Austria and nationalism

Some studies of the origins of the war have focused on the intractable nationality issues which caused so much conflict in eastern Europe in the late nineteenth and early twentieth centuries. In his Historical Association pamphlet 'The Origins of the First World War' (1958), Bernadotte Schmitt argued that the primary cause of war in 1914 was the denial of self-determination to minority groups. 'More than any other circumstance', he maintained, 'this conflict between existing governments and their unhappy minorities was responsible for the catastrophe of 1914.' The tensions which arose throughout eastern Europe as a result of political frontiers cutting across lines of nationality was especially acute in the Habsburg empire, and gave rise to the bitter conflict between Austria-Hungary and Serbia.

There has been much debate among historians about the foreign policy pursued by the Habsburg rulers, and the extent to which it was motivated by defensive or aggressive considerations, and by internal or external factors. Many historians have portrayed Austria's external policy in the years before 1914 as primarily defensive, aimed at keeping peace in the

Balkans and working to prevent any change in the balance of power there. They argue that this strategy of containment was fatally undermined by the sudden collapse of Turkish power in Europe in 1912, and that after this date, Austria faced the prospect of a desperate struggle for her own survival as a great power. F. R. Bridge, in his Historical Association pamphlet 'The Coming of the First World War' (1983) argued that both Austria and Russia were motivated in their Balkan policies by a quest for security which brought them into constant conflict. However, the existence of the Turkish empire in south-east Europe acted as a stabilising factor, operating as a 'shock absorber in the international system'. It was only when this buffer between the great powers was suddenly removed, after the Balkan Wars of 1912–13, that serious conflict in the Balkans became inevitable, and a peaceful solution to Austria's problems proved impossible to achieve.

Some historians have depicted Austria's attempts to crush Serbia as aggressive and totally reckless. Unable or unwilling to solve internal problems, its government has been perceived as embarking on a suicide mission against Serbia which was bound to involve the country in war with Russia, and possibly with other powers as well. Others, however, have argued that Austria's external policy between 1912 and 1914 was not unduly influenced by domestic considerations. They believe that a much more important consideration influencing Austrian policy was the German government's reluctance to support Austrian interests during the Balkan Wars or to recognise the growing danger posed by Serbian ambitions. Because the German government sought to distance itself from the Balkan crisis, the Austrian government felt itself increasingly isolated in the face of a mounting challenge from Serbia, behind which lurked the prospect of a Balkan Federation linked to Russia. It was this threat, it is argued, rather than domestic considerations, which motivated Austria's policy in the Balkans in 1914 and caused it to become more and more desperate.

However, there is general agreement that German decision-making was a crucial element in the tense situation after the June assassination. Without the assurance of German support, given so instantly and unequivocally to Austria on 5 July by the Kaiser and German Chancellor, Austria would not have embarked on its fatal confrontation with Serbia. It has been widely asserted that German policy held the key to the situation in the summer of 1914, and that it was the German desire to profit diplomatically and militarily from the crisis which widened the conflict from an east European one to a continental and world war.

The historiographical impact of the outbreak of war in 1939

It was the circumstances of the outbreak of the Second World War which made historians look again at German policy-making in 1914. Was Hitler a freak, a historical accident? Or was there some underlying continuity of aggressive German ambition, an aim to expand into eastern Europe and to dominate Russia, which was relevant to 1914 too? Those interested in the causes of the First World War began to look again at German policy before 1914. The first person to do this exhaustively was Luigi Albertini, an Italian journalist. He went through all the available documents, interviewed all the surviving participants, and wrote a three-volume work *The Origins of the War of 1914*, between 1942 and 1943, though this was not published in English until the 1950s. Albertini's view was that the German declaration of support for Austria in July 1914 constituted a very risky gamble, and that German mobilisation was equivalent to war because of the **Schlieffen Plan**.

This view was shared by A. J .P. Taylor in his 1954 publication *The Struggle for Mastery in Europe 1848–1914*. He asserted that 'the sole cause for the outbreak of war in 1914 was the Schlieffen Plan', because, while Austrian and Russian mobilisations were diplomatic moves, Germany's

---

The Schlieffen Plan

This was a military plan, first put forward by the Prussian Field-Marshal Alfred Schlieffen (see photo) in 1895, to defend Germany against possible simultaneous military attacks by the allied powers France and Russia. He advocated a rapid German breakthrough in Belgium and the defeat of France within six weeks by a major wide-flanking movement which would cut Paris off from the sea. Because it took the Russian government some weeks to mobilise its army, only a small number of German troops would need to be deployed on Germany's eastern frontier, leaving the great majority to complete the defeat of France, before rejoining them for the war in the east against Russia.

Though Albertini acknowledged the fact that Russian policy escalated the crisis, that the Serbs had no intention of compromising with Austria, and that Grey could have warned the Germans earlier of likely British intervention, he concluded that 'final, definite responsibility for the outbreak of the war lies with the German plan of mobilisation'.

meant war. Within western Germany, Gerhard Ritter had already embarked on an extremely thorough and critical examination of the problem of militarism in Germany, which resulted ultimately in a four-volume publication, which appeared in an English translation in the early 1970s as *The Sword and the Sceptre*. While he found much to criticise in the growing power and ascendancy of the military elites in Wilhelmine Germany, he nonetheless still believed, in 1960, that German political and military leaders had been overwhelmed by the crisis of 1914, and that 'we have no right to doubt the genuineness of their basic desire for peace. No one in a position of authority wanted to bring about a world war; in this sense the "war-guilt question" no longer exists.' However, contrary to Ritter's belief, within a year the 'war-guilt question' was brought to centre-stage once more with the publication of a lengthy work by Fritz Fischer, entitled *Griff Nach der Weltmacht*, published in England in 1966 under the rather different title *Germany's Aims in the First World War*.

The Fischer controversy

Fischer's book caused a sensation, and provoked a great outcry in West Germany, particularly among fellow historians, for it presented three provocative theses. The first one asserted that the German government in July 1914 accepted, and indeed hoped, that a major European war would result from its backing of Austria against Serbia. The second suggested that the war aims of the Kaiser's government not only pre-dated the outbreak of war, but also showed a remarkable similarity with the plans made by the Nazis for conquest after 1933. The third argued that the sources of German expansionism were to be found less in Germany's international position than in her social, economic and political domestic situation on the eve of war.

In coming to such conclusions, Fischer had the benefit of being allowed access to the Imperial archives in Potsdam, located since 1945 in the newly created state of East Germany. This in itself annoyed the West German historical establishment, but it was the way in which he utilised his documentary findings to frame a charge of general German responsibility for the outbreak of war in 1914 which really enraged his critics. He did not share Ritter's belief that civilian leaders, such as Chancellor Bethmann-Hollweg, had been misled or dominated by the military. Indeed, he argued that the sources revealed no substantial difference in approach or in objectives between the civilian and military decision-makers.

For the next few years, Fischer's work was the subject of great controversy, and he himself became the subject of bitter personal attacks. The

West German government cancelled funding for a lecture tour Fischer had arranged to undertake in the United States. But the staunchness with which Fischer defended his views, and the documentary material which became available during the 1960s, much of it collected by Fischer's former pupil, Immanuel Geiss, forced Fischer's critics to look again at the policies pursued by German leaders in 1914. They began to admit, grudgingly, that German strategy in 1914 had been a high-risk one, but argued that it had been justified by the growing Russian military build-up and construction of railways in her western provinces. Pessimism about the future and in particular about the inexorable growth of Russian power affected both civilian and military leaders in Germany in 1914, it was argued, and made them willing to run the risk of war in 1914, not to achieve aggressive objectives but to secure Germany's position as a great power.

This view was strongly challenged by Fischer in his second major book which came out in 1969, and appeared in English in 1975 as *War of Illusions*. The focus of this book was on German policy between 1911 and 1914, and Fischer drew on detailed documentary evidence to substantiate his charge that there was a strong 'will to war' among German leaders before 1914. In particular, he drew attention to the personal diary of Admiral Müller, which had only been published in 1965, and which referred to a meeting between the Kaiser and his chief military and naval advisers on 8 December 1912. The Kaiser had been informed by his new ambassador to London that, in the event of a German attack on France, Britain would come to France's aid. This provoked a general review of the European situation which led the Chief of the General Staff, von Moltke, to comment, 'In my opinion war is inevitable, and the sooner the better'. This view appeared to be generally agreed, as was the desirability of a war against Russia being 'better prepared' in the press. Fischer laid great emphasis on this 'war council' meeting, and argued that it revealed a clear intention on the part of Germany's leaders to wage European war at the earliest favourable opportunity.

Fischer's researches also laid great emphasis on the social and political structure of Wilhelmine Germany, and on the power wielded by a set of autocratic, militaristic Junkers, who were violently anti-democratic and anti-modern. They felt their domestic position to be under threat from the forces of social democracy, and their world aspirations to be increasingly blocked by the 'encirclement' policies of France, Russia and Britain, and by their own lack of investment capital.

The debate since Fischer

Fischer's claim that it was domestic, social and political factors which were instrumental in shaping Germany's increasingly aggressive foreign policy after 1911 was taken up by a younger generation of German historians in the 1970s. In particular, Wehler developed further the concept of the 'primacy of domestic politics', and Herwig portrayed the German ruling elite as 'ridden with anxiety, guilt, fear and paranoia, yet at the same time dominated by a remarkable egoism'. He argued that 'German statesmen and soldiers by the second decade of the twentieth century could see escape from their predicament only in a "mad bolt"'.

The publication in 1972 of the diaries of Kurt Riezler, Bethmann-Hollweg's closest adviser, only served to substantiate this view of the German leadership being willing to pursue a dangerous, high-risk strategy in 1914, though there remained disagreement over whether this was to further long-nurtured, aggressive designs or because of defensive motives.

By the mid 1980s, Fischer's interpretation of German policy was becoming accepted as the new orthodoxy. Writing in *Europe Transformed* in 1983, Norman Stone commented that 'not many historians nowadays dissent from the proposition that the German government, egged on by its generals, deliberately provoked the war of 1914'. James Joll, in *The Origins of the First World War*, published in 1984, argued that by December 1912 German rulers had 'accepted war as inevitable' but were concerned to wage it at the most opportune time. One of the most recent reviews of writing on the origins of the First World War, published in 1992, suggests that three-quarters of Fischer's assertions are now accepted as valid. However, disagreements remain, largely over the importance of the 'war council' meeting of December 1912 and of the extent to which it supports the view that Germany was planning for war since that time, and over the nature of Germany's aims in 1914. Were Germany's leaders really trying to 'grab at world power' in July 1914, or were their aspirations based on continental Europe? Were their policies the product of confident, determined, expansionist ambitions, or did they result from feelings of increasing insecurity and growing pessimism about the future?

Much work has also been carried out over the past few years into the pre-war planning and domestic situations of the other major European states. Meticulous research has suggested that neither Russia nor France wanted war in 1914; Britain also wished to avoid a military conflict, but did not know how best to achieve this. There is still disagreement on the point that if Grey, early on in the crisis, had given a firmer assurance that

Britain would stand by her entente partners and intervene on their side in a general European conflict, it might have caused a rethink of German policy. The latest study of Habsburg foreign policy suggests that by 1914, Austria was determined to wage war against Serbia, and that July of that year saw a 'fateful meshing of aggressive German *Weltpolitik* with an even more aggressive, irresponsible Habsburg *Balkanpolitik*'.

So by the late 1990s, the verdict of the Treaty of Versailles, which aroused so much controversy between the two world wars, had become endorsed by the majority of historians. Writing in *The Coming of the First World War*, published in 1991, Hartmut Pogge von Strandmann observed that 'in the present state of research, the evidence that Germany and Austria started the war and dragged the rest of the powers into it is even stronger than in the early 1960s when Fischer published his analysis of German war aims policies'. We await the publication of new source material or of future books and articles seeking to challenge what has now become the standard interpretation of the origins of the First World War.

Further reading

V. R. Berghahn, *Germany and the Approach of War in 1914* (Macmillan, 1973) – detailed analysis of German decision-making in the years before 1914.

F. R. Bridge, *The Coming of the First World War* (Historical Association pamphlet, 1983) – useful general survey of the issues.

Ruth Henig, *The Origins of the First World War*, Lancaster pamphlet (Routledge, 1989).

James Joll, *The Origins of the First World War* (Addison Wesley Longman, 1984) – excellent broad analysis of the issues.

W. O. Simpson, *The Second Reich*, Cambridge Topics in History (Cambridge University Press, 1995) – chapter 5.

K. Wilson (ed.), *Decisions for War, 1914* (UCL Press, 1995) – the most recent country-by-country assessment of responsibility for the conflict.

9 Why did the First World War go on so long?

Time chart

1914: 28 June Assassination of Archduke Ferdinand at Sarajevo

28 July Austria-Hungary declares war on Serbia

1 August Germany declares war on Russia

3 August Germany declares war on France and invades Belgium

4 August Germany declares war on Belgium; Britain declares war on Germany

23 August Battle of Mons

26–30 August Battle of Tannenberg

5–10 September Battle of Marne

6–15 September Battle of Masurian Lakes

15 September First trenches dug

18 October–22 November Battle of Ypres

17–29 December Battle of Artois

1915: 25 April Allied landings at Gallipoli

22 April–27 May Gas first used at second Battle of Ypres

7 May Sinking of the *Lusitania*

4 May–18 June Second Battle of Artois

25 September–14 October Third Battle of Artois

1916: 9 January Allies evacuate Gallipoli

21 February–18 December Battle of Verdun

31 May–1 June Battle of Jutland

6 June Arab revolt in the Hejaz

4 June–10 October Brusilov Offensive

1 July–19 November Battle of the Somme

7 November Woodrow Wilson re-elected president of USA; death of Franz Josef, Emperor of Austria-Hungary

7 December Lloyd George becomes Prime Minister of Britain

1917: 15 March Abdication of Tsar Nicholas II of Russia

6 April USA enters war on Allied side

19–29 April Nivelle's Offensive at Chemin des Dames

31 July–10 November Battle of Passchendaele

24 October–10 November Battle of Caporetto

7 November Bolsheviks seize power in Russia; Clemenceau becomes Prime Minister of France

20 November–8 December Battle of Cambrai

1918: 8 January Woodrow Wilson publishes '14 Points'

3 March Russia and Central Powers sign Treaty of Brest-Litovsk

21 March–18 July German Spring Offensive

18 July–10 November Allied counter-offensive

28 October Mutiny of German sailors at Kiel

9 November Kaiser abdicates

11 November Armistice between Allies and Germany

Everyone expected the war to be short. The enthusiasm of young men across the whole of Europe to join their country's armies (see Figure 9.1), was based on the expectation that it would be 'over by Christmas'. Generals and politicians had planned for a short war of rapid movement. For Germany, the basis of their war-planning was the daring but risky Schlieffen Plan (see chapter 8). Five German armies would sweep across Belgium and Luxembourg into France, capturing Paris and knocking out the French Army in precisely 42 days. They would then turn to deal with the huge Russian army, but with the aim of forcing an advantageous peace in under a year.

Britain in 1914 had no intention of, or capability for, fighting a long land war. The French Plan XVII was designed to recapture Alsace and Lorraine in rapid pincer movements. In both armies, soldiers were trained for a war of movement, with cavalry playing an important role and infantry soldiers in hand-to-hand combat. Through the autumn of 1914 all these plans came unstuck. Once the Battle of the Marne had ensured that the Schlieffen Plan was not going to work, once the trenches had been dug and occupied, all hopes for a short war were cancelled. How can we explain why it took so long, over four more years, before the conflict was resolved?

Strategy and operations

The historian Paul Kennedy explains it simply: 'Until one of the coalitions had a distinct superiority at all levels of military effectiveness, it was not possible to overcome the stalemate that was the First World War.' For most of the war there was no distinct superiority but a combination of strengths and weaknesses on both sides. Kennedy defines four levels of military effectiveness:

- political (Are the resources of the country fully committed to war?)

- strategic (How is the war to be won?)

- operational (How is each battle to be won?)

- tactical (How good are the soldiers at fighting?).

In this chapter we will combine the first two, and call it 'strategy', and the last two as 'operations'.

Strategy

Operations

Case study: the war at sea

1 *The surface war*

Let us see how these two elements of military effectiveness – strategy and operations – worked in the surface war at sea. The German Naval Commander, Admiral von Tirpitz, saw his battle fleet in the form of a 'sharp knife, held gleaming and ready only a few inches away from the jugular vein of Germany's most likely enemy'. He had no strategic plan other than to lure the British navy to come out and fight him.

British strategic planning was much more clearly thought out. Their superior fleet controlled the seas on the western approaches to Germany and so could operate a blockade. This was the main function of the fleet and its main contribution to the Allied victory. This advantage could be lost in an afternoon if a battle went wrong, so the British avoided engagements. When it did come to a battle, at Jutland in 1916, the German fleet showed some operational superiority, sinking more British ships and causing more damage. Admiral Jellicoe's decision to turn away from the engagement, although not very glorious, was wise. The British retained their superiority and the German Fleet was sentenced to languish in harbour, eventually collapsing into mutiny.

2 *The U-boat war*

For Germany, unrestricted U-boat warfare was a strategy of high risks and potentially high gains. The risk was that sinking ships on their way to Allied ports could cause the deaths of American citizens (most famously on the *Lusitania*, sunk on 7 May 1915 with the loss of 128 US lives, but on other vessels too). This could well hasten the entry of the USA into the war on the Allied side. The possible strategic benefit was the crippling of the British economy and food supply. For this reason unrestricted U-boat warfare, which began in February 1915, was called off in September, re-commenced in March 1916, but halted in April following American protests, and begun again in earnest in February 1917.

Operationally the U-boats were very successful. The worst month for British shipping was April 1917, when 545,000 tons of ships were sunk. If this had gone on for only a few more months Britain's ability to carry on with the war would be in doubt. British anti-U-boat warfare was ineffective, as Winston Churchill later described:

'In one week in September 1916 three U-boats operated in the Channel between Beachy Head and the Eddystone lighthouse, an area patrolled by 49 destroyers, 48 torpedo-boats, 7 Q-ships and 468 armed auxiliaries, 572 anti-submarine vessels, not counting aircraft. They sank 30 ships and were entirely unscathed themselves.'

The Navy had dismissed the idea of escorted convoys as a way of protecting merchant ships but after the losses of April 1917, Lloyd George insisted that an experimental convoy should be tried. It was a success and by September 1917 convoys were in general use. Losses never came near the figures of Spring 1917 again; this analysis from a German U-boat commander, Karl Dönitz, explains why:

'The oceans at once became bare and empty. For long periods of time the U-boats, operating individually, would see nothing at all. Then suddenly up would loom a huge concourse of ships, 30 or 40 of them, surrounded by a strong escort of warships of all types. The solitary U-boat would then attack, for perhaps several days and nights, until physical exhaustion of commander and crew called a halt. The lone U-boat might sink one or two ships, even several. But that was a poor percentage of the whole. The convoy would steam on. In most cases no other German U-boat would catch sight of it and it would reach Britain, bringing a rich cargo of foodstuffs and raw materials safely to port.'

Breaking the stalemate

The war at sea was important in contributing to the eventual Allied victory, but the war as a whole could not be won at sea. There had to be a resolution of the stalemate on the Western Front. The reasons for the stalemate are clear: strategically, both coalitions could use the resources of government, industry and transport to put huge numbers of men into the war. There was no overwhelming superiority of numbers on one side or the other, given the nature of the fronts they had to hold. (The arrival of the USA was to tip this balance, of course, but not until well into 1918.) Operationally, the balance of firepower lay with the weapons of defence – machine-guns, heavy artillery – rather than offence. The problem was the same for everyone and was concisely put by the British Major-General Money:

> 'How to surprise, over-run and penetrate a well-sited defence system, some four miles deep, the front edge of which was only a short distance from one's own, protected by massive wire entanglements, and covered by the flanking fire of machine-guns and a wall of fire from artillery and mortars of all calibres, sited in depth.'

There was also the sheer scale of the war on the Western Front. Figure 9.2 shows the extent of the trenches from November 1914 to March 1918: over 700 kilometres from the sea to the Swiss border. Although this was partly a modern, mechanised war, it was quite old-fashioned in other ways. When it came to the action, soldiers were simply required to get out of their trenches and walk or run over to the enemy trenches. If a breakthrough was made, supplying advancing troops was enormously difficult.

All of this was entirely unprecedented. One cannot blame the generals for being stumped. What the situation demanded was lateral thinking, openness to new ideas, widespread discussion with the men who were actually doing the fighting, and readiness to investigate new technological responses to the problem. These qualities seem to have been in short supply on all sides.

Germany

Industrial developments in Germany in the later nineteenth and early twentieth century had supplied the army with newer and better weapons in ever increasing quantities. But industrial Germany was not the Army's Germany; this was still aristocratic, landowning Prussia. It was an army in

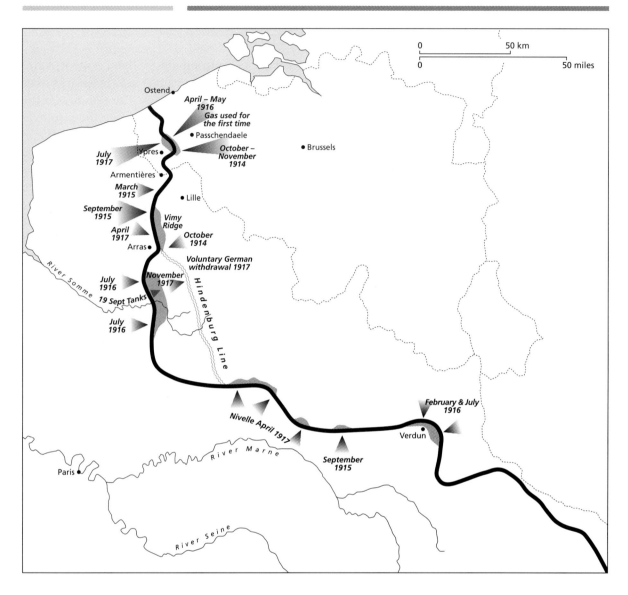

Figure 9.2 The Western Front,
November 1914 to March 1918

which a young man could become an officer if he came from the right family even if his educational achievement was poor. It was an army with no Jews or members of the German Social Democratic Party, the SPD. The army was seen by the Kaiser as the guarantor of social order against the new forces unleashed by industrialisation.

It was true that the army had created modern Germany, in wars with Denmark in 1864, Austria in 1866–7 and France in 1870–1. But these great victories were now increasingly remote, part of the hallowed traditions of the army which its supreme commander, the Kaiser, loved and cultivated. The curious state which Bismarck created, apparently democratic but in fact profoundly monarchical (see chapter 1), was in part designed to keep the army away from democratic interference. This meant that all final military decisions revolved around the erratic enthusiasms of the Kaiser. Decisions were not discussed in an open forum by those who had to implement them. Loyalty and tradition were the watchwords. All these factors meant that hard-headed strategic planning did not take place.

The Schlieffen Plan, for example, was worked out, largely on his own, by Field-Marshal Alfred Schlieffen. It was initially proposed in 1895 but the War Ministry did not hear of it until 1912. There was no discussion of whether the gamble of invading Belgium was worth the risk of bringing in Britain. There was no attempt to involve the Navy in preventing a British force crossing the Channel. There was no joint discussion with Germany's oldest ally, Austria-Hungary. In the event, one major reason for its failure was its impracticability in detail. German troops at the beginning of the Battle of the Marne had been marching 15 miles a day for three weeks, fighting all the way.

Nor should we assume that the German army had the best of the technology. They rejected the development of lorries for transporting supplies, preferring horses. Von Kluck's army in 1914, for example, included 84,000 horses which consumed two million pounds of fodder a day. The sheer logistics of this supply problem help to explain why a war of movement could not be sustained.

 At this level the German army excelled. Their officers had a narrow but effective training. They learned fastest and most logically from the experience of the first few engagements in the trenches. They:

- built better trenches, communication posts and dugouts;
- made better use of barbed wire, sandbags and camouflage;
- developed better flame-throwers, parapet-piercing bullets, hand-grenades, trench-mortars, steel helmets and machine-guns.

Their defence in depth wrecked Haig's attack at the Somme in 1916 and nearly destroyed the French army completely. The system was up to 8,000 yards (7.3 km) deep: 600 yards (0.5 km) behind the outposts were a triple line of trenches; these included bunkers deep enough to withstand the heaviest possible artillery pounding; then a battle zone, preferably hidden from the enemy, with new artillery placements.

What sort of strategic war should Germany fight? General Falkenhayn proposed a war of attrition, expecting his attacks on Verdun in 1916 to produce three French casualties for every dead German. In the event the figures were much more equal. Falkenhayn was sacked. By the end of 1917 the Germans could see that a long defensive war was not to their

KEY TERM:

Storm-troopers

These were small groups of well-armed foot soldiers. (See also KEY TERM on page 281.)

strategic advantage. Accordingly, General Ludendorf developed ideas for attacking in depth. These had been put forward by soldiers in several armies, notably the French Captain Laffargue and the Russian General Brusilov (see page 134). A sudden, brief artillery barrage or gas attack to disrupt the enemy was followed by rapid advances of **storm-troopers**. Over the winter of 1917–18, in 12 special training schools, his men practised these techniques. 'Operation Michael', Ludendorf's Spring 1918 offensive, restored movement to warfare again: the soldiers saw open country in front of them.

Again, however, lack of strategic planning let the Germans down. What were Ludendorf's strategic objectives? He seems never to have discussed them, either with the War Minister, the Kaiser or his Austro-Hungarian allies. In fact, he seems to have had none, other than to 'punch a hole in the enemy line'. He was short of support, with no plans for supplying an extended advance. He had no tanks, and few lorries. Operationally, the attack was a success, but it soon became too difficult to supply his advancing troops. Nor was the morale of his troops what it was in 1914. They had been led to believe that the Allies were as short of food and supplies as they were. When they reached Allied supply depots too many of them turned to looting food and wine.

The Allies had learned too: Marshal Foch held some troops in reserve so that he could regroup and counter-attack in July. In August Haig led a successful assault in the Somme area, combining secrecy and the deployment of tanks. The final assault by French, British and US troops began on 26 September 1918.

Britain

British strategy in 1914 was the same as it had been in the Napoleonic wars 100 years earlier: using naval superiority to blockade the enemy's ports, keeping a small army, and giving economic aid to the Allies. Sir Edward Grey, Foreign Secretary, summed up the calculations behind this 'business as usual' approach in 1911:

> 'To give the French such support as would prevent her from falling under the control of Germany and estrangement from us. This would mean the virtual break-up of the Triple Entente; if France retired, Russia would at once do the same and we should again be faced with the old troubles along the frontiers of India. It would also mean the complete ascendancy of Germany in Europe.'

PROFILE: *Lord Kitchener*

Horatio Herbert Kitchener, born in 1850, was from an Anglo-Irish family. He joined the army in 1871 and served in Britain's Imperial wars in Egypt and the Sudan, and in South Africa, as well as being Supreme Commander in India. As Britain's best-known soldier, he was Asquith's choice for Minister for War. His face is still famous from his recruiting poster. He hoped to recruit 700,000 men by April 1915; in fact, one million men had signed up by Christmas 1914. Kitchener, however, found it hard to deal with politicians. He died when his ship was blown up by a mine in 1916.

One of the first people to realise that the situation by late 1914 was completely different, requiring a different strategy, was **Kitchener**. He saw that the balance of forces in Europe would lead to a long war. A large British Army could tip the balance. His plan was to put together an army of a million men, ready by 1916, when the other armies would be exhausted. Britain could then use this army to force an advantageous peace.

However, as the war went on, the plan of keeping 'Kitchener's army' in reserve became difficult to sustain. The French army was crippled, British losses were high, Russia was retreating and the Gallipoli Campaign had failed. There seemed a real danger that one or both of Britain's Allies could make a separate peace. With some opposition, the decision was taken to introduce conscription in 1916 and throw in British forces on the Western Front, whatever the cost. The danger of defeat seemed greater than the danger of bankruptcy.

Gallipoli Campaign

In an attempt to break the stalemate of the Western Front, Churchill proposed opening another front in south-east Europe. The plan was to land forces at Gallipoli, in Turkey, and seize Constantinople. This would knock Turkey out of the war and open up another route to help Russia. The strategy was fine, but it was an operational failure. There were no good maps, an enquiry in 1907 which investigated the idea and rejected it was ignored, mine-sweeping was inadequate and troops – many of them Australians and New Zealanders – badly-equipped and ill-prepared. Most of all, the military capability of the Turks was seriously underestimated. Troops were landed in April 1915 and never got much beyond the beach. They were eventually withdrawn in January 1916.

The rapid expansion of the army was obviously going to present problems. One was shortage of trained officers:

> *'One battalion had just three trained officers: a pre-Boer War commanding officer aged 63, a regular subaltern with a broken leg, and a stone-deaf quartermaster who had retired in 1907.'*
>
> C. Barnett, *The Swordbearers* (1963).

Haig had never commanded more than 3,000 men when the war started; he was soon to be in charge of a million.

Discussion of the operational effectiveness of the British army sooner or later encounters the controversy over Sir Douglas Haig. Judgements still vary between John Terraine's defence ('He won the war: what else can you ask of a general?') and that of Sir Llewellyn Woodward ('Fortunately the enemy generals were equally obtuse.'). Haig was not stupid or lacking in ideas: he was prepared to support the use of tanks quite early on, for example. However, the British Army in 1914 was 'locked into a traditional nineteenth-century set of ideas and a traditional, hierarchical method of decision-making'. Officers had their own code, in which it was not done to be too clever; loyalty was the most admired virtue; and criticism of current wisdom, especially to politicians or the press, was not on. Haig could have done something about this when he took over from Sir John French in 1915, but he did not. He was aloof, not keen on discussion. His conferences were just ways of passing on his plans. He was distant, both psychologically and physically, from the trenches. There were also some serious lapses of intelligence (*i.e.* supply of information): he did not know about the deep bunkers used by German forces to survive the artillery barrage which preceded the Battle of the Somme; nor did he know of the waterlogged ground at Passchendaele.

The first response of commanders on all sides to the trench stalemate was to call for more artillery.

> *'Breaking through the lines is largely a question of the expenditure of High Explosive ammunition. If sufficient ammunition is forthcoming a way can be blasted through the line.'*
>
> Sir John French (January 1915).

The demand for shells was eventually met, as can be seen by comparing the 18,000 shells fired at the Battle of Hooge, May 1915, with the 4,300,000 fired at Passchendaele in July 1917. The latter took 321 trains to supply, consumed the annual output of 55,000 workers and cost £22 million – the total cost of the army in 1914. Yet the promised result was not forthcoming.

The problem with the massive artillery barrage, as demanded by French and used in just the same way by Haig, was that it:

- lost all element of surprise
- churned up the ground across which the infantry were then supposed to advance
- destroyed landmarks so that maps became useless
- did not necessarily destroy barbed-wire entanglements and certainly did not destroy troops in deep bunkers.

While it may be possible to defend Haig for the failure at the Somme in 1916, it is hard to find any defence for the near-repetition of the same tactics at Passchendaele in 1917.

There also seems to have been a profound confusion over British aims: was this a war of attrition or were Haig's attacks designed to win the war there and then? Haig always claimed the latter, but some of his commanders clearly saw it as a war of attrition. His own intelligence officer, Sir John Charteris, was ambiguous:

> 'We are fighting primarily to wear down the German armies and the German nation, to interfere with their plans, gain some valuable position, and generally prepare for the great decisive offensive which must come sooner or later.'

By 1918 Haig had instituted new ideas of defence in depth, although not all his commanders had implemented them, leading to some of the panic of March 1918. He had also learned some of the lessons of attack, and put these into effect in summer 1918.

France

The wartime government of the Third Republic proved most efficient at stepping up production of war materials in spite of having almost half their iron and coal in enemy hands. By the end of the war shells were being made at 300,000 per day, tanks at 30 per day, rifle production had increased 290-fold and machine-gun production 170-fold. French aircraft production was also the best.

But was all this being used to good effect? The problem was that there seemed no other way of responding to the German invasion and occupation than to seek to drive them out as soon as possible. Rational strategic planning seemed unpatriotic in this situation. Indeed, in a democracy the will of the people had to be listened to, even by generals. Joffre could not wage a defensive war: he had to attack. His replacement by Nivelle in 1916 was to make way for an even more aggressive strategy. Only when millions of lives had been lost and total collapse actually faced, could Pétain seek a more rational approach from 1917, and then not without opposition.

French expectations for a short war of movement meant that their army was ill-supplied with heavy guns and machine-guns. There was also a tradition in the French Army that the artillery were the elite, and had little contact with the rest of the army. It was soon clear that coordination between gunnery and infantry was an essential element in a successful advance. This was hard to achieve in most armies, but in the French Army it was hardly attempted. Instead, commanders called for more and more shells.

> 'The vastness of material and mechanical power seemed to produce a kind of dull megalomania in which ingenuity of execution was sacrificed to the intensity and elaboration of preparations.'
>
> R. Crutwell, *History of the Great War* (1936).

Alongside this reliance on the guns to do the job was the belief that the 'poilu' (nickname for the ordinary French soldier), still in his red and blue uniform for the first few months of the war, would overcome all obstacles through sheer patriotic fervour. Training was rigid, leaving little room for initiative, mobility or surprise. Indeed, in training, the enemy was expected to behave just as rigidly; unfortunately, in real life it rarely did.

Casualties were enormous: 143,000 lost their lives in the Champagne offensive of 1915; 380,000 were killed defending Verdun; 120,000 in Nivelle's offensive in 1917. At the end of 1917 Pétain implemented a programme of improvement, involving defence in more depth and with better coordination. Its effects were postponed by the German Spring offensive but contributed to the successful counter-attack later in 1918.

Russia

The Russian effort in the First World War is usually dealt with by historians as part of the causes of the revolutions of 1917: bumbling incompetence, corruption and defeat. Certainly the war imposed strains on the distribution of food and fuel; this led to shortages in which prices rose faster than wages, producing industrial unrest (see chapter 12). However, considered as a war effort Russia's record is not one of unrelieved disaster. There were supply problems and stupid generals, but these were not confined to Russia. On the other hand, from August 1914 until early in 1917 Russia was certainly a serious combatant on the Eastern Front.

 Russia had always been a state geared around the needs of war. The Tsar was ultimately the supreme commander of army and navy; many of the upper classes had traditionally served in the army and most peasants regarded military service as an onerous but necessary duty. Nor was there any disagreement about war aims in 1914. The initial mobilisation went well. Alongside the heavy defeats inflicted by Germany at Tannenberg and the Masurian Lakes must be set Russian advances into Galicia, threatening Hungary, and a spirited repulse of the Turkish attack in the south.

Like everyone else, the Russians had expected a short war: 1915 was therefore a year of difficulties, of stepping up supplies of weapons for an extended conflict. In fact, Russia did not do too badly. Some weapons were imported from France and Britain, but Russian industry expanded production dramatically: shell production by 2,000 per cent by late 1916, artillery by 1,000 per cent, rifles by 1,100 per cent.

If everyone at the time (and to some extent since) underestimated Russian industrial capacity, they overestimated the country's manpower. The expected 'Russian steamroller' simply did not roll. By the time Russia withdrew from the war about 14.5 million men had been mobilised, out of a population of 180 million. This is fewer than Germany managed out of a population of 65 million.

The reasons for this lie in Russia's unique size, as well as the problems caused by the level of development and its particular social and political system. There was first the problem of collecting large numbers of men from their homes, equipping them, arming and training them and getting them to the Front. In the west, railways played a crucial role in this. Russia was vast, and the Eastern Front far longer and more widely spread than the Western Front. There were only 1.2 kilometres of railway track per 100 square kilometres of Russian territory, compared to 10.7 kilometres in Germany and 6.7 kilometres in Austria-Hungary.

Russian soldiers were usually illiterate, with little idea what the war was about. The massive casualty rate put paid to large numbers of regular officers. There were fewer NCOs in the Russian army – two per company, compared with 12 in the German army. By 1915 many of the middle classes were ambivalent about the war: defeats and difficulties were ammunition in their struggle to wrest democratic concessions from the Tsar. Many in the Duma were openly critical of the conduct of the war, and they had plenty to be critical about (see chapter 13).

The Supreme Commander, the Grand Duke Nicholas, was arrogant and incompetent. Many of his officers were totally unable to grasp the scale of the war they were involved in. Their gross underestimate of hospital facilities required, for example, contributed to the enormous casualties Russia sustained: 7 million by the end of the war. As German forces came to the aid of their allies on the Eastern Front in 1915, the Russians were driven out of Poland and Galicia. The High Command panicked and the retreat became a rout in which thousands of tons of precious weapons and ammunition were abandoned.

In August 1915 Tsar Nicholas II took over supreme command himself. He restored some calm and rationality to the conduct of the war and promoted competent officers. The Russian war effort was still hampered by transport, manpower and supply problems, but was far from being a spent force.

From what has been said, it is clear that the Russian army was less effective than the Germans but capable of being more than an equal match for the Austro-Hungarians. In 1916 General Brusilov showed himself to be one of the first commanders on any front in the war to have learned its lessons and devised new operational plans.

In May 1916 he prepared a plan of attack which rejected conventional wisdom. To achieve surprise, normal leave went on as usual; preparation work went on at night; deep bunkers were dug for the assault troops and well camouflaged; the attack was not preceded by a long artillery barrage and his forces went forward in strength at several points. He achieved several breakthroughs and only ground to a halt through inability to follow them up.

In December 1916 and January 1917 similar tactics were used in the Mitau Offensive, showing that his ideas were beginning to spread to other commanders. By then, however, revolution was almost upon them.

Conclusion

By the middle of 1918 the conditions for an end to the war had been reached. Strategically, Germany was played out. Once the Schlieffen Plan had failed they were likely to be in difficulties, although events in Russia nearly delivered them the one-front war they needed. By mid 1918, however, the scales of resources were tipping strongly against them: the blockade had reduced supplies and crippled morale. The Kaiser's state was falling to pieces under mutinies and uprisings. The support of the USA was beginning to make a serious difference to the Allies' position. Operationally, the Allies had learned sufficiently from the preceding four years to be able to launch their counter-offensive effectively. The German High Command knew that they were defeated when they sued for an armistice on the basis of the Fourteen Points in November 1918.

Task

The charge that British generals in the First World War were incompetent, and so sent millions of young men to their deaths, has been made ever since the war itself. This task invites you to make a judgement about the abilities of one of the most important, and most controversial, military leaders in the First World War, Field Marshal Douglas Haig.

The historian John Laffin has entitled a book about British generals *British Butchers and Bunglers of World War One*. Many veterans of the war despised their generals. The poet Siegfried Sassoon turned his bitter ironic humour on the generals in 1917:

> *'Good morning, good morning!' the general said*
> *When we met him last week on the way to the line.*
> *Now the soldiers he smiled at are most of 'em dead,*
> *And we're cursing his staff for incompetent swine.*
> *'He's a cheery old card', grunted Harry to Jack*
> *As they slogged up to Arras with rifle and pack.*
>
> *But he did for them both by his plan of attack.*

The military historian John Terraine has taken on the task of defending Douglas Haig. Here are some of the points he makes:

A

'It is simple historical fact that the British generals of the First World War did not fail in their duty. It was not a British delegation that crossed the lines with a white flag in November 1918. No German army of occupation was stationed on the Thames, the Humber or the Tyne.'

B

'Behind the bristling moustaches and the granite jaw was a surprisingly high degree of broad-minded flexibility, unexpected adaptability to change, readiness to accept and use novelties, which is absolutely contrary to the normally accepted image.'

a Make a summary list of the points John Terraine makes in defence of Haig.
b Make a list of the charges you could make against Haig.
c Are the differences matters of fact or judgement?
d How far does the information in this chapter help to resolve the differences?

Further reading

J. M. Winter, *The experience of World War I* (Edinburgh, 1988) – very readable and well supported with pictures and statistics.

Keith Robbins, *The First World War* (Oxford University Press, 1984) – wittily written.

A. R. Millett and W. Murray, *Military Effectiveness*, vol. I (Allen and Unwin, 1988) – provides the basis for much of the analysis in this chapter.

D. French, *British Strategy and War Aims, 1914–16* (Allen and Unwin, 1986) – also examines these issues.

10 Peacemaking and peacekeeping, 1919–25

Time chart

1916: **November** Woodrow Wilson re-elected as United States President, and pledges to make the world 'safe for democracy'

1917: **February/March** Tsarist regime falls in Russia
April United States enters war on allied side as an 'Associated Power'
October/November Bolsheviks seize power in Russia

1918: **January** Wilson outlines '14 Points' peace programme in speech to Congress
March Treaty of Brest-Litovsk between Germany and Bolshevik Russia takes Russia out of First World War
September/October Disintegration of Habsburg empire, and surrender of Bulgaria
4 October German government seeks armistice on basis of Wilson's '14 point programme'
5 November US and allies agree to armistice based on 14 points, but Britain and France express reservations to points 2 and 8. Republican Party gains majority in US Congress in mid-term elections
11 November Armistice signed between Germany and allies; Clemenceau says 'we have won the war, now we have to win the peace'
December British general election results in victory for Lloyd George and his coalition of Liberals and Conservatives. Electorate clamour to 'make Germany pay' for the war

1919: **January** Paris peace conference starts
14 February Delegates reach agreement on a League of Nations
March Council of Four – Wilson, Lloyd George, Clemenceau, Orlando – established to thrash out most contentious issues
May Treaty of Versailles handed to German representatives; Germans make lengthy written criticisms
21 June Germans scuttle their own High Seas Fleet at Scapa Flow
28 June Treaty of Versailles with Germany signed at Palace of Versailles
10 September Treaty of St Germain signed with Austria
27 November Treaty of Neuilly signed with Bulgaria

KEY TERM:

Maginot Line

This was a line of defensive fortifications built in France, close to and following the French border with Germany. It was to defend France against invasion by German troops and tanks. Construction of the **Maginot Line** began in July 1925.

1920: **10 January** Treaty of Versailles and League of Nations come into force

19 March Final attempt to ratify Treaty of Versailles in US Senate fails. US signs separate peace treaty with Germany

4 June Treaty of Trianon signed with Hungary

10 August Treaty of Sèvres signed with Turkish empire

1921: **January** Allied conference sets Germany's reparations bill at 132 billion German marks

League of Nations supervises partition of Upper Silesia

1921–2: Washington Naval Conference draws up treaty limiting capital ships of Britain, USA, Japan, France and Italy; also Four-Power Pact between USA, Japan, Britain and France replaces Anglo-Japanese alliance

1922: **March** Genoa Conference on disarmament and economic recovery of Europe convenes; its only outcome is Treaty of Rapallo between Germany and Russia, signed on 15 April

1923: **January** Belgian and French troops invade Ruhr to force Germany to pay reparations. Collapse of German currency and massive inflation

July Treaty of Lausanne finally brings peace between allies and new nationalist government of Turkey

1924: **August** Dawes Plan agreed – lays down reduced schedule of German reparations payments. German currency stabilised

1925: **October** Mutual security pact signed at Locarno

France begins construction of **Maginot Line** along frontier with Germany

Economic and social consequences of the First World War

When the peacemakers finally assembled in Paris in January 1919, their prewar world had been completely shattered. They had to deal not just with immediate and pressing crises, but with the longer-term consequences of the war which were not always clearly apparent to them as the fighting ended. We cannot form a balanced judgement on the work of the peace negotiators and on the treaties they drew up between 1919 and 1920 without taking into account the economic, social and political consequences of the war of 1914–18. As we shall see, the problems which were facing Europe by 1919 were so great that one can argue that it would be virtually impossible to construct a lasting peace settlement in a postwar environment which was so unstable.

Physical damage

Figure 10.1 *Numbers of soldiers killed during First World War*

Numbers killed (millions)	
Germany	2
Russia	1.5–2
France	1.4
Austria-Hungary	1.1
Britain and Italy	0.75 each
Total	**8 million soldiers** (about 15 per cent of all combatants)

In addition, millions were totally disabled, physically or psychologically. Nearly all the dead and disabled were males in the 18–40 age range, a 'lost generation' for the countries concerned (see Figure 10.1).

Five million civilians died from famine and disease in the chaos at the end of the war. Fifteen million died from a flu epidemic in the winter of 1918–19. This left a huge legacy of dependants: widows, orphans and war-wounded. They now looked to the state, in whose service lives had been given, or wrecked, for sustenance. (Germany alone had 2.7 million permanently disabled ex-servicemen, 0.5 million war widows and 1.2 million orphans to look after.)

KEY TERM:

Départements

Départements are the local government units into which France is divided.

Land and buildings   Wherever the fronts had been, or invaders passed through, farmland was laid waste, factories, mines and houses destroyed (see Figure 10.2), railways smashed. Belgium, Italy, Serbia, Poland and the ten rich northern *départements* of France were the worst affected areas.

Technological changes

In addition to bringing about political changes, the war had also accelerated the march of technology. By 1918, tanks, aeroplanes and submarines had demonstrated their prowess, and had transformed the nature of war. Britain was no longer cut off from the European continent; she was as open to aerial bombardment as any other European country. Indeed, the combination of air and submarine power made Britain more vulnerable to attack than it had ever been in its history. Populations across Europe became war targets in a way they had never been previously. The realisation of what war might entail in the future, combined with the devastating impact of the war of 1914–18, had an enormous psychological impact on political leaders throughout Europe.

Figure 10.2 *Mine crater in France, October 1918*

Economic consequences

European economic growth was retarded by about 8 years. In Germany, France, Belgium and eastern Europe, manufacturing output was 30 per cent lower after the war than before. In central and eastern Europe industrial production was half the prewar level; in Belgium, Germany and Austria it was 60 per cent below. Britain sold 25 per cent of its foreign investments, France 50 per cent and Germany 100 per cent.

European export markets were lost, economies were distorted, food and equipment had had to be imported. Into the gap came non-European nations, notably USA and Japan: both these were debtor nations in 1914 and ended the war in surplus. The Americas as a whole accounted for 22.4 per cent of world trade in 1913; 32.1 per cent by 1920. Asia's rose from 12.1 per cent to 13.4 per cent. Europe's (including Russia) fell from 58.4 per cent to 49.2 per cent. Thus Europe's economic decline, as against the rest of the world, was accelerated.

Financial consequences

The total cost of the war was $260 billion, equivalent to six times the national debt accumulated by all nations from the eighteenth century to 1914. All the belligerent powers financed their war efforts by borrowing money. By 1918 the USA had lent $2,000 million, mainly to Britain and France. Through the 1920s debt charges and repayments consumed between one-third and one-half of the total public expenditure of these countries. The problem was exacerbated by the Bolsheviks' repudiation of Russia's share of the debt.

This situation weakened currencies and produced inflation, worst of all in Germany. In 1913 there were 2,000 million paper marks in circulation; by 1919 there were 45,000 million. The national debt rose from 5,000 million marks in 1914 to 154,000 million by 1918. It would have taken more than 100 per cent of Germany's budget in the 1920s just to service these loans, never mind repay them.

At the end of the war the German mark had lost about three-quarters of its value. In 1920 it stood at one-tenth of its prewar value, by 1922 one-hundredth and by January 1923 one prewar gold mark was worth 2,500 current paper marks. The German wartime government had expected to repay their debts from the spoils of victory. Defeat, and reparations, simply made a bad situation worse.

These financial problems hampered European recovery in the 1920s, especially because they were not widely recognised. Trying to put their country's economies back to 1914 was not only impossible, it distracted governments from dealing with the social and political consequences of the war.

Social consequences

A vigorous debate is still raging about whether the war initiated social change or served to accelerate it.

Women's employment   The war brought lots of jobs for women, often in totally new areas, such as munitions, engineering, offices and transport (see Figure 10.3). In Britain, by April 1918, 5 million women were employed, compared to under 3.5 million in 1914. In Germany, the number of women working in factories rose by 50 per cent.

Once the war was over, women were pressurised into giving up work and returning to their homes. Nevertheless it had given women the opportunity to show what they could do. It had given them a taste of life outside

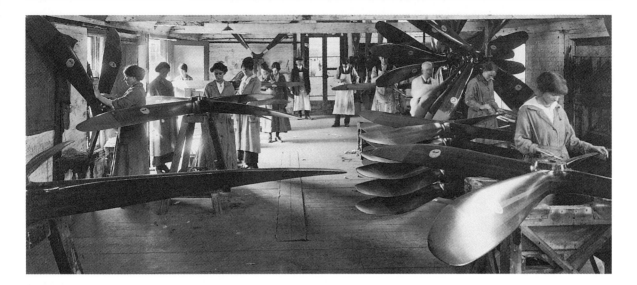

Figure 10.3 Women workers in a British aircraft factory

the narrow confines of the home and increased their expectations and confidence. Over the next few years there were clashes between those who wanted to return to the norms of the pre-1914 period, and those, often younger women, who wanted to build on the gains of the war years.

Organised labour   Governments desperately needed the cooperation of workers, especially in military production. Across Europe, organised labour worked closely with governments and sought greater social and political power in return. They wanted better wages, housing, working conditions and political rights. This brought them into conflict after the war with employers and others seeking to put the clock back to 1914.

Ideological consequences

As leader of the successful Bolshevik coup in Russia, Lenin encouraged socialist groups to rise up against their governments and seize power. Many of the war-weary people of Europe were ready to listen. In Germany there were one million workers on strike by January 1918. In Britain, the red flag was flown over Glasgow Town Hall and there was talk of revolution in south Wales. Socialist regimes appeared briefly in Hungary and Bavaria. Postwar Italy was racked by large-scale strikes and brutal counter-revolutionary measures from landowners and employers.

Fear of revolution was a powerful force in interwar politics. It gave a boost to right-wing parties and helped to bring to power Fascist regimes in Italy, Germany and elsewhere. Europe, already economically and financially weakened by the war, was further destabilised by these massive conflicts.

Political effects

When the peacemakers gathered in Paris in January 1919 to construct a peace settlement, the political map of Europe as it had existed in August 1914 had been swept away. In the course of the war, or soon after it, four empires collapsed – the Russian Empire, the Habsburg Empire, the German Second Reich and the Ottoman Empire. In their wake, they left a huge swathe of central and eastern Europe in turmoil. A whole host of competing ethnic and politically motivated groups fought to establish successor states, and the result was a series of fierce struggles, many of which continued into the early 1920s. Boundaries were marked out not in the salons of Paris but on the ground in eastern and south-eastern Europe, and the peacemakers for the most part had to accept them. Decisions were not reached quickly: it was only in 1921 that a provisional frontier was agreed between Poland and Russia; it was not until 1923 that a peace treaty was finally concluded between the new nationalist Turkey and the allies.

At the end of the war, there was a power vacuum in central and eastern Europe. Instead of three powerful, conservative empires competing against each other in the area, there were a number of small, new states, trying to establish themselves politically and economically. Russia had retreated eastwards, and Germany was temporarily defeated. But for how long would these two powers accept the new situation? If, in the future, either or both of them looked to expand, it was unlikely that Britain or France, weakened as they were by the war, would be in any position to offer a challenge.

Thus Europe in 1918 was war-weary and impoverished. It had suffered both short-term and long-term political and economic damage. Its populations looked to the leaders of the victorious powers to bring about lasting peace and economic and financial recovery. But the damage had been so widespread and had brought about so much instability that recovery was bound to be a slow and difficult process. As a result, disillusionment spread and compounded the problems which faced the peacemakers in the aftermath of war.

The peacemakers

The traditional view of the Treaty of Versailles has been to see it as a harsh and vindictive settlement, a 'diktat' imposed on a helpless Germany. This interpretation has been challenged in recent years by a number of historians who now portray the Treaty as relatively lenient, and certainly the best compromise that could be reached in the prevailing circumstances. The truth was that a number of serious obstacles faced the peacemakers:

- the divergent attitudes towards the settlement of its principal architects;
- the potentially strong position in Europe still occupied by Germany after 1919;
- the enduring instability bequeathed by the Great War.

In the face of such difficulties, a strict enforcement of the Treaty was never likely. Instead, German resentment would ensure that piecemeal revision of the settlement was a much more likely outcome, leaving Germany in a potentially stronger position than before 1914.

Political problems facing the Allies in late 1918

The position of the USA The United States played an increasingly important role in the First World War, first as the provider of loans and of crucial war supplies to the allied powers, and then as a military partner, throwing desperately-needed fresh troops on to the battlefields of the Western Front. With economic and military power came political leadership, which US President **Woodrow Wilson** was determined to exercise to the full.

PROFILE: *Woodrow Wilson*

Thomas **Woodrow Wilson** was born in Virginia in 1856. He trained as a lawyer before becoming a university professor and president of Princeton University. He was elected state governor of New Jersey in 1911, and won the Democrat Presidential nomination, being elected President in 1912 and securing re-election in 1916. His Fourteen Points peace programme, delivered to the American Congress in January 1918, became the basis on which the Germans sued for peace in the autumn. He was the first American president to leave the USA to negotiate a peace settlement in Europe, and his support for the establishment of a League of Nations aroused hostility among his Republican opponents. He returned to the United States in the summer of 1919 and embarked on an arduous speaking tour to drum up support for the Treaty of Versailles. However, he suffered a serious stroke, and spent the rest of his presidential term in the White House, communicating only through his wife. He was unable to prevent the American Senate from rejecting the Treaty of Versailles on two separate occasions. He left office in 1920 and died in 1924.

It became very clear in the course of the war that Wilson's views on the nature of the conflict and on how to prevent wars in the future differed radically from those of the British and French leaders. Wilson saw the outbreak of war in 1914 as tangible proof of the bankruptcy of traditional European diplomacy, based as it was on balances of power, armed alliances and secret negotiations. Wilson resolved to use his influence to construct a more just system of international relations, based on clear principles of international law and on a global association of nations working through agreed procedures to maintain world order. He believed passionately that the United States should take the lead in the creation of such a system, pursuing at the same time a related goal, the extension of democracy throughout the world.

Wilson saw this as a moral commitment entrusted to the American people and their leaders by the country's founding fathers. In 1916 he proclaimed that the object of the war should be 'to make the world safe for democracy'. In that same year, his views were endorsed by the American voters when, albeit by a narrow margin, he was re-elected President. America's entry into the war was portrayed as a crusade for the right of self-determination and for democracy, under the leadership of the United States. Wilson emphasised the gap between American principles and the more selfish war aims of the allied powers, as he saw them, by entering the war not as an ally of the entente powers but as an 'associated power'. He made it clear that he would use all the considerable influence at his disposal to modify allied war aims to try to bring them into line with his more exalted principles. And in the course of late 1917 and 1918 he outlined his peace programme in a number of well-publicised speeches.

The most famous of these was a carefully-prepared address delivered to the American Congress on 8 January 1918, which became known as the 'Fourteen Points' speech because of the number of heads under which he itemised his proposed settlement. Wilson had not consulted his allied partners before delivering the speech, and they were not impressed with its contents; the British Foreign Secretary Balfour declaring them 'admirable but very abstract'. In the succeeding months, however, Wilson was successful in widening the scope of allied war aims from the restoration of Belgium and Serbia and the return to France of the provinces of Alsace and Lorraine to include self-determination for Czechs, Poles and other subject peoples in eastern Europe and the estab-lishment of a League of Nations.

However, his biggest coup came in September 1918. Although the German High Command had been scathing about the Fourteen Points in January 1918, when victory still seemed to be within their grasp, the sit-uation looked very different by late summer. The German offensive had failed, tired German troops were being pushed back towards the Rhine, while at the same time more and more fresh American troops were arriving in Europe. The possibility of defeat was now very real, and the German High Command moved to put out peace feelers before the situation became desperate and Germany was threatened with invasion. Civilian leaders were instructed to sue for peace on the basis of Wilson's 'Fourteen Point' peace programme, which promised a more lenient peace than British or French demands. On 4 October, the German government formally asked Wilson to take steps to bring about a ceasefire as a preliminary to the negotiation of peace terms on the basis of his 14 points. Britain and France, though far from happy, were forced to agree to an armistice on this basis when Wilson threatened to deal with their objections by concluding a separate peace with Germany. The only obstacle to peace now was the Kaiser, whose removal from power Wilson insisted on as a precondition for the opening of peace negotiations. On 9 November 1918 the Kaiser was prevailed upon to abdicate, and on 11 November the armistice was signed.

The nature of the armistice settlement The armistice agreement was drawn up by allied and American military and naval commanders. It was wholly unconnected with Wilson's peace programme on which the Germans had sued for peace. In practice, however, the armistice was bound to constitute an important element in the subsequent peace negotiations, as the French were acutely aware. The armistice terms were therefore designed both to remove Germany's ability to continue the war, and to serve as the basis for a more permanent weakening of Germany. German troops were ordered to withdraw beyond the Rhine, former German territory on the left bank was to be occupied, and a ten-mile-wide zone on the right bank, stretching from the Netherlands to the Swiss frontier, was to be neutralised. Allied and American garrisons were to be established at the three principal Rhine crossings and in 30-mile-deep bridgeheads on the other side of the river. The Germans were also to be deprived of large quantities of war material, including all their submarines and much of their surface fleet, air force and transport. Finally, the blockade of Germany was to continue until peace terms had been drawn up and accepted.

Even before the peace conference assembled, new battle lines had been drawn between Wilson's Fourteen Point peace programme and French plans to weaken Germany permanently by pushing her back beyond the Rhine. This was to be only one of many serious conflicts which disrupted peace negotiations and made a final settlement so difficult to reach.

Popular sentiment in the allied countries One of the most important factors influencing the shape of the peace settlement was the strength of popular feeling in Britain, Italy, and more particularly in the countries which had suffered German invasion, France and Belgium. Four years of warfare, with its associated loss of life, civilian suffering, hardship and disruption inevitably meant that by the end of 1918 emotions were running high. In Britain and France in particular, a strong current of opinion looked to the peacemakers to lay the blame for the war with Germany, and to exact appropriate punishment, including the surrender of territory, the hanging of the Kaiser and the payment of substantial reparations. The British First Lord of the Admiralty, Eric Geddes, captured this mood very well when he urged the victorious allies to 'squeeze the German lemon until the pips squeak'.

Such strong currents of feeling were echoed and sustained by the popular press which had developed during the war into a major influence on the formation of public opinion. The popular press made its presence felt at the Paris peace negotiations, forcing leaders to negotiate in the full glare of publicity, in the certain knowledge that details of their discussions would be carried the next day in newspaper columns throughout the world. Wilson in particular developed a loathing of the Parisian press during his stay in Paris; he became acutely aware of French government attempts to manipulate it as a powerful weapon in their fight for a more stringent settlement.

The British Prime Minister **Lloyd George**, the French Prime Minster **Clemenceau** and the Italian Prime Minister Orlando were well aware that they would have to answer for their decisions not just in the press but to their electorates. Lloyd George, in particular, came to Paris shortly

PROFILE: *Lloyd George*

David **Lloyd George** was a Liberal politician, born in Manchester in 1863 but brought up in Wales. He was first elected as MP for Caernavon Boroughs in 1890 and represented the area for 55 years. He served as Chancellor of the Exchequer between 1908 and 1915 in the Liberal government, and in 1916 replaced Asquith as prime minister of a war coalition government. He pursued a forceful war policy to a victorious conclusion, and fought the election of December 1918 at the head of a coalition with the Conservative Party, against his former colleagues, the Asquithian Liberals. The coalition won a crushing victory, and Lloyd George went to Paris at the head of the British peace delegation. After the conference, he served as Prime Minister until 1922, when his Conservative allies deserted him. He contested the election of that year as the leader of an independent party. He remained out of office for the rest of his long Parliamentary career. He died in 1945.

PROFILE: *Clemenceau*

Georges Clemenceau was born in 1841. He started his political career in 1870 by serving for a year as Mayor of Montmartre in Paris. He entered the French National Assembly as a Radical in 1871, and founded a radical newspaper *La Justice* in 1880. A supporter of Dreyfus (see chapter 2), he served in the French Senate from 1902 to 1920. He was Prime Minister from 1906–9 and again from 1917–20, and was instrumental in securing the appointment of Marshall Foch as chief of allied forces in March 1918. At the Paris peace conference he survived an assassination attempt, but returned to the negotiations within a month to continue his dogged defence of French security interests. He failed to secure election in the French Presidential elections of January 1920 and retired from public life. He died in November 1929.

after a general election which left him in no doubt as to what the British voters wanted. The election campaign which began in November 1918 was the first since 1910, and the first to be conducted on the basis of full manhood suffrage and the vote for women of 30 and over. Meetings up and down the country were heated, with widespread calls for a punitive settlement, and for Germany to be made to pay for the costs of the war. Those candidates who called for a peace based on Wilsonian principles were howled down and for the most part defeated. Lloyd George and his coalition partners were returned with large majorities, and knew that their political futures depended on the maintenance of a hard line towards Germany.

Feelings in France ran even stronger. After the war the French Chamber of Deputies was nicknamed the 'one-legged chamber' because of the number of maimed ex-soldiers it contained. These men would be satisfied with nothing less than a punitive peace. They had a doughty champion in Marshal Foch, allied commander-in-chief during the final stages of the war, who was present at the Paris peace negotiations and could be relied upon to ensure that Clemenceau did not sacrifice French interests. Similar sentiments inspired the Italians, who looked to the peace treaties to give them territorial and economic gains which would compensate them for their heavy losses in the war, and would make Italy at last the great power they longed for her to be. Orlando was well aware that if he failed to deliver the goods, he would be charged with betrayal by more extreme nationalists seeking to expand their own political influence.

The defeat of Woodrow Wilson in America It was ironic that while allied leaders were receiving massive public support for a harsh peace settlement, Wilson's own peace programme was being rejected by the American people. American mid-term elections traditionally voiced criticisms of the incumbent President and administration. To try to combat this, Wilson made a particularly strong appeal to American voters to support him so that he could impose his peace programme at Paris on the allies with maximum authority. Instead, the elections held on 5 November 1918 saw sweeping gains made by Republican opponents who had been very critical of his methods of conducting foreign policy and of the idealism of his peace programme. The Republican Party now had majorities in both the House of Representatives and the Senate, and its view was that the United States should withdraw from involvement in Europe and let the European leaders conclude a peace with Germany. Any peace treaty to which the USA was a party would first have to be submitted for detailed scrutiny to the Foreign Relations Committee of the Senate, now chaired by a hostile Republican opponent of Wilson, Henry Cabot Lodge. It would then require approval by a two-thirds majority in the Senate. Wilson's chances of gaining acceptance in the United States of any settlement he might negotiate on the basis of the 'Fourteen Points' – particularly if it involved active American participation in commissions or in a League of Nations – were seriously imperilled. When Wilson set sail for Europe in December 1918 (the first American President to travel overseas during his term of office, thus attracting further Republican criticism), both he and the European leaders with whom he would have to negotiate were well aware that he could no longer make commitments on behalf of his country with any certainty that they would be honoured.

The mood in Germany   The final political problem facing the peacemakers was the mood of the German people and of their leaders. When the Germans sued for peace, there was widespread shock that Germany appeared to have lost the war, since people had been told until recently that its armies were about to win. The end of hostilities came about not as a result of a crushing allied victory in the field, or after the invasion of Germany, but because it had become perfectly clear to German military leaders that her allies were at breaking-point and that the civilian effort necessary to sustain her armies could no longer be guaranteed. The High Command had consequently instructed the politicians to sue for peace on the best terms available.

German troops, however, were still in occupation of parts of France, Belgium and the Baltic states, and had scored a crushing defeat of Russia on the Eastern Front. When they returned home to Germany after the armistice was signed, they were greeted by cheering crowds and by political leaders as 'undefeated heroes' who had 'stood their ground undefeated up to the last minute'.

So why had Germany not won the war? An explanation was not slow in coming – Germany had been betrayed by internal enemies, by Jews and by communists and socialists. With the end of the war in sight, in the autumn of 1918, Germany had erupted into revolution. There had been mutinies in naval dockyards, occupations of factories, and the establishment of workers' councils. Civil war threatened the country, as struggles for power erupted in the different states of Germany. Order was not fully restored for several months, when the army was brought in to crush revolt.

While much of the revolutionary turmoil was due to war-weariness and to frustration after months of food shortages and spiralling inflation, there were groups who sought to emulate the Bolshevik example and to establish a socialist government in Germany. It was activity of this kind which fuelled the infamous 'stab in the back' myth which began to take hold on the right – a myth alleging that Germany could have won the war had she not been betrayed in the autumn of 1918 by internal enemies. Prussian textbooks in the 1920s alleged that:

> 'In hand-to-hand fighting the German showed his superiority up to the last moment. But . . . the resistance of the Austrians, Bulgars and Turks had collapsed . . . Worse news came: "Sailors revolt in Kiel!" – "Revolution in Berlin!" – "The Emperor in Holland!" Thus all possibility of a final resistance on the shortened line between Antwerp and Strasbourg was gone.'
>
> Gordon Craig, *Germany 1866–1945* (1978).

One of the most gallant soldiers in the German trenches on the Western Front, Corporal Adolf Hitler, was gassed in early October 1918, and was taken to hospital, playing no further part in the war. As he began to recover, he was told that Germany had been defeated. He could not understand how victory had been snatched from Germany's grasp, and came to the conclusion that conspiracy and betrayal was the only possible explanation. Henceforth he referred to those who had agreed to an armistice in November 1919 as the 'November Criminals'. Hitler was not alone in refusing to accept the bitterness of defeat. A determined search began for traitors who had brought such humiliation to Germany.

Since it was not the High Command but the political leaders who had sued for peace, they were the target of hatred and, in some cases, of assassins. Wilson's insistence that the Kaiser could not be trusted to conclude a just settlement, and that he must be replaced by a democratic regime before peace talks could begin, compounded the political problems facing Germany. It was the new regime which had to shoulder the burdens of an onerous peace and to face the attacks from right and left.

Not only did the German population have no sense of defeat; their leaders expected to play an important part at the forthcoming peace conference. As a strong nation at the heart of Europe, they saw themselves as playing a crucial role in the fight against Bolshevism, and in efforts to re-establish European finances and to bring about economic recovery. They waited to be summoned to Paris, hopeful that a peace based on Wilsonian principles would be reasonably lenient; they were also well aware of the new opportunities opening up for Germany in eastern Europe as a result of the collapse of the Habsburg and Romanov empires.

As we have already seen, the victors were deeply divided, even before they reached Paris. While it was anticipated that a preliminary peace settlement would be drawn up, followed by a more definitive treaty negotiated directly with the Germans, protracted disputes among the allies prevented even a preliminary settlement from being drawn up for many months. In the end, the Treaty of Versailles was hastily put together and simply presented to the Germans. Not one of the victorious powers was completely happy with it, and the Germans were outraged by its proposed terms.

Let us now look at its terms, and assess how harsh they really were.

The terms of the Treaty of Versailles

The League of Nations

The first 26 articles of the Treaty of Versailles – and of the other treaties concluded with Germany's former allies – formed the Covenant of the League of Nations, and will be discussed in detail in the next chapter. There was general agreement that Germany and the other ex-enemy states should not be eligible to join the new body until they had demonstrated their commitment to uphold international agreements and to carry out the peace terms.

Germany's colonies

These had been seized by British, French and Japanese troops during the war; South Africa, Australia and New Zealand, now called Dominions of the British Empire, had also taken the opportunity to gain additional territories. There was complete agreement at Paris that they should not be returned to Germany. Woodrow Wilson was persuaded that Germany

151

had treated her colonial subjects harshly before the war, but he also argued that the wishes and well-being of the colonial inhabitants should be an important factor in the disposition of the colonies. He was opposed to their outright annexation by the allied powers, and successfully pressed that they be administered as 'mandated areas' by more politically and economically advanced nations who would help them to develop into more modern states under the general supervision of the new League of Nations.

Military and naval terms

At the time of the armistice, it had been agreed that the German navy should be interned in a neutral or allied harbour. Soon afterwards, it was escorted to Rosyth in the Firth of Forth, and thence to Scapa Flow in the Orkneys, where it was to remain while the peace negotiations settled its fate. There was much discussion among British, American, French and Italian naval chiefs as to whether the ships should be sunk or distributed among the powers in some agreed ratio. The Germans themselves finally decided the issue by sinking their own fleet on 21 June 1919, when it had become very clear that it would not be allowed to return to Germany.

The Germans had already handed over substantial numbers of submarines to the British naval authorities, and it was decided that in future they should be forbidden to possess submarines or naval aircraft. Furthermore, they were to be limited to six battleships, six light cruisers, 12 destroyers and 12 torpedo boats. The entire navy was to have no more than 1,500 officers and warrant officers, enlisted on a voluntary basis. Fortifications and harbour works at Heligoland were to be demolished, and the Kiel Canal was to be given the same status in international law as the Suez and Panama canals.

The future German army was also to be strictly limited, and forbidden the use of tanks, military aircraft or heavy artillery. There was considerable discussion among the negotiators about the basis on which the army should be recruited. The French were prepared to allow an army, based on annual conscription, of about 200,000 men. Lloyd George, however, insisted that the army should be a volunteer army, with its recruits serving 12-year contracts. Clemenceau finally agreed to this, but only on condition that the size of the army be reduced to 100,000 since its quality and fighting capacity would obviously be considerably greater than that of an army of raw conscripts.

Wilson's hopes for the future could be clearly discerned in the preamble to the military section of the treaty with Germany. Germany was to be disarmed 'in order to render possible the initiation of a general limitation of the armaments of all nations'. Allied commissions of control were set up to supervise the carrying out of the military, naval and air clauses, but it was left to the German authorities to cooperate in the process. As the 1920s wore on, allied commissioners repeatedly complained that Germany was not complying with the disarmament provisions of the treaty; the Germans counter-charged that, since the allies were not themselves disarming, Germany should be allowed to rearm.

Reparations

No single issue caused more acrimony at the peace talks than reparation payments. In accepting a peace settlement based on the Fourteen Points which included the French definition of what was meant in point 8 by the 'restoration' of invaded territory, the Germans agreed to pay compensation for damage caused by German aggression 'by land, by sea and from the air'. But how was the damage to be assessed, and was Germany to pay for all of it? If interpreted as including such government costs as war pensions and separation allowances paid out during the war, Germany's total liability would double. Could the country afford to pay? Claims of £30,000 million were being advanced as entirely reasonable. How could Germany pay such sums when the war had crippled its economy? On the other hand, France and Belgium had suffered terrible damage in the course of the German invasion – should they have to bear the costs of restoration themselves?

United States delegates tried to limit Germany's liability by basing it on the country's ability to pay rather than on the total amount of allied claims. In pursuit of this aim, their representative on the Reparations Commission, John Foster Dulles, proposed that a formula be adopted requiring Germany to admit a moral and theoretical responsibility for the entire cost of the war, while accepting an actual liability only for civilian damage. This ingenious but lethal formula was incorporated into the Treaty of Versailles as article 231 – to become known as the infamous 'war guilt' clause:

> 'The Allied and Associated Governments affirm and Germany accepts the responsibility of Germany and her allies for causing all the loss and damage to which the Allied and Associated Governments and their nationals have been subjected as a consequence of the war imposed upon them by the aggression of Germany and her allies.'

This clause, more than any other in the entire Treaty of Versailles, was to cause lasting resentment in Germany. Ironically it was inserted only in the financial section of the Treaty in order to provide a clear basis on which reparations could be exacted, and to limit the overall sum Germany had to pay. Only with respect to Belgium was Germany ordered to pay the full war costs, because its invasion was seen as a flagrant violation of the Treaty which in 1839 had guaranteed Belgian neutrality.

As we have seen, the populations in Britain and France were clamouring for Germany to be made to pay for the costs of the war. A settlement based on Germany's capacity to pay was not likely to be substantial enough to satisfy this public demand. Clemenceau was under pressure to exact from Germany the astronomical sums the French people had been led to expect. In April 1919, Lloyd George received a telegram signed by 376 Members of Parliament urging him to 'present the bill in full to the Germans'. The consequence of all these conflicting pressures was that an exact total of reparations to be paid by Germany was not stated in the Treaty. Instead, a Reparations Commission, drawn from the allied and associated powers, was established to settle the figure after detailed consideration. The Germans complained angrily that they were being asked to sign a 'blank cheque'. In 1921, Germany's liability was set at £6,000 million, and this sum was progressively reduced, and payments rescheduled, to ease her burden.

Punishment for war criminals

Not all the allied leaders were happy to endorse a move to 'hang the Kaiser'. The Japanese, conscious of the semi-divine status of their own Emperor, were particularly reluctant to agree to such a course of action. Besides, the Kaiser had fled to Holland, and the Dutch government refused to hand him over to the allies, despite threats that Holland might not be allowed to join the League of Nations until it did. It proved equally difficult to draw up a list of lesser war criminals.

Eventually, a handful of German military commanders and submarine captains were tried, not by the allies themselves, but by a German military court at Leipzig. The sentences imposed were light – fines or short terms of imprisonment – but this was the first time that the concept of 'crimes against humanity' was given legal sanction.

Germany's frontiers

The West   Negotiations about national frontiers were, not surprisingly, extremely contentious. While expert commissions laboured to demarcate frontiers in eastern Europe to accord, as far as possible, with Wilson's insistence on 'self-determination of peoples', Clemenceau and Foch battled with Lloyd George and Wilson to weaken Germany in the west. The French demands for a Rhine frontier for Germany, the establishment

Plebiscite

A political process in which all the citizens of a state who are deemed eligible to vote give their views on a particular issue or set of questions prepared by the government or some other official body. Thus through a **plebiscite** a whole community or national population can express its opinion.

of an independent Rhineland state and a Saar under French occupation almost brought the conference to a premature end in early April 1919. Wilson ordered his ship to stand by to take him back to the United States. Painfully, however, a series of compromises was hammered out.

Wilson had already accepted the French argument that, as partial compensation for the German destruction of coalmines and iron-ore works in north-east France, the French government should be allowed unrestricted access to the coalmines of the Saar, which had produced 8 per cent of Germany's coal before 1914. He was not prepared to agree to the further French demand that the Saar be separated from Germany and placed under French or allied control. The agreement finally reached was that the Saar should be administered by the League of Nations for 15 years, with French ownership of the mines, and that after that time the inhabitants should choose in a **plebiscite** whether they wished to continue under the League, revert back to Germany or become a part of France.

The argument over the Saar was part of a larger argument over the whole Rhineland area. Neither Wilson nor Lloyd George was willing to agree to the central French demand that the German frontier in the west should follow the course of the river Rhine. Lloyd George saw only too clearly that this could sow the seeds for future conflict, just as the German annexation of Alsace and Lorraine in 1871 had been one of the long-term causes of the First World War. As a substitute for a Rhine frontier, Wilson and Lloyd George on behalf of their respective countries each offered Clemenceau a treaty of guarantee of military assistance against unprovoked aggression, to operate under the League of Nations.

Germany therefore retained possession of the Rhineland, but Wilson came to an agreement with Clemenceau that it should be occupied by allied troops for 15 years to ensure that the terms of the peace treaty were carried out. The area under occupation was to be divided into three zones, the most northerly to be evacuated after five years, the middle zone after ten years and the most southerly after fifteen years, providing that Germany was meeting all her treaty obligations. Germany herself was forbidden to keep military forces or military installations in the Rhineland, and no time limit was set on this demilitarisation. As a further part of the territorial settlement in the west, Germany ceded Eupen and Malmedy to Belgium (see Figure 10.7).

The East   In eastern Europe, the disputes were not about existing frontiers, but about the establishment of new ones, following the collapse of the Habsburg and Russian empires. Given the mix of nationalities and races in this area, drawing frontiers along clearly defined national boundaries, as Wilson was urging, would be well-nigh impossible. The

Figure 10.7 *Germany after the Treaty of Versailles*

difficulties were clearly revealed in the demarcation of Poland's frontiers. Wilson's thirteenth point promised an independent Poland to include territories inhabited by 'indisputably Polish populations' which should be guaranteed 'free and secure access to the sea'. However, this access to the sea was bound to cut through the German provinces of Posen and West Prussia, inhabited mainly by German-speaking peoples. And if Poland obtained the port of Danzig, with its half a million German inhabitants, about two million Germans would be included in the new Polish state.

It was initially agreed that Danzig, the east Prussian provinces of Marienwerder and Allenstein, and a substantial corridor of land carved out of West Prussia, should be assigned to Poland. Lloyd George, however, strongly disagreed and, largely as a result of his pressure, Danzig was finally established as a Free City, to be administered by a Commissioner responsible to the League of Nations, and to be connected with Poland by a customs union and port facilities. Lloyd George also secured plebiscites for Allenstein and Marienwerder, and in March 1920, both districts voted decisively to be included in Germany.

Upper Silesia was another racially-mixed area on the German-Polish frontier, of immense economic value. Before the war, it had provided Germany with 23 per cent of its coal, 80 per cent of its zinc and a large part of its iron. The Polish territorial commission at Paris assigned it to Poland on the grounds that it was 'indisputably Polish in origin'. Only after violent German objections in late May did Lloyd George press for a change of heart and, at the least, for a plebiscite to be held. Again he was successful, and a plebiscite was arranged for 1921. However, the populations in this region were so inextricably mixed that it proved almost impossible to fix a frontier in accordance with the expressed wishes of the inhabitants. In the end, a special League of Nations commission divided Upper Silesia between Germany and Poland, with the western, predominantly agricultural, section going to Germany and the smaller, but wealthier, eastern section being assigned to Poland.

While there were strong attempts to reflect claims of nationality and self-determination in eastern Europe, on behalf of Czechs, Slovaks, Poles and Romanians, the Germans themselves could justifiably complain that these were not extended to them. Substantial German minorities, who had been subjects of the Austro-Hungarian empire, now found themselves in Poland or in Czechoslovakia. A notable example were the Sudeten Germans, from 1919 subjects of the new Czech republic. Furthermore, the Treaty stipulated that Germany should respect the independence of the new Austrian republic, despite calls for union from Germans in both countries. It was understandable that the allied leaders should take measures to prevent Germany from becoming a more extensive territorial power in 1919 than she had been in 1914. But it was equally understandable that German governments would cite the 'Fourteen Points' in support of their claim that they had been unfairly treated by the peacemakers.

Reactions to the Treaty

The Treaty of Versailles was completed in great haste at the end of April 1919 and handed to German representatives at Versailles on 7 May. Few of its 440 clauses had not been the subject of intense bargaining and serious disagreement. The Germans were given 15 days, later extended by a week, to comment on the treaty. This they did at great length. Their bitter and sustained objections, documented in great detail, were received by the allied and associated powers at the end of May. They reinforced growing feelings, especially among British representatives, that the treaty was too harsh, and departed too much from Wilson's Fourteen Points.

The British delegation now pressed for modifications in response to the

German objections. They succeeded in gaining a plebiscite for Upper Silesia, but failed to secure admission for Germany to the League, or to shorten the military occupation of the Rhineland and secure reconsideration of the reparations settlement. Thus the treaty which the Germans finally signed on 28 June 1919 was only a slight modification of the original version. The French insisted that the ceremony should take place in the same splendid Hall of Mirrors at the Palace of Versailles in which the French had been forced to acknowledge their submission after the Franco-Prussian war in 1871 (see Figure 1.1 on page 5). French revenge was sweet, but the humiliation for Germany was bitter and lasting.

Overall assessment of the Treaty of Versailles

How harsh was the peace settlement with Germany? The Treaty of Versailles deprived Germany of about 13.5 per cent of its territory, including Alsace and Lorraine, about 13 per cent of its economic productivity and of about 10 per cent of its population, as well as all of the country's colonies and large merchant vessels.

Compared to the Treaty of Brest-Litovsk, which Germany had negotiated with Russia in March 1918, Versailles could be said to be fairly lenient. The Germans, however, argued that they had sued for peace on the basis of the Fourteen Points, and that the final treaty bore little resemblance to Wilson's peace programme. In particular, they resented the 'war guilt' clause, the imposition of a blank reparations cheque, the loss of western Prussia, Danzig and much of Upper Silesia, and the forbidding of *Anschluss* or union with Austria. Within a short time of the conclusion of the treaty, an influential body of opinion in Britain began to sympathise with German grievances. Even before the treaty was ratified, in January 1920, Britain's Treasury representative at Paris, John Maynard Keynes, had written a devastating critique of the way the treaty had been negotiated. He drew attention in particular to the unworkability and undesirability of the reparations section of the treaty. The publication of Keynes's *Economic Consequences of the Peace* fed a growing movement in Britain which pressed for substantial revision of what was being seen, particularly on the left, as an unfair treaty.

In France, however, there was growing alarm that the treaty might not be harsh enough to contain renewed German aggression in the future. While the fighting had devastated France's richest ten provinces, Germany itself had not been invaded. The Treaty of Versailles left it largely intact, with a population almost double that of France, and with no powerful east European neighbours. Many in France denounced Wilson's insistence on self-determination and its effect in fragmenting eastern Europe as 'folly'. And such anxieties turned into alarm at developments in the United States, when the Senate failed to ratify the peace settlement in the autumn of 1919.

On his return to the United States in the summer of 1919, Wilson had embarked on an extensive speaking tour to whip up support for the Treaty of Versailles and in particular for US participation in the new League of Nations. But the effort was too much for him, and in the autumn he suffered a serious stroke. In November 1919 and again in March 1920 the US Senate failed to ratify the Treaty of Versailles – with reservations – by the necessary two-thirds majority.

Within a year of the peace conference, therefore, the victorious alliance which had defeated Germany and had negotiated a set of peace terms had crumbled away. France was left without a Rhineland frontier and without the treaties of guarantee she had been promised as a substitute. The USA withdrew from political involvement in Europe, and negotiated a separate peace with Germany, but at the same time reminded the allies of the substantial financial debts which they owed to it. Britain was left feeling guilty about the severity of the terms, particularly anxious that they would weaken a valuable prewar trading partner, and limit its ability to withstand the western march of Bolshevism. Most crucially, Germany was left resentful and determined to cooperate as little as possible in the carrying out of the treaty. Indeed, within a short time, the Weimar republic and Bolshevik Russia were working together to undermine the settlement. When the British government took the lead in organising a conference at Genoa in 1922 to promote European economic recovery, the only tangible outcome was a treaty of cooperation between Russia and Germany signed at nearby Rapallo.

Recent historians have argued that it was a lack of agreement among the victorious powers about enforcing the treaty which was much more important in helping to explain the failure of the 1919 peace settlement than the terms themselves. These are now seen as 'relatively lenient', and about as reasonable a compromise as it was possible to construct in the circumstances. Indeed, if you compare the Treaty of Versailles with the Treaties of St Germain and Trianon (see below), you will see that in respect to territorial losses it is much less severe.

The real problem was that no power was really happy with the Treaty of Versailles and there was an ongoing struggle between French leaders who sought to strengthen its terms, and British governments seeking revision in favour of the Germans. The treaty itself had been constructed on the assumption that the Germans would help to carry it out, and when they refused, there was no agreement on how to force them to comply.

The other peace treaties

The **Treaty of St Germain** with Austria, September 1919, was modelled on the Treaty of Versailles. The Covenant of the League of Nations formed the first 26 articles, and there were war responsibility and reparation clauses similar in form to the treaty with Germany. Austria was to be permitted a conscript army of no more than 30,000 officers and men, and was forbidden to unite with Germany. It lost to Italy the South Tyrol, with a German-speaking population numbering about a quarter of a million, and the prosperous provinces of Bohemia and Moravia to the new republic of Czechoslovakia. Austria also ceded to the allies Galicia and land around the northern Adriatic. The new Austrian republic was left with little more than a quarter of the territory that had formed the Austrian half of the prewar Habsburg monarchy. Nearly a third of its population was concentrated in Vienna.

The **Treaty of Trianon** with Hungary, June 1920, was also modelled on the Treaty of Versailles, with similar war responsibility and reparation clauses, and with the Covenant of the League of Nations forming its first 26 articles. Almost one-third of prewar Hungarian territory – principally Transylvania and most of the Banat – were ceded to Romania, taking about two million Magyars into the newly-enlarged Romanian state (see Figure 10.8). The rest of the Banat, along with Croatia and Slovenia were incorporated into the new state of Yugoslavia. Slovakia, Ruthenia and Bratislava were transferred, along with their 700,000 Magyar inhabitants, to Czechoslovakia, and Fiume was surrendered to the allies. Altogether, Hungary lost rather more than two-thirds of its prewar territory, and was limited to a professional army of 35,000 officers and men.

Like the above two treaties, the **Treaty of Neuilly** with Bulgaria was modelled on the Treaty of Versailles. Bulgaria had to cede some territories to Romania and to Yugoslavia, and surrendered western Thrace to the allies, who passed it on to Greece by treaty in August 1920. Bulgaria was charged with war responsibility and with reparation payments, and her army was limited to 33,000 professional men.

Peacekeeping, 1920–25

The early 1920s witnessed continuing conflict between the British and French governments over how to deal with Germany. An earlier generation of historians was critical of what they saw as French intransigence towards Germany, but recent verdicts suggest that French policies were more realistic than those of Britain. The French recognised that German

Figure 10.8 Europe after the Treaties of St Germain, Trianon and Neuilly (dotted line represents the former borders of Germany and Austria-Hungary)

governments would only carry out the terms of the treaty under duress, and would try to evade as far as possible the payment of reparations. A recent assessment of the early 1920s concludes that:

> 'As France and Germany both understood, but Britain and America rarely seemed to, reparations constituted the primary battlefield in the continuing contest over who won the war and over whether Germany would again dominate the continent. Indeed, one German official termed this struggle "the continuation of war by other means" ... If reconstruction costs were transferred from the loser to the continental victors and added to their domestic and foreign war debts while Germany paid effectively nothing ... eventual German predominance would be virtually assured.'
>
> Sally Marks, *Genoa, Rapallo and European Reconstruction in 1922* (1991).

Thus when France and Belgium invaded the Ruhr in January 1923 to try to collect the reparations which they alleged Germany was refusing to

161

pay, Britain strongly disapproved and remained on the sidelines. The Germans embarked on a campaign of passive resistance, and the German economy, which was already very weak, completely collapsed. As hyper-inflation swept through the country and threatened to undermine European economic recovery, Britain and the United States sought to put together a package of measures which would rescue the German economy, provide a formula to guarantee regular German reparation payments and reassure the French government of Germany's peaceful intentions.

The Dawes Plan

This took its name from American banker General Charles Dawes and was based on a report on Germany's economic problems adopted in 1924. The plan brought the Ruhr occupation to an end and laid down a schedule of annual German reparation payments. At the same time, it stabilised the German economy by outlining the reorganisation of the German Reichsbank, and recommending a large foreign loan for Germany. The loan was successfully taken up, with American investors proving particularly keen to invest in the German economy.

As a result of the influx of funds coming into the country after 1924, Germany was able to recover economically and to pay reparations to the allies. They, in turn, then paid their war debts to the United States. But these financial arrangements rested on fragile foundations, and the Wall Street Crash of 1929 caused the sudden recall of American short-term loans, with fateful consequences for the German economy and ultimately for the rest of Europe.

The Locarno settlement

Following the economic settlement, the Germans, under the leadership of Foreign Secretary Gustav Stresemann, pressed for political negotiations to bring further stability to Europe. At the Locarno conference of October 1925, Germany, France and Belgium pledged to uphold the territorial settlement in western Europe, including the demilitarised status of the Rhineland, with Italy and Britain acting as guarantors, on behalf of the League of Nations.

What this meant in practice was that Britain and Italy guaranteed Belgian and French frontiers against German attack, and German frontiers against French aggression. It was also agreed that Germany should be admitted to the League of Nations. However, there was no such unequiv-ocal German acceptance of its frontiers in eastern Europe; the most it would agree to in this region was to enter into arbitration treaties with her neighbours Poland and Czechoslovakia.

Locarno appeared to mark a giant step in the direction of lasting European peace. The chief architects of the settlement – Stresemann, Briand of France and Chamberlain the British Foreign Secretary – were collectively awarded the Nobel Peace Prize for their efforts. Germany entered the League in 1926, and allied troops began leaving the Rhineland. By 1930, all occupation troops had left the area, five years ahead of schedule.

Considerable tensions still remained, however, particularly in Germany. Stresemann was the target of virulent attacks from the Right for not bringing about a quicker or more wholesale revision of the Versailles Treaty. French governments were aware of the strong nationalist senti-ment which existed in Germany, and pressed for the continued enforce-ment of the Versailles Treaty. British governments, however, saw the Locarno treaties and German membership of the League as ushering in a new era of diplomatic equality, in which German pleas for progressive revision of the treaty would be sympathetically received.

Germany's position in Europe by the mid to late 1920s was once again potentially a very strong one. Though its military strength had been limited by the Treaty of Versailles, its army chiefs had found ways of circumventing the restrictions and of keeping a small, but highly efficient, military force in operation, which could quickly be expanded if the opportunity arose. The United States had retreated from active involvement in Europe, and Russia had largely withdrawn into self-imposed isolation after the adoption of 'socialism in one country' (see chapter 11). Eastern Europe lay open to German penetration, while the entente partners – Britain, France and Italy – continued to disagree over the extent to which the peace treaties should still be enforced.

There is no doubt that the terms of the Treaty of Versailles were contentious, inevitably so given the scale of the First World War. They were not as harsh as the French wanted, but nor were they as lenient as the Germans hoped for. The settlement was a compromise which pleased no one and which was never effectively enforced. As a result, a resentful Germany was given the opportunity to stage a rapid recovery, and before too long right-wing groups would be urging eastward expansion and a renewed attempt to gain mastery of Europe.

Task: making notes

Good note-taking is essential to making sense of detailed material, such as that presented in this chapter. The following guidelines should help you to see how to clarify in your own mind what are the key points. You could use a similar strategy when you tackle similar chapters.

1 Make brief notes on the problems facing the peacemakers, under the following headings:

■ The position of the USA

■ The armistice

■ Popular sentiment among the victorious allies

■ Popular sentiment in Germany.

2 Take two sheets of paper. Head them both 'The terms of the Treaties'. Then add a subhead to one of 'Bad news for Germany'; and to the other: 'Not so bad for Germany'.

Make notes under the following six headings on whichever sheet is more appropriate (it may be necessary to write on both sheets under the same heading):

– League of Nations
– Colonies
– Military terms
– Reparations
– War crimes
– Frontiers.

3 Make brief notes on 'Reactions to the Treaties', under the headings:

– in Germany
– in France
– in the USA
– in Britain
– reparations
– Locarno Pact.

Further reading

Derek Aldcroft, *From Versailles to Wall Street 1919–29* (Penguin, 1987) – chapter 1 is a useful summary of the aftermath of the war, focusing particularly on economic issues.

Gerd Hardach, *The First World War* (Penguin, 1987) – chapter 10 provides succinct coverage of the financial and economic legacy of the war.

Ruth Henig, *The Origins of the Second World War*, Lancaster Pamphlet (Routledge, 1985) – section 1 has a short general survey of the impact of the war.

Ruth Henig, *Versailles and After*, Lancaster Pamphlet (second edition, Routledge, 1995).

James Joll, *Europe since 1870* (Penguin, 1976) – chapter 10.

Martin Kitchen, *Europe between the Wars* (Addison Wesley Longman, 1988) – a clear account of peacemaking and peacekeeping.

11 The League of Nations

Time chart

1920: League begins to operate from its base at Geneva.
Aaland Islands dispute between Sweden and Finland

1921: League divides Upper Silesia between Germany and Poland

1923: Corfu crisis breaks out
Draft Treaty of Mutual Assistance drawn up to strengthen
League's peacekeeping machinery. Rejected by Britain, among
others

1924: Geneva Protocol drawn up by League Assembly. Rejected by
Britain in March 1925

1925: League successfully intervenes to prevent spread of military
conflict between Bulgaria and Greece

1926: Germany joins League

1931: Manchurian crisis breaks out. Japan ignores recommendations of
Lytton Commission and leaves League in 1933

1932: League Disarmament Conference meets, but fails to agree on
general scheme for arms limitation

1933: October Germany leaves Conference and the League

1934: Disarmament Conference ends in failure. Russia joins League

1935: Italian troops invade Abyssinia. Half-hearted League sanctions fail
to stop Italian aggression and Abyssinia annexed by Italy, who
leaves League and concludes Rome–Berlin Axis with Hitler (in
1936)

The League of Nations was the first peacekeeping agency which operated
on a worldwide scale. It was set up as part of the peace settlement in
1919, with the aim of ensuring that no conflict on the scale of the First
World War ever happened again. Clearly it failed, in the sense that
another major war broke out 20 years later. However, the potential of the
organisation and the work it did achieve ensured that a similar body, the
United Nations, was established after the Second World War. Assessing
the record of the League of Nations is no easy task: it was a complex
organisation which succeeded in some of its aims and failed in others.
This chapter will look at the reasons why it was set up and will attempt to
assess how effectively it carried out the functions for which it was
established.

Why was the League set up?

There were a number of developments in the late nineteenth and early twentieth centuries which highlighted the need for an international agency to bring nations together on a regular basis to deal with specific issues.

1 The scientific and technological revolution created the need for a network of international agreements which required central coordination – such as those to oversee postal deliveries, link telegraph systems, draw up international labour regulations and regulate major waterways.

2 There was a growing acceptance that disputes between states could be resolved by legal means, through arbitration agreements, rather than by resorting to force. The USA took a lead in this by concluding a number of arbitration treaties with other powers before 1914.

3 As powers built up their armaments before 1914, the costs of their armies and navies and of the equipment they demanded rose dramatically. The Russian government took the lead in 1899 in calling other major governments to a disarmament conference at the Hague in Holland. A second disarmament conference took place in 1907. Some limited agreements were concluded, and a third conference was scheduled for 1915. Before it could convene, it was overtaken by events – the outbreak of the First World War.

4 Throughout the nineteenth century, the great European powers had attempted to resolve conflicts, particularly among smaller powers, by working together – first in the congress system established after the Vienna settlement of 1815, and later through the Concert of Europe. Such bodies proved to be useful in a variety of crises, but they had no regular machinery. It was left to individual states to try to convene meetings when specific problems blew up. As the Balkan crisis unfolded in the summer of 1914, the British government desperately tried to convene a conference of the leading European powers, but was unable to force Germany or Austria-Hungary to agree to meet. Many people in Britain believed that if there had been an international body in existence in the summer of 1914, which member states had to attend on a regular basis or in a crisis situation, the First World War could have been prevented.

5 The length and intensity of the First World War was the final, and certainly most decisive, factor which led to the establishment of the League of Nations. As casualties mounted, and costs soared, demands to stop any repetition of a conflict on this scale grew louder. By 1918, an international peacekeeping agency of some kind had become a political necessity – to assure populations which had suffered great personal losses that their sacrifices had not been in vain.

6 It was the US President, Woodrow Wilson, who was responsible for putting the issue of the League at the top of the peace conference agenda in Paris in 1919. The outbreak of war convinced him of the bankruptcy of traditional European diplomacy. He believed that standards of international conduct and of diplomacy needed to be established, and that a body like the League was essential to supervise and to regulate a new international order. The last of his Fourteen Points (see chapter 10) called for the formation of a 'general association of nations . . . for the purpose of affording international guarantees of political independence and territorial integrity to great and small states alike'.

What were to be the League's functions?

A commission to draft a constitution for the League was set up in Paris in January 1919, under Woodrow Wilson's chairmanship. Progress was rapid, and by the middle of February a first draft had been completed. Indeed, the creation of the League was one of the first tasks to be completed by the peacemakers at Paris. Its constitution, containing 26 articles, was called the Covenant and at Wilson's suggestion it constituted the first section of each of the peace treaties concluded at Paris in 1919.

Fourteen states were represented on the Commission, including the five major powers at Paris: the USA, Britain, France, Italy and Japan who each had two delegates; nine smaller powers provided one delegate each. Their agreed aim was to set up a body which would be effective in preventing wars in the future, but it soon became apparent that delegates had different ideas on how this could best be achieved. The result was that the League was equipped with a range of mechanisms which it was hoped would preserve peace and enable conflicts to be settled peacefully, and to some extent these mechanisms overlapped. But this was not seen at the time as a major problem. Delegates believed that the League's most important task would be to provide as many avenues of escape from war as possible, and it was in this spirit that they constructed a body with a wide range of different functions. We can list them as follows:

1 a permanent inter-state conference
2 the League as a disarmament agency
3 the League as a guarantee scheme

4 prevention of conflict
5 the peaceful settlement of disputes
6 the League as an administrative body
7 the League as an economic and social agency.

A permanent inter-state conference

The first seven articles set out how the League was to be constituted, how often it was to meet, and that its headquarters were to be at Geneva in Switzerland. It was to have a Council of great-power members, with four representatives of smaller powers, meeting regularly during the year, and an Assembly of all members meeting once a year. Thus the League was to be a permanent international organisation which could deal with crises as they arose, rather than relying on the diplomatic initiatives of individual states. It was hoped that nearly all states would in due course become members and therefore be bound by the procedures laid down in the Covenant.

Ex-enemy powers were not invited to become members at the outset. It was felt that they should first have to demonstrate their fitness to join by carrying out the terms of the peace treaties. Nor was Bolshevik Russia a founder member – it condemned the new body as a capitalist organisation dominated by imperialist states. There were to be 45 founder members, and it was hoped that this number would soon grow.

However, a body consisting of 45 different nation states, each jealously guarding their independence and national interests, was not likely to find it easy to agree on many issues. Wilson's original idea had been for membership of the League to be restricted to democracies, whose electorates, he believed, would maintain a constant pressure on their governments to work for peace. But his rather narrow conception was overruled by delegates urging a more broadly-based organisation. Thus the League was really, as its French translation suggests, a 'society of nations' covering a wide variety of states, and on most issues, under article 5, 'decisions...shall require the agreement of all the Members of the League represented at the meeting'. Concerted action was therefore likely to be difficult to bring about. Nonetheless it was hoped that the mere fact that member states would meet on a regular basis and get to know each other would contribute to international peace.

The League as a disarmament agency

Article 8 spelled out that one of the major functions of the League was to bring about the reduction of national armaments to the lowest point consistent with national safety. The fact that disarmament was the first major role of the League reflected the strong belief of those who drafted the Covenant in 1919 that the build up of armaments before 1914 had been a major cause of war. Britain's Foreign Secretary in 1914, Sir Edward Grey, asserted in the 1920s that 'great armaments lead inevitably to war' and that it had been 'the enormous growth of armaments in Europe, the sense of insecurity and fear caused by them' which had made the outbreak of war in 1914 'inevitable'.

In the immediate aftermath of a war which had been responsible for so many deaths, the conviction that disarmament was a vital task that should be carried out by League members as a matter of urgency was too strong to be challenged.

The League as a guarantee scheme

Article 10 of the League Covenant specified that member states should protect the 'territorial integrity and existing political independence of all Members of the League' against external aggression. This was the role which Wilson thought would be the most crucial of all the League's tasks, and he argued that without this provision the League would simply be a 'talking shop'. However, other delegates at Paris warned that under this clause the League would in effect be policing the 1919 peace settlements, which might be seen by the defeated powers as unjust. The guarantee provision offered no scope for peaceful change or revision of frontiers in the future, nor did it spell out what action should be taken if aggression against a member state took place. It was left to the League Council to 'advise' on how the obligation members had agreed to under this clause was to be fulfilled.

Many delegates, and particularly the British representatives, were unhappy about the 'guarantee' role of the League, and tried to persuade Wilson to drop it altogether or to amend it. However, Wilson remained adamant that article 10 would constitute the backbone of the League machinery, and its guarantee provision therefore remained as one of the League's main functions.

Prevention of conflict

To try to balance article 10, delegates pressed for the League Covenant to contain provisions which would provide machinery for the prevention of disputes. This was achieved in two ways. Article 11 gave members the right to bring to the League any issues which they thought might threaten war, so that the League could take action to tackle the problems before war actually broke out. Article 19 empowered the League Assembly to 'advise the reconsideration of treaties which have become inapplicable' and the discussion of 'international considerations whose continuance might endanger the peace of the world'.

However, member states could only 'advise' consideration, and all major powers had to be in agreement before changes could be sanctioned. Clearly, powers who had gained substantial territory from the Paris peace settlements – like Poland, Czechoslovakia and Romania – were not likely to agree to territorial changes which would weaken their position and power. Thus the League's capacity to operate effectively as an agent of peaceful change was in question from the outset.

The peaceful settlement of disputes

Those who drafted the Covenant accepted that armed conflicts might break out again in the future. Their concern was to draw up a set of rules which League members would agree to follow in the event of a dispute. The aim was to prevent that dispute from escalating out of control, as it was believed that the Austro-Serbian conflict in 1914 had done, and to bring about a peaceful settlement as quickly as possible.

Articles 12–17 laid out the rules which member states agreed to observe. In the event of a dispute in which they were involved, they were to submit it to the League Council who would investigate it, and they were not to resort to a forcible solution until three months after the League had reported on the dispute. The League was given six months to despatch a commission of enquiry or set up an investigation, and to bring a report back to the League Council. If that report was agreed to unanimously by Council members (obviously excluding parties to the dispute), then it was to be enforced. If, however, there were divided views, then the parties were free to fight it out after the requisite three months.

If members failed to follow these procedures, by resorting to war before submitting the dispute to the League, or by failing to wait for the requisite period of time after a report, then sanctions were to be applied against the offending member by the other Members of the League. In the first instance, these sanctions were to be economic, prohibiting trade and financial relations with the offending state. If these failed to bring about compliance with the League's procedures, then the Council could recommend 'what effective military, naval or air force the Members of the League shall severally contribute to the armed forces to be used to protect the covenants of the League'.

These, together with article 10, were the celebrated 'collective security' provisions of the League. They were regarded as the 'teeth' of the League, to enforce peace when all other measures had failed. It was believed in 1919 that economic sanctions on their own would prove sufficient in most cases to compel an aggressor to lay down arms. Military sanctions were seen as a last resort. The League was not to have its own armed forces, as the French had demanded. It was to ask member states to furnish military assistance as and when required by circumstances, and any advance planning or organisation was therefore out of the question.

The sanctions provisions of the League were therefore carefully defined and fairly limited in extent to what those drafting the covenant believed states would be willing to do in the event of a major dispute breaking out. It is unquestionably the case that the League was set up to prevent the First World War from breaking out! All its mechanisms were designed with 1914 in mind, on the assumption that the big danger to peace in the future would not be deliberate aggression but disputes spiralling out of control. Hence the emphasis on mechanisms designed to contain crisis situations and to resolve them as quickly as possible. Whether the machinery would work so effectively in the face of deliberate aggression by one of its members was a more difficult issue, which the French raised on a number of occasions but which delegates in 1919 did not wish to dwell on at any great length.

The League as an administrative body

Arising out of the peace settlements of 1919, the League was entrusted with a range of duties relating to the supervision of agreements and of treaties. It was to oversee the running of Danzig and of the Saar, through League Commissioners, and a number of minority agreements entered into by east European governments. It was also to supervise the administration of ex-German colonies and former Turkish provinces in the Middle East, through a system of mandates which were to be operated by League members on agreed conditions, who had to furnish an annual report to the League.

The League was also to 'encourage and promote' voluntary national Red Cross organisations, and to take over the coordination of 'all international bureaux already established by general treaties' with the consent of the parties involved.

The League as an economic and social agency

Finally, the League was charged under article 23 with a wide range of humanitarian concerns. It was to:

■ 'secure and maintain fair and humane conditions of labour for men, women and children', and to that end a separate International Labour Organisation was established to draft international conventions and try to secure their acceptance by member states

■ try to outlaw 'traffic in women and children' and 'the traffic in opium and other dangerous drugs'

171

- supervise and try to regulate 'the trade in arms and ammunition' across the globe
- secure and maintain 'freedom of communications and of transit and equitable treatment for the commerce of all Members of the League'
- try to prevent and control the spread of disease.

The League in operation

You can see that the scope of the League's activities was potentially enormous. In coming to any judgement on how effectively the League operated between 1920 and 1939, it is necessary to look at all the different roles which the League was trying to carry out. You will see that while it failed to perform well in some roles, it had a modest success in others and encountered total failure in one or two. Let us therefore consider the League's record in relation to the functions which we have already listed.

A permanent inter-state conference

In this role, the League was greatly handicapped from the start because of the refusal of the United States to join the organisation. The absence of one of the world's leading powers inevitably narrowed the scope of the League's operations, and made its member states nervous of taking any initiatives which the United States might oppose. Many historians argue that American membership would have made the League a much more effective organisation. Certainly this would have been true had the United States taken an active role in the League. On the other hand, the presence of a United States concerned to limit the operation of the League and only prepared to act in certain specified circumstances and in restricted ways might not have increased the League's effectiveness to any great degree.

Until 1926, the League was also without Germany and Russia, and its Council therefore had as many representatives from minor powers as it did from major ones. However, in 1926 Germany joined the League and stayed until 1933. In that year, both Germany and Japan gave notice of their intention to leave, but Russia joined in 1934. Italy also left in the mid 1930s. Thus the League never contained all the world's major powers, and in that sense it could be seen to have failed in one of its major objectives. However, the members it had did meet regularly, and the friendships forged among many of the delegates helped to oil the wheels of international diplomacy. Between 1926 and 1929, the leaders of Britain, France and Germany met regularly at Geneva and made considerable progress in resolving a number of European problems.

After the mid 1930s, the League did not play a major role in the events leading to the outbreak of the Second World War. It was bypassed in the crises which arose over the Sudetenland and over Danzig and the Polish corridor. Its existence therefore failed to prevent another major war from breaking out, and as several historians have pointed out, there was a paradox right at the heart of the League's activities. If its members were willing to act peacefully and in a law-abiding way, then a body like the League was not really necessary. If states were determined to go to war, and were not prepared to be League members or abide by League rules, then the League would not have enough power to stop them.

Disarmament

This was the role in which the League most disappointed its ardent supporters. It was unable to persuade its members to disarm to any great extent, and its failure in this area led many people both then and later to dismiss it as a totally ineffective body. However, we can now see more clearly that the League faced a number of obstacles in its endeavour to bring about arms limitation, and that its task was virtually impossible from the start.

The 1920s was a period of great international instability, with the consolidation of a communist government in Russia, the emergence of fragile new states in eastern Europe, and at the heart of Europe a Germany unreconciled to the peace settlement. In this situation, countries like France, Poland and Czechoslovakia were reluctant to embark on major schemes of arms limitation. Article 8 of the League Covenant required reduction of national armaments 'to the lowest point consistent with national safety'. Eastern European states, perched uneasily between Germany and Russia, two potentially powerful expansionist states, would certainly not feel secure enough to reduce their armies in the short term. France, with its population of 39 million, faced a Germany which had a population of nearly 65 million and greater industrial resources. Without the promise of support from the United States or Britain, France was also not prepared to disarm.

No amount of persuasion from other powers that disarmament would bring about security had any effect. Many League members demanded security first, before they would agree to reduce their armaments.

Britain was willing to reduce its military and naval forces, but with the United States out of the League, naval disarmament talks took place through conventional diplomatic channels, at conferences like Washington in 1921–2 or London in 1930. Substantial naval limitation agreements were concluded between the United States, Britain and

Japan, but it proved very difficult to extend them to cover a wider range of countries. Britain took the lead at Geneva in urging members to set up a commission to begin discussions to draw up a possible League disarmament convention. From 1926 to 1930 a Preparatory Disarmament Commission met at Geneva, and invited to its meetings representatives from both the United States and Russia. However, substantial disagreements soon arose, partly from political factors and partly because of technical difficulties. Powers with one type of military organisation, such as the use of conscription, favoured the disarmament of volunteer-style armies but demanded special concessions for their own situation. Those who had naval strength but negligible military strength, like Britain, demanded across-the-board reductions in military strength but a rather different approach, by category of ship, to naval reductions. Bolshevik Russian representatives urged total disarmament on all other powers, and then castigated them for insincerity when they found reasons not to proceed too rapidly in this direction. The Russians soon found they could count on German support for many of their proposals; this situation filled other members with alarm and caused them to make minimum concessions.

As well as political obstacles to agreement, there were substantial technical problems, relating to limiting different types of weapon, weighing the capability of one armed force against another, and deciding whether, for example, aeroplanes in civil use were to be left out of agreements, or whether they might rapidly be converted to military purposes. Then there were the problems arising out of enforcement of agreements – how was this to be done, how was periodic inspection to be carried out – with many powers threatening not to cooperate with outside inspection and insisting that enforcement could only be done on a voluntary basis.

A disarmament conference was finally convened at Geneva in 1932. Not only did delegates have to try to resolve the sorts of problems which had already bedevilled the Preparatory Commission's labours, but they were then faced with a German threat that if League members failed to bring about substantial disarmament they would demand the right to rearm (see chapter 10). The rise of extremist nationalism in Germany not unnaturally frightened not just the French government, but eastern European regimes as well. In this situation, no significant measure of disarmament was likely to be adopted. Hitler ostentatiously led the German delegation out of the League disarmament conference in October 1933, and the conference limped on for a further few months before ending in failure in 1934.

Clearly the League failed to operate effectively as a disarmament agency. In the first place the international situation was too fraught with difficulty. In the second place, the problems of trying to limit weapons which were becoming more and more complex and sophisticated, and of trying to equalise the ways in which different countries organised their armed forces were too intractable. The real problem, however, was that expectations in 1919 about what could be achieved were totally unrealistic. We have a better idea today of the complexities of arms limitation negotiations, and of the need to concentrate on specific aspects and on particular weapons rather than taking a broad, general approach. Unfortunately the League's quest for substantial, across-the-board armament limitations was not only doomed to failure, but fatally divided its members and therefore made cooperation in other fields more difficult.

The League as a guarantee scheme

We have already seen that there was considerable opposition to this aspect of the League's activities in 1919. Many members, particularly non-European ones, felt that article 10 potentially put far too great a burden on them, and Canada unsuccessfully campaigned in the early 1920s to have the article removed. Meanwhile, the decision of the United States not to join the League made other members, such as France and its eastern European allies, feel more insecure and more determined to try to use the League to enforce the peace settlement.

Indeed, France led the way in trying to strengthen the operation of article 10, and the sanction provisions in article 16, refusing to discuss disarmament schemes until the League's collective security mechanisms had been tightened. The Draft Treaty of Mutual Assistance of 1923 and the Geneva Protocol of 1924 were schemes designed to strengthen the League as a guarantor of the 1919 settlements and of the global political and territorial *status quo*. They were strongly opposed by Britain, its **Dominions** and the Scandinavian powers, who believed that members would not be willing or able to carry out the vast liabilities and commitments which would inevitably result from such a role. Thus article 10 stayed as it was. The League's members remained divided between those who wanted it to operate strongly to enforce the existing territorial settlement, and those who believed that a more selective approach was necessary to promote peaceful change and prevent the build-up of dangerous tensions in Europe. With its members divided in this way, the League could not operate effectively either to enforce territorial integrity and political independence or to promote peaceful change.

The prevention of conflicts

The League did record some success in resolving issues which might otherwise have brought powers into serious conflict. In 1920, Britain brought to the Council of the League the problem of the future of the

KEY TERM:

Dominions

The settlers who had gone to Australia, Canada, New Zealand and South Africa had all, by 1910, been granted internal self-government, though retaining the British monarch as head of state. Britain, however, was still responsible for their foreign policy and defence, at no inconsiderable cost. In the interwar period they became generally known as **Dominions** – autonomous countries but freely associated with Great Britain.

Aaland Islands, situated in the Gulf of Bothnia between Sweden and Finland (see map on page 161). They were populated largely by Swedes, but on the collapse of the Russian Empire, Finland claimed sovereignty over them. By using independent members to investigate and report, the League was able to settle the matter. The same approach was also successful in relation to Mosul, an oil-rich province coveted by Turkey and Iraq, and with the final division of Upper Silesia between Poland and Germany.

However, there were many situations in which the League of Nations was unsuccessful in imposing an agreed solution. Both Lithuania and Poland claimed Vilna, and the League was unable to prevent the Poles from seizing and retaining it by force. Italy occupied Fiume which had been assigned in the peace settlements to the new state of Yugoslavia. The more distant from Europe a territorial dispute was, and the more powerful one of the contending parties was, the more unsuccessful the League was likely to be in preventing conflict or a forcible seizure of the disputed area by one party. Thus the League could claim some success in preventing conflict, but its achievements in this area were limited.

The peaceful settlement of disputes

The League's successes in this area were even more limited. Where conflict broke out between two small member states, which could be threatened easily with military reprisals from the leading League powers, the League was strong enough to impose a settlement. This was the case in 1925 when Bulgarian and Greek forces stationed on the frontier between the two countries started to fight. However, in a situation where a major member state broke the rules and defied the League's authority, it quickly became clear that a united response from all the other League powers was unlikely to occur.

In 1923, Italy seized the Greek island of Corfu in the Mediterranean, in retaliation for the murder of an Italian general delimiting the Albanian-Greek frontier which the Italians claimed was Greece's fault. Benito Mussolini demanded the payment by Greece of an enormous indemnity before Italian troops would evacuate Corfu (see chapter 15). He refused to submit the dispute to the League of Nations, claiming that the Italian general had been working for a different international body, the inter-allied Conference of Ambassadors. The dispute was eventually resolved, but not before significant doubts had been cast on the League's ability to settle disputes peacefully. In the first place, Italy had shown that it was prepared to take the law into its own hands. Secondly, it secured significant support from France, which was unwilling to take action against a power which had cooperated with it in the invasion of the

Ruhr earlier in the year (see chapter 10). Thirdly, when the British government considered whether it might be feasible to take either economic or naval sanctions against Italy, Treasury and Admiralty experts warned of the damaging consequences they would have on Britain, with no guarantee that they would actually help to resolve the crisis. All League powers breathed a sigh of relief when Greece paid the indemnity and Italy evacuated Corfu. But the episode showed up weaknesses in the League's structure and limits to the actions which its members were prepared to take. These were fully exploited by expansionist member states in the 1930s.

The Manchurian dispute

In September 1931, Japanese troops guarding railway lines in South Manchuria, a distant northern province inhabited largely by Chinese settlers, fanned out and invaded the entire province. All attempts by the League and by the civilian Japanese government to bring the troops under control or force them back to their original bases failed. The League despatched a commission of enquiry, under the British representative, Lord Lytton, to tour Manchuria, northern China and Japan. The commission's lengthy and complex report blamed both sides for inflaming the situation in Manchuria, but demanded that Japan should return the state she now called Manchukuo back to the Chinese. The Japanese refused to consider this, and announced that they were leaving the League (see Figure 11.1).

The League was now unable to enforce the Lytton Commission's proposals. Member states were reluctant to enforce economic sanctions on Japan, in the midst of the Depression. In any case, Japan's main trading links were with the USA, who supplied her with oil, scrap iron and many other vital resources. The USA was not a member of the League, and was not willing to work with the League to impose a solution on Japan, though it deplored Japan's aggression and called on other powers to join in refusing to recognise the territorial changes which Japan had brought about in northern China. Military action was even more problematical. Manchuria was geographically remote, and only Britain and the United States had the naval resources to confront Japan successfully. The United States made it clear that they were not prepared to engage in military action against Japan and Britain was unwilling to act alone. France and Italy were preoccupied with the European situation, so neither were prepared to agree to military or naval action in the Far East. Britain took the lead in 1933 by calling for a League arms **boycott** of both Japan and China. It quickly became apparent that such a measure would hit China far more heavily than it would Japan, and it was soon abandoned. Japan remained in control of Manchuria,

KEY TERM:

Boycott

The origins of the word '**boycott**' lie in the nationalist agitation in Ireland in the late 1870s. Tenants during the depression of the late 1870s were frequently evicted and the land taken over by others. Frequently, those who took over the land from evicted tenants were treated with extreme hostility and given no help to farm their land. This fate befell Captain Boycott in County Mayo. 'Boycott' therefore came to mean refusing to have any dealings, particularly trade, with someone.

THE DOORMAT.

Figure 11.1 *Cartoon entitled 'The doormat', which appeared in* The Evening Standard, *1931*

now independent state of Manchukuo. The League had proved itself powerless to do anything to combat Japanese military expansion.

The Abyssinian affair

The Manchurian dispute revealed that the League was not able to operate effectively to settle disputes far from Europe. It was similarly unable to intervene successfully to settle conflicts which broke out in the interwar period in South America. However, in 1935 a challenge arose to League authority nearer to Europe, in north-east Africa, which revealed a different set of problems. Italian troops launched a full-scale military invasion of Abyssinia, a League member, in a bid to expand the Italian empire in Africa. It was a clear-cut case of aggression. Abyssinia's ruler, Haile Selassie, travelled to Geneva to appeal to League members for assistance.

Neither France nor Britain was willing to engage in military hostilities with Italy on behalf of the League of Nations. France was still hopeful of gaining Italian support for an anti-German alignment which might serve to contain Nazi expansionism. Britain was facing the prospect of Japanese hostility in the Far East and the threat of an aggressive Germany in Europe. British troops were spread across the globe in peacekeeping activities in different parts of the empire, so the last thing the British government wanted was to make an enemy of Italy, especially since she occupied such an important strategic position in the Mediterranean Sea, the vital artery linking Britain with her empire. While the National government in Britain pledged itself to uphold the authority of the League in the general election of 1935, it then tried to negotiate a compromise deal with Mussolini, which would have given him much of the Abyssinian territory he coveted, through the Hoare–Laval pact of December 1935. (Hoare and Laval were the foreign secretaries of Britain and France.) However, a public outcry in Britain against the pact forced the British and French to abandon it, and Hoare resigned.

League members now agreed to the imposition of mild economic sanctions against Italy, but neither Britain nor France was willing to extend these to include oil, for fear that they might drive Mussolini into some 'mad dog' act of aggression in the Mediterranean. While the British navy in the area was strong enough to feel reasonably confident of victory in a conflict against its Italian counterpart, such an encounter would inevitably affect on British strength elsewhere and on Britain's overall global position. Britain was not willing to run the risk of a naval war in the Mediterranean without French support, which the French were unwilling to give. The truth was that neither Britain nor France believed that its own national interest would be well served by fighting a League war on behalf of Abyssinia against Italy.

Thus the Abyssinian dispute starkly revealed, as the Manchurian crisis had earlier, that the leading League powers were not prepared to enforce the Covenant against another major League power who was not directly threatening their own interests. The machinery was there to be used, but member states were not willing to use it fully in case it provoked a war which might uphold the general interest of the League but at the same time undermine their own power and effectiveness.

Some economic sanctions continued to be applied half-heartedly against Italy in 1936, but they failed to prevent her from completing her conquest of Abyssinia. The only tangible result of the sanctions was that they forced Italy to look elsewhere for vital imports and therefore strengthened Italy's trading links with Germany. They also convinced Mussolini that he could achieve more international success by working closely with Hitler than he ever could from allying with Britain and France (see chapter 15). Thus ironically the only outcome of the League's half-hearted attempts to combat Italian aggression over Abyssinia was to drive Mussolini into the arms of Hitler.

The League had totally failed in its attempts to settle disputes peacefully because its leading members, who were individual sovereign states, were not prepared to subordinate their own interests in support of one overall 'League' interest. They might take concerted action if it suited them, or enforce sanctions if they thought that this action would have some effect without damaging their own position. They saw the League machinery essentially as an addition to conventional diplomatic channels, to be used or not as appropriate, rather than as a new approach to international affairs. As we have seen, the League enjoyed limited success in settling disputes involving minor powers, but its 'collective security' provisions could only work if its members shared a common interest in preserving peace and similar views on how to deal with those who broke the rules. It soon became apparent that there was no widespread common interest in peace or agreement on the extent to which powerful aggressors could or should be coerced into submission to the League. In such a situation, the League was unable to settle major disputes or to enforce settlements.

The League as an administrative body

The League of Nations proved to be a useful international agency for supervising agreements and monitoring treaties, though it was less successful in authorising action when breaches of treaty provisions were alleged. It kept reasonable order in the Saar and in Danzig, and received reports from **mandatory powers** on an annual basis. The League's Mandates Commission scrutinised the reports closely, and called for changes in policy in certain areas or for the mandatory powers to justify some of the actions they were taking. While its members were not able to intervene directly, they did keep up a constant pressure on the mandatory powers to rule in accordance with the agreements they had registered with the League.

KEY TERM:

Mandatory powers

Germany's colonies were taken over by various Allied nations following the Treaty of Versailles. However, under pressure from US President Woodrow Wilson, they were not simply annexed, but the Allies became **'mandatory powers'** – responsible to the League of Nations for the good government and development of these areas, leading them eventually to independence.

Minority provisions, however, were more difficult to administer. There was a stream of allegations of flagrant violations of minority rights on the part of Germans in Poland and of other minorities throughout eastern Europe. While the League endeavoured to investigate complaints, it was often very difficult to gain a clear picture of the true state of affairs, and even more difficult to pressurise the offending government into taking corrective action. While the involvement of the League in protecting minorities could not be ignored by governments in eastern Europe, they were able to evade their responsibilities on a wide scale, and the League had no effective way of forcing compliance with its demands on behalf of specific minorities. Furthermore, minorities provisions covered only the new states of eastern Europe, and therefore could not be used to protect Jews from persecution in Germany after 1933.

Social and economic activities

The League undertook a wide range of humanitarian activities in the interwar period. It was active in trying to assist refugees in Russia in the early 1920s, and in facilitating an exchange of populations between Greece and Turkey after the war of 1920–22. It undertook investigations into the extent of the white slave trade, and into drug smuggling. It also carried out much valuable work in combating tropical diseases and the spread of infections. The International Labour Office became a very active body, promoting labour agreements among employers and workers and trying to improve working conditions on a worldwide basis.

The League Council took the lead in organising economic help for Austria and Hungary in the 1920s, and the League Secretariat drew up an agenda designed to try to bring about a world economic recovery. Conferences were held to examine the impact of tariffs and the possibility of promoting trade agreements among the world's leading economic powers. In the late 1920s, Aristide Briand's ideas for closer European economic and political cooperation were examined by the League, to see how and in what ways they could be incorporated into a world framework. League members then found themselves faced by the Depression, and various League bodies worked hard to try to mitigate its impact.

There was general agreement among member states that the League's social and economic activities had proved to be effective in a variety of ways, and on the eve of the Second World War, a League of Nations report called for an expansion of League efforts in these areas. It was acknowledged that the League had failed in a number of its aims, but in this area of 'non-political' activities, it was extremely successful. Indeed, much of the humanitarian work pioneered by the League was continued and expanded by its successor, the United Nations.

Conclusion

You can see that the League had more than one function. Its establishment was an ambitious attempt to prevent any more major wars from breaking out, by a variety of means. While it had some successes, it failed in its major objective. Some have argued that far from preventing a second world war, it actually helped to bring one about by its weak and half-hearted efforts to deter dictators from their aggressive designs. Undoubtedly, the expectations people had about what the League could achieve were unrealistic. The main concern of its member states was to protect their own national interests and it proved almost impossible for them to agree to the pursuit of collective goals on any sustained basis.

However, the League of Nations was not a total failure. It did achieve some successes, most notably by providing the foundations of the United Nations. We now have a whole range of international bodies bringing nations together in a variety of activities. They have learned from the League's failures, and at the same time are building on the foundations established by the world's first international organisation.

Task: essay writing

'The League of Nations failed because of the actions of states in the 1930s, not from its own weaknesses. How far do you agree with this view?'

This essay title is in quite a common style: it provides you with a view of events which you are expected to debate. As in this case, the view is usually in the form of a rather dogmatic statement. You will often find yourself agreeing with part of the statement but disagreeing with much of it. In this case you might say that the actions of states, especially over Manchuria and Abyssinia, showed the League to be failing, but that this failure was inherent in the structure of the League, not just a new factor in the 1930s. You will also want to show that the League had some successes to its name. This gives you the beginnings of a plan. The seven points which provide the focus of this chapter (pages 167–172) give the rest.

An essay should have an introduction, a paragraph in which you pick up the issues in the title of the essay, show that you understand what the question is driving at, and say how you are going to tackle it. In making a plan, it may well be that you decide what you are going to say in the introduction after you have outlined the focus and content of the rest of the essay.

An essay should also have a conclusion. The easy way of doing this is to summarise what you have just said. It is better, however, to add another perspective. In this case you might show your wider knowledge by pointing out that, although the League of Nations seemed to have failed, it provided much of the structure for the United Nations, set up before the end of the Second World War.

Further reading

Ruth Henig (ed.), *The League of Nations* (Oliver and Boyd, 1973) – contains some useful documentary extracts.

F. S. Northedge, *The League of Nations: Its life and Times* (Leicester University Press, 1986) – the most recent appraisal of the League.

George Scott, *The Rise and Fall of the League of Nations* (Hutchinson, 1973) – a lively account of the League's activities.

Frank Walters, *A History of the League of Nations* (Oxford University Press, 1952) – very thorough and detailed study by a former League official.

12 Russia, 1917–24: why did the Bolsheviks succeed?

Time chart

(*Note:* Dates are given according to the Julian calendar which was used in Russia until February 1918. In the twentieth century, this was 13 days behind the Gregorian calendar, which was used in the West.)

1914: **1 August** Germany declares war on Russia
26 August Russia defeated at Battle of Tannenberg
5 September Russia suffers serious losses at Battle of Masurian Lakes

1915: **6 September** Tsar assumes supreme command of the armed forces
16 September Tsar **prorogues** Duma

1916: **June–October** Brusilov Offensive secures some advances but costs over a million casualties
30 December Murder of Rasputin

1917: **January–February** Strikes and civil unrest in Petrograd
26–27 February Troops refuse to fire on demonstrators and go over to revolutionary movement
Formation of Petrograd Soviet of Workers' Deputies
March Order no. 1 of Petrograd Soviet drafted; election of soldiers' committees called for. Nicholas II abdicates. First Provisional Government formed, which announces programme of democratic reform and civil liberties
3 April Lenin returns to Russia and formulates *April Theses*; calls for 'all power to the Soviets'
3 June First all-Russian congress of Workers' and Soldiers' Deputies opens
2 July Trotsky joins Bolsheviks
3–4 July Violent anti-government demonstrations in Petrograd, known as 'July Days'
5–7 July Arrest of Bolshevik leaders ordered; Lenin goes into hiding
16 July Kornilov appointed Commander-in-Chief of Russian army
18 July Kerensky becomes Prime Minister
27–30 August Arming of Red Guards; Kornilov's 'coup' defeated

KEY TERM:

Prorogue

To cease the holding of meetings for the time being, without actually dissolving the Duma as an organisation.

1917: September Trotsky becomes chairman of Petrograd soviet; both Petrograd and Moscow Soviets get Bolshevik majorities

10 October Lenin attends meeting of Bolshevik Central Committee and his call for armed insurrection is agreed

20 October First meeting of Military Revolutionary Committee of Petrograd Soviet

24–25 October Armed workers and soldiers, led by Bolsheviks and organised by Military Revolutionary Committee, take over key buildings and installations in Petrograd

25–27 October Provisional Government ministers arrested; Bolshevik coup announced at 2nd Congress of Soviets. Congress adopts Decree on Peace and Decree on Land, and appoints first Soviet government, the all-Bolshevik Council of People's Commissars, with Lenin as chairman

December Establishment of Cheka

1918: January Constituent Assembly forcibly dissolved

February Introduction of Gregorian (western) calendar

March Treaty of Brest-Litovsk signed with Germany.
Soviet government moves capital from Petrograd to Moscow. Trotsky appointed People's Commissar of War

April–May Civil war breaks out

16 July Imperial family executed at Ekaterinburg

1920: November End of civil war

1921: March Kronstadt uprising of sailors crushed. At 10th Party Congress, New Economic Policy is introduced by Lenin

1922: Lenin suffers two strokes

December Formation of Union of Soviet Socialist Republics (USSR), containing Russia, the Ukraine, White Russia and Transcaucasia

1923: Lenin has a third stroke

1924: January Death of Lenin

Russian government and society was undergoing considerable changes before 1914. Historians are divided over the direction in which Russia was heading by 1914, and some argue that a revolutionary upheaval was highly likely. However, there is general agreement that this would not have been a Bolshevik revolution, and that only the disastrous war against Germany gave Lenin and the Bolsheviks their opportunity to seize power. We will examine this view by looking at different factors which contributed to Bolshevik success, not only in 1917 itself but more crucially in the civil war which followed. We shall also look at the revolutionary ambitions which Lenin proclaimed in late 1917 and consider the extent to which they were realised by the time of his death in 1924.

The impact of the war, 1914 to February 1917

Like all other European governments involved in the First World War, the Russian government was totally unprepared both for the length of the conflict or for the scale on which it was fought. Even the prospect of a short war filled many advisers and government ministers with gloom. One commented in the summer of 1914 that if Russia became involved in a war with Germany, 'Russia will be flung into hopeless anarchy, the issue of which cannot be foreseen'. However, Russia's entry into the war initially generated considerable enthusiasm. Cheering crowds appeared in the towns; young men showed themselves eager to enlist, exchanging a humdrum life in the fields or factories for action on the battlefield and the chance to sport a new uniform, a new pair of boots and a gun.

Within weeks, the Russian army had suffered a massive defeat at the Battle of Tannenberg in east Prussia, when the German army encircled the Russians and captured hundreds of thousands of prisoners. A subsequent defeat at the Masurian Lakes in September saw the Russian army in temporary retreat from east Prussia, though the forces pitted against Austria further south were initially more successful. However, by the end of 1914 it had become clear that the war would not be over quickly, and that massive amounts of men and munitions would be required to fight it.

The Russian government was soon struggling to sustain a war on the scale required. It did manage to mobilise about fourteen and a half million men between 1914 and 1917 – a considerable feat – but was not able to provide them with enough equipment or munitions. The army required about 18 million rifles. The government managed to get hold of about 7 million, and of a small number of machine-guns, though nowhere near the 133,000 or so demanded. As a result, soldiers found themselves restricted in the number of rounds of ammunition they could fire, and there were not enough weapons to go round. Morale among the troops fell disastrously, and was reduced further by incompetent leadership and by the contempt with which all too many officers treated their men.

As Russian factories switched to the production of war munitions and equipment, output of consumer goods plummeted, and there were serious shortages of crucial raw materials. Groups of businessmen, politicians and workers came together to try to improve levels of planning and output, but their efforts were not effectively harnessed by the government.

Indeed the Russian government became more and more isolated as the war proceeded. All attempts by the Duma to assist in the running of the war were rebuffed, and in September 1915 the Duma was dismissed. The same month, Nicholas II took the fateful decision to assume personal command of the Russian army, and he entrusted the government of the country to his wife Alexandra, who was deeply under the influence of 'our friend' Rasputin. The fact that Alexandra was German by origin gave rise to all sorts of suspicions about pro-German sentiments at court, but much more damaging to the royal family were the antics of Rasputin (see page 82). His irresponsible approach to affairs of state, and public displays of drunken debauchery alienated the Russian nobles and professional classes whose support the government so desperately needed. By the time Rasputin was murdered in 1916 by a young noble, the Tsar and his family had precious few friends left in Russia.

The economy

The growing unpopularity of the government was due not only to the absence of firm leadership, but also to the spiralling cost of living and the increasing shortages of food. As the war dragged on, the government paid for it partly by taking out loans from its allies and partly by printing more and more paper roubles. Thus Russia, in common with other countries during the war, suffered from massive inflation. Workers soon discovered that the wage increases they received were quickly swallowed up by high prices which for many commodities had quadrupled by the end of 1916.

In the rural areas, the situation was somewhat better. The loss of so many young men to the army relieved what had been a serious problem of overpopulation on the land in many parts of Russia. Peasant families therefore had fewer mouths to feed. They also received income if they had horses which could be used by the army. The problem facing the peasants now was a novel one: there was little on which they could spend their money, and therefore the incentive to produce and sell grain in large quantities was no longer so great. The result was that peasants ate more, stored grain for an uncertain future, and deposited money in the bank. Most of the surplus grain they produced was directed to the army, and only a relatively small amount found its way to the towns.

Given the fact that Russia was being blockaded during the war, and was therefore unable to export grain, as it had done in such large quantities before 1914, there should still have been enough food to go round. But the government lacked the ability to organise and to plan the war effort effectively. Foodstuffs which could have been sent to the cities perished beside railway lines because there was no transport to carry them or storage facilities to preserve them. The army demanded more and more grain, and at the same time populations which were fleeing from the fighting zones crowded into the major Russian cities. A swollen urban population began to experience food shortages and lengthy queues for basic necessities. By the winter of 1916–17, there was serious talk of food rationing. It was the panic buying of bread in late February 1917, combined with a strike by metal-workers and women textile operatives in Petrograd (renamed from the too German-sounding St Petersburg in 1916) which triggered off the first revolution of 1917.

The Revolution of March 1917

Within four days – 27 February to 2 March – revolutionary disturbances in Petrograd, at the naval base in Kronstadt and in Moscow spiralled out of control. The soldiers ordered to crush the uprisings mutinied and joined the protesters. The government lost all authority and the Tsar was forced to abdicate. No single individual or revolutionary group master-minded the revolution. It was the culmination of both long-term griev-ances against the Tsarist government and short-term protests about the effects of the war. In the cities, workers seized control of their factories and workshops, and singled out particularly objectionable bosses and foremen for rough treatment, daubing them with red paint or bundling them unceremoniously into wheelbarrows and tipping them into nearby rivers. In the rural areas, as the weeks went by, peasants began to chop down trees illegally, to seize parts of noble estates and to demand sweeping land reforms. Minority peoples in Finland, Poland, the Ukraine and in the Caucasus declared their independence from Russian rule. Most seriously of all, in the Russian army, soldiers' committees were formed to curtail the powers of officers over them, and to demand more say in military decision-making.

In the middle of this increasingly chaotic situation, members of the Duma agreed to form a provisional government. It was to be provisional, until elections could be organised to produce a Constituent Assembly which would exercise democratic power on behalf of the Russian people. Meanwhile, all Russians were to be granted freedom of speech, of associ-ation and of religious worship. There was to be a free press, a political amnesty and the freeing of political prisoners, the abolition of the death penalty and no more discrimination on the basis of class, nationality or religion. At a stroke, Russia became, in Lenin's words, 'the freest of all the belligerent countries'. Before long, the government had acceded to workers' demands to introduce an eight-hour day and to accept the principle of workers' control in factories.

'Dual Power'

All the direct action which was being taken by workers, soldiers and sailors, and later by peasant groups, quickly resulted in the formation of local soviets or committees. The most prominent and influential of these was the Petrograd Soviet of Workers' Deputies which was established in the early days of the revolution to organise food supplies and guard against a counter-revolutionary attack by Tsarist supporters by setting up a workers' militia. It was quickly joined by revolutionary soldiers, anxious to extend the responsibilities of the Soviet into the military sphere, to prevent the army from being used to crush the revolution. They extracted from the Soviet 'Order number 1' on 2 March 1917, which called for the setting up of soldiers' committees in every military unit which would send deputies to the Soviet and take political orders only from that body. Soviets modelled on that of Petrograd were soon established in major cities throughout Russia.

Thus the new Provisional Government found its authority increasingly challenged by the network of Soviets which sprang up around the country, and in particular by the Petrograd Soviet. A system of 'Dual Power' existed, which made the difficult task of restoring order to Russia almost impossible. The Soviet did not directly challenge the Provisional Government's right to rule. Indeed, many deputies who were familiar with Marxist theory saw the Provisional Government as representing the bourgeois class in Russia which had overthrown feudalism, and would now set to work to build up a capitalist regime in Russia. Only when this process was well advanced – possibly after years or even decades – would Russia have a working class strong enough to rise up and carry through a socialist revolution. However, while the introduction of a socialist government might be some way off, it was the duty of the Soviet to protect the interests of its workers and soldiers, and to guard against any attempt by discredited feudal elements to seize back power.

Problems facing the Provisional Government

The war

Russia's allies, Britain and France, put great pressure on the new Russian government to continue fighting Germany. Clearly, the end of fighting on Germany's eastern borders would enable the German government to switch considerable numbers of troops to the Western Front. This would be a potentially disastrous development for the British and French governments, and so they offered considerable loans to the Provisional

Government to persuade them to carry on fighting. The Petrograd Soviet, on the other hand, reflected the mood of the great majority of the Russian population in urging the Provisional Government to seek peace with Germany as quickly as possible, on the basis of no annexations of territory and no indemnities.

This offered no easy solution to the government, however. The German peace terms were bound to entail huge losses of territory, almost certainly including such economically important areas as the Ukraine. Peace at this price would undoubtedly make the government extremely unpopular. Furthermore, if the fighting suddenly ended, seven million armed Russian peasants would be discharged from the army and would all flock back to their villages making the country ungovernable. A compromise position on the war was therefore reached between the Provisional Government and the Petrograd Soviet – that Russia should continue to fight, but with the aim of defending Russian territory and the Russian revolution, rather than of seeking territorial gains in what many people were now calling an 'imperialist' war. Continuing with the war ruled out any possibility of an improvement in the Russian economy. Instead, as the year progressed, there were growing shortages of fuel and raw materials, leading to the closure of factories and to strident demands from workers for direct action to protect their livelihoods. Food shortages continued, and the harvest of 1917 was disappointingly low. Inflation worsened, fuelling more resentment and discontent. With no money, and no way of enforcing law and order, the Provisional Government faced an uphill struggle to maintain such authority as it had in the face of a great increase in militant demands and direct action by workers and peasants.

The land

The members of the Provisional Government were reluctant to embark on any programme of land reform before the Constituent Assembly was established. The most they would do to meet peasant demands was to agree to the establishment of Land Committees to gather information on land ownership in different parts of Russia in preparation for any reforms the Constituent Assembly might decide to introduce. But peasants all over Russia were not prepared to wait so long. As the months went by, the number of rural disturbances and illegal seizures of land, livestock and machinery increased dramatically. The nobility and the church had no force at their disposal to prevent their large estates from being divided up by an increasingly determined peasantry, whose targets also included wealthier peasant families who had opted out of communes under the Stolypin reforms and had worked to consolidate their holdings. The village commune became once again the focal point of peasant activities, where land seizures, division of plots, distribution of animals and rent levels were decided upon. The Provisional Government was powerless to prevent the Russian peasantry from realising their long-held ambitions, to gain more land and to farm it under the general supervision of the village commune.

Factory committees

Workers in factories in the major industrial areas of Russia were determined that the February revolution should bring them gains in the form of the eight-hour day, higher wages and a greater say in the running of factories. But the worsening economic situation brought shortages of fuel and of supplies, a slowdown in production and the threat of factory closures. Factory committees therefore emerged to represent the interests of the workers, and played an increasingly prominent part in decision-making. Fierce clashes ensued with employers and managers. As more and more factories were forced to close, workers became increasingly adamant that only direct workers' control of factories would improve the situation. This was not a view shared by the Provisional Government who looked to factory bosses to increase output by restoring discipline in their factories.

The army

It was the disaffection of soldiers in the barracks around Petrograd which had enabled the revolution to gather such momentum, and their support for the Petrograd Soviet which gave it power and authority. Increasingly, soldiers' committees were formed in the different army units, not just those stationed near Petrograd, but in the field armies on the Northern, Western and later the South-Western and Romanian fronts. Their aims were, in general terms, to curtail the power of officers, to remove particularly hated officers, and to propose that in future officers should be elected. Increasingly, the expansion of influence of the committees undermined the structure of command in the army, though until the summer army discipline was maintained. The failure of an offensive launched from the South-Western Front in June, and a German counter-attack in early July, led to rapid retreat and a breakdown of discipline. Troops rounded on their officers, and ransacked local depots and shops, looting and rioting. Desertions from the army were also a serious problem. By August, over a quarter of a million soldiers had deserted, not just because of war-weariness, but also to be in a position to claim their share of land from the village commune when plots were re-apportioned after the peasant land seizures.

Increasingly, the army command demanded powers from the Provisional Government to re-impose discipline in the army ranks, to bring back the death penalty and to curb the influence of the soldiers' committees. The

Provisional Government was torn between the obvious need to restore order in the army and the fear that a strong army could be used by unscrupulous generals to crush the revolution.

The return of Lenin

The amnesty which the Provisional Government had granted enabled many political activists to return to Petrograd from exile in Siberia. But for those like Lenin who were in exile abroad, a return to Russia was a more difficult exercise. Without the assistance of the German General Staff, who arranged for a train to carry Lenin and other political exiles across Sweden to Finland and then down to Petrograd, it would have been very difficult for Lenin to make his way back to Russia. The Germans were happy to facilitate his return in the confident expectation that he would do his utmost to end Russia's involvement in the war, thereby ending the need to keep a German army in the east. Few could have foreseen the long-term consequences of their strategy!

Lenin arrived at the Finland Station in Petrograd on 3 April 1917. Here he found a city in revolutionary ferment, but one in which most radical parties were supporting the Provisional Government and the continuation of a defensive war. Even Lenin's own party, the Bolsheviks, had not established any clear alternative strategies on how to advance the socialist phase of the revolution. Within days, Lenin had set to work to outline the main policies which the Bolsheviks should pursue in the ensuing months. The result was his *April Theses* which were to be crucial in bringing the Bolsheviks to power some six months later. The three main propositions were:

1 The Bolsheviks must oppose the continuation of the war, which was an imperialist war, benefiting only capitalists and not workers.

2 The party should offer no support to the Provisional Government.

3 Instead, power should pass to the Soviets which had sprung up all over Russia. Members of these Soviets should be encouraged to withdraw their support for the Provisional Government, and to assume control of affairs in their own localities.

Lenin's proposals shocked not only the members of other socialist parties, but most Bolsheviks as well. For the theses assumed that the bourgeois stage of the revolution was at an end and that the working class was now strong enough to contemplate taking power alone. Most socialists in Russia did not believe this was the case. Far from being ripe for a workers' revolution, they saw Russia as only just embarking on its capitalist

phase. The Provisional Government had promised to call a Constituent Assembly, and most members of Soviets were happy to await the elections and to support the result. As for pulling out of the war, a separate peace with Germany would almost certainly deprive Russia of much of its territory and economic resources in the west and south, and would impoverish the nation still further.

The initial impact of the theses was to isolate the Bolsheviks from other socialist parties. Many even pitied Lenin – he was obviously out of touch with the situation in Russia, and it would take him time to grasp the full extent of the new political realities. As the months wore on and the situation facing many urban workers became more and more desperate, it increasingly appeared to be the case that Lenin was the realist, and that only the installation of a socialist government and the ending of the war would offer some relief. What Lenin had done was to disassociate the Bolsheviks from the failures of the Provisional Government. He now set to work to persuade the Bolshevik Party and then the Soviets that peace, bread and land could only be achieved by advancing to the socialist phase of the revolution.

The July Days and the Kornilov Uprising

In May, the composition of the Provisional Government was broadened when the Petrograd Soviet agreed to participate in a coalition on certain agreed terms, including a speedy peace, the further democratisation of the army, the imposition of State control over the economy, and the preparation of plans for land reform. When the first All-Russian Congress of Soviets met in early June in Petrograd, it passed a sizeable vote of confidence in the coalition government, by 543 votes to 126, with the opponents of coalition predictably being the Bolshevik delegates. A military offensive was launched in mid June which, it was hoped, would relieve the pressure on the government and rally the forces of order and discipline in the country. Unfortunately, the attack failed and was quickly followed by a German counter-attack which caused a major retreat by the Russian army. This severe military setback precipitated a collapse of the coalition government, which was quickly followed by a number of demonstrations in Petrograd by workers, soldiers and sailors. While these demonstrations – which became known as the July Days – had not been organised by the Bolshevik Party, prominent party members were soon prevailed upon by the demonstrators to march at the helm of the protests under the slogan, 'All power to the Soviets'.

The Provisional Government was able to crush the demonstrations, with the help of loyal troops. One factor in their success was the leaking of information to the newspapers that Lenin had links with the German General Staff and was being financed by the Germans. Such allegations discredited the Bolsheviks, who were already unpopular with other socialist groups for attacking the Provisional Government and trying to overthrow it. The Provisional Government ordered the arrest and trial of all those involved in 'the organisation and leadership of the armed insurrection against the State power'. Lenin went underground to avoid arrest, but other Bolshevik leaders, including Trotsky, were arrested and imprisoned. It seemed that the Bolsheviks had tried to force events and had completely misjudged the mood of the country.

They were saved, and the situation completely transformed, by the Kornilov affair. The details surrounding the affair are unclear, but we do know that the Prime Minister, **Alexander Kerensky**, appointed **Kornilov** to be Supreme Commander-in-Chief of the Russian armies on 19 July. Kornilov agreed, on condition that steps were taken to curb the power of soldiers' committees and to restore military discipline. By August, Kornilov was asking the Provisional Government to agree to the restoration of the death penalty for military as well as civilian personnel, for the authority of army officers and the use of courts martial for disruptive soldiers to be restored, and for revolutionary-minded regiments to be disbanded and held in concentration camps. While the Provisional Government hesitated, troops began to be deployed in the direction of Moscow and Petrograd, and Kornilov extended his demands to the imposition of tougher discipline on workers producing war materials, including sending workers who failed to produce agreed production quotas to the front and banning strikes and factory meetings. He

PROFILE: *Alexander Kerensky*

Born in Simbirsk in 1881, **Alexander Kerensky** studied law in St Petersburg and later joined the Social Revolutionary Party. He entered the Duma in 1912 and was a strong critic of the Tsarist government. He took a leading part in the March revolution of 1917, and became a member both of the Petrograd soviet and of the Provisional Government. He served as Minister of Justice and of War, before becoming Prime Minister in July. He moved against Kornilov's troops which were advancing towards Petrograd in August 1917, but was then deposed by the Bolsheviks in November. Kerensky escaped to France, and finally settled in the USA where he wrote many books on the Russian Revolution, before his death in 1970.

PROFILE: *Kornilov*

Lavr Georgyerich Kornilov was born in 1870. He was a Russian soldier who fought in the Russo-Japanese war of 1904–5, and commanded Russian troops in Galicia during the First World War. He was appointed Supreme Commander-in-Chief of the Russian army in July 1917, but just over a month later was accused of planning a military coup against Kerensky, and arrested. Kornilov managed to escape and fought against the Bolsheviks in the civil war, until he was killed in action in 1918. He was described as having 'the heart of a lion and the brains of a sheep'.

also wanted the railways placed under military control. The Provisional Government was torn between the undoubted need to try to halt the lawlessness and anarchy which was gathering pace in Russia and the equally important objective of preserving the support of the Petrograd Soviet and the gains of the revolution. As talks continued with Kornilov, Riga fell to the Germans, and the military front came ever closer to Petrograd.

Amid rumours of a planned Bolshevik rising, Kornilov now demanded that martial law be proclaimed in Petrograd, that all military and civilian authority should be placed in his hands, and that the Provisional Government should resign. Kerensky interpreted this as an ultimatum from Kornilov, and as the first stage of a plot to overthrow the government. He accused Kornilov of mutiny and sent a telegram dismissing him. Kornilov meanwhile was intent on sending troops to Petrograd to crush the Bolsheviks and to establish martial law, with the support, as he always maintained later, of the Provisional Government whom it was his aim to protect.

The situation deteriorated into farce, as the soldiers despatched to Petrograd were intercepted on the way and persuaded to turn back. At the same time, the Petrograd Soviet organised itself to combat a military rebellion and formed a committee for revolutionary defence, a step which was repeated in other parts of Russia. Suspected counter-revolutionaries were arrested, and Red Guards of armed workers were set up, many of them with Bolshevik sympathies. From this point onwards, there was a great increase in support for the Bolshevik Party and a corresponding decline in trust of the Provisional Government. Bolshevik support in the Petrograd and Moscow soviets grew substantially, and it seemed to many that only the uncompromising Lenin and his party could guarantee to workers and peasants a share in power and the peace, bread and land that they craved.

The Bolshevik seizure of power

While events were clearly moving in Lenin's direction, and party membership had leapt from about 23,000 in February to 200,000 at the beginning of October, the Bolsheviks were still a small revolutionary faction. There was considerable disagreement among the leadership about when and by what means power should be seized. From mid September, still under cover in Finland, Lenin urged an immediate seizure of power. Two other leaders, Zinoviev and Kamenev, wanted to wait to see the results of the Constituent Assembly elections, since they believed that economically and socially Russia was completely unready for a successful socialist uprising. Trotsky suggested a different course, working through the Petrograd Soviet and using the Second Congress of Soviets, due to convene towards the end of October, as a platform from which to launch a socialist revolution. The appeal of Trotsky's strategy, which to some extent represented a compromise position, was strengthened by the spread of panic in Petrograd about the possibility of a German capture of the city, and the formation by the Soviet on 9 October of a military revolutionary committee to control troop movements in the area. The very next day, the Bolshevik Central Committee met, and by 10 votes to 2 (the dissenters being Kamenev and Zinoviev) agreed that 'an armed rising is inevitable and that the time for it has come'.

Two weeks later, between 24 and 25 October, with the support of the Petrograd Military Revolutionary Committee, and in the name of the Second Congress of Soviets, the Bolsheviks drove the Provisional Government out of the Winter Palace and seized key points in Petrograd. Kerensky escaped to try to make contact with troops loyal to the government who would march to the capital to defend it. He was unsuccessful; no strong support could be found to save the Provisional Government.

Many Menshevik and Social Revolutionary deputies left the Congress at this point, opposed to what they saw as a premature and irresponsible uprising which was bound to bring reprisals from the army and from other right-wing groups opposed to the revolution. Undeterred, Lenin used the remaining Congress sessions to announce two decrees – one proposing that peace be immediately concluded by all belligerent nations, and the second that landed estates be abolished and the land be handed over forthwith to peasant communes. It was agreed that a workers' and peasants' government, the Council of People's Commissars, should be formed which would exercise power on behalf of the Congress of Soviets. The chairman was to be Lenin, with Trotsky as Commissar of Foreign Affairs, and the lesser known Stalin, a Georgian, as Commissar for Nationalities.

The consolidation of power

The events of late October 1917 gave the Bolsheviks only a tenuous grip on power. It was widely believed that they, in their turn, would be quickly overthrown. The Bolsheviks had to conclude a demoralising peace with the Germans and fight a savage civil war which lasted for two years and stretched their resources almost to breaking-point before their revolutionary seizure of power was consolidated. By that time, Russia was in an even more enfeebled economic and social condition than it had been in 1917.

The Treaty of Brest-Litovsk

Peace was finally agreed with the Germans in early March in the Belo-Russian town of Brest-Litovsk. The terms were very harsh on Russia. It had to recognise the independence of the Ukraine, of Latvia, Lithuania, Estonia, Finland and Poland and to recognise the demands for autonomy of Georgia and Armenia. Thus Russia lost 27 per cent of its grain-producing area, 26 per cent of its population, over a quarter of its railways and three-quarters of its iron and steel works. Russian delegates had to agree not to spread revolutionary propaganda, to disarm and to keep its navy in home waters. While the Russian population welcomed peace, the price was demoralisingly high, and contributed to widespread disillusion towards the new government.

The civil war

Civil war broke out as a result of a number of factors. Czech prisoners-of-war, trapped in Siberia, tried to fight their way out to continue the struggle against the Germans. The British landed troops in northern Russia at Murmansk and at Archangel, to guard munitions supplied by the Allies, and to try to form an independent Russian army to resume the struggle against the Germans. They were also involved alongside the French in military operations in south Russia. Meanwhile, former Tsarist military and naval officers tried to recruit armies to fight against the Bolsheviks, and the new government faced attack on several fronts. Four principal factors saved them.

1 *Divisions among the Whites* The White armies, though more numerous, were not able to coordinate their attacks, and one by one they were driven back by the Red Army.

2 *Geography* Having moved their capital to Moscow, the Bolsheviks controlled the heartlands of Russia, which possessed a reasonable rail network which was effectively used by Bolshevik forces. Their enemies were trying to attack them from different peripheral areas of Russia, and had longer supply routes and difficulties with transport.

3 *Bolshevik ruthlessness* The Bolsheviks pursued the civil war with the utmost ruthlessness. They requisitioned food at gunpoint from peasant villages, raised armies, and utilised the skills and experience of ex-Tsarist officers while holding their families hostage. They used violence and terror against enemies, known or suspected. They were fighting for their political lives, and used every possible means to secure their victory. Trotsky was particularly effective in his role as Commissar for War, travelling in his personal train from one battle front to another, ensuring that necessary troops were raised, supplied and despatched, that they fought vigorously and did not surrender.

4 *The peasants* In the last resort, the Bolsheviks were saved by the Russian peasantry. While peasant communities had little preference for Red armies over White ones, they were determined to hang on to the land which they had gained as a result of revolution. In areas which were recaptured by White armies, estates were returned to former landlords, and peasant 'ringleaders' were hanged. While the Bolsheviks also meted out brutality, in particular to get their hands on crucial grain supplies, they supported – at least for the time being – the sweeping land reforms which had transformed rural Russia. Peasant communities might be reluctant to fight for them, but they would not oppose them, and this was even more true of non-Russian communities who feared the Great Russian aspirations of many White leaders.

Russia after the civil war

By the end of the civil war, Russia was in a desperately weak condition. The economy had collapsed. Industrial production was less than 20 per cent of its 1914 level, and steel production had plummeted to 5 per cent. Food was scarce, and populations were resorting to barter to get hold of the supplies they needed in order to survive. Millions died as a result of the fighting or through disease and starvation. People fled from the towns back to rural areas, where at least there was a chance of food and some work. Whereas the urban population of Russia in 1917 reached about 19 per cent, by 1920 it had fallen back to 15 per cent. Moscow lost half its population, and Petrograd about two-thirds. The proletariat was even smaller in number than in 1917, and the prospects for the successful introduction of socialism even more unfavourable.

Furthermore, by 1920 it became apparent that no successful workers' revolutions were likely to take place in neighbouring countries. Lenin had justified the seizure of power in 1917 in a predominantly rural country like Russia by arguing that the Bolshevik example would trigger off revolutions in other more advanced European countries such as Germany, the Habsburg Empire and Italy. The workers' governments which were set up would then give economic and financial assistance to their fellow socialists in Russia to enable them to overcome their economic backwardness. Instead, governments across Europe took strong measures to combat socialism. Socialist regimes appeared briefly in Hungary and in Bavaria, and there were revolutionary struggles in Germany and in Italy, but by 1920 the flames had largely been put out. Russia would have to recover from its own resources. The Bolshevik repudiation of Tsarist debts had ensured that no government or international consortium would extend credit to a government which was not prepared to honour commercial agreements.

What kind of state did the Bolsheviks establish, 1917–24?

A workers' state

The aim of the Bolsheviks was to create a workers' state, in which each individual contributed to the best of their ability and profits were distributed according to need. Factories, mines, banks, food production – all were to be run by the state on behalf of the workers.

Workers needed guidance, so the Bolsheviks argued, before they could adjust fully to this new system. The role of the Bolshevik Party was to give leadership, just as they had done in organising the revolutionary movement before 1917 and in choosing the moment to seize power. Thus Lenin argued for the party to constitute a 'dictatorship of the proletariat' for a period of time, while society was transformed. In due course, the state apparatus would wither away, since there would be no class antagonisms to repress, and workers would be free to run their own affairs. The new government used posters, films and theatre to get these ideas over. Figure 12.3 shows a 'theatre-on-a-train' carrying the Bolshevik message to rural Russia.

However, this long-term vision was quickly obliterated by the problems arising from Russia's economic and social weakness, and by the destructiveness and savagery of the civil war. It was vital for the new state to try to bring about economic recovery and, in particular, an increase in industrial production. Thus discipline was gradually re-imposed in factories. Workers' committees were replaced by managers and officials answerable to the party, and trade unions were brought under party control. The Bolshevik Party ran the state on behalf of workers, and very quickly a

Figure 12.3 Propaganda train carrying the Bolshevik message, 1920s

state bureaucracy mushroomed to carry out policies on behalf of the Bolshevik government.

Those who were not workers but were class enemies – the nobility, the professional and commercial classes – were to be destroyed. By the end of 1918, the Tsar and his family, rich peasants, industrialists, priests, and many thousands of supporters of the Whites had been killed. Many more fled abroad.

The peasantry

A crucial question which the Bolsheviks needed to address was: were the peasants to be classed as workers? Karl Marx had argued that peasants were a reactionary force, interested only in acquiring land, and that, when capitalism was overthrown, land along with other property would be appropriated by the workers. The peasant seizures of land throughout 1917 therefore had profound consequences for the new Bolshevik state. For while in the towns the capitalist system was overthrown, on the land the vast estates of Russia had been divided up into 25–30 million private plots jealously guarded by individual peasant families under the watchful eye of the village commune. The revolution had given peasant communities property, which they would not lightly surrender. As the historian Isaac Deutscher pointed out, the Bolshevik revolution was at one and the

Kulaks

A Russian term meaning 'tight-fisted people'. **Kulaks** were prosperous peasants who benefited from Stolypin's agrarian reforms after 1906 and became independent peasant landowners. The Bolsheviks denounced them for their greed and growing bourgeois tendencies.

same time a proletarian revolution in the cities and a bourgeois revolution on the land. Or to put it another way, the state 'superstructure' was now socialist, but its base consisted of millions of private peasant plots of land.

Lenin rationalised the situation by arguing that the interests of poor peasants were identical with those of workers, and that gradually state policies would enable poor peasants to acquire the land of their more wealthy class enemies, the **kulaks**. But the reality was that whatever divisions existed in peasant communities, they were not as great as the division between peasant villages on the one hand and the urban-based state on the other. The state wanted grain from the peasants, at low prices, and as the civil war progressed, more and more force was used to extract grain and other food supplies. Peasants resisted as best they could, and continued to farm in their traditional manner. They supported the Bolshevik Party but only insofar as it confirmed their right to keep hold of their land. Bolshevik doctrines were of little interest – as late as 1928, only about 170,000 peasants, out of a rural population of 120 million, were Bolshevik Party members.

Sooner or later, the Bolsheviks would be forced into some sort of struggle with the peasantry. To underpin a workers' state, Russia had to industrialise and this would inevitably entail radical changes in the rural base of Russia. The problem was postponed during Lenin's lifetime, but it would not go away.

One-party rule

To begin with, as we have seen, the Bolsheviks took power on behalf of the Congress of Russian Soviets and with the support of other radical revolutionaries, particularly from the Social Revolutionary Party. Given their revolutionary slogan 'All power to the Soviets', many thought that they would try to broaden their political base and draw in socialists from other parties, and assumed that this would be done when the long-awaited Constituent Assembly met.

Elections had been held in late 1917 – the first, and until recently only, freely-contested elections in Russia's history. While the Bolsheviks had done well in the towns and secured 21 per cent of all votes, the Social Revolutionaries, with massive rural support, gained 38 per cent and had extra support from similar parties in non-Russian areas. When the deputies assembled on 5 January and refused to support a Bolshevik declaration endorsing the decrees of the second Congress of Soviets, the building was surrounded by armed guards and the Assembly was forcibly dispersed, with many being shot in street demonstrations. Lenin declared, 'The breaking up of the Constituent Assembly by the Soviet Power is the complete and public liquidation of formal democracy in the name of revolutionary dictatorship. It will be a good lesson.' But for whom?

What it clearly showed was that the Bolsheviks, having seized power, intended to rule as a one-party dictatorship, imposing their policies on a reluctant population. Just as their rule became ever more dictatorial, so did the power of the party over its individual members.

The Bolshevik Party

There were increasing complaints from party members about the growing power of the leadership. The Central Committee increased its grip over the party structure, partly to enable it to prosecute the civil war more effectively. It set up two new committees: the Politbureau to decide grand strategy and overall policy; and the Orgbureau to oversee internal administration. Scope for ideas to filter upwards was restricted, and increasingly policies and decisions only went in one direction – from the top downwards. The domination of the party leadership was reinforced by the establishment, in December 1917, of the Extraordinary Commission, or Cheka. Its intention was to root out counter-revolution and sabotage, but it was increasingly used to check on the loyalty of party members and to keep them compliant. As an arm of 'revolutionary justice' the Cheka operated outside soviet or party control, and was a weapon which brought fear and terror not just to Bolshevik enemies, but also to friends and to critics within the Bolshevik Party.

Stalin was given the post of Commissar of Workers' and Peasants' Inspection between 1919 and 1922. He helped to ensure that a stream of hand-picked and suitably docile party members and supporters were available to fill the expanding party and state bureaucracies. By 1921 Lenin had banned all factions within the Bolshevik Party. There could be discussion of policies at the highest level, at the Party Congress and in the Central Committee, but once a line had been decided upon and a policy adopted, it had to be accepted and enforced without question.

The Kronstadt Uprising

By the end of 1921, many socialists, ordinary workers, peasants, and even some erstwhile Bolsheviks, were completely disillusioned with the dictatorial way in which power was being exercised by the new regime. Coinciding with the fourth anniversary of the February revolution, the sailors of the Kronstadt naval base, near Petrograd – formerly among the most fervent of Bolshevik supporters – mutinied. Significantly, among their demands were:

- new soviet elections – since 'the present Soviets no longer expressed the will of the workers and peasants'
- the establishment of freedom of speech and of the press for workers and peasants and for left socialist parties
- freedom of assembly for trade unions and peasant organisations
- the release of all political prisoners.

The rebellious sailors were gunned down by unwilling soldiers, but even Lenin admitted that while 'they do not want the White Guards . . . they do not want us either'.

Kronstadt showed how quickly and how ruthlessly revolutionary hopes could be crushed. Undoubtedly, the civil war had contributed to this outcome, but it also has to be emphasised that Lenin's view of the role of the Bolshevik Party and his decision to seize power in the circumstances of October 1917 were equally, if not more, important factors. Lenin had always exercised strong leadership over his party, and had worked hard to ensure that it retained its own identity and did not work closely with other factions. Thus a small party seized power in the name of a minority of urban workers in the chaotic conditions of 1917. Their right to rule was bound to be contested, and they could only survive by closing ranks and by exercising power in an ever more dictatorial way.

The New Economic Policy

Kronstadt did bring about one temporary reform, the introduction of the New Economic Policy. In an attempt to placate workers and peasants, and to begin to generate some sort of economic recovery, it was agreed that there would be no more forced grain collections. After selling a set quota of grain to the state, peasants could sell any surpluses which remained on the open market. Small-scale trading would also be tolerated, but would exist alongside the public-sector enterprises which had been nationalised and would continue to be run by the state.

The New Economic Policy reflected the realities of rural Russia but it caused great opposition in the Bolshevik Party since it seemed to signal a retreat from socialism. However, Lenin justified it on the basis of 'one step backwards to achieve two steps forward' and it was pushed through and endorsed by the party in the expectation that sooner rather than later, the private-sector enterprises would wither away as the public sector expanded. Lenin's willingness to negotiate a compromise with Russia's peasant producers, albeit on a short-term basis, was crucial in enabling the Bolsheviks to consolidate their power effectively at the end of the civil war period.

The state of Russia on Lenin's death in 1924

Lenin suffered a series of strokes from 1922, and died in January 1924. He was mourned as a great revolutionary leader and a man who had done more than anyone else to establish socialism in Russia. Yet the Russia of 1924 was overwhelmingly a rural country, in which over 80 per cent of the population lived in village communities, and earned their livelihood from agriculture. In output and productivity per head Russia was on a par with Turkey and with India, rather than with France or Britain. Its urban working class numbered about 4.5 million, scarcely 5 per cent of the population. The state employed a further 3.5 million, and there were a million unemployed. Russia was impoverished, had experienced severe famine and epidemics since the ending of the civil war, and its population was weary.

Had the revolution been successful, and if so, what were its achievements? There was a workers' government, but precious few workers. There was a socialist regime, yet capitalism, far from having been overthrown, had scarcely developed. The biggest beneficiaries were the peasants, yet inevitably their small private plots stood in the way of economic reform and industrialisation. Lenin was certainly one of the dominant figures of the twentieth century. Yet he bequeathed to his successor a host of intractable problems which would have to be tackled to bridge the gap between revolutionary aspiration and the reality of Russian backwardness. He also bequeathed weapons with which to bring about change – a party dictatorship, a strong state bureaucracy and the apparatus of terror being constructed by the secret police.

Task: essay writing

'Why were the Bolsheviks able to seize power in Russia in October 1917?'

This is a straightforward enough title: a 'gift' you might say (they do happen sometimes!). But there are some things to think about when planning your essay:

■ Don't just say what happened in the period up to October 1917. To describe is not to explain.

■ This is a 'gift' question, so you need to think of ways of making your essay more distinctive. The introduction and conclusion give you scope for your own ideas. You could, for example, start by describing how unlikely a Bolshevik coup seemed in the early autumn of 1917, how many factors were against them (their size, the failure of the July Days, the belief of Marxists in the processes of history, which would lead to a bourgeois democracy in Russia as the next step).

■ Note the last phrase: 'in October 1917'. Even an apparently straightforward title might have a twist in its tail. If you see a reference to a precise time, you should take it as a clue to comment on timing. Your plan should therefore include some reference to 'why October 1917?' rather than March or July 1917 or even March 1918. That should get you thinking about what was special about the autumn of 1917.

■ At A and AS levels you are expected to do more than just list possible reasons for the Bolshevik success in any old order. You should weigh them up. Carry out the task below, in groups, before writing your essay plan.

Discuss the reasons why the Bolsheviks were able to seize power in Russia in October 1917. Here are six possible elements:

a The continuation of the war
b The weakness of the Provisional Government
c The strong support of workers and soldiers
d Peasant land seizures
e The Kornilov coup
f The strategy and leadership of Lenin.

Place these factors in order of importance from 1 to 6: 1 being the factor you think *most* helped the Bolsheviks to seize power; 2 the second most important factor and so forth. Justify your order as against the views of those who have a different order of factors. Add any important issues which you think the list above leaves out.

Further reading

Edward Acton, *Rethinking the Russian Revolution* (Edward Arnold, 1990) – a stimulating discussion of the different ways in which the Russian revolutions of 1917 have been interpreted.

Sheila Fitzpatrick, *The Russian Revolution* (Oxford University Press, 1982) – a very clear and relatively concise study.

Geoffrey Hosking, *A History of the Soviet Union* (London, 1985) – excellent textbook on Russian history since 1917.

Adam Ulam, *Lenin and the Bolsheviks* (Fontana edition, 1969).

Robert Service, *The Russian Revolution 1900–27* (Macmillan, 1986) – a useful introductory survey.

James White, *A Short History of the Russian Revolution, 1917–21* (Edward Arnold, 1994) – an up-to-date and detailed but easy-to-follow account of this crucial period.

Alan Wood, *The Origins of the Russian Revolution, 1861–1917* (Methuen, 1987) – good introductory survey.

13 Collectivisation and industrialisation in the Soviet Union, 1928–41

Was Stalin really necessary?

The Soviet Union remained an overwhelmingly rural country when Lenin died in 1924. While both agriculture and industry were beginning to recover after six years of war and civil war, the Soviet Union lagged far behind other industrialised European powers both in terms of industrial and manufacturing output, and in levels of productivity per head. She was still the 'backward, semi-Asiatic Russia' Lenin had described before the First World War. Any government would have faced the need to introduce programmes of modernisation as a matter of urgency, but for the socialist government of the USSR the task was even more pressing. It was pledged to build a workers' state and to defend it against attack from capitalist enemies. In 1924, workers formed a tiny minority of the Russian population, and the fledgling socialist state was isolated from, and ostracised by, nearly all of Europe's governments. Industrialisation, and a parallel modernisation of the agricultural base of the country, was vital if the revolutionary momentum in the Soviet Union was to be sustained and protected. At the same time, the peasants, who had achieved their long-standing goal to acquire more land as a result of the 1917 revolutions, would certainly resist any attempts to reorganise or amalgamate land-holdings. Any programme of modernisation was likely to bring peasant communities into conflict with a Communist government.

Whoever succeeded Lenin was clearly going to face a daunting challenge. The Soviet Union lacked the capital to invest in industry, and the repudiation of Tsarist debts by the Bolsheviks immediately after their seizure of power meant that investors abroad would not be queuing up to offer financial help. While the German government was interested in establishing some contacts in a bid to circumvent the Treaty of Versailles military restrictions, for the most part socialist Russia would be left to solve her problems alone. This situation was bound to pose enormous social and economic challenges to the Bolshevik Party under its new leadership.

While there is general agreement on the size of the difficulties facing the Soviet Union in the mid 1920s, there is a considerable debate about the approach adopted by Lenin's successor, **Josef Stalin**. His ruthless drive

PROFILE: *Josef Stalin*

Josef Stalin was born, the son of a cobbler, near Tblisi in Georgia in 1879. He was educated in a theological seminary but was expelled in 1899. He became an active revolutionary and was twice exiled to Siberia, in 1902 and 1913. He became a leading member of the Bolshevik Party and was active in the October revolution of 1917, becoming People's Commissar for Nationalities in the first Soviet government. In 1922 he became General Secretary of the Bolshevik Party's Central Committee, and kept this post for the rest of his life (he died in 1953). After Lenin's death, he outmanoeuvred his political rivals, notably Trotsky, and took over the leadership of the Soviet Union. He was instrumental in launching a series of five-year plans to industrialise Russia, and forcing through a collectivisation programme on the land in which millions of peasants died. In 1939 he signed the Nazi-Soviet pact with Germany, but this did not prevent a German invasion of Russia two years later. Though Russia suffered enormous population and economic losses as a result of the war of 1941–5, Stalin provided strong leadership. Russian military strength finally drove Nazi troops back into Germany in 1945 and established control over a large part of eastern Europe.

to collectivise agriculture and to bring about substantial industrialisation in little more than a decade provoked, on the one hand, enormous criticism and condemnation and, on the other hand, grudging respect and occasionally open admiration.

What were the options facing Stalin? Did his policies promote the establishment of socialism in Russia or ensure its failure? As more and more evidence has come to light about the high price large numbers of Russian people paid to ensure the achievement of Stalin's policies, such questions have inevitably generated a wide-ranging debate, to which survivors of the regime in post-communist Russia have increasingly contributed in the last few years. This chapter will examine a range of interpretations of collectivisation and industrialisation and of the great purges of the 1930s. It will evaluate the ways in which Lenin's one-party state of 1924 had changed under Stalin by the end of the 1930s. We will start, however, by looking at different views of Stalin's character and personality and at some of the main factors in his rise to power.

Stalin's personality

While Stalin has been portrayed in many different guises – from mass murderer and Byzantine despot to great genius and revolutionary leader

– it would be fair to say that most assessments, particularly by non-Marxist historians, have stressed his negative rather than positive qualities. Edward Acton commented that he was 'a singularly repulsive concoction of power lust, megalomania, cynicism and suspicion'. An early biographer, the French writer Souvarine, portrayed him as a twentieth-century Ivan the Terrible. One critic drew attention to his 'pathological personality' and another asserted that he was 'criminality enthroned'. His arch-rival Trotsky contemptuously dismissed him as 'neither a thinker, a writer, nor an orator' and delivered the crushing verdict that he was 'the grave-digger of the revolution'.

Even before he became party leader, serious reservations about his suitability for high office were expressed by Lenin in what became known as his *Testament* written in December 1923, a month before he died. He wrote of Stalin that he was 'too rude' and should be replaced as General Secretary by a comrade 'more tolerant, more loyal, kinder, less capricious'. However, by this time Stalin was far too entrenched in the party apparatus to be vulnerable to criticisms even by the dying Lenin. Since his appointment as General Secretary in 1922 he had used his position to establish for himself a virtually unassailable power base, as Trotsky acknowledged when he commented that Stalin took power with 'the aid of an impersonal machine. And it was not he who created the machine but the machine that created him.' A later historian agreed that Stalin was the 'product of his time and place'.

A number of historians have agreed that Stalin was a grey committee man of no particular distinction, who rose to prominence as the party bureaucracy mushroomed. While other more eloquent and highly-educated colleagues concentrated on the major political problems facing the Soviet Union after the civil war, Stalin – a home-spun, less intelligent but unscrupulous political operator – made himself indispensable as the man in charge of the party machine. While there is some truth in this view, it undoubtedly underestimates Stalin's capabilities. We know that Stalin spent most of his teenage years in a theological **seminary**, to which he would not have gained admittance had he not been bright and a good student. He undoubtedly possessed considerable political skills, which he developed during his time as a young revolutionary. He played his part in the construction of the new state after 1917, and was regarded as vigorous, intelligent and energetic, if very short-tempered. Stalin was clearly not an easy man to work with – he was suspicious, cynical and on occasions extremely rude – but he was also perceptive, adroit and hard-working. He harboured slights and bore grudges not for years but for decades. He could also conceal his own ambitions, using patience, manipulative and political skills to consolidate his own position and to undermine and ultimately destroy his rivals and opponents.

KEY TERM:

Seminary

Special college for training priests.

'Socialism in one country' and the future of the NEP

Though Stalin was in a strong political position at the time of Lenin's death, he was not regarded as the automatic choice to succeed the revolutionary hero. Trotsky was seen by many in the Bolshevik Party as a more likely successor, and Zinoviev and Kamenev also had strong support in some quarters. Stalin skilfully appealed to many party members by the respectful attitude he displayed towards his deceased leader, and by his assiduous efforts to promote a Lenin cult. In 1924 he published a book entitled *The Foundations of Leninism* which won him considerable authority among many new, young party recruits. He also won support as a result of his line of argument in the major policy debates consuming the Party in the mid 1920s.

More recent interpretations of Stalin's rise to power, such as *Stalinism* by Graeme Gill, stress the importance of the stance he adopted in crucial party discussions relating to the problems facing the country. The failure of revolutions to materialise in other European countries posed a major dilemma for the Bolshevik Party. Was industrialisation in the Soviet Union dependent on developments elsewhere in Europe? Should efforts to bring about revolutions in the wider world take precedence over attempts to modernise Russia? Trotsky was in no doubt that the answer had to be 'yes'. He argued uncompromisingly that 'the contradictions in the position of a workers' government in a backward country with an overwhelming peasant population can only be solved on an international scale in the arena of the world proletarian revolution'.

But what if the world proletarian revolution failed to materialise? Did that then condemn Russia to continuing backwardness? Here Stalin cleverly played on the patriotic feelings of rank-and-file members of the Party by suggesting that though the regime might not be able to achieve the 'final victory of socialism', it could surely start on the process of constructing a 'complete socialist society'. Stalin skilfully emphasised the positive aspects of the doctrine of 'socialism in one country' to attack Trotsky for taking an anti-Leninist stance and for lacking faith in the abilities of the Russian working class to construct a socialist state.

Trotsky outmanoeuvred

With the assistance of Zinoviev and Kamenev, Stalin succeeded in outmanoeuvring Trotsky and discrediting him in the Party. By the time they realised how powerful Stalin had become, and tried to ally with Trotsky against him, it was too late. Stalin had accumulated support not only because of his position as General Secretary, but because of the backing he was getting from large numbers of party members in key strategic positions and in the lower ranks of the Party. Stalin followed up his success with 'socialism in one country' by his skilful manoeuvring in the debates about the future of the New Economic Policy (NEP).

Lenin's tactical retreat (see previous chapter) had not turned out as the Party had hoped. Although the volume of heavy industrial output had recovered almost to 1913 levels, there were over a million workers unemployed in public-sector industries in 1927. At the same time, private, small-scale and handicrafts production had also recovered to prewar levels, and many NEPmen, as they were called, made a reasonable living plying their wares from village to village, although they were resented by party members as a new manifestation of the despised petty bourgeoisie.

The greatest gainers from the adoption of the New Economic Policy had been the peasants. Agricultural production recovered during the mid 1920s and became more diversified. Modest rises in standards of living were experienced; peasants ate more of their produce, bought a range of consumer goods from travelling salesmen and kept more animals. Only about 10–15 per cent of their grain harvest was going to the towns by 1926–7, and the government faced difficulties in trying to get its hands on more. The Bolshevik Party had little support in rural areas and there was therefore little understanding of peasant village organisation or sympathy for peasant aspirations.

Stalin and Bukharin

All sections of the Bolshevik Party agreed by 1927 that a greater level of industrialisation had to be brought about, and that public-sector enterprises had to be expanded. Many members called for a rapid strengthening of the proletariat, and a move in rural areas towards collective farms. The debate centred on the pace of change, and in particular on the policy to be adopted towards the peasantry. Some of the party's leading figures, including Trotsky, Zinoviev and Kamenev, had been dubbed 'super-industrialisers' because they had called for the adoption of ambitious plans for industrialisation, and a campaign against rural capitalism and what was referred to as the 'kulak danger'. By 1927, the three discredited leaders had been expelled from the Party for fomenting opposition, and Trotsky had been despatched to distant Alma Ata on the Chinese border. Stalin at this stage aligned himself firmly with the party's leading theorist, Nikolai Bukharin, who believed that economic growth depended crucially on cooperation with the peasants. He argued that they needed to be drawn gradually into schemes of modernisation through economic incentives, and that the Party should therefore 'travel at the pace of the peasant's nag'.

However, a growing shortage of consumer goods and the low prices paid by the state for grain caused peasants in 1927 to hold on to even more of their crops than usual. If the state could not sell sizeable surpluses abroad, there would be little capital available for even modest industrial development. Lack of grain in the cities meant the possibility of widespread hunger and urban unrest. It seemed that the peasants, and particularly the wealthier 'kulaks', were holding the workers' state to ransom in order to force higher prices from it. Stalin now moved against Bukharin and the advocates of 'wooing' the peasantry and won considerable support in the Party for a rather different approach, a policy of forcible seizure of grain. It was employed in Siberia in early 1928, and repeated in other parts of the country.

Peasant resistance and the accompanying turmoil contributed to a disastrously bad harvest in late 1928. As the amount of grain delivered to the state fell sharply, and rationing had to be introduced in Russian cities, Stalin broke completely with Bukharin and the right of the Party and in 1929 called for a 'decisive offensive' against rural capitalists. Soon afterwards, he announced that the kulaks would be 'liquidated as a class'. A campaign to seize the land of wealthier peasants, and to promote rapid collectivisation, coupled with the adoption of a five-year plan in 1928, marked the end of the NEP. Stalin had skilfully negotiated the rapids of party debate and the intricacies of shifting coalition groups to emerge as Lenin's successor, the man who would lead the party faithful and the USSR into the promised industrial land. As Graeme Gill has commented, Stalin won because 'he was able to play the rules of the political game and to generate political support far more ably than his opponents'.

Collectivisation

The aim of collectivisation was to relocate Russia's peasants into either state or cooperative farms, which would have to meet state quotas for food production and to pay local taxes and levies in return for services and modern equipment such as tractors. The five-year plan of 1928 assumed that the process would be gradual – covering about 20 per cent of peasant households by the end of the plan, and be directed in the first instance at expropriating the land and possessions of the kulaks, who comprised about 4 per cent of the rural population. But by January 1930, the Party's Central Committee decided that the pace of collectivisation should be stepped up dramatically and that all peasants should be brought into the new collective farms. Local party officials were sent into villages across the Soviet Union to liquidate and to deport kulaks and to 'persuade' peasants to move into hastily-formed collectives. By March 1930, 58 per cent of Russian agriculture had been collectivised.

This operation was carried out by urban party officials ignorant of peasant village structures and generally contemptuous of rural traditions. Violence was inevitable. Peasants regarded the intruders into their world with deep suspicion and often hatred. As a French historian, Hélène Carrère-d'Encausse, has noted, 'From the beginning, collectivisation assumed the aspect of a class war'. Peasants resisted as best they could; they slaughtered their animals to prevent them from falling into the hands of the state, they tried to hide away their possessions, and when they were herded into half-prepared collectives, they refused to work. But party officials had a monopoly of armed force, and the contest was therefore an unequal one. Those who resisted were branded as kulaks. Many died, either immediately or from starvation and disease, as they were driven east towards Siberia. The rest cowered sullenly in their unfinished new quarters, or tried to flee to safety in neighbouring areas.

By the spring of 1930 it was clear that the campaign would completely disrupt vital sowing of grain, and result in another disastrous harvest. A temporary reprieve was granted: *Pravda*, the party newspaper, published an article by Stalin entitled 'Dizzy with success' in which he denounced local officials for being over-zealous, and assured peasants that collectivisation was voluntary. Immediately, peasants streamed out of the hated collectives, back to their own homesteads. The vital sowings took place, and at least a modest harvest was assured. At the beginning of 1931, the process began again, somewhat more gradual, but this time irreversible. By 1933, 60 per cent of peasant households had been collectivised, and by 1934 over three-quarters.

Consequences

The process of collectivisation has been universally condemned by historians as brutal and as incredibly destructive. Livestock holdings declined sharply in the struggles – the numbers of horses and pigs were reduced by 55 per cent, cattle by 40 per cent and sheep by 66 per cent. Production of cereals fell dramatically; in 1932 the harvest was 25 per cent below average. But the biggest toll was in human lives. Stalin himself estimated the number of dead and deported at 10 million; the Soviet writer and dissident Alexander Solzhenitsyn has suggested that during collectivisation 5 million peasants were sent to camps in Siberia and the Arctic North. Many historians agree that deportations affected more than 10 million people, and that the famines which spread across the Soviet Union in 1932–3 killed more than a million peasants.

Furthermore, the whole structure of Russian agriculture was drastically altered, in a way which alienated generations of peasants. Productivity on collective farms remained low and the state had to use mass coercion to

Figure 13.2 *Tractors gathered for propaganda photograph*

get hold of the grain, bringing in a system of controls which, as one historian has commented, 'contributed heavily to the hardening of Stalin's Russia into a bureaucratic police state'. In contrast, however, amounts of produce soared in volume from the small cottage plots which peasants were finally, as a great concession, allowed to farm privately in their spare time. By the end of the 1930s, nearly three-quarters of the nation's milk and meat and nearly half of its wool was coming from private plots, providing most families with half of their total income. Collectivisation did little to improve productivity overall, and the much-heralded mechanisation of farming – through tractors and more modern implements – was extremely slow in arriving. Fleets of tractors came together for propaganda purposes only (see Figure 13.2).

Judgement

Stalin has received most of the blame for all these disastrous consequences. He has been condemned for the single-minded and callous way in which he drove through collectivisation without any evidence of concern for the human cost. However, in recent years historians have pointed to the fact that Stalin received considerable support from the Bolshevik Party, both at national and at local levels, for the policy of collectivisation. Many party members believed that a crusade against the capitalist peasantry constituted a vital 'renewal of the revolution' of 1917. Thousands of workers volunteered for collectivisation brigades. One young party member enthused to a correspondent in the United States, 'I am off in villages with a group of other brigaders ... It is a tremendous job but we are making amazing progress ... We shall yet smash the last vestiges of capitalism and for ever rid ourselves of exploitation.'

Not only was collectivisation seen as a necessary political stage in the progress of the revolution; it was also seen as vital for the success of industrialisation. Despite the chaos caused by collectivisation, the state was successful in increasing the amount of grain it collected from the peasants. It was easier to collect from a smaller number of large farms, and the prices paid were low, often less than the cost of production. The result was that the state made a huge profit out of the grain, selling it abroad and purchasing much-needed machinery and manufactured goods. At the same time, many displaced peasants helped to build new roads, industrial complexes and factories, and were available to join the increased labour force which the five-year plan required. Many historians have emphasised the important role which collectivisation played in the successful industrialisation of Russia.

Recent surveys of Soviet history have emphasised the enormous social changes which occurred between the 1930s and the 1960s. At the end of 1929, three-quarters of Russia's population were peasants. By the end of the 1960s the figure had dropped to just over 30 per cent. Huge numbers of peasants had become urbanised, had become educated and had taken up factory or office jobs. Many younger peasants felt that they had gone up in the world, and that their status had risen. There is no doubt that industrialisation and modernisation could not have occurred so rapidly in Russia without a brutal shake-up of the peasantry.

Historians are agreed that the peasant base of Russia had to be changed in some way if the Russian economy and Russian society were to be successfully modernised. Debate has therefore centred on the means employed, and on the degree of brutality and of deaths involved. As Chris Ward has commented, 'No one would challenge the assertion that collectivisation was a tremendous national tragedy'. But given peasant attitudes, and the general backwardness of Russian agriculture, could the disaster have been avoided? Was there not bound to be a struggle between the modernising state and traditional peasant communities, with peasants refusing to change their way of life except at gunpoint? Or could the peasants have been wooed towards change? This would have slowed down the process, not just of agricultural change but also of industrial development. Could a Soviet state surrounded by capitalist enemies afford to wait so long to tackle its problem of backwardness?

Industrialisation

By the late 1920s, the 16th Bolshevik Party conference had voted to adopt an ambitious five-year plan to lay the foundations for rapid industrialisation. The development of heavy industry was seen as vital, not just for political or economic reasons, but for considerations of security. Stalin explained what he saw as the dilemma facing the country in a famous speech to factory managers in 1931:

> *'Do you want our socialist fatherland to be beaten and to lose its independence? If you do not want this, then you must end its backwardness in the shortest possible time. We are 50 or a 100 years behind the advanced countries. We must make good this lag in ten years. Either we do it or they crush us.'*

The five-year plan presented to the Party contained two suggested levels of achievement: one basic and the second 'optimistic'. The proposals of the discredited 'super-industrialisers' of the mid 1920s paled into insignificance beside the targets now suggested. As Chris Ward has pointed out, the 'optimistic' variant envisaged 'the doubling of Soviet industry's fixed capital stock between 1928–9 and 1932–3'. On the basis of the electrification of the entire economy the rises in output were to be as shown in Figure 13.3.

Even these targets were progressively raised as the 'socialist offensive' got under way. Exhortations were made to 'fulfil the five-year plan in four years' and to transform Russia through 'socialist emulation'. No allowances were made for the slump in world commodity prices or for

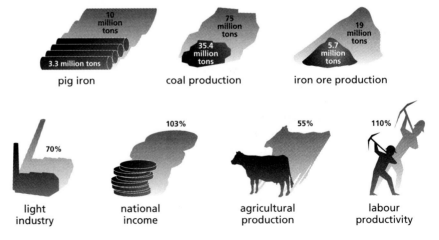

Figure 13.3 *Planned development for industrial output under the first Five Year Plan*

the savage deflation which hit western economies after the Wall Street Crash of 1929. The Soviet Union would pioneer a new way forward, based on rational socialist planning, in spite of plummeting prices on world markets for Soviet grain and the internal chaos of collectivisation. It was obvious to many economic planners that the targets were too high and could not be reached, but Stalin castigated any who dared to criticise as having a 'hopelessly bureaucratic' approach.

Most targets were not reached by the end of the first five-year plan. Some, indeed, were not met until the 1950s or even later. Nonetheless spectacular progress was recorded, and was trumpeted by the party leadership. While old industrial centres in areas like the Urals expanded dramatically, new giant complexes were constructed, notably at Magnitogorsk and at Stalinsk. New industries – such as chemicals and the manufacture of cars and tractors – sprang up, and there was a great increase in the production of machine tools. A dam and Europe's most powerful hydroelectric power station was built on the river Dnieper. Railway networks were expanded, and new canals dug, one linking the Volga river with the White Sea. Overall, Soviet production rose by some 250 per cent, and the foundations were firmly laid for a further two five-year plans which were increasingly geared to military needs and to the requirements of defence. Industries were progressively relocated from vulnerable western regions to the east. Whereas 1,500 new enterprises had started under the first five-year plan, 4,500 became operational under the second. Although western historians do not accept Soviet estimates that between 1928 and 1940 industrial production increased by 852 per cent, they do agree that enormous industrial expansion did take place, especially in the production of oil, steel and coal and the output of electricity. Steel output increased fourfold between 1928 and 1941. Figure 13.4 shows other impressive increases.

Figure 13.4 *Soviet production compared*

	1927	1939
Coal (millions of tons)	35	145
Oil (millions of tons)	12	40
Iron (millions of tons)	6	32

This tremendous economic transformation, though, was achieved at the expense of socialist values. To try to achieve targets and to keep controls on workers, labour workbooks, and later internal passports, were introduced. Savage punishments were meted out for absence or for lateness. Incentives were introduced to reward 'model' workers, and a new breed of 'super-workers' appeared. These were called Stakhanovites, named after Alexis Stakhanov, a miner who had heroically over-fulfilled his target on the night of 30 August 1935 by allegedly mining 102 tons of coal single-handed. By 1937, a group of elite workers and officials had emerged, rewarded by the regime with a range of benefits. The spread of wage differentials in the Soviet Union was greater than in the USA.

Repression

Alongside exhortation went coercion and repression. Labour camps multiplied, and inmates were used as forced labour to develop industrial construction in regions such as the Arctic North, the Ural mountains and Siberia where workers would not venture of their own free will. Labour camps were responsible for much of the country's lumbering industry, extraction of copper and goldmining. Political prisoners built canals and roads and set up major industrial centres in remote areas. The casualty rate was high, but as workers succumbed to hunger and disease, there were always more inmates to replace them.

Two other major accompaniments which powered the massive drive to industrialise were great Russian chauvinism and ceaseless propaganda. The regime portrayed industrial progress as reflecting the innate qualities of the Russian worker, brought to maturity through socialism. Non-Russians were more harshly treated than their ethnic Russian counterparts. They were attacked as representing reactionary 'bourgeois nationalisms'. A wide range of cultural forms portrayed factory workers as 'heroes of socialist construction', optimistically overcoming all obstacles as they toiled to build the new state.

As Russians starved in the famines of 1933, Stalin depicted the progress and promise achieved by the socialist regime as being in stark contrast to the miseries inflicted on workers in other European countries by the Depression and by capitalism in crisis. But the Russian worker was not totally deceived and even managed to retain a sense of humour. A popular riddle of the period ran, 'Why were Adam and Eve like Soviet citizens? Because they lived in paradise and had nothing to wear.'

The 1930s saw Russia finally catch up with the other powers of Europe. As Paul Kennedy notes, 'By the late 1930s ... Russia's industrial output had not only soared well past that of France, Japan and Italy but had probably overtaken Britain's as well.' But at what cost had this unprecedented industrial expansion been achieved? Bukharin was no detached observer, but one cannot help sympathising with his view that 'Stalinism is one way of attaining industrialisation just as cannibalism is one way of attaining a high protein diet'. The standard of living of an entire generation had been sacrificed, and countless numbers of lives. Workers and peasants starved, and housing conditions were appalling, as families crowded into inadequate barracks and improvised shelters. Far from withering away, the state had become overbearing and coercive, operated by a party elite and a mushrooming bureaucracy. On the other hand, Russia became strong enough to face a German invasion and ultimately to drive it back. Many historians argue that without the industrial feats of the 1930s, Russia's wartime resistance and subsequent victories would not have been possible. And if Russia had been defeated in 1941–2 by Nazi Germany, the whole course of recent history would undoubtedly have been very different.

Judgement

Many historians have suggested that it was Stalin's interference and constant upping of targets which necessitated coercive measures in a desperate bid to achieve them. There is a view that his approach hampered industrial progress and prevented plans from being implemented more coherently and effectively. Others argue that without ambitious targets, achievements would not have been so great, and that given the low standards of education and lack of discipline of many workers, constant pressure and strict discipline was necessary to achieve substantial increases in output.

In recent years, historians have switched their attention to the social revolution which accompanied the industrial and agrarian upheavals. In one important respect, Stalin achieved the aims of the Bolshevik revolution, by greatly expanding the urban working class from 11 million in 1928 to over 38 million by 1933, and by increasing the urban population overall from 18 per cent in 1926 to 33 per cent in 1939. Educational facilities, especially technical ones, expanded greatly. Whereas in 1926 only 1.8 million students were enrolled in secondary higher schools, by 1938–9 the figure was 12 million. In particular, the regime trained large numbers of engineers and technical specialists. It thereby gave opportunities to many young Russians. It was possible to rise up the social ladder, from unskilled worker to skilled worker to official or party functionary, and many took their opportunities. Industrialisation had many supporters in Russia. It did promote a social revolution of massive proportions which brought benefits to considerable numbers of Russian people.

The Purges and the Great Terror

Millions of innocent people in Stalin's USSR died or were sentenced to years in labour camps in the 1930s because they had been wrongly denounced, or had a distant acquaintance with a party member suspected of 'wrecking' or sabotage. While denunciations of capitalist 'deviationists' and 'wreckers' had already surfaced in the late 1920s, the substantial change after 1934 was that the search for such spies and traitors shifted to the Bolshevik Party itself, and not just to the rank and file, but to its highest echelons.

Historians believe that this change was brought about as a result of the tremendous disquiet within party ranks caused by the upheaval of collectivisation. Covert but substantial opposition to Stalin emerged at the 1934 Party Congress, and in elections to the Central Committee about 300 delegates crossed out Stalin's name. Earlier in the proceedings, several provincial delegates had asked Kirov, a rising party star from Leningrad (as Petrograd had been renamed after Lenin's death) to take over as General Secretary. Only three out of the 1,225 delegates failed to vote for him in the Central Committee ballot. There can be no doubt that Stalin felt his position to be extremely insecure and brooded over the situation. However, not all historians conclude that he was therefore implicated in the assassination of Kirov which took place in December 1934. Some accounts argue that the secret police, fearful that their influence was about to be curtailed by the party, acted on their own initiative.

Whatever the truth about Kirov's murder, it unleashed a period of mass arrests, show trials involving former leaders such as Kamenev and Zinoviev who confessed to a range of crimes under torture, and a flood of prisoners in the labour camps, known as the 'Kirov flood'. Stalin introduced an 'extraordinary law' denying those accused of terrorism against the state any protection in the investigation of charges. Furthermore, he directed that investigations should take as little time as possible and that those found guilty should be executed. Millions of people were subjected to repression and to torture for various alleged crimes against the regime, and were either shot or imprisoned for long periods of time. According to some accounts, there were periods in 1937–8 when up to 1,000 people a day were shot in Moscow alone. Most significantly, the terror was unleashed against the Bolshevik Party itself. The majority of the delegates to the 17th Party Congress in 1934 were killed before the next congress convened in 1939. About a third of party members were purged, and their places taken by new recruits. Zinoviev, Kamenev, Bukharin and other long-serving leaders were shot after torture and lengthy interrogation which brought forth charges of wrecking, undermining the Red Army, plotting to kill Stalin and to overthrow socialism. A contemporary painted a chilling picture of the final executions: 'Bukharin and Rykov died with curses against Stalin on their lips. And they died standing up – not grovelling on the cellar floor and weeping for mercy like Zinoviev and Kamenev.'

The armed forces did not escape the terror. Indeed, the army and navy suffered particularly severely: three out of five marshals were purged, three-quarters of the full generals, all 12 lieutenant-generals, 60 out of 67 camp commanders and 136 out of 199 divisional commanders. Carnage in the navy was even worse. Some argue that German spies had managed to convince Stalin that the army was plotting against him. Others believe that army leaders had tried to intercede on behalf of peasant recruits during the collectivisation process, fearing that recruitment to the army would be badly affected, and that Stalin resented their criticisms. Whatever the truth, it took many years for the armed forces to recover their morale, and Russia's military performance in the early stages of the war cannot fail to have been affected by the scale of the purges.

Historians have struggled to explain, let alone justify, such actions. Some have argued that by the mid 1930s Stalin was suffering from paranoia or from some other mental disability, and that the terror was therefore unleashed by an irrational, demented tyrant. Others have viewed Stalin as a despotic descendant of Ivan the Terrible or of Peter the Great, corrupted by absolute power and bent on destroying all opposition. In more recent years, attention has shifted away from Stalin to other party leaders, particularly those in distant regions, who not only faithfully carried out Stalin's orders, but who also indulged in political revenge of their own against some of their fellow party members. While some have stressed the totalitarian nature of the regime, with Stalin firmly in control, others have pointed to the poor communications and vast distances of the Soviet Union. They have argued that Stalin had supporters as well as enemies, and that many took advantage of the purges to improve their own prospects. Yet others have laid some of the blame on the Leninist legacy which bequeathed to Stalin a one-party state, the notion of the dictatorship of the proletariat by a small group of professional revolutionary leaders, and a secret police apparatus responsible to the leader alone. Some historians completely reject the idea that Lenin would ever have sanctioned the excesses and the random terror of the 1930s, or have allowed colleagues to undergo the humiliations and the ritual denunciations of the show trials. Instead they argue that such developments were the direct result of Stalin's sadistic nature.

Conclusion

On one point, however, nearly all are agreed: the Stalinist system which emerged by the late 1930s was a far cry from the socialism which so many in Europe had aspired to achieve. Its excessive political and economic centralisation, coercion and cultural values had far more in common with previous Tsarist regimes than with the aspirations of Russian socialist parties before 1914. To what extent was this due to the ill-judged decision of Lenin to try to construct a socialist state in the largely peasant-based Russia of 1917? Bolshevik aims were far from being realised at the time of Lenin's death; the workers' state was a fragile construction, perched uneasily on a traditional, economically backward peasant base. In such an environment, modernisation was a daunting prospect. While we can condemn Stalin's way of approaching problems and attack the outcome of his policies, we have to acknowledge that his options were limited. He did succeed, where Witte and Stolypin before him failed, in dragging Russia into the twentieth century. E. H. Carr has observed that 'Seldom perhaps in history has so monstrous a price been paid for so monumental an achievement'. There can be no doubt that the price, in terms of the impoverishment and virtual slavery of an entire generation of Russians, was monstrous. You must decide for yourselves how monumental you think Stalin's achievements were.

Task

1 Divide into groups and discuss your opinions of Stalin as a Bolshevik leader. On a scale of 1 to 10 (1 equalling 'grave-digger of the revolution'; and 10 equalling the 'successful construction of a workers' state') decide where you would place Stalin. Give reasons for your views, for example that he betrayed socialism, or that he had little room for manoeuvre and achieved a great feat in industrialising Russia. Swap your conclusions with the other groups.

2 Imagine that you are members of the Bolshevik Central Committee in 1928. What would you do about the New Economic Policy, and about the peasant problem? How would you aim to bring about industrialisation? Debate these issues in small groups, and explain the reasoning behind your suggested solutions. See if you can come up with alternative ways of solving the problems facing Russia, and report the main points back to the full class.

Further reading

Hélène Carrère-d'Encausse, *Stalin: Order Through Terror* (Addison Wesley Longman, 1981) – detailed study of the Soviet Union under Stalin.

Graeme Gill, *Stalinism* (Macmillan, 1990) – good general introduction to the debates about Stalin and Stalinism.

Alec Nove, *An Economic History of the USSR* (Penguin, 1969).

Adam Ulam, *Stalin* (Allen Lane, 1974) – detailed but very readable biography.

Chris Ward, *Stalin's Russia* (Edward Arnold, 1993) – the best recent survey of the debates and controversies.

Alan Wood, *Stalin and Stalinism*, Lancaster Pamphlet (Routledge, 1990) – good introduction.

14 Why did Spain's democratic government of 1931–6 end in civil war?

Time chart

1873–4: First Republic

1875: Liberal monarchy of Alfonso XII

1885: Alfonso XIII becomes king

1898: Loss of Spanish colonies of Cuba, Puerto Rico and Philippines

1923: Primo de Rivera becomes dictator

1930: Fall of Primo de Rivera. Pact of San Sebastian

1931: **April** Local elections. Proclamation of Second Republic and flight of Alfonso XIII
October Azana becomes Prime Minister

1932: **January** Anti-clerical legislation
September Agrarian Law Reform and Statute of Catalan autonomy

1933: **September** Azana resigns
October Foundation of Falange
November Election victory of Radicals and CEDA. Radical leader Lerroux becomes Prime Minister

1934: **October** Asturias Rising

1935: **May** CEDA leader Gil Robles becomes Minister of War
September Lerroux resigns

1936: **January** Popular Front formed
February Election victory for Popular Front
July Military rising. Beginning of social revolution in Republican zone. Germany and Italy begin to send aid to Nationalists
September Largo Caballero becomes Prime Minister
October Franco becomes head of Nationalist state. Soviet aid to Republic begins
November Franco besieges Madrid. Republican government moves to Valencia

1937: **February** Nationalist advance at Jarema stopped
March Italians defeated at Gudalajara

1937: **April** Bombing of Guernica by German Condor Legion
May Communists and POUM fight each other in streets of Barcelona. Caballero succeeded as Prime Minister by Juan Negrin
June Bilbao falls to Nationalists
October Negrin government moves to Barcelona
December Republican advance at Teruel

1938: **April** Nationalists reach the Mediterranean
July Republican counter-attack along river Ebro
September Munich Crisis
December Nationalists advance into Catalonia

1939: **March** Nationalists take Madrid
April End of Civil War

The Second Republic in Spain (there was a short-lived First Republic 1873–4) was proclaimed in April 1931. At first sight, democratic government seemed likely to succeed. There were free elections, a free press and a range of political parties. The Republic began to tackle the social and economic problems facing the country. Yet Spain in the early twentieth century was deeply divided, and had already experienced widespread violence on several occasions. As we look at these divisions and outbreaks of violence, you must decide for yourself whether, and at what point, civil war in Spain became inevitable.

A divided land

Economic and social divisions

By twentieth-century European standards Spain was a backward country. In 1930 46 per cent of the population worked in agriculture, with another 10 per cent in agricultural industries. Peasant holdings in northern Spain were very small and old-fashioned. They were crippled by debt, high rents and insecure tenure.

They were, however, better off than their compatriots in the south. Here the land was still owned in huge estates, called 'latifundia'. In Cordoba, for example, 3 per cent of landowners held 57 per cent of the land and in Badajoz 459 individuals, many related to each other, held 31 per cent of the land. Many were absentees, living in towns, while managers organised the work of the estate. This was done by millions of landless day-labourers. Their wages were half the national average. They were only paid when they worked, which might be only 150–180 days a year. Whether they worked or not depended on the whim of the estate. This dependence forced them into abject servility and bred bitter resentment. Meanwhile the great landowners, many of them relatively new families as the old nobility and the Church were forced to sell up in the nineteenth century, held all social, economic and political power in rural Spain. The hated 'Guardia Civil' (Civil Guard) protected their property from the land-hungry labourers.

The only industrialised areas were on the margins of Spain: textile manufacture in Catalonia, iron, steel and shipbuilding in the Basque north and coalmining in the northern Asturias (see Figure 14.1 on page 230). Some parts of Spain therefore had a working class and an urban bourgeoisie, but they were not spread evenly over the country, so they found it difficult to make their voices heard.

Political divisions

The Left   The working class in the industrialised areas of Spain, together with older craftworkers in some cities – such as the printers of Madrid – formed the nucleus of the socialist party, the PSOE (*Partido Socialista Obrero Espanol*) and the socialist trade union, the UGT (*Union General de Trabajadores*). Like many European socialists, members of the PSOE were split over whether they should take part in bourgeois democracy. The PSOE only gained its first elected representative in 1910, so had little in the way of tradition of participation in parliamentary politics. There was, however, a rival force in left-wing politics, unique to Spain: the **Anarchists**. Anarchist ideas arrived in Spain before Marxism, and took firm root.

KEY TERM:

Anarchists

Anarchism was developed mainly by Russian thinkers Bakunin and Kropotkin. **Anarchists** oppose all forms of imposed government, including democracy, as a loss of freedom. Instead, people should come together voluntarily to achieve their basic needs. Anarchists usually abstain in elections and may support local or regional demands for more autonomy as a way of bringing power closer to the people. Some anarchists believe in violent action: 'One assassination is worth a thousand pamphlets', as the slogan went.

By 1917 700,000 workers, mainly in Catalonia and Andalucia, had joined the anarcho-syndicalist trade union, the CNT (*Confederacion Nacional del Trabajo*). They hoped to revolutionise Spain through General Strikes and, in the case of some extremists, political assassinations.

The Right   Until the 1930s there was no conservative party in Spain: there did not need to be, when the forces of the Right were so strong outside party politics. Apart from the vested interests of the big landowners and industrialists, there were the great institutions of the monarchy, the Church and the Army.

1 Monarchism as a force was weakened by a split dating back to the 1830s: the Carlists were ultra-conservative, and strong in Navarre; the Alfonsists supported the more constitutional monarchy established in 1874.

KEY TERMS:

Mass

The Roman Catholic Eucharist service (usually called Holy Communion by the Church of England).

Last rites

The religious ritual performed for someone on the point of death.

2 The Roman Catholic Church had, of course, always been extremely powerful in Spain and was deeply embedded in Spanish life. The Church expected to continue to wield this power through a monopoly of religion and morals and control of all forms of education. The seminary education of most priests was narrow and old-fashioned. The Church was hated by many intellectuals, who wanted a secular, progressive state. It was also ignored by many Spaniards, especially in the towns. In working-class Madrid, for example, only 7 per cent of the population went to **Mass**, only 25 per cent of children were baptised and only 10 per cent received the **last rites**.

3 The Army was grossly over-officered: there was a ratio of one officer to 10 men, when the norm in the rest of Europe varied from 1:17 to 1:24. There were nearly 300 generals, far more than could hold a command. Officers were often recruited from military families and education in the military academies was narrow minded. There was widespread suspicion and lack of understanding of working-class grievances or regionalism.

With time on their hands, officers had got used to intervening in politics. At one time they had been a force for liberalism but by the twentieth century they saw themselves only as a bastion of traditional Spain. They were used to acting as arbiters in politics, supporting one group or another.

The Centre   In most of Europe, successful democratic institutions relied on the active support and participation of the middle classes, who shied away from the extremes and sought consensus in the centre of politics. However, we have seen that Spain, for economic and social reasons, did not have a large middle class. In Third Republic France (see chapter 2) the combination of peasants and small-town middle classes kept the Radicals in power for years. In Spain, no such alliance was made. The commercial and industrial middle classes mostly joined forces with the old landed Right. No effort was made, as Gambetta made in France, to win the support of the peasants who were only politically active through Church-based organisations.

Regionalism

Spain is a country of regions, with strong regional traditions, dialects, even regional languages. By 1900 two regions in particular were demanding more autonomy from central Spanish (which they called 'Castilian') control:

1 *Catalonia*   Nineteenth-century Catalan nationalism had begun with interest in the Catalan language and a revival of its literature.

However, industrial developments in Catalonia meant that the region was a powerful but separate economic force. The demand for autonomy for Catalonia therefore had meaning for all classes. It was supported by the Anarchists and contributed to the strength of the CNT in Catalonia.

2 *The Basques* The Basque language is also entirely different from Spanish, but Basque nationalism was much more conservative. The presence of industry in the Basque provinces was resented by Basque nationalists because it drew in a non-Basque workforce.

Before the Republic

In the 50 years up to the proclamation of the Second Republic in 1931, Spain became more socially complex as the population rose and industrial growth deepened the divisions described above. Democracy in the so-called 'liberal monarchy' set up in 1874 was a farce. Elections were rigged. The same politicians alternated in power. Local bosses, the *caciques*, intimidated voters: if they did not vote for the *cacique's* candidate they would never work again.

In 1898 Spain lost the last of its major colonies in a humiliating war with the USA: Cuba, Puerto Rico and the Philippines. This led to a call for 'regeneration' and real democracy. Neutrality in the First World War helped the industrialised sectors of the economy to prosper, but added to tensions as more workers were sucked into industry. From 1917 there were serious outbreaks of violence in Barcelona and Andalucia.

In 1923 General Primo de Rivera took over the country and ruled as dictator with the total acquiescence of King Alfonso XIII. He crushed the anarchists, had new roads and railways built and worked with the UGT. He seemed to offer to trade prosperity for democracy. However, by 1930 he had alienated nearly everyone to the Left and the Right, so he resigned. King Alfonso tried to find other generals to take his place, but failed. The monarchy was now hopelessly tarnished by association with the dictatorship. Republicanism was rapidly gaining support among the urban middle classes. Even some on the Right saw a republic as a better defence of the existing order than a monarchy which might provoke a revolution on the Russian model.

The various Republican groups signed a pact at San Sebastian in 1930. They were joined by the Socialists in a 'Revolutionary Committee'. The local elections of April 1931 brought victory for the monarchists in the old rural areas under the control of the *caciques*, but defeat in most towns and cities. Alfonso abdicated and the Second Republic was declared.

The Republicans in power, 1931–3

Elections were held for a Cortes (parliament) to draw up a new constitution. The Socialists won 113 seats, the Left Republicans 85, their allies from Catalonia and Basque Galicia 55, other pro-Republicans about 60; the Radicals won 89 and various rightist parties about 50. For the next two years Spain was governed by coalitions, at first embracing nearly all republican groups, but from the end of 1931 made up of Socialists and Left Republicans.

Many hopes were pinned on the new Republic: hopes for radical change, social reform, land reform and regional autonomy. But many on the Right feared the new government too; feared it would destroy the traditional order or unleash forces which would. The reform programme had four aspects:

1 *Land reform*   The Socialist Minister of Labour, Largo Caballero, issued decrees to deal with the appalling situation of southern labourers. Landowners were not allowed to hire labourers from outside if any local person was unemployed. Wage boards were set up to decide wage rates and an eight-hour day was decreed. Landowners were furious and tried to ignore the decrees.

The government began to draw up a detailed plan to redistribute the land of the great estates. It was blocked at every stage by the Right in the Cortes. The Agrarian Law Reform was not passed until September 1932. Even then it was too cumbersome to operate and alienated many peasant-owners, who found themselves included in the land redistribution.

2 *The Church*   For many Republican intellectuals – like Manuel Azana, Prime Minister from October 1931 to September 1933 – weakening the hold of the Church on Spanish life was a high priority. He appeared to act very slowly when churches were attacked and burnt in May 1931. By Article 26 of the new constitution there was to be no state support for clergy, and orders such as the Jesuits, owing allegiance outside Spain, were to be dissolved. A major effort was made to build state schools: 7,000 by 1932. There were also petty regulations, such as the banning of church bells and religious processions.

This programme had three results: first, it alienated millions of ordinary Spanish Roman Catholics; second, it drove conservative Republicans to resign from government, so Azana became more dependent on Socialist support; third, it pushed the Right into organising itself into a political party, based on defence of traditional Spain, especially the Church.

This was the CEDA (*Confederacion Espanola de Derechas Autonomas*), founded in March 1933.

3 *The Army* Another requirement for a fully democratic state was a non-political army. Azana had studied the French Army and set about reforms in Spain. Army interference in civil law was stopped and 8,000 officers were retired on full pay. This was hardly a policy designed to endear the new Republic to the army.

4 *Regional autonomy* The Republicans were committed to granting autonomy to the Catalans, if not the Basques, whom they regarded as reactionaries. The army regarded regional autonomy with horror and the Right fought the Statute of Catalan Autonomy all the way through the Cortes. It was not passed until September 1932.

Results and rhetoric

The Socialists had asked their supporters to exercise self-discipline while they worked with the new Republic to bring the reforms they desired. By 1933 these reforms were seen to be too feeble, too late. The Socialists were always outflanked on the left by the anarchists, who had no stake in the Republic. There were anarchist risings in 1932 and 1933. The government used the Civil Guard to put them down, sometimes with bloodshed. Abroad, the Nazis were crushing socialist opposition in Germany and there were fears the same thing could happen in Spain. The CEDA leader, Gil Robles, was an unashamed admirer of Mussolini and Hitler and had met both of them.

By 1933 Largo Caballero's rhetoric turned more and more to talk of revolution, of seizing the initiative in direct action. He did nothing about preparing for a left-wing rising, but gained enormous support on the Left. At the same time, he scared the middle classes stiff.

The middle classes were even more alarmed because this revolutionary talk was fuel to right-wing orators like Gil Robles. The fairly mild reforms of the Republic were represented as the opening moves in a rabid Bolshevik assault on property, the Church and family life. The violence of anarchist strikes and risings of these years only seemed to confirm that law and order was breaking down and that the Republic could not be relied on to keep control. Gil Robles had absorbed the Fascist and Nazi rhetoric of Mussolini and Hitler. He made no secret of his hostility to democratic politics:

> 'We must reconquer Spain. We must give Spain a true unity, a new spirit, a totalitarian polity [government]. It is necessary now to defeat Socialism inexorably. . . What does it matter if we have to shed blood? We need full power and that is what we are demanding. To realise this ideal we are not going to waste time with archaic forms. Democracy is not an end but a means to the conquest of a new state. When the time comes, either parliament submits or we will eliminate it.'
>
> Raymond Carr, *The Spanish Tragedy* (1977).

Not surprisingly, this rhetoric lent support to the Socialists' own inflammatory demands for revolution.

Women voted for the first time in the elections of November 1933. The Left parties went into them disillusioned and disunited. Many anarchists had voted in 1931 in order to achieve regional autonomy. Now they reverted to their policy of abstention. CEDA worked in alliance with the Radicals, who had drifted right during the last two years, with a well-financed campaign. The results were: Socialists 58 seats, Republican Left 38, CEDA 117 and Radicals 104.

The two black years, 1933–5

Although CEDA was the largest party, the president was not prepared to ask them to form a government as he doubted their commitment to democracy. Instead he turned to the Radical leader, Lerroux, who governed with support from CEDA. Gradually the reform legislation of the last two years was undone. Agrarian reform laws were ignored. Catalan autonomy was declared invalid. Wages were cut. Workers were dismissed and peasants evicted. Strikers were arrested, taken hundreds of miles from their homes and dumped. Their leaders were imprisoned.

In September 1934 CEDA refused to support the Radicals any longer. The prospect of a CEDA government led to a rising of Socialists all over Spain in October 1934. In Catalonia the leader, Companys, refused to arm the workers and the rising failed, as it did everywhere except in the Asturias region. There the PSOE, the CNT, the UGT and the Communists worked together. They took over the local administration for two weeks and were only crushed by ferocious army action commanded by General Franco.

Both Left and Right learned from the Asturias Rising. The Right learned that parliamentary methods were not enough to suppress the forces of revolution. Robles began to lose influence. On the streets this passed to

Fascism

Fascism is an illiberal and highly nationalistic political ideology, aiming to overthrow democracy and set up a dictatorship. Central to fascism is the heroic leader. Also vital is the extensive use of propaganda, which aims to ensure the conformity of citizens.

the Falange, an overtly **fascist** organisation, led by José Primo de Rivera, son of the dictator. The real initiative, however, lay with the army; it became a matter not of whether there would be a coup, but when.

The Left saw that a rising, accompanied by a social revolution, was tremendously powerful. They also learned the need to make common cause. Over the next few months a Popular Front was formed. In the elections of February 1936 the Popular Front won 257 seats against 139 for the Right. It was a sweeping victory, but the voting showed that Spain was deeply divided: 4.65 million voted for the Popular Front, but 4 million voted for the Right.

The outbreak of civil war, 1936

Violence flared in the weeks after the 1936 election. Peasants in the south seized land and, in some cases, killed priests and landlords. Pastures dedicated to breeding fighting bulls were ploughed up; the bulls were eaten. The Falange paraded and brought violence to city streets. Between February and July 269 people were killed in political disorders.

The Socialists were in a quandary now. Moderate leaders like Prieto realised that any reforms would have to be suspended. He wanted to concentrate on enforcing law and order, disarming the Falange, de-politicising the army and, even at this stage, trying to build up support in the centre. Caballero, however, talked more of revolution and a merger with the Communists, nullifying Prieto's efforts.

The military rising had been planned for some time, coordinated by General Mola. It came on 17 July 1936.

The Republic had failed primarily because not enough people were committed to it. In the end, too many people were prepared to resort to extra-parliamentary means to get what they wanted or protect what was theirs. Many would have seen themselves as driven to civil war by their opponents: the Right saw Bolshevism in everything and the Left saw fascism in everything.

The civil war, 1936–9

Why did Spain have to endure a long civil war, rather than a quick military coup?

The Generals, of course, expected to carry out a quick, efficient coup. In

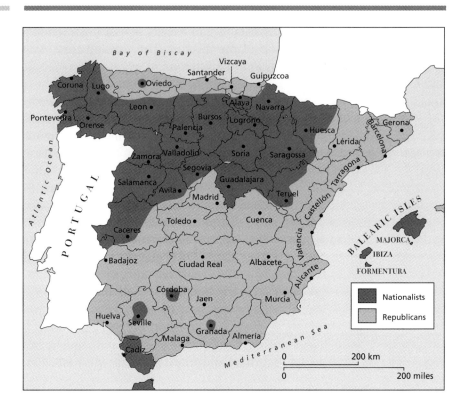

Figure 14.1 *The division of Spain, July 1936*

Figure 14.1 *The division of Spain, July 1936*

fact, they precipitated a civil war in which at least 2 million died, which lasted three years and overshadowed the next 40 years of Spanish history.

1 *Divisions in the rising* The plotters did not manage to take all Spain with them (see Figure 14.1). Even the armed forces were split: 75 per cent of generals, 70 per cent of brigadiers, and a majority of officers stayed loyal to the Republic. Younger officers supported the rising and the actual forces split 62,000 for the rebels and 55,000 for the Republic. The air force split about 3:2 in favour of the Republic and mutinies in the navy brought it to the Republican side.

2 *Republican militias* Apart from loyal soldiers in about half of Spain, the government rapidly armed UGT and CNT militias. In several cases it was these who disarmed the army units who attempted to join the rising.

3 *Foreign intervention* Even though Spain was about equally divided, it was foreign intervention which prolonged the war and made it all the more bloody. Despite the deliberations of the Anglo-French inspired 'Non-Intervention Committee', Italy and Germany sent troops, weapons and, crucially for a modern war, planes to help the Nationalists. The USSR sent enough help to the Republicans to enable them to resist until April 1939.

Why did the Nationalists win?

German and Italian aid

The initial, more or less equal, balance of forces could be tipped in Franco's favour if the 34,000 pro-Nationalist troops in Africa could be transported to Spain. Hitler intervened personally to send 30 Heinkel transport planes. Mussolini sent a force of 40,000 Italian troops (supposedly 'volunteers'). Hitler sent far fewer, but his commanders, and especially his pilots, used the war as convenient battle practice. This was not an unmixed blessing to Franco. The Italian forces could not be split up and deployed separately; the Germans hardly recognised his command. It was ironic for the proudly Nationalist **Francisco Franco** to come to power on the backs of Italian, German and African troops.

Franco's command

Franco was an able, but ultra-cautious, commander. In the end his mistakes did not matter, except that they served to prolong the war, and his successes were sufficient. He was declared head of the Nationalist state in October 1936. His position was unassailable and this unity contrasted sharply with the situation in the Republic (see page 232). He formed his first government in January 1938. It was clear from the start that it was to be traditional and right-wing, but not really Fascist. The Falange were only allowed to involve themselves with the Ministry of Labour. The tone was one of stifling Catholic puritanism, as it was to be for the next 40 years. Women were not to wear 'immodest' dress; men were not to wear shirtsleeves in cafés; advertisements were not to show swimming costumes 'with women inside them'. Films were censored: an extract from Abraham Lincoln's Gettysburg address was cut, for example.

PROFILE: *Francisco Franco*

Francisco Franco was born in 1892. He went to military academy at 15 and was a general at 41. He was Commandant of the Military Academy at Saragossa, closed down as part of the Republican Army reforms. In October 1934 he was director of operations against the Asturian miners' rising. After the Popular Front victory of 1936 he was regarded as a threat to the Republic and sent to the Canary Islands. He was always cautious and it was uncertain right up to the last minute whether he would join the rising of 1936. He flew to Morocco in a British plane and was soon the most obvious leader of the Nationalists. He was dictator ('El Caudillo') of Spain from then right up to his death in 1975.

Terror

Civil wars are invariably savage affairs, but in this situation it was bound to be a fight to the death. There were unlawful killings on both sides, but at least the Republican government made an effort to stop them. For the Nationalists, terror was part of their campaign. General Mola had explained even before the rising:

> 'It is to be borne in mind that our action will need to be very violent in order to crush a strong and well-organised enemy as soon as possible. Hence, all leaders of political parties, societies or unions not pledged to the movement will be imprisoned. Such people will be administered exemplary punishment so their movements or rebellions or strikes will be strangled.'

An early example of this policy was the massacre, in the bullring at Badajoz, of all those the Nationalists termed 'enemies' – Republican town councillors, trade unionists and freemasons.

Even more ominous was the destruction, on 26 April 1937, of the historic Basque town of Guernica by German bombers of the Condor legion. They may not even have told the Nationalist Command that they intended to do this and probably wanted to see the effect of hundreds of incendiary bombs on a small town. It is hard to assess the effect of terror as a weapon of war. At first it may have stiffened Republican resistance, but later, when their morale was lower, contributed to defeatism.

Republican disunity

The Republican side was divided: in 1936 there were Catholic Basque Nationalists, Catalan Nationalists, moderate and left Republicans, moderate and left Socialists, Stalinist Communists, Trotskyists and Anarchists. There were also, famously, International Brigade soldiers from many countries, who saw this war as the crucial anti-Fascist struggle.

For many Republican militiamen, the revolution was as important as the war and their political views affected how they fought. In *Homage to Catalonia* the British writer George Orwell describes the unusual military methods of the Trotskyist POUM (Partido Obrero de Unificacion Marxista) which he joined: 'No titles, no badges, no heel-clicking, no saluting – a model of the classless society'.

Alongside units of the Regular Army which stayed loyal to the Republic

Figure 14.3 *Republican militiamen, 1936*

there were anarchist militiamen who discussed orders before carrying them out, and refused to wear uniform (see Figure 14.3). It was hard for Republican commanders to wage a concerted war with these forces.

Non-intervention

There is no doubt that the Republican government was the legally elected government of Spain. As such they were entitled to buy weapons from whoever would sell to them. Britain, however, closely followed by France, put an embargo on sales of weapons to Spain and set up the Non-Intervention Committee. Some British Conservatives sympathised with Franco, but non-intervention was partly an attempt to limit the war, partly a fear that they would be drawn into a European conflict. Nonetheless, with Hitler and Mussolini blatantly sending all sorts of military aid to one side, non-intervention was a hypocritical farce.

Soviet aid and its consequences

The effect of non-intervention was to throw the Republicans into Stalin's arms, as the USSR was prepared to give them the help they needed. It was, however, on Stalin's terms. He wanted a long war which would embroil Germany and Italy indefinitely and keep them from attacking him. A defeat for Franco might provoke an anti-Communist war in Europe.

He therefore sent enough troops, supplies and aeroplanes to step up Republican resistance, but not enough to assure them of outright victory. He also sent military advisers. They pressed the Republican government to introduce orthodox military practices and tactics.

Stalin also wanted to bring the Left in Spain under Soviet control. This meant weakening and eventually eliminating other political groups. In May 1937 the Prime Minister Largo Caballero was replaced by Juan Negrín. Caballero had objected to the changes in the army and the attempts by the Communists to take over the PSOE; Negrín was more acceptable to the Communists. At the same time, Communist and rival militia groups such as the anarchists and POUM fought each other in the streets of Barcelona.

Many people flocked to join the Communists at this time: they claimed over 300,000 members by mid 1937. They attracted considerable middle-class support because they opposed the revolutionary excesses of the anarchists, were not anti-clerical and were capable of military success.

In the end, however, the Communist takeover contributed powerfully to the Republican collapse. Idealism was sapped from the Republican cause, and without idealism, what was the point of fighting? It was the clash of ideas, the belief that a new society could be built in Spain, that had put together the Popular Front, brought them election victory and then foiled the Nationalists' coup. The Communists only tolerated those who followed the Moscow line. They substituted slogans for debate and required total loyalty to the Party. In fact, Party advantage was often put above the needs of the Republic: commanders whose views they disapproved of would not get reinforcements. Some were sent into battles from which it was unlikely they would escape alive; others were harassed by accusations of cowardice. After years of this, and the gruelling deprivations caused by war, many on the Republican side lost the will to carry on.

The International Brigade

Here was the stuff of romance and heroism in what W. H. Auden called 'a low dishonest decade'. The International Brigade was made up of volunteers from all over Europe who wanted to fight Fascism. Many came from countries where they had already lost the battle once, for example Germany, Austria and Poland; others came from countries which appeared to prefer self-interest to principles, such as Britain, USA and France: of the 50,000 volunteers about 25 per cent came from France. Among the British volunteers were upper-class intellectuals, but the overwhelming majority were working class.

The International Brigade was run by Comintern, the international organisation of the Soviet Communist Party. Volunteers met at their office in Paris and travelled on to Spain. Several units became quite effective fighting forces. However, many were soon disillusioned by the bitter infighting, Communist infiltration and self-interest, if not by the hardship and danger. By 1938 the International Brigade bore little resemblance to what it was at the beginning of the war.

The War

Franco took most of western Spain at the beginning of the Nationalist rising and attacked Madrid in November 1936. The Republican government left for Valencia. However, Republican forces in the city prevented it falling to the Nationalists and repulsed Nationalist attacks. The Republican army showed itself capable of dogged resistance, but not of successful attacks.

In the north, Nationalist forces cut off the Republicans from the French border by taking Irun in September 1936. Through 1937 the Nationalists concentrated on the north, where they had defeated all Basque resistance by October.

The Republicans captured Teruel in December 1937 but lost it early in 1938 to a Nationalist advance which enabled them to cut the Republic in two by reaching the Mediterranean in April. Franco's forces were now 80 miles from Barcelona. However, he made the mistake of trying to attack Valencia and was driven back by a Republican counter-attack along the river Ebro in July 1938.

The Munich Crisis of September 1938 (see chapter 19) was a terrible blow for Negrin and the Republic. Soviet aid was clearly not enough to enable them to tip the balance of the war in their favour. The Republicans' only, and continued, hope was that Britain and France would come to their aid. However, Munich showed that if Britain and France could toss Czechoslovakia to Hitler in order to avoid war, they would never change their minds and help the Republic.

By 1939 the Nationalists had superiority in the air and in artillery. In January they entered Barcelona and Negrin's government fled across the Pyrenees. In March 1939 Madrid fell.

Task

Who do you think was to blame for the civil war?

As this chapter makes clear, there were dire problems in Spain in the early twentieth century which were making it almost ungovernable. But the actors who took part in the unfolding tragedy could only behave as their beliefs and experiences led them to. Why did they do what they did? How were their motives shaped by events? Could anyone have behaved differently?

1 For *each* of the people in the list below, write a few sentences outlining their aims and motives.

2 Working in pairs, give each of them a mark out of 20 for their degree of blame for the civil war (0 for innocent, 20 for totally to blame).

3 Discuss your decisions with the rest of the class.

4 How important were the roles of key individuals in bringing about the Civil War?

Alfonso XIII	General Franco	The Anarchists
Largo Caballero	Gil Robles	Catalan nationalists
Manuel Azana	José Primo de Rivera	Church leaders

Further reading

Martin Blinkhorn, *Democracy and civil war in Spain 1931–9*, Lancaster Pamphlet (Routledge, 1988) – succinct narrative with some useful analysis.

Paul Preston, *The Spanish Civil War 1936–9* (Weidenfeld and Nicolson, 1986) – chronological account with lots of photographs by a writer with enormous knowledge of Spain.

Gabriel Jackson, *A concise history of the Spanish Civil War* (Thames and Hudson, 1974) – a similar book to Paul Preston's; older, and with a different viewpoint.

George Eisenwell and Adrian Shubert, *Spain at War* (Addison Wesley Longman, 1995) – this book incorporates much recent re-thinking, especially in Spain, and has some readable and original analysis.

Raymond Carr, *The Spanish Tragedy* (Weidenfeld and Nicolson, 1993) – has more on the war than is covered by this chapter, and is written by the doyen of British scholars of this topic.

15 Italy under Mussolini

Time chart

1915: Italy enters First World War

1915–17: Mussolini fights in Italian army and is wounded

1917: Italy suffers severe defeat at Caporetto

1919: Italy takes part in peace conference at Paris and is dissatisfied with its gains, particularly its failure to acquire the Adriatic port of Fiume

1918: Universal male suffrage is introduced in Italy

1918–20: Two turbulent years of industrial protest and of land seizures, often referred to as the *Biennio rosso* (two red years)

1919: **March** Fascio di Combattimento founded
September D'Annunzio seizes Fiume

1920–2: Rise of Fascism as a mass movement

1921: **May** General election – 35 fascists elected
November Foundation of PNF – Fascism becomes a political party

1922: **October** Mussolini offered post of Prime Minister – March on Rome takes place
December Fascist Grand Council created

1923: **February** Nationalists join PNF
September Corfu crisis

1923–4: Italy obtains Fiume

1924: General election under revised electoral system results in fascist victory
June–August Matteotti murder – opposition parties walk out of parliament

1925: **January** Mussolini announces dictatorship

1926: Ministry of Corporations created

1929: Lateran Accords between Italy and Papacy

1935: **April** Stresa conference held between Italy, Britain and France
October Outbreak of Ethiopian war which lasts until 1936

1936: Outbreak of Spanish civil war – Italy intervenes in July
October Axis with Germany formed

1938:   Racial laws enacted
      September Munich Agreement

1939:   Chamber of Fasces and Corporations instituted
      April Italy annexes Albania
      May Pact of Steel concluded with Germany
      September Outbreak of European war – Italy stays neutral

1940:   **June** Italy enters war

1943:   **July** Mussolini deposed at Fascist Grand Council meeting
      September Italy surrenders

1945:   **April** Death of Mussolini (shot by Communist partisans); his body taken to Milan where it is suspended upside-down, flanked by his mistress and an aide

Italy experienced considerable political, social and economic problems in the decades after unification. On the eve of the First World War, it remained an agriculturally-based country, though it possessed a highly developed industrial belt in the north centred on Milan and Turin. While a mass electorate had emerged, there was a considerable sense of alienation from the political process, particularly in the south where illiteracy rates remained high.

This chapter will look at the impact of the war on Italy, and on the post-war disillusionment which followed. It will look at the rise of the fascist party, and at the means by which Benito Mussolini consolidated his position as Italian leader. We shall try to establish whether the Italian fascist party had a clear set of domestic and foreign policy objectives, and, if so, whether they bore any resemblance to those pursued by Nazi Germany.

Impact of the war on Italy

Italy entered the First World War on the allied side only after a bitter public debate about the respective merits of intervening or of staying neutral. The prospect of territorial gains, especially of the German Tyrol, the Trente region and Habsburg lands around the Adriatic Sea, helped to pull Italy into the war, but the military price was high. Nearly six million Italian men were conscripted into the Italian armies, and of these, half a million were killed, over half a million were captured and a million wounded, nearly half of them permanently disabled. In October 1917 Austrian troops inflicted a crushing military defeat on Italy at Caporetto, and were only pushed back in the final stages of the war.

The economic costs of the war were great. Like other participants, Italy piled up debts which would have to be repaid in the postwar period. The country also experienced substantial inflation; the lira fell from 30 to the pound sterling in March 1919 to 100 in December 1920. The rapid expansion of war-related industries, which generated handsome profits for a few industrialists in the short term, inevitably led to problems of economic adjustment after the war for those in shipbuilding, heavy industry and armaments. Unions had built up a strong position during the war, and were determined to hang on to their gains. However, as supplies dried up and orders became scarce after 1918, unemployment spread and the situation was made worse by two and a half million returning soldiers.

There was increasing violence as postwar economic and social problems intensified. Strikes and occupations of factories and of land, which began in earnest in the last year of the war, escalated between 1918 and 1920. Factory workers, rural labourers and peasants in north and central Italy pressed for wage increases and for the nationalisation of industry. They demanded the establishment of factory councils through which they could bargain with employers, and used strikes and then factory occupations to push their demands. As a result of the economic and social impact of the war, nearly 900,000 farm workers, 160,000 metal workers, 200,000 building workers and 47,000 railway and transport workers 'were organised and in a militant mood'. In 1920 alone, there were over 1,800 strikes, and in August workers occupied factories and shipyards in several northern cities.

At the same time Italy experienced a wave of 'land occupations', particularly in southern Italy, as returning soldiers and bands of peasants seized uncultivated or barren land, or forced landlords to sell them plots cheaply. They were helped by local priests or by ex-servicemen's organisations. The result was that by 1921 there were around 3.5 million peasant owners, twice as many as in 1911. In southern Italy, between 30 and 40 per cent of rural heads of families now owned land. As Martin Clark has pointed out in his book *Modern Italy 1871–1982*, 'The turmoil of 1919–21, so alarming and revolutionary in appearance, in reality established a new, deeply conservative social structure in much of rural Italy'.

However, those who were on the receiving end of such militant action believed that it was not the effects of the war or postwar problems which were fuelling them but anarchist beliefs or communist doctrines. Employers and landlords looked to the government to take strong action to curb what they regarded as unacceptable revolutionary demands on the part of workers and peasants. When the government backed off, they

KEY TERM:

Tenant farmers

Tenant farmers did not own their own land. They rented it from landowners and were responsible for keeping it productive. The tenant farmer would pay an agreed sum for a lease from the landlord which gave him the right to farm the land.

took the law into their own hands, determined to crush what many saw as an attempt to establish a socialist regime, inspired by the example of the Bolshevik Revolution. Employers resolved to beat trade unions into submission and to humiliate their leaders by a variety of means, including the use of force and intimidation. On the land, wealthy agriculturalists took a similar approach towards peasant leagues, subjecting them to violence and harassment and intimidating them into accepting the conditions laid down by landlords. The employers and landlords found no shortage of veteran soldiers and disaffected sons of **tenant farmers** and of the urban middle class willing to lend a hand and mete out punishment to alleged 'reds' and socialists.

Nationalists and the traditional landed and industrial elites were contemptuous of the government not just because of its refusal to crush workers' and peasants' uprisings, but also as a result of the peace settlement. While Italy had gained territory at the end of the war, its leaders felt they had not been treated fairly by the other great powers at Paris (see chapter 10). In particular, they demanded additional colonial spoils in Africa and the port of Fiume on the Adriatic Sea. The Italian writer and romantic nationalist Gabriele D'Annunzio denounced the settlement as a 'mutilated peace'. In September 1919 he seized Fiume from the newly constituted Serbo-Croat-Slovene state (later to be called Yugoslavia). He remained there for 15 months, supported by 2,000 'legionaries', an example of what the 'new Italy' could achieve, given the will. D'Annunzio's exploits in Fiume were enormously popular throughout Italy, and increased discontent with the weak, colourless government, who took until the end of 1920 to negotiate a settlement and to eject D'Annunzio.

Birth of the Fascist Movement

It was in this violent postwar environment that Italian Fascism was born. The movement was officially inaugurated in March 1919, as the *Fascio di Combattimento* (Combat Group) by a former schoolteacher and socialist agitator, Benito Mussolini.

While Mussolini originally saw the Fascist Movement as a left-wing challenger to socialism, it soon began to develop in a rather different direction as an anti-socialist force. In 1920 it spread rapidly in the rural areas of northern and central Italy, joining forces with other movements to fight against socialist unions and Catholic peasant leagues. As local fascist groups established themselves in provincial capitals such as Bologna and Florence, they were sought after by employers and by landlords anxious to recruit allies in the fight against the forces of the Left.

Fascist squads attracted notoriety and considerable support for their willingness to use violence, including knives, guns and clubs, to intimidate left-wing leaders. Martin Clark has given us a vivid description of fascist tactics:

> *'A lorry-load of ex-officers or students would descend on some village at night, beat up the local unionists, "purge" them of their iniquities by making them drink castor-oil, burn down the local party offices, and depart. The police would stand by, when not actively joining in; the Prefect would wring his hands, but stay well clear.'*
>
> Martin Clark, *Modern Italy 1871–1982* (1984).

By such means, the 'red' provinces of the Po Valley and of Tuscany were rapidly transformed from being the centre of the most powerful peasant unions in Europe into fascist strongholds.

Between 1920 and 1922, the Fascist Movement grew rapidly as local groups mushroomed across Italy. By 1922 there were over 3,000 such groups, with a total membership of nearly 300,000, covering most regions, with the notable exception of the south where the Fascists were relatively weak. Their leaders and active members were drawn from the ranks of war veterans and former officers, students, and professional and landowning families. Rank-and-file members came from middle-class urban occupations and from respectable peasant families rather than from urban working-class backgrounds and the ranks of poor peasants and seasonal agricultural labour. As the movement grew, it was responsible for the destruction of socialist and Catholic trade union networks across north and central Italy. But what were its more positive aims? As Martin Blinkhorn has written:

> *'Fascism offered comradeship and excitement in a dull and ungrateful postwar world; for the more politically conscious it represented a continuation of the war in peacetime, Italy's enemies now being socialist and liberal "traitors"; for many more, fascism promised the revolutionary overthrow of liberal Italy's tired ruling caste by a new elite, broadly middle class in composition, steeled in battle against Italy's foreign and internal enemies, and therefore qualified to govern.'*
>
> Martin Blinkhorn, *Mussolini and Fascist Italy* (1984).

Fascism was a movement of action rather than of revolutionary messages, and it posed an increasing challenge to the liberal governments of postwar Italy.

The rise to power

In the parliamentary elections of May 1921, the fascists lined up with the anti-socialist 'nationalist' bloc, and 35 of their members were elected. Six months later, in November 1921, the rather loose collection of fascist groups declared itself a political party, the *Partito Nazionale Fascista* (PNF), supporting the monarchy and free trade, and violently anti-socialist. As the Fascists became an increasingly popular movement, with a colourful, charismatic leader and strong grassroots support, Italy's leading political leaders sought to ally with the new political force and to 'tame' it by bringing it into a government coalition. Businessmen and landlords hoped it would stiffen policies towards organised labour; nationalists looked to it to inject some life and energy into the political system; even the Vatican welcomed the possibility that a new force in government might bring an end to the long-running feud between church and state and result in some concessions for the Catholic Church. The expectation was that the new fascist party would be so grateful to be brought into power that it would be willing to work within the established political structure. But the leaders of the movement had very different ideas.

After the failure of an anti-fascist general strike organised by the socialists in August 1922, fascist groups let it be known that they were laying plans for a march on Rome to overthrow the existing government and install a new regime, modelled somewhat loosely on D'Annunzio's colourful and highly nationalistic rule over Fiume. The Italian authorities were caught in two minds, some wanting to organise military resistance to any fascist move, and others feeling that it would be preferable to avoid a confrontation and take some fascists into the government. In the end the King decided the issue, when he proved to be unwilling to declare martial law to counter any fascist march. The Prime Minister resigned in protest, while Mussolini refused to join any government unless appointed its leader. On 29 October 1922, Mussolini was offered the post of Prime Minister, and only after he had accepted did the March on Rome take place!

The consolidation of power

For two years, Mussolini was at the head of a series of coalition governments which included fascists, nationalists and right-wing liberals. His coalition partners hoped that power would tame the wild and revolutionary elements in the fascist movement; grassroots and local fascist organisations, however, eagerly anticipated a move towards an outright fascist regime. Mussolini therefore bided his time, on the one hand working to consolidate his political power within the government, while on the other hand trying to keep together a network of fascist groups throughout Italy which had strong independent power bases and different ideas about what the aims of a fascist regime should be. In a bid to create a more unified party, in 1923 Mussolini coordinated the individual fascist military squads into a national fascist militia and created a Fascist Grand Council. But his authority as Prime Minister rested not on this fascist network but on the traditional machinery of state – the support of the king, the loyalty of the army and the cooperation of the state bureaucracy and of industrial and landed elites.

In a bid to strengthen the position of the fascist party within the decision-making structure, Mussolini introduced a significant measure of electoral reform in July 1923. The Acerbo Law was designed to give the leading party or alliance at a general election two-thirds of the seats in parliament. In the general election of April 1924, the official fascist-led list of candidates polled two-thirds of the votes cast, and therefore won 374 seats out of a possible 535. The fascists had greatly strengthened their position in Parliament; as a result, Mussolini's authority as Prime Minister was enhanced. Nonetheless, radical and left-wing parties, and in particular the Socialist Party, polled particularly well in the north of Italy and still posed a threat to fascist dominance.

In the summer of 1924, a socialist deputy, Giacomo Matteotti – a particularly outspoken critic of Mussolini – was seized by a gang of fascists and stabbed to death. This brutal murder of an opponent of fascism aroused widespread opposition. Many socialist, Catholic and democratic opposition deputies withdrew from parliament in protest. For a time, Mussolini's position seemed very shaky. But the nationalists and conservatives continued to support him, in a bid to ensure that no revival of left-wing power took place. The King did not demand his resignation. Fascist forces throughout Italy urged him to move to a more dictatorial regime. Accordingly, Mussolini told the remaining deputies in parliament in January 1925 that he intended to establish a more autocratic government.

In the course of the next two years political opposition and free trade unions were banned. A free press disappeared. Elected local governments were replaced by appointed officials, and Mussolini made himself responsible to the King alone. Fascists were brought into the civil service, and the state's machinery to deal with dissent was enormously strengthened, by giving powers of arrest and detention, increasing the scope of the death penalty, introducing a court for 'political' crimes and forming a special 'political' police force.

Nonetheless, it was the powers of the state which were increased, rather than the authority of the Fascist Movement. In the mid to late 1920s, the independence of local fascist groups was increasingly curbed and their demands for 'active' and radical policies were checked. In 1926, Mussolini was officially acknowledged as head of the fascist party for the first time. The Fascist Grand Council retained the right to formulate policy, and all party posts were to be filled in future by appointment rather than through election. By the end of the 1920s, the Fascist Movement was fully subservient to the Italian state, and Mussolini wielded power as the dictatorial head of state rather than as the leader of the movement. His authority rested on the state apparatus, the army and police, on the goodwill of the king, and on the support of important interest groups and centres of influence such as the church and industry.

Indeed, fascist Italy by the late 1920s was, as Martin Clark has pointed out:

> 'based essentially on the old bureaucratic-military ruling class, and designed to protect that class from the new political and economic forces that had arisen . . . – organised industrial labour, militant agricultural labour, political Catholicism, and indeed Fascism itself . . . the important institutions of the new State were the old traditional ones writ large – the army, the Prefects, the police and the courts.'
>
> Martin Clark, *Modern Italy, 1871–1982* (1984).

Local councils had been dissolved and mayors dismissed. The men now controlling local affairs, and handing out patronage and local contracts were local aristocrats, landowners or retired colonels. At national level, the Chamber of Deputies was still needed to pass laws, the Senate remained untouched and Italy was still a monarchy. Thus while 'Il Duce', as Mussolini was increasingly called, was seen as indispensable to orderly government in Italy, his rule was very much a personal regime and not a party one.

Domestic policies

The decline in influence of the local fascist networks, and Mussolini's need to cooperate with important interest groups meant that no sweeping programme of economic or social change was introduced in fascist Italy. However, there were three areas in which Mussolini claimed significant success:

■ church–state relations

■ introduction of the 'corporate state'

■ the modernisation of the Italian economy.

The Lateran Accords, 1929

In 1929, Mussolini became the first Italian leader in 60 years to establish cordial relations with the Papacy, when he signed an agreement with the Catholic Church. For his part, Mussolini received the support of the Papacy, and therefore increased his political legitimacy as Italy's leader in the eyes of many Catholics who had hitherto been rather distrustful of him. The Vatican gained more influence in Italian schools and over teachers, and Catholicism was established as the sole religion of the Italian state. Vatican City was to be sovereign and independent, but in return the Vatican recognised the kingdom of Italy, under the rule of the House of Savoy, with Rome as its capital. There can be no doubt that the establishment of harmonious relations between church and state in Italy was a notable achievement for Mussolini, and boosted both his authority and that of the Papacy.

The 'corporate state'

The creation of a 'corporate state' (**corporatism**) in Italy in the 1930s was claimed to be one of the major achievements of fascism. In 1926 a Ministry of Corporations was established, and it was followed four years later by a National Council of Corporations. The next stage was the creation of individual 'mixed' corporations of employers and employees, 22 in all, each one covering a specific area of economic activity. They were to determine wages and conditions in their particular spheres, regulate apprenticeships, advise on economic issues and encourage improvements in production. They were to be accountable to a Chamber of Fasces and Corporations, set up in 1939.

That was the structure of the 'corporate state' which was to promote both workers' self-management and managerial authority. In practice, however, the supposedly new concept did little other than promote jobs for officials. The corporations operated very much in the interests of employers. Workers were represented in negotiating bodies by fascist officials. Employers, however, were directly involved in the new bodies, and at the same time could deal with the government through traditional channels of influence, while workers had lost their trade unions. Not surprisingly, Martin Blinkhorn concluded that 'Corporatism in practice, especially during the Depression of the 1930s, thus represented a means of disciplining labour in the interests of employers and of the state'. Workers suffered officially imposed pay cuts in 1927, 1930 and 1934, and levels of unemployment and of part-time working rose significantly in the early 1930s. Far from being a major new departure, the machinery of the 'corporate state' in fact reinforced traditional structures and the existing authority of the state and of individual employers.

The modernisation of the Italian economy

There is considerable debate about the extent to which the Italian economy was modernised under Mussolini's fascist regime. There was certainly an attempt to increase economic resources in order to strengthen the regime in its quest for 'greatness' and imperial expansion. That tended to result in the protection of the older, heavier industries of the north rather than encouraging newer, more export-orientated firms. At the same time, increasing intervention in finance and in industrial development did promote expansion and modernisation in some sectors.

In 1926, the exchange rate of the Italian lira, which had reached almost 150 to the pound, was revalued to 90 lira to the pound. The move may have enhanced Italian prestige, as it was no doubt designed to do, but it had unfortunate economic effects. Italian cars, more than half of which were being exported in the early 1920s, and Italian textiles, were now priced out of world markets as they became uncompetitive in price. At the same time, high tariff barriers were imposed to keep cheap imports out of Italy and to protect heavy industry and selected agricultural products. Such measures were designed not to make Italy's industry and agriculture more competitive but to promote economic stability. This was achieved, but with the consequence of creating a sluggish and complacent domestic market. Steel and chemicals were the only industries which really flourished. Thus the government's economic policies were boosting those sectors of heavy industry 'which stood to gain the most from Empire and rearmament'.

Increasingly, the government provided industrial credit and long-term loans to industry through agencies which it established such as the IMI (*Istituto Mobiliare Italiano*) and the Institute for Industrial Reconstruction (IRI), founded in 1933. As a result, a considerable amount of new industrial investment helped Italy to weather the economic storm between 1929 and 1933 somewhat better than some other industrial countries. By 1939, the IRI and its subsidiaries controlled major steelworks, shipping lines and shipbuilding yards. It also dominated the electricity and machine-tool industries as well as the telephone system. By the end of the 1930s the Italian state controlled over four-fifths of Italy's shipping and shipbuilding, three-quarters of its pig-iron production and almost half that of steel. The state owned a proportionally larger part of industry than any other state in Europe except the Soviet Union, far greater than the level of state intervention in Nazi Germany. However, it is important to add that the firms involved were not wholly state-owned, and stock was sold off at regular intervals to private investors.

Unfortunately, the resources generated by the state's economic activities were increasingly used to finance Mussolini's ambitious foreign and colonial policy objectives. In the late 1930s, military spending was accounting for over a third of all public spending, and was therefore placing an enormous strain on Italy's economic resources.

Military considerations also influenced agricultural policies after 1925. To try to avoid the import of large quantities of wheat, which had been necessary in 1925 because of a poor harvest, Mussolini proclaimed a 'battle for wheat' (see Figure 15.1). High tariffs were placed on imported grain, which pushed up the price of bread but benefited Italian farmers. Though wheat yields in the 1930s were still low by British or French standards, fascist policies certainly led to the production of more wheat. Unfortunately, this was often achieved by switching resources away from other crops such as maize, or by taking over pasture land and vineyards. Martin Clark tells us that 'the South lost 20 per cent of its cattle and 18 per cent of its sheep between 1918 and 1930 as pasture was ploughed up'. Thus Italy's dairy industry suffered, as did her fruit and wine export trade. The gap between the north and south of Italy, which was so marked before 1914, was not narrowed to any great extent as a result of fascist economic or agricultural policies.

The fascist regime also laid great emphasis on land reclamation and improvement schemes. Though marshland had been drained on an extensive scale before 1914, Mussolini declared that land reclamation schemes should be given priority in public spending and should cover irrigation, road building and housing schemes and the construction of aqueducts. There were some successes, such as the draining of the Pontine marshes near Rome, but in the country as a whole, and especially in the south, achievements were modest rather than spectacular. Nonetheless, there were important advances. Malaria, long the scourge of central and southern Italy, was reduced by half. Schemes financed by the state accounted for a third of all public works jobs and helped to cushion the impact of the Depression. But Italy remained a poor country, in which impoverished peasants were increasingly driven to the cities in search of more money and better prospects.

In general terms, it was not the small-scale peasant-farmers and workers

Figure 15.1 *Mussolini addressing farmers in the 'battle for wheat', 1925*

who benefited from the government's economic policies but the industrialists and large landowners. They received subsidies and secure outlets for their products, while wages were held down. But workers and the rural masses saw their standards of living fall as a result of the Depression. They were protected to some extent by increasing state insurance schemes, to cover unemployment and industrial injury, and new social networks were established to provide workers with a range of cultural and sporting facilities. But they received no real economic benefits from the regime.

The economic policies pursued by Mussolini undoubtedly did promote a degree of modernisation. At the same time, the Fascist leader was concerned to appease important agricultural and industrial interests, to make the country economically more self-sufficient and to gear the economy to the support of an ever more ambitious foreign policy. These were the regime's prime concerns and they did not always contribute to economic modernisation.

Foreign policy

The dynamism that was lacking in domestic policy was to be a central element in fascist foreign policy ambitions. Mussolini was determined to raise Italy's status as a European power, by increasing her influence in the Mediterranean region and by expanding her empire. Like many other ardent nationalists, he believed that Italy had been badly treated at the 1919 Paris Peace Conference by its allies and that its legitimate claims for territorial gains at the end of the First World War had largely been ignored. D'Annunzio's enormously popular occupation of Fiume had raised passions which Mussolini had to try to satisfy once he became prime minister. However, any attempt to try to revise the peace settlement in Italy's favour was bound to run into stiff French opposition, and therefore Mussolini had to try to counter that by establishing cordial relations with British leaders.

The Corfu crisis

Ten months after taking office, Mussolini sought to avenge the murder of an Italian official working in the remote border area of Greece and Albania. Blaming the Greeks for the outrage, he ordered the seizure of the Greek island of Corfu and demanded a 50 million lira indemnity from the Greek government. Though Italy was one of the four permanent members of the Council of the League of Nations, Mussolini argued that the dispute did not involve the League, since the official had been working for a different body, the Conference of Ambassadors in Paris.

At this stage Italy's relations with France were good, because both powers were involved in the allied occupation of the Ruhr in Germany. However, Mussolini's seizure of Corfu aroused strong opposition from Britain. After tortuous negotiations, Britain agreed to Mussolini's demand that the dispute should be settled by the Conference of Ambassadors, but only on condition that Italy handed Corfu back to Greece. This demonstration of Italy's need to work with, and not against, Europe's most powerful naval power was not lost on Mussolini. For the next decade, he tried to work closely with Britain at Geneva, and established effective links with Austen Chamberlain, the British Foreign Secretary between 1924 and 1929. Together, they acted as guarantors of the Locarno settlement of 1925 (see chapter 10).

Italian gains in the 1920s

To retain British support, therefore, Mussolini had to find a way to pursue expansion in the Mediterranean area in a less flamboyant and threatening way. In 1924 Mussolini completed an agreement with the

Yugoslav government as a result of which the urban area of Fiume, though not its **hinterland**, was to be incorporated into Italy. In 1926 this triumph was followed by another: the declaration of a protectorate over Albania. At the same time, Italy secured some small pieces of territory in Africa, and strengthened her colonial position by signing a treaty of 'friendship' with Abyssinia in 1928.

These gains, though they could be loudly trumpeted, were in fact relatively modest in scope. Mussolini's problem was that to achieve more substantial expansion for Italy, he needed a strong economic base and well-equipped, effective military forces. Neither of these were in prospect by the early 1930s, and the onset of the Depression made it even harder for Mussolini to achieve them. Therefore, he was forced to seek glorious expansion on the cheap – hence his attempt to persuade Britain and France to turn a blind eye to Italian annexation of much of Abyssinia.

The Abyssinian crisis

The rise to power in Germany of Hitler temporarily increased Mussolini's status and diplomatic bargaining power. Hitler's emulation of Mussolini and of his fascist squads was immensely flattering to Mussolini. Figure 15.2 shows Hitler's first visit to meet Mussolini in 1934. Mussolini had been in power for 12 years; Hitler, in a shabby suit, had been in power for only a year.

The alarm caused in Paris and London by events in Germany after January 1933 made French and British leaders eager to work with Mussolini to contain German power. Mussolini himself had cause to worry when Austrian Nazis launched an unsuccessful *coup d'état* and murdered the Austrian Prime Minister Engelbert Döllfuss in July 1934. Italian troops were quickly moved to the Austrian frontier to warn Germany against invasion, and in 1935 Mussolini met with French and British leaders at Stresa to discuss with them ways of countering possible future German aggression.

It was at this point that Mussolini revealed his price for working with Britain and France in Europe: a free hand for Italy in Africa. How explicitly, and in what ways, Mussolini spelled out his demands we do not know. Evidence suggests that British and French leaders were prepared to turn a blind eye to Italian expansion in Africa, provided that it was carried out discreetly and through negotiation, in return for cooperation in Europe against Germany. But Mussolini was set on military conquest in Africa, and after border skirmishes between Italian and Abyssinian troops in late 1934, plans were expedited for a full-scale Italian offensive against Abyssinia. War broke out in October 1935, and

the League of Nations was forced to intervene in this conflict between two League members (see chapter 11).

Britain and France were torn between their obligations as the League's two leading members and their anxiety not to incur Mussolini's hostility or drive him to some 'mad dog' act. The League invoked economic sanctions against Italy but these did not include the vital commodity of oil. Furthermore, the British government made no move to close the Suez Canal to Italian shipping. With little effective opposition, the Italian army completed its conquest of Abyssinia, and Mussolini had achieved his coveted east African empire. The fascist regime had recorded a major triumph and its prestige in Italy stood high. Ironically, the victory was the high-water mark of Mussolini's rule, and from that point on he began the fatal descent which ended with his overthrow in 1943.

The Spanish Civil War

Victory in Africa had stretched Italy's resources. It had also given Mussolini an exaggerated notion of how powerful a role Italy might play in the Mediterranean region. The outbreak of the Spanish Civil War in July 1936 (see chapter 14) appeared to offer a further prospect for the expansion of Italian influence. Mussolini decided to back the rebels, led by General Franco, and to send Italian troops, aeroplanes and weapons to Spain. Altogether, 70,000 Italian troops fought in the war between 1936 and 1939, though they brought little direct reward to Italy. Instead, the Italian economy was put under further strain, and Italy's military pretensions were completely overshadowed by those of Nazi Germany.

The Rome–Berlin Axis

As a result of the Abyssinian conflict and the outbreak of the Spanish Civil War, Mussolini became contemptuous of the weakness of the 'decadent' democracies, as he saw them. Franco's challenge to the Republicans in Spain, and Hitler's remilitarisation of the Rhineland in March 1936, reinforced his view that the future belonged to the fascist powers. Increasingly, Mussolini drew closer to Germany, and the first agreement between the two powers was reached in October 1936.

The decision to work with Hitler was to have disastrous consequences for Mussolini. He had to stand by in 1938 and watch helplessly as Hitler triumphantly completed the *Anschluss* with Austria. He was pressurised by the German dictator into introducing racial laws against the 45,000 Jews in Italy, which caused great resentment and anti-German feeling among large sections of the Italian population. Italy seemed ever more the junior partner as German power increased menacingly in eastern Europe. By March 1939, Hitler's occupation of Prague provoked Mussolini into proclaiming the Italian annexation of Albania. In May, Italy bound itself to Germany in a military alliance, the 'Pact of Steel', but Mussolini had no intention of actually fighting a war. When a European war broke out over Poland in September 1939, Mussolini told Hitler Italy could not participate unless it received huge quantities of arms and raw materials from Germany. Italy therefore remained neutral until the following spring, when Mussolini felt impelled to join in alongside Hitler, as the whirlwind progress of German armies across western Europe suggested that the war would soon be over.

The war went badly for Italy from the start. A string of disasters exposed military weaknesses and caused tremendous economic pressures. Discontent spread, and Mussolini lost all the support and respect he had once commanded. He became a rather pathetic figure, plagued by illness and by the constant strains which the war was imposing. As Italy faced invasion from the Allies in 1943, the Fascist Grand Council turned against their leader and he was dismissed by the King. The final bizarre episode of the dictator's life followed: seized by the Germans, he was installed at the head of a new fascist regime in German-occupied northern Italy. But the relentless advance of allied troops through Italy, and growing resistance among the Italians, brought his new reign to an ignominious end in the spring of 1945. As he tried to flee, he and his mistress were killed by the Italian Resistance. Their bodies were publicly hung on display in Milan to the delight of the spitting and jeering crowds.

Conclusion: Italian Fascism and German Nazism compared

Was there a general European Fascist ideology? Or were Italy and Germany just two, very different, one-party states? Historians are divided over whether the term 'fascist' should be used to cover a number of right-wing and nationalistic movements in Europe between the wars. Clearly Nazism and Fascism had similarities as movements, but sharp differences emerge as soon as we look at their actions in power.

Similarities	
Anti-Liberalism	Both criticised liberal parliamentary democracy as a source of national weakness and called for more authoritarian government. Both exploited the parliamentary system for their own ends as well as advocating and using violence.
Anti-Communism	Both gained considerable support through their opposition to Socialism and Communism. Communism was seen as weakening the nation by promoting class conflict and because of its links with the USSR.
Anti-big business	Both contained a radical economic element: supporting small-scale farmers, shopkeepers and skilled workers against big corporations, department stores and banks (in Germany identified with Jews).
Exploiting instability	The First World War brought tremendous political, social and economic instability. Both gained support from the lower middle class particularly; their group felt threatened by depression and unemployment, in Italy after 1919, in Germany after 1929.
Leadership	Both Hitler and Mussolini came from modest social origins and were charismatic orators, with enormous mass appeal. Both made much of their war record and posed as selfless patriots. Both headed mass movements whose uniforms, flags, rituals and comradeship appealed to nationalistic ex-soldiers in the unhappy aftermath of the war.
Opposition to the Paris peace settlement	Both exploited their country's resentment of the peace treaties. Both gained support by pledging to revise them and to win territory: Italy in Africa, Germany in eastern Europe.

Differences

Ideology

a Fascism had no clear set of aims. It took Mussolini several years to bring disparate Fascist groups into line.

b Hitler's books (*Mein Kampf*, 1924, and *The Second Book*, 1928, see pages 288–9) expressed Nazi ideology: German racial superiority, anti-Semitism, belief in the need to expand Germany eastwards. These ideas gave Nazism a coherent set of beliefs, important during its rise to power.

Revolutionary regimes?

a Italy under Mussolini retained the monarchy and the Roman Catholic Church; civil servants, local police and local loyalties still remained powerful factors in Italian life. Mussolini took some years to become dictator and then worked through these traditional elements, while ordinary Fascists had little influence. Mussolini's main claim to revolutionary status – the corporate state – did not, as we have seen in this chapter, amount to much.

b Hitler carried out a sweeping revolution in 1933–4. He became Führer, Nazis took over control of local government, labour, education and youth and purged the civil service. Other groups – the army, industrialists, the churches – retained influence, but under Nazi leadership. Hitler's revolution was different: his aim was to create a strong racial state, capable of seizing territory in the east through war.

Preparing for war?

a Despite Mussolini's bluster, he did little to prepare Italy for war. Certainly he hoped to acquire territory, but not necessarily by force. Italy was totally unprepared for the Second World War and took little part in it at first.

b Hitler made rearmament a priority and, from 1936, put Germany on a war footing, through the Four Year Plan (see chapter 18).

Extent of change

a No attempt was made to change the structure of Italian society. Italians did not feel they were living through a dynamic and successful new order. Mussolini's grandiose foreign policy may have led to an increase in patriotism but this probably did not survive the humiliating defeats of the Second World War.

b Hitler's aim was the complete recasting of Germany as a militant racial state. He was not completely successful in this but, as we shall see in chapter 18, many Germans both supported and benefited from his policies.

Task: making notes

Ideally, your notes on a topic should include not just essential factual information in an easily revisable form, but some ideas about the topic too. Here is a way of making notes on the career of Mussolini which will cover the main factual points but also requires you to reach some judgements about him.

Take four sheets of paper. Head them:

■ Mussolini the fascist

■ Mussolini the dictator

■ Mussolini the popular leader

■ Mussolini the political operator.

Read through this chapter carefully as far as page 253. Write key points from the text on whichever sheet of paper you think is most appropriate.

When you have finished, add a sentence or two on each sheet giving your own views on this aspect or interpretation of Mussolini's career.

Further reading

M. Blinkhorn, *Mussolini and Fascist Italy*, Lancaster Pamphlet (Routledge, 1984) – an excellent starting-point for this topic.

M. Clark, *Modern Italy 1871–1982* (Addison Wesley Longman, 1984) – very useful student text.

D. Mack Smith, *Mussolini* (Weidenfeld and Nicolson, 1981) – comprehensive biography.

A. de Grand, *Fascist Italy and Nazi Germany* (Routledge, 1995) – recent, invaluable comparison between the two regimes.

R. Griffin, *The Nature of Fascism* (Routledge, 1993) – broad-ranging discussion.

W. Laqueur (ed.), *Fascism: A Reader's Guide* (Penguin, 1979) – covers a good range of fascist movements and regimes.

16 Was Weimar Germany 'doomed from the outset'?

Time chart

1918: **1 October** Ludendorff asks German Parliament to sue for peace

3 October Prince Max of Baden is appointed Chancellor and asks USA for a peace on the basis of the '14 Points'

3 November German Grand Fleet mutinies at Kiel. Sailors set up workers' and sailors' councils for redress of grievances

9 November General strike in Berlin. The Emperor flees to Holland. Prince Max resigns and hands over office to Ebert, Social Democratic Party leader. The Republic is declared

11 November Armistice signed between Allies and Germany at Compiègnes

30 December German Communist party (KPD) founded

1919: **8 February** National Constituent Assembly meets at Weimar

11 February Ebert becomes President of Weimar Republic

29 June Signing of Treaty of Versailles

1920: **March** 'Kapp putsch' – attempt by army extremists to overthrow the government – fails as workers in Berlin call a general strike

1921: **August** Erzberger, Centre Party leader, assassinated by right-wing extremists

1922: **June** Rathenau, Jewish Foreign Minister and former industrialist, also assassinated by right-wing extremists

1923: **January** Invasion of Ruhr by French and Italian troops

August Stresemann becomes Chancellor

September Massive hyper-inflation

November Unsuccessful 'putsch' in Munich by Hitler

1924: **April** Dawes Plan settles reparations issue

1925: **February** Death of President Ebert

April Hindenburg elected President for seven years

October Germany signs Locarno pacts with France and Belgium

1926: **September** Germany enters League of Nations

The failure of democracy in interwar Germany has been debated endlessly in the 60 years since the collapse of the Weimar Republic. Because Weimar was succeeded by the Third Reich, a regime which pursued brutal and aggressive racialist policies, discussions about the reasons why it failed have been particularly heated. It has been argued that Weimar was 'doomed from the outset' because of the circumstances in which it was established. Many historians have pointed out that the Weimar regime was a 'republic without republicans' committed to upholding it, and that therefore the establishment of such a form of government in Germany immediately after the Great War was 'a gamble which stood virtually no chance of success'. Other historians disagree. They have suggested that the regime was gaining in popularity, after a shaky start, and that it was principally the disastrous economic impact of the Great Depression which caused its downfall.

This chapter will consider the nature of the problems facing Weimar governments in the 1920s and will seek to establish how stable and how widely supported the regime was by the late 1920s. In particular, it will examine the impact of the First World War on Germany, the circumstances in which the new democratic regime was established, and the policies pursued by early Weimar governments. We shall see that although the new republic survived the turbulent years immediately after the war, it struggled to establish its authority over the country and its support remained fragile. Even before it was hit by the full impact of the Depression, it was facing serious political, economic and social problems.

The impact of the war on Germany

As we saw in chapter 9, the First World War was not a short, 'jolly' affair but a long and punishing slog between mass armies. Thirteen million men served in the German Army; of these around 2 million were killed. Nearly 5 million more were wounded, and over half of these were permanently disabled as a result (see Figure 16.1). The war also left behind 600,000 war widows and nearly 2 million children without fathers. In the 1920s there was considerable bitterness as war casualties battled with the Weimar government for pensions and for social assistance. They complained that their sacrifices were being ignored by an ungrateful country. Even so, over one-third of the country's budget in 1925 went on payments to wounded soldiers, war widows and orphans.

Economic consequences

Germany did not pay for the war out of current tax receipts but by borrowing and by printing more money. The result was rocketing inflation and a vastly increased national debt. The dilemma facing any German government after 1919 was that it would take all of the Reich budget just to service the wartime loans, let alone to begin to pay them off.

Figure 16.1 *Disabled soldier begging in a German street, 1918*

By the end of the war, the German mark had lost about three-quarters of its value. It plummeted further by 1920 to 10 per cent of its prewar value, and in 1922 to 1 per cent. By this time, the country's internal debt had risen to 469,000 million marks. This parlous economic situation owed nothing to reparations, which the Germans had scarcely started to pay in the early 1920s, and everything to the cost of the war. The truth was that the First World War had impoverished Germany. At the end of it, real national income was only about two-thirds of what it had been in 1913, and income per head of the population was less than three-quarters. Industrial production had slumped to two-fifths of its 1914 output, and grain production was about half of the prewar level. Any postwar government was therefore going to face the enormous challenge of how to restore Germany's financial and economic position. Faced with the options of a massive rise in taxation, which was bound to be unpopular and to provoke political opposition, or letting inflation escalate and wipe out some of the debts, it is scarcely surprising that political leaders took the second course.

The confident expectation of the military chiefs during the war had been that war costs would be more than covered by the spoils of victory. The consequences of defeat were never considered. Therefore, rather than trying to tackle the serious economic problems facing them after 1919, all governments preferred the easier option of blaming the harsh reparation demands of the Allies for all their economic difficulties. Given that they were also faced with the consequences of the social upheavals that the war had caused, such a response was hardly surprising.

Social consequences

Sharp price rises during the war sharpened social tensions. As food and fuel became difficult to obtain, the gap between the rich for whom 'everything is still available in any amounts, at a high price' and growing numbers of the poor widened greatly. While as late as 1918, some families were still taking luxury holidays at choice Baltic coast spa resorts, a quarter to a third of the population in many major German cities were desperately struggling to make ends meet on family support payments.

Increasing numbers of women were drafted into German factories to replace men who had been called up to the army. While their contribution to the war effort was obviously vital, it caused great disquiet among many sections of the population. There were allegations that the greater freedom being enjoyed by working women was encouraging the spread of 'promiscuous behaviour'. Women were neglecting their homes and their children, with the serious consequence, some people alleged, of a marked increase in thieving and in delinquent behaviour by unsupervised young people.

By the end of the war, therefore, social expectations among many groups had markedly changed. Workers resented the profiteering and ostentatious display of wealth of rich financiers and industrialists. They vowed to press for increases in their own standards of living. Many women, particularly younger ones, had seized the chance to escape from the confines of home, and were reluctant to return to the strict social conventions of prewar Germany. Returning soldiers, on the other hand, demanded their jobs back, and women were summarily dismissed from their wartime occupations and despatched home. The battle between traditional values and a quest for modernity was fought throughout the 1920s and centred particularly on the wave of American culture and Hollywood films which swept through Germany. While many young people flocked to Berlin to the new dance halls and cinemas, people in other parts of Germany increasingly regarded their capital city as a centre of sin and iniquity, where good, old-fashioned German virtues were being replaced by American decadence.

Political consequences

The scale of the war had a number of political consequences. In the first place, the Kaiser was increasingly relegated to the sidelines, as the

PROFILE: *Hindenburg*

Paul Hindenburg (1847–1934) was a German soldier who fought in the Franco-Prussian war and became a general in 1903. He retired in 1911 but was recalled to service during the First World War and became Chief of the General Staff in 1916. He advised the Kaiser to abdicate, arranged the armistice and then retired again in 1919. He was elected as the second President of the Weimar Republic in 1925, and re-elected for a second term in 1932. He was finally persuaded to appoint Hitler as Chancellor in January 1933, before dying in 1934.

military authorities took charge of operations. **Hindenburg** and **Ludendorff** were appointed by the army to the Supreme Command in 1916, and they effectively ran Germany until the end of the war. The eclipse of the Kaiser gave encouragement to those political parties who wanted to see the development of a more democratic parliamentary regime. While they did not wish to take any action which would jeopardise military success, their hopes rose that significant political change could be achieved once hostilities ended. Those who had opposed the war from the start, though a small minority, won increasing support as the costs of the war escalated and food and fuel shortages spread. Signs of growing radicalism, however, only spurred the military into even greater efforts to achieve a glorious victory which would vindicate the existing imperial structure; they refused to contemplate any negotiated peace of the sort outlined in the Reichstag's celebrated peace resolution of July 1917 calling for a peace 'of understanding and lasting reconciliation'.

The Russian Revolution of February 1917 had far-reaching effects in Germany, heightening anti-war sentiments and leading to an increase in the numbers of strikes. By January 1918 there were more than a million workers on strike, voicing political demands as well as economic ones. In the course of the next few months, a majority of parties represented in the Reichstag intensified their efforts to extend parliamentary government, and to strengthen the democratic elements of the constitution. At the same time, the great German Spring Offensive failed. As more and more American troops arrived on the Western Front, increasing numbers of German soldiers began to desert. Nearly a million men in the course of the year tried to escape from combatant duties or simply failed to return after leave. By the autumn of 1918 it was becoming frighteningly clear to the Army High Command that, far from heading for victory, they were facing certain defeat.

Their response was to 'order' the political parties to take over with the

---

PROFILE: *Ludendorff*

Erich von Ludendorff (1865–1937) was a German soldier who entered the army in 1882 and had risen to the rank of major-general by 1914. He took an increasing share in the direction of the war effort with Hindenburg after 1916. As the German armies began to retreat on the Western Front in 1918, he pressed for a transfer of power to the civilian authorities and an approach to Wilson for peace terms. He was involved in the 1920 Kapp putsch (see page 266) and in Hitler's attempted coup in Munich in 1923. He founded an extreme nationalist party in 1925 and was an unsuccessful candidate in the Presidential election of that year. He continued to be involved in extreme nationalist politics but ended his association with Hitler. By 1933 he was warning that Hitler was a dangerous fanatic intent on establishing a personal dictatorship.

---

aim of securing an armistice from the American President on the most lenient terms they could get. The German Reich was suddenly transformed into a parliamentary monarchy whose first act was to sue for peace on the basis of Woodrow Wilson's Fourteen Points (see chapter 10). The High Command clearly hoped that a parliamentary regime would secure more favourable terms from the US President than a military delegation. They also demonstrated considerable political skill in ensuring that it was the civilian authorities and not they themselves who shouldered the responsibility for ending the war and who would therefore get the blame.

The final push towards the establishment of a parliamentary democracy came from Wilson, who was not willing to negotiate a peace based on his Fourteen Points with a regime headed by the Kaiser. With the German population now clamouring for peace, and revolution breaking out in various parts of the country, the Kaiser was left with no option but to abdicate. On 9 November 1918, the last imperial chancellor, Prince Max of Baden, handed political authority over to the Social Democratic leader Friedrich Ebert. An hour later, the new Republic was declared.

The German revolution

The sudden turn of events, and the prospect of an end to hostilities, brought about a release of tensions which erupted into revolution. It was triggered by a naval mutiny at the end of October at Kiel, where sailors refused orders to put to sea for a final battle against the British navy. They argued that the Naval High Command was disregarding the government's policy of ending the war, and seized control of Kiel harbour and of the ships anchored there, raising the red flag on each vessel that they 'captured'. The uprising spread to other bases and ports, and workers', solders' and sailors' councils sprang up in towns and cities across Germany. In Bavaria, a socialist republic was proclaimed. Separatist movements in other regions gathered momentum. Left-wing groups in many big cities, such as the Berlin Revolutionary Shop Stewards' movement, appealed to the disaffected masses to support the establishment of workers' soviets.

Fearful that the mood for change was being exploited by extreme left-wing forces, and that further uprisings would leave Germany open to invasion by her enemies, Ebert and the army leadership came to an agreement whereby the army would support the new government and work with it to suppress the Communists and other left-wing groups. During the turbulent weeks that followed, many left-wing leaders – such as Kurt Eisner in Bavaria and Karl Liebknecht and Rosa Luxemburg in Berlin – were brutally murdered by irregular volunteer army units.

The revolutionary interlude was finally brought to an end, but it had three serious consequences for the new republic:

1 On the Left, a deep rift opened up between the emerging German Communist Party and the Social Democrats which grew wider throughout the 1920s. The Communists never forgave the Social Democrats for the betrayal, as they saw it, of the revolution and the deliberate murder of revolutionary comrades. For their part, the Social Democrats felt the need to make a public display of their credentials as representatives of the working class, and for most of the 1920s remained in opposition, rather than participating in government.

2 For many Germans, the outbreak of revolution had been a tremendous shock. While they welcomed the end of the war, they were vehemently opposed to what was called 'The Russian solution', which embraced the establishment of workers' and soldiers' soviets, and the spread of disorder. The writer Thomas Mann spoke for millions of ordinary Germans when he said 'I don't want politics. I want a matter-of-fact approach, order and decency'. Fear of the spread of communism remained strong in Germany, and played a decisive role in Hitler's rise to power, as we shall see.

3 On the Right, there was a conviction that the revolution had robbed Germany of a chance of military victory. Re-read the quote on page 150 to see how a school textbook, used in Prussia in the 1920s and 1930s, explained the end of the war.

The myth was spread that Germany was poised for victory when she was betrayed by a combination of traitors at home and enemies abroad. This idea of the 'stab in the back' exercised a powerful hold on many sections of the German population after 1919. It explained the widespread denunciations of 'November Criminals' and 'Jewish traitors' which were the stock-in-trade of extreme nationalist speeches and propaganda throughout the 1920s.

The peace settlement

As if it was not enough for the new regime to be associated with defeat and revolution, it was then saddled with an enormously unpopular peace settlement. The German people had been led to believe that their conversion to democracy would guarantee a relatively lenient peace. Instead, they were faced by what they attacked as a 'diktat', a treaty which laid the blame on them for causing the war, which demanded an unspecified sum for reparations, stripped them of their colonies, and of most of their navy. They lost territory in the east to the hated Poles, the French were to get unlimited access to the Saar coalfields, the army was to be limited to a derisory 100,000 men and the Rhineland was to be demilitarised and occupied by allied troops. To add insult to injury, the much vaunted doctrine of self-determination was not to be applied to Germany or to Austria, who were forbidden to unite, and substantial German minorities found themselves outside the new German state (see chapter 10).

Evidence about the kind of peace settlement the German High Command was preparing to impose upon their enemies suggests that this was not an unduly harsh peace. Germany was not dismembered nor even subjected to serious loss of territory. The reparations bill which was eventually demanded represented some 6 per cent of Germany's national income, a considerable sum but one which many historians believe would not have been an impossible burden for the German economy to bear, had German leaders chosen to try to meet it. However, the German people had been expecting victory, not defeat. Then they had braced themselves for a peace negotiated among equals, which would have taken from them Alsace and Lorraine and one or two other small areas, but would have left them as one of the leading powers of postwar Europe. Now they found themselves excluded from the League of Nations, branded as the aggressor who single-handedly caused the First World War, and facing territorial losses in the east along with stringent military restrictions. No wonder the civilian leaders who reluctantly agreed to sign the Treaty of Versailles in June 1919 incurred so much hostility.

The contrast between the reception accorded to the German troops who returned back to Germany in late 1918 and to the peacemakers of 1919 could not have been greater. To greet the returning soldiers, the authorities ordered festive receptions and commended the bravery of those who had 'stood their ground undefeated up to the last minute'. They were hailed in their local communities as 'undefeated heroes' who had patriotically and selflessly served their country. Those who had supported an armistice and had then agreed to the signing of the Treaty of Versailles, on the other hand, had signally betrayed their country. One of them, the Catholic Centre Party leader Matthias Erzberger, was murdered in 1921, and others were the targets of extreme right-wing violence. The new republic could not have had a more inauspicious start.

The Weimar Constitution

The constitution of the new republic was drawn up in Weimar, the small town in which both Göthe and Schiller, the greatest German poets, had once lived. It established a political system based on the Reichstag, whose members were to be elected by **proportional representation**. All men and women over the age of 20 could vote, at least once every four years for a Reichstag deputy, and once every seven years for a President.

1 The President was to have extensive powers. He could appoint and dismiss governments, dissolve the Reichstag and rule by decree in an emergency.

2 There was also to be a Cabinet, headed by a Chancellor, which was responsible to the Reichstag.

3 Under the new constitution, the German regions were to retain considerable powers, appointing their own teachers and judges, and retaining control of their own police force, though they lost their power to raise local taxation.

4 The Weimar Constitution gave the new governments municipal and welfare responsibilities as well as legislative functions. They had a duty to secure 'a healthy dwelling for every German' and a place of residence and work for every German family 'appropriate to their needs.'

5 They also had to supervise the new labour laws under which workers were granted statutory rights against arbitrary dismissal. All factories had to establish factory councils to give workers a say in how the factories were run. There was to be a system of legally-binding collective wage agreements, and trade unions were to gain recognition. If labour disputes could not be resolved directly between employers and workers, the state had powers to arbitrate.

These social and economic responsibilities turned Weimar governments into uncritical upholders of the demands of workers and tenants in the eyes of industrialists and landlords. Many on the Right saw the new regime as a 'workers' government' and sought to undermine its authority. Furthermore, the political parties which contested the early elections and formed coalition governments were unused to operating on a national scale or to working with each other. The largest party was the Social Democratic Party which secured about a quarter of the votes. As we have seen, it could not work with the Communists to the left, and found difficulty in agreeing on a common set of policies with the Catholic Centre Party or the small Democrat Party to its right. Industrialists and rural interests supported the more right-wing German National Party or the even more nationalist German National People's Party. These two groups did manage to work together, often in coalition with the Catholic Party. But the right-wing parties never gave the new parliamentary system their wholehearted support, although they were prepared to work through it to secure their particular interests.

The result was a series of weak coalition governments. Between 1919 and 1928, there were 15 different cabinets, none lasting longer than 18 months, and some only surviving for three. The Social Democrats, who along with the Democrats were the most enthusiastic supporters of a republican democracy, played a prominent part in the first five governments from 1919 to 1921. They spent the next seven years in opposition, apart from a brief spell back in government in the crisis year of 1923.

Coalition governments found it difficult to reach agreement on a common set of policies, and the German electorate became increasingly exasperated by political in-fighting, the frequent disintegration of coalition cabinets and what seemed to be an endless cabinet crisis. The one platform on which all parties could unite was a denunciation of the peace terms and a full-blooded attack on the Treaty of Versailles. No government wished to be seen to be a lackey of the allied powers, helping them to find concealed stocks of weapons and to extract reparations payments. Governments therefore tried to show that they were exerting authority by refusing to comply with the treaty terms, and by branding those who tried to carry them out as 'pacifists' and traitors.

The early years

The Weimar Republic faced a number of daunting challenges in its first few years. In 1920, there was an attempted coup by Free Corps army units who marched into Berlin and installed a Prussian bureaucrat, Wolfgang Kapp, as Chancellor. Ominously, the army refused to intervene, and Ebert and the legitimately elected government fled from Berlin. They were saved by the actions of workers who called a national strike and refused to cooperate with Kapp's regime, forcing him to withdraw with his troops.

In the following years, the behaviour of many Germans in prominent positions showed that they shared the army's contempt for the new regime. Judges meted out ridiculously light sentences to right-wing extremists who were brought to trial for the murder or attempted murder of political opponents. Accused parties who had left-wing sympathies, however, were dealt with savagely. Civil servants pledged their loyalty to the German state rather than to the Weimar Republic. And the new republican flag was widely condemned. One of the earliest Free Corps commanders was interviewed by a journalist after attracting notoriety for describing the hated flag as a 'Jewish rag' and the Weimar government as 'a rabble'. He no doubt expressed the sentiments of many Germans when he said:

> *'I make no bones of the fact that I am a monarchist. My God! When one has served his king and country faithfully for 30 years he can't suddenly say, "Starting tomorrow I'm a Republican". But you don't have to be afraid. I don't believe it's possible to set up a monarchy again in a minute. The Allies wouldn't let us do that in any case. But what will happen in ten years' time . . .'*

Economic weakness, resulting from the war, compounded the problems facing the early governments. Inflation continued to rise steadily, and any politician who genuinely tried to get to grips with the twin problems of war debts and reparations was treated with suspicion, if not worse. The Jewish industrialist and Foreign Secretary, Walter Rathenau, was murdered by extremists in 1922, as foreign governments became increasingly impatient with Germany's attempts to evade reparations payments.

The invasion of the Ruhr

At the end of 1922, the allied reparations commission, which consisted of French, Italian, Belgian and British representatives, declared Germany to be in default on her reparations payments. The French government, with Belgian and Italian support, now insisted on an invasion of German territory to seize directly from factories the reparations payments which they argued Germany was refusing to pay. Troops marched into the Ruhr area which provided over 80 per cent of Germany's coal and 80 per cent of its steel production. The French were also intent on trying to stimulate independence movements in the Rhineland area, but their policies failed in both respects. The German government met the Ruhr invasion with a tactic of passive resistance, and soon the great industrial heartland of Germany lay idle. The government now gave assistance to workers who were without income, and could only afford to do this by printing more paper money. The German economy, which had been under increasing strain since the end of the war, escalated into hyper-inflation and currency became worthless. A loaf of bread cost millions of marks. Prices changed hourly; goods, and especially food, became scarce. Those on fixed incomes, or with large savings, saw their money disappear. Those, on the other hand, with large debts, or access to foreign currency, could speculate their way to huge fortunes.

Stresemann

The Ruhr invasion nearly destroyed the Weimar Republic. It left a legacy of bitterness, and certainly undermined the confidence of millions in the new regime. Yet it survived, and even gained in strength from the crisis. The danger of a total collapse forced many Germans to adopt a more constructive attitude to the regime, and to work to build it up, lest Germany's enemies should profit from its weakness. A notable example was Gustav Stresemann, who took over as Chancellor in the summer of 1923. A former monarchist and fervent supporter of Germany's expansionist aims in the First World War, he now shouldered the responsibility of repairing relations with France and Britain, and agreeing to fulfil the terms of the Treaty of Versailles. At the same time, he accepted the US offer of substantial loans, which poured into Germany between 1924 and 1929 and enabled the German economy to recover. The loans enabled the Germans to pay the hated reparations, through an American-sponsored scheme called the Dawes Plan (see chapter 10), and gave them the opportunity to re-equip their factories and industrial plants.

This change in approach was not without its critics. Many nationalists attacked what they saw as a German 'sell-out', and plotted to overthrow Stresemann's government and install a more patriotic nationalist regime. Bavaria had become a particular hotbed of extreme right-wing nationalism and in the autumn of 1923, a 'half-crazed fanatic', as a contemporary described him – leader of a small fringe group called the National Socialist Party (Nazis) – organised a coup in Munich. Hitler's plan was to seek the support of the Bavarian authorities for the installation of a military regime in Bavaria and for a march to Berlin to overthrow the government. Despite the support of Ludendorff, his grandiose scheme turned into pantomime farce as the local police and army refused to participate, and arrested him instead. It seemed that all over Germany, the threats to the Weimar Republic from right and from left were receding, and that the new regime was finally becoming accepted by the majority of German people.

Even so, in the 1924 Reichstag elections, a third of German voters supported parties who professed their total opposition to the Republic and to Stresemann's policy of international rehabilitation.

Weimar support, 1924–8

Many historians have portrayed the period between 1924 and 1928 as the 'golden years' of the Weimar Republic, an all-too-brief interlude during which the new political system became more fully accepted. They have argued that the economy was stabilised, and that great social and cultural progress was achieved. It is certainly the case that under Stresemann's leadership, relations with Britain and France improved markedly and Germany was once more accepted into the international fold. Germany signed the Treaty of Locarno in 1925 (see chapter 10) and was admitted to the League of Nations in the following year. Historians remain divided about Stresemann's ultimate foreign policy objectives, particularly with regard to the revision of Germany's frontiers in eastern Europe. However, his twin strategy of cultivating cordial relations with his French and British counterparts while at the same time retaining Germany's links with the new Bolshevik regime, put Weimar Germany at the forefront of European diplomacy.

Yet Stresemann was bitterly attacked by nationalist politicians through-out this period. They claimed that the payment of reparations under the Dawes agreement represented 'a second German enslavement' on top of the Treaty of Versailles. They attacked the Locarno treaties as a further betrayal. What they advocated was the complete repudiation of Versailles with its affront to national honour, and a tactical alliance with Russia and possibly with other south-eastern European powers to enable Germany to establish her authority over eastern Europe. Meanwhile, Communists were attacking Locarno as a 'capitalist conspiracy' against the Soviet Union led by Britain to which Germany should never have agreed. It is undoubtedly the case that Stresemann's prestige abroad was considerably higher than his popularity at home.

Great progress was made during this period in social and economic policy. A large number of new housing units were built, about half of them financed from state funds. An ambitious unemployment insurance scheme was introduced, and real wages rose steadily. Increasing numbers of ordinary Germans found themselves with time to devote to leisure pursuits, at a time when popular entertainments, such as the cinema, radio and spectator sports were developing rapidly. In 1926, a publisher lamented that 'books are nowadays the most dispensable objects of everyday life. People go in for sport, they dance, they spend the evenings listening to the wireless or watching a film.'

In addition to the spread of popular culture, the 1920s in Germany saw the development of modern forms of expressionism in art, literature, music and architecture. An early example of this was the establishment in 1919 of the Bauhaus, a new school of art, architecture and design at Weimar, founded to 'conceive and create the new building of the future'. Its first exhibition in 1923, with its striking posters, created tremendous interest and attracted 15,000 visitors. The Bauhaus symbolised a new age, ready to experiment with modern ideas and different forms. These themes were taken up by writers and musicians. Paul Hindemith pioneered new and diverse musical forms and Arnold Schönberg composed 'atonal' musical works which were not written in a set key but were based on different series of musical notes; Schönberg's pupils, Anton von Webern and Alban Berg, developed 'atonal' music in ever more diverse, but to many, unmelodious ways. At a more popular level, Kurt Weill's music brought some of these new musical idioms to audiences in provincial theatres and concert halls throughout Germany.

Literary works emphasised new codes of behaviour and a general revolt against authority. At the same time, writers such as Thomas Mann and Hermann Hesse drew attention to what they saw as a general decline of western society, resulting in decadence and depravity. This seemed to be borne out in the behaviour of many young people in Weimar Germany, especially women, many of whom were now to be seen in public smoking, drinking and exhibiting a willingness to enter freely into pre-marital sexual relationships. Even less 'forward' young women cut their hair and adopted new American fashions. Berlin was to many young Germans the exciting centre of a new, liberated and modern Germany; to others, however, it represented a dreadful new 'Sodom on the eve of its destruction', where decadence and debauchery of every kind flourished.

The experimentation and new 'modernism' of Weimar culture aroused fierce criticism and often outrage from traditionalists who attacked what they regarded as signs of 'cultural Bolshevism'. Their fears that the foundations of Germany's strength were being fatally undermined by a decline in morals and in standards of public and artistic life were reinforced by such books as Spengler's *Decline of the West* (first published in 1918) which painted a gloomy view of the impact of capitalism and of democracy, and argued that only a new 'elite of heroes' could save Germany.

Therein lay Weimar's great weakness. Social and cultural changes, which were supported by some groups as being progressive and modern, were attacked by many others as decadent and leading inevitably to national decline. While workers appreciated new municipal housing, shopkeepers and farmers resented paying for it through their taxes. Industrialists warned that their businesses were facing bankruptcy because of unrealistic wage demands and the high taxes required to finance Weimar's social security payments. It was by no means clear that those who supported the regime were gaining the upper hand by 1928. Indeed, it could be argued that considerable sections of the population remained uncommitted, and that Weimar's critics and declared opponents were in a strong position even before the Depression hit Germany.

Hindenburg's election

The election of Field-Marshal Hindenburg as Weimar's second president in 1925 was a clear indication not just of the nostalgia for past glories felt by large sections of the German electorate but also of their strong desire for authority and order and their respect for military leaders. By 1925 Hindenburg was 78 years old, and certainly not in sympathy with democratic or progressive trends. He was one of many Germans who hated the new republican flag and pressed for German embassies in ports throughout the world to fly the merchant marine flag, with its colours similar to the old imperial flag, alongside the republican one. Such a man had now been democratically elected to the highest position in Germany. As one historian has commented, 'one of the commanding heights of the republic was now in all but hostile hands'.

Industrialists

While the German economy had been stabilised in 1924, with the help of a considerable influx of American loans, there were clear signs by 1928 that it was slowing down. German coal and steel bosses blamed this on the fact that real wages were rising faster than productivity, and that too great a proportion of national expenditure was being spent on wages and on social handouts rather than on industrial investment. While this may have been one cause of the economic problems Germany was experiencing, there were also others:

■ investment being misdirected

■ employers not willing to introduce innovations and new technology

■ banks being very restrictive in granting credit facilities.

By 1928, employers were increasingly looking to reduce wages and if necessary to ignore arbitration awards backed by the government. There was an ugly confrontation between employers and workers in the Ruhr when a quarter of a million workers were locked out of their factories as employers defied the government and tried to force down wages. Employers and industrialists saw the Weimar regime as favouring workers, and were becoming increasingly antagonised by its social and economic policies.

Farmers

Farmers were also turning against the government. Throughout the 1920s, they were battling against the effects of a worldwide agricultural depression brought about by the wartime need to stimulate and to extend agricultural production. With too much produce flooding on to world markets, prices tumbled and small-scale farmers in northern Germany and particularly in Prussia were severely hit. By the later 1920s, they were getting little, if any, return on their capital, yet many farms were heavily mortgaged and interest rates were high. Increasingly the beleaguered farmers and disgruntled industrialists joined forces in nationalist organisations and parties to attack the government.

Small shopkeepers and artisans

The farmers and industrialists were joined by many shopkeepers and artisans who resented all the help being given to unskilled industrial workers and to the urban poor, paid for out of their hard-earned profits. On the one hand, these groups saw people who they regarded as being their social inferiors – factory and industrial workers – increasing their standard of living. On the other hand, they themselves were facing stiff competition from a growing number of large department stores which were attracting more and more of their traditional customers. Once again, they blamed Weimar for their plight. Along with other middle-class groups, such as teachers and civil servants, they turned increasingly to support nationalist opponents of the regime.

The army

The army operated with considerable independence during the 1920s. Desperate to evade many of the restrictions of the Treaty of Versailles, army leaders concluded secret deals with the Bolsheviks which enabled them to assemble and test weapons forbidden to Germany, such as aeroplanes and tanks, on Soviet soil. The much-reduced German army operated almost like a 'state within a state', and though it never intervened actively in German politics, it remained deeply hostile to the new regime.

Extremist opponents

While the Weimar regime was struggling to establish its authority, its opponents on the extreme left and right were busily engaged in campaigns designed to bring about its destruction. The German Communist Party struggled to attract workers away from the Social Democrats, but the National Socialists were increasingly successful in drawing into their ranks those on the right. Adolf Hitler had gained something of a national reputation during his trial for treason against the state in 1924. He won widespread sympathy for his argument that he could not possibly have committed treason against the revolution of 1918 which was itself an act of treason. His sentence of 'five years' honourable confinement' was extraordinarily lenient, and he spent scarcely a year in Landsberg jail. While there, he was allowed to communicate with the outside world, and was given every facility to dictate his lengthy and rambling autobiography *Mein Kampf* ('My Struggle') which was subsequently published.

Once released from jail, Hitler set himself the task of rebuilding the Nazi Party under his strong leadership with the aim of capturing the hated Weimar Republic and destroying it from within, rather than overthrowing it from outside. As he told a friend who visited him in jail:

> *'When I resume active work it will be necessary to pursue a new policy. Instead of working to achieve power by an armed coup we shall have to hold our noses against the Catholic and Marxist deputies. If out-voting them takes longer than out-shooting them, at least the results will be guaranteed by their own Constitution!'*

To put into effect the new strategy, party branches were established all over Germany and considerable effort went into developing Nazi Party propaganda, organising meetings and designing eye-catching emblems. Hitler found that farmers, small Protestant rural communities, teachers and students were particularly receptive to the Nazi message centred on the need for national regeneration and for a government of all the classes committed to restoring German pride and removing from their midst traitors, class and racial enemies.

In the 1928 Reichstag elections, the Nazis did not do particularly well, gaining only 12 seats and 2.6 per cent of the vote. But ominously for Weimar's supporters, the 1928 election saw voters in the centre and on the right deserting the main political parties who seemed to do nothing but quarrel among themselves, and giving their support to regional parties or to single-issue candidates. This 'fragmentation of the centre', as historians have called it, was overshadowed at the time by a resurgence of support for the Social Democrats who received nearly 30 per cent of the vote. No one would have predicted in 1928 that within four years the

Nazi Party would be the major beneficiary of this political disillusionment. What was clear, however, was that substantial opposition remained to the Weimar Republic. Even more ominously, large sections of the population, having witnessed 15 different cabinets between 1919 and 1928, were not yet convinced of the merits of a democratic system and any serious setback was likely to reinforce their doubts. Unfortunately the Wall Street Crash of 1929 faced the Weimar Republic not with a setback but with the most catastrophic economic crisis of the twentieth century. As we shall see, it was a crisis which the regime had little hope of surviving.

Task

Classwork task as preparation for an essay on *'Was Weimar Germany doomed from the outset?'* Work in groups on this analysis of the Weimar Republic in the years up to 1930.

1 Use a large sheet of paper to record your conclusions. Draw up a table like the one below, though yours will need to be bigger.

	Economic	Social	Political	External factors
Consequences of the war				
The German revolution and its consequences				
The peace terms				
Germany up to 1923				
Germany 1923–30				

2 Use a smaller sheet simply divided into two down the middle. On one side, record which groups, trends and attitudes in Germany were PRO-WEIMAR in 1930 and, on the other, those which were AGAINST WEIMAR.

Use these two analyses to plan your essay. The main sections will follow the sections on the larger sheet; the smaller sheet gives you a conclusion. In the introduction you could give an overview of what you intend to say in the essay. This will either outline the forces ranged against the Weimar Republic, or make the point that its collapse was not inevitable from the beginning and outline the forces in support of Weimar.

Further reading

Gordon Craig, *Germany, 1866–1945* (Oxford University Press, 1978) – very full treatment of Weimar political and cultural developments.

J. A. S. Grenville, *A World History of the Twentieth Century* (Fontana, 1987) – chapters 10 and 16.

Helmut Heiber, *The Weimar Republic* (Blackwell, 1993) – up-to-date and very detailed assessment.

Ian Kershaw (ed.), *Why Did Weimar Democracy Fail?* (Weidenfeld and Nicolson, 1990) – very interesting debate, centred on a number of contributions from leading historians of the Weimar Republic.

Eberhard Kolb, *The Weimar Republic* (Unwin Hyman, 1988) – the standard textbook of recent years.

A. J. Nicholls, *Weimar and the Rise of Hitler* (Macmillan, 1968).

17 The Nazi seizure of power

Time chart

1929: 3 October Death of Stresemann
29 October Wall Street Crash leads to cessation of American loans to Europe

1930: March Head of coalition government, Müller, resigns. Brüning forms a minority coalition of Right
July President Hindenburg authorises German budget by decree as Reichstag fails to pass it
September In Reichstag elections, Hitler and Nazi Party emerge with 107 seats, second only to Socialists

1931: July Unemployment rises to over 4.5 million; banks face crisis as economy worsens

1932: March In Presidential elections, Hindenburg gets 18 million votes, Hitler 11 million and Communist candidates 5 million. Since Hindenburg fails to secure a majority over all other candidates, a second election is called
April Hindenburg is re-elected President with 19 million votes, against 13 million for Hitler and 3 million for the Communists
May Brüning resigns
June Franz von Papen forms a ministry with von Schleicher as Minister of Defence
July Nazis win 230 seats in Reichstag election, becoming largest party
August Hitler refuses Hindenburg's request to serve as vice-chancellor under von Papen
September Von Papen dissolves the Reichstag
November In new Reichstag elections, Nazi vote falls but they remain the largest party. Von Papen resigns
December Von Schleicher becomes Chancellor but his government is unable to secure a majority in Reichstag

1933: January Von Schleicher resigns and Hindenburg accepts a Cabinet with Hitler as Chancellor and von Papen as vice-chancellor (only 2 other Nazis in Cabinet)
February Reichstag fire breaks out and is blamed on Communists. Civil liberties suspended
March In new Reichstag elections, Nazis make gains, winning 288 seats but failing to secure overall majority. Hitler obtains Enabling Act with support of Centre Party, giving him dictatorial powers for 4 years

1933: April National boycott of Jewish shops and businesses

July Centre Party disbands. All other parties are suppressed and the Nazi Party is declared the only legal political party in Germany

1934: 30 June 'Night of the Long Knives' – Nazis liquidate thousands of opponents, including over 70 leading Nazis and von Schleicher

August Hindenburg dies. Hitler becomes President but keeps title of Der Führer. Army swears oath of allegiance.

The face of German politics was dramatically changed in the five short years between 1929 and 1934. This chapter looks at two related but separate processes: the collapse of the Weimar Republic and the rise to power of the National Socialist German Workers' Party (Nazis, for short). We saw in the previous chapter that support for the democratic regime in Germany remained fragile. It was by no means inevitable that it would be succeeded by an extreme nationalist one-party dictatorship under Hitler's leadership. Why did the Depression bring to power the Nazis rather than some other extremist group? Were they 'voted into power' by the German electorate or was it 'backstairs political intrigue' which gave them the vital entry into government? This chapter will examine the economic and political impact of the Depression on Germany and then consider how important the role of popular support was in bringing Hitler into government as Chancellor in January 1933 and in enabling him to create a one-party dictatorship in little more than a year thereafter.

The impact of the Depression

Unemployment

Germany felt the impact of the 1929 Wall Street Crash earlier than many other European countries because so much US money had been pumped into the German economy since 1925 in the form of short-term loans. These loans were rapidly called in by American banks, resulting in a sudden contraction in industrial output. Some factories closed; others reduced their workforce and put the remainder on to short-time working. The result was spiralling unemployment which soon brought millions of families to the brink of poverty and despair. By 1932 the number of people officially registered as unemployed stood at 6 million; if seasonal workers, casual labourers and unregistered female workers are included, the true figure was nearer to 9 million, or over a third of the country's workforce.

The strain on the unemployment insurance fund was enormous; industrialists demanded a progressive increase in contributions to enable the fund to be self-supporting, but this was vigorously opposed by those who wanted to safeguard the interests of those still in work. As early as 1930, this issue precipitated the break-up of the last great coalition government of the Weimar Republic, when the Social Democrats pulled out in protest at the increase in contributions being proposed. As the German economy contracted, national income fell steeply and by 1932 was 39 per cent less in real terms than it had been in 1929. (In Britain the comparable reduction was 15 per cent and in France 16 per cent.)

Brüning and political consequences

With the memory of the hyper-inflation of the early 1920s strong, the new government under Heinrich Brüning, the Catholic Centre Party's leader and President Hindenburg's choice as Chancellor, was determined to bring order into the Weimar's overstretched public finances. However, while he protected the farmers, he refused to stimulate demand or reflate the economy. Brüning urged Germans to make the necessary sacrifices and to enable unrestricted market mechanisms to sort out the crisis.

Brüning also wanted to persuade the allied governments to cancel Germany's reparations payments. The more serious Germany's economic position became, the greater the chances were of reaching agreement on cancellation. Brüning was eventually successful; reparations were finally ended in 1932. But by that time the situation facing large numbers of German families was so desperate that, rather than continuing to support the Brüning government, they had begun to be attracted to more extreme political remedies.

Hindenburg was determined to use his presidential powers to modify the Weimar Constitution, considerably reducing the powers of the democratically-elected Reichstag. Brüning supported him in this endeavour, believing that a strong patriotic government was essential in the prevailing crisis. Both leaders concentrated their efforts on securing a more pliable Reichstag, and to this end Hindenburg used his emergency powers in 1930 to dissolve the existing Reichstag and to call fresh elections.

The 1930 Reichstag elections

The decision had catastrophic consequences, both for the immediate future of Weimar democracy, and in the longer term for Germany as a nation. In the climate of economic panic and spiralling unemployment, the Nazi vote rocketed from 2.6 per cent to over 18 per cent, giving them 107 seats in the new Reichstag. The Communist Party vote also increased from 10 to 13 per cent, giving them 77 seats – a gain of 23. The Nazis took votes away from the more moderate nationalist parties, and attracted new voters in 'an uprising of stupidity' as one commentator put it. Hitler certainly attracted a considerable amount of middle-class support. Recent research has suggested that unskilled workers from smaller urban centres and rural communities, and those employed in small workshops, also voted for the Nazis. The Nazi Party was justified in its claim that it was now 'a national movement cutting across classes', with an appeal to all sections of the population. Those who remained most resistant to Nazi propaganda were Catholics and workers from the industrial heartlands of Germany.

Presidential rule

Brüning and Hindenburg now had to work with a Reichstag in which they could only count on the full support of about a third of deputies. Another third of its members, Nazis and Communists, subjected it to constant attack and were frequently prepared to turn its proceedings into an unruly rabble. Brüning desperately needed backing from the Social Democrats but Hindenburg was not prepared to re-admit them to the governing coalition. Despite the difficulties of managing an increasingly fractious Reichstag, and the worsening economic situation, Hindenburg insisted that Brüning continued to give financial support to landowners, particularly in east Prussia, and to the army. As violence escalated throughout the country, and street fights between Nazi gangs and formations of communist Red Guards or Social Democrat Reichsbanner groups became a regular occurrence, the Reichstag met less and less often. It was in session for 94 days in 1930, for 42 days in 1931 and for only five days in 1932. Weimar democracy was being replaced by an autocratic President ruling through an emergency powers provision.

Hardly surprisingly, Hindenburg struggled to keep control of the political situation. Brüning lost his confidence by 1932 and was replaced by a political nonentity, Franz von Papen, a backbench member of the Prussian Landtag (provincial assembly). The real power behind the throne now was General Kurt von Schleicher, the defence minister, who nursed political ambitions of his own. He wanted to 'tame' the Nazi movement by bringing it into government, and making it shoulder some of the responsibility for unpopular measures. Since Hindenburg was reluctant to be drawn into any direct dealings with the 'Bohemian corporal', as he contemptuously called Hitler, for the time being, von Papen took over as Chancellor in what became known as the 'cabinet of barons', none of whom were members of the Reichstag. The Weimar Republic was now unquestionably dead, and the von Papen cabinet consciously aimed to establish a 'new state' no longer reliant on the ballot box, on parties and on parliament, but authoritarian in structure and offering an alternative to discredited democracy on the one hand and a Nazi-run state on the other.

The growth of support for the Nazis

Nazi electoral support doubled in the years 1930–32. The Nazi Party recorded spectacular advances in regional elections in 1931, and by the summer of 1932 was consistently attracting around 37 per cent of the vote in the Presidential and Reichstag elections and in regional contests. In the spring of 1932, the 84-year-old President Hindenburg grudgingly had to submit himself for re-election, after Brüning failed to persuade the Reichstag to extend his term of office. On the first ballot, he narrowly failed to win an overall majority, though he was convincingly ahead of his principal rival, Hitler, who received 30 per cent the votes. He was therefore forced to a second ballot, in a head-to-head confrontation with the Nazi leader, in which several members of the traditional German elites, including the Crown Prince, declared their support for Hitler. While Hindenburg won, Hitler secured nearly 37 per cent of the votes cast; over 13 million Germans now preferred him to the ageing President.

Reichstag elections in July 1932 confirmed this level of support. The Nazi Party, cashing in on Hitler's manifest popularity, referred to themselves as 'Hitler's party' and secured over 37 per cent of the votes cast. In a second Reichstag election in November, Nazi support fell to 33 per cent, but the party still had the largest number of elected deputies. It faced an opposition fragmented between the Communists who received 17 per cent of the vote, the SPD who received 20 per cent and the Catholic Centre at nearly 12 per cent. Its support in regional elections remained strong, reaching over 40 per cent in some states.

There can be no doubt that by the summer of 1932 Hitler was attracting a huge level of mass support. The electorate was reacting to the economic and social crisis which was engulfing them, and to the Nazi message, which was both simple and at the same time carefully calculated to give them hope for the future.

Economic factors

Brüning's cabinet had found no answers to the continuing economic crisis, except to cut spending, reduce the levels of welfare payments, and increase contributions to the unemployment insurance scheme. Parties on the left and in the centre had few alternative proposals. About a third of unemployed families had barely any income at all; millions more feared that they too would soon face destitution. Only the Nazis were prepared to pledge themselves to provide work for all Germans, without being too specific about how they would achieve this goal.

Nationalist appeal

Which voters supported Nazi ideology? While a range of evidence seems to suggest that the party's strident anti-semitism and racial doctrines were not great vote winners, people were attracted by calls for national regeneration and for an end to class-based politics. The electorate hankered after the national unity established during the early stages of the First World War, when there were 'no longer parties but only Germans'. Hitler's calls for a *Volksgemeinschaft* (a 'people's community') received strong support. Furthermore, his denunciations of the Treaty of Versailles and of the 'November Criminals' who signed it, and his pledge that he would work to restore German honour and Germany's rightful position in Europe, undoubtedly added to the Nazi appeal.

Fear of Communism

As the votes of unemployed workers helped the Communists to win the support of around a sixth of the German electorate, the strong anti-Communist sentiments of the majority of the population increased. Large numbers of people were scared stiff about the emergence of workers' soviets and a Bolshevik-type regime in Germany. The Nazis emphasised their total opposition to Communism and to class-based politics, under-lining the message with street attacks on alleged Communists. They also linked together the twin threats to Germany of a world Jewish conspiracy and of revolutionary Bolshevism, and pledged that they would combat both vigorously and unceasingly.

The role of Hitler

Hard as it may now seem for us to believe, Hitler commanded mass support because voters believed that he was a selfless patriot, concerned only to rescue the country from the slough into which it had fallen after 1918. Though born in Bohemia in the Habsburg Empire in 1889, Hitler was a German who had fought bravely for his adopted country in the First World War and had twice been rewarded with the Iron Cross. He was no corrupt politician, but a man of the people, pledging himself to rid Germany of political in-fighting, bribery and self-interest.

If Hitler possessed one skill above all others, it was his eloquence as a public speaker. He had the ability to mesmerise and to arouse an audience to a frenzy of approval for his message. Tales abound of political

Figure 17.1 Nazi gathering in 1931. Both SS and SA are present, including their leaders: Heinrich Himmler (front row, black hat and trousers) and Ernst Röhm (to the right of Himmler).

KEY TERM:

Stürmabteilung

The **SA Brownshirts** were a paramilitary force in Germany in the early 1930s. They numbered about four and a half million men. The SA was an organisation of Nazi party members who fought street battles against their opponents. After Hitler came to power, it became commonplace to see groups of 'storm-troopers', armed with revolvers and pieces of piping, roaming the streets looking for Jews and other 'opponents of the Nazis' to beat up. They were disbanded after the 'Night of the Long Knives' (see page 284). The name 'storm-trooper' was borrowed from the small units of soldiers successfully used on the Western Front in the First World War – see page 128.

opponents attending his meetings to heckle, and being carried along with the rest of the audience. Hitler also possessed considerable charisma as a performer – he therefore managed to portray himself as ordinary, while at the same time possessing an extraordinary ability to arouse interest and attract support.

A party of the future

Party members presented an image of colour, of purpose and of unity. Their emblems and uniforms brought back memories of the prewar period and of the war itself (see Figure 17.1). The *Stürmabteilung* (SA, 'Storm-Troopers') wore brown shirts; while the SS (*Schützstaffeln*, or rifle squadrons) wore sinister black uniforms. At the same time, their propaganda and sense of theatre were totally modern. They took great pains to disassociate themselves from the unpopular Weimar regime. They looked to the future, to the establishment of a government which would bring order instead of chaos, and expansion instead of humiliation. While the excessive levels of brutality from which many party members derived such sport repelled a considerable number of voters, they appear to have attracted others who were keen to see the 'lefties' being beaten up.

Nazi organisation

The Party had spent a lot of time in the late 1920s establishing branches throughout Germany. Literature was produced and circulated with a careful eye to targeting specific issues at particular groups of voters. Not only had the Nazi Party built up a formidable election machinery, but it had also achieved financial solvency, through the contributions it levied on its membership, which by 1932 had passed the half-million mark. While the question of the extent to which big business gave donations to the Nazis has been extensively discussed, by far the greatest part of the party's finances came from membership dues and from small individual donations.

Popular support, as against manipulation

It has frequently been asserted that electoral support for the Nazi Party was falling by the end of 1932, and that there was no need for Hindenburg to bring Hitler into power. The conclusion has therefore been drawn that it was the scheming and intrigue of unscrupulous careerists and extreme right-wing sympathisers which was responsible for bringing Hitler to power.

As we have seen, the Nazis were polling a third of the vote in the Reichstag and regional elections held at the end of 1932, which in a multi-party system still gave them the largest number of deputies and a strong political position. It is possible that a prolonged period of inactivity might have seen the Party fragment, but Hitler was a skilled operator when it came to holding the Party together. As the leader of the largest Reichstag party he was able to exert considerable pressure both on von Papen and on his successor after the November elections, von Schleicher, to appoint him as Chancellor.

What political alternatives did Hindenburg and his advisers have? Von Papen and von Schleicher had virtually no popular support, and Hindenburg was reluctant to sanction a military coup to overthrow the Weimar Constitution, or to see the German army drawn into active politics to help in the formation of a military-style regime. As long as the Reichstag existed, it would oppose any attempt to establish an autocratic system, and a move to abolish the Reichstag might trigger off violent opposition and possibly civil war. It is perhaps not surprising that Hindenburg finally succumbed to the persuasion of his son and of many of his aristocratic and army friends, and agreed to the formation of a new government with Hitler as Chancellor, von Papen as vice-chancellor, and with only two other Nazis in the cabinet. Von Papen was convinced that such a move would result in Hitler being 'framed in'. He predicted in a letter to a friend that 'In two months' time we will have squeezed Hitler into a corner until he squeaks'.

It was not only on the Right that such illusions were held. Communists, divided from other parties on the Left by the memories of the betrayed revolution of 1918, confidently anticipated that Hitler's accession to power would hasten the collapse of capitalism and usher in a workers' revolution.

Hitler's rapid consolidation of power

It quickly became clear that it would not be Hitler who would be tamed but his Nationalist colleagues. He had agreed to become Chancellor only on condition that the Reichstag be dissolved and new elections held. To a small gathering of industrialists two weeks before election day on 5 March, Hitler and fellow Nazi leader Hermann Göring confided that this would be the last election 'for the next ten years, probably even for the next hundred years'. Hitler was already scheming to take over the powers of the newly-elected Reichstag, but meanwhile he wanted to use the elections to underline the strength of popular support for the Nazis.

The Reichstag fire

Two weeks before the elections, on 17 February, the Reichstag building was set on fire. There has been disagreement ever since about whether the Nazis plotted it, or whether the Dutch Communist found on the scene was genuinely working on his own. Whatever the truth of the matter, the fire enabled Hitler to claim that it was the signal for a communist uprising and that action needed to be taken as a matter of urgency to protect the country. Not only were large numbers of Communists arrested, but an emergency decree was introduced under which all political rights guaranteed under the Weimar Constitution were temporarily suspended. Though Hitler pledged that 'Once the Communist threat is removed, things will return to normal', the Emergency Decree remained in force until 1945.

The end of democracy

The elections were accompanied by widespread street violence and by strident Nazi propaganda. The Nazi share of the vote rose to 43.9 per cent. The Party now had 288 seats in the Reichstag and their Nationalist allies had a further 52, giving them a majority. Communist deputies were jailed. Two weeks after the election, Hitler attended a church service with Hindenburg to mark a Day of National Awakening. Two days later, through a mixture of intimidation of left-wing deputies and reassurance aimed at the Centre Party, the Reichstag passed an Enabling Act, giving to the Government the power to enact laws and decrees. As Noakes and Pridham noted in *Nazism, 1919–45*, 'It gave the destruction of parliamentary democracy the appearance of legality'. The Nazi Party newspaper analysis was more brutal:

> 'The will of the German people fulfilled: Parliament hands over power to Adolf Hitler. Passing of the Enabling Law with the overwhelming majority of 441 votes to 94 SPD votes ... Hitler's historic revenge on the men of November ... Capitulation of the parliamentary system to the new Germany.'

The whirlwind political revolution continued. The Nazi Party consolidated its position in the individual German states, and at the end of March appointed special Reich Governors from among senior local Nazis in the different localities, to rule them. The next targets of attack were trade unions and the SPD (see chapter 18). Their offices were broken into and ransacked by local Nazi thugs; officials and party members were beaten up. Soon the SDP was forcibly dissolved on the grounds that it was 'hostile to nation and state', and its leaders were taken into 'protective custody'. Trade unions were the next to go, and the Catholic Centre Party was also persuaded to dissolve its organisation. By 14 July, scarcely six months after Hitler's accession to power, the Nazi Party was declared to be the only legal political party in Germany and 'whoever undertakes to maintain the organisation of another political party shall be punished with penal servitude of up to three years or with imprisonment'. Nazi control of the press and radio was also tightened, as was their grip on all areas of German life. Only two separate bastions of power remained: the army and the powers of the President.

The 'Night of the Long Knives'

On 30 June 1934, in a move calculated to consolidate the support of the army for the new regime, Hitler launched a pre-emptive strike against members of the Nazi SA Brownshirts, under the leadership of Ernst Röhm. Hitler feared that Röhm was building up an independent political force and was provoking the hostility of the army. In what became known as the 'Night of the Long Knives', Röhm, other SA leaders and assorted suspected opponents of Hitler were murdered. The opportunity was taken to settle old scores – those killed included von Schleicher and

Strasser who had plotted together in late 1932 and the Bavarian State Commissioner who had thwarted the Hitler coup in 1923. Von Papen was placed under house arrest.

Just over a month later, Hindenburg died, and Hitler now proceeded to combine the office of Reich President with that of Chancellor. Henceforth those entering office as civil servants or joining the army had to swear an oath to 'Hitler, Führer of the German Reich and People'. In a plebiscite held on 19 August to approve the merging of the two offices, nearly 96 per cent of those eligible to vote went to the polls, and over 89 per cent approved of the change. Only four and a half million people disapproved, and there were 870,000 spoiled papers. Most crucially, the army gave its support to Hitler, underlining the fact that his authority was now supreme. In little over 18 months he had established a Nazi dictatorship.

The speed with which Hitler succeeded in carrying through his 'National Revolution' shows just how discredited the Weimar system of government had become. The Nazis unleashed terror on an escalating scale after January 1933, while at the same time voters supported Hitler in the hope that he would restore order and promote economic recovery. Whatever the reasons for the widespread support which Hitler received, there can be no doubt that the purposeful way in which he consolidated his power was an impressive achievement and a far cry from the outcome predicted by so many in January 1933.

Task

Read the following passages, along with the above chapter, and then answer the questions which follow:

1

'When the speech was over, there was roaring enthusiasm and applause . . . How many look up to him with touching faith! as their helper, their saviour, their deliverer from unbearable distress – to him who rescues the Prussian prince, the scholar, the clergyman, the farmer, the worker, the unemployed, who rescues them from the parties back into the nation.'

Account of an election meeting in 1932 addressed by Hitler, given by a Hamburg schoolteacher, Frau Solmitz.

2

'...the supporters of the National Socialists expected the destruction of the Marxist labour movement and the "party state"; they hoped for a rigid authoritarian regime, which would cease to tolerate class struggles and ideological conflict.'

Historian H. A. Winkler, writing in 1976.

3

'The nucleus of the NSDAP's following was formed by the small farmers, shopkeepers and independent artisans of the old middle class...It was among these groups that the fear of social and economic displacement associated with the emergence of modern industrial society was most pronounced...

'By 1932 the party had won considerable support among the upper-middle-class student bodies of the universities, among civil servants, even in the middle and upper grades and the affluent electoral districts of Berlin, Hamburg and other cities. Motivation was myriad, including fear of the Marxist Left, frustrated career ambitions, and resentment of the erosion of social prestige and security...they cannot be described as uneducated, economically devastated or socially marginal. They belonged, in fact, to the established elites of German society.'

T. Childers, *The Nazi Voter: The Social Foundations of Fascism in Germany, 1919–33* (1985).

a To what extent do the three passages support the Nazi contention that theirs was 'a national movement cutting across classes'?
b Compare and contrast the explanations offered in the three passages of why people voted for the Nazis between 1930 and 1932.
c On the basis of these three extracts and the material in the chapter, how far do you agree with the view that the Nazis were 'voted into power'?

Further reading

Noakes and Pridham, *Nazism 1919–45* vol. I, 'The Rise to Power' (University of Exeter, 1983) – indispensable collection of primary source material.

E. J. Feuchtwanger, *From Weimar to Hitler* (Macmillan, 1993) – recent detailed study of the final years of the Weimar Republic.

William Simpson, *Hitler and Germany* (Cambridge University Press, 1991).

Michael Kater, *The Nazi Party* (Basil Blackwell, 1983) – very detailed study of membership of Nazi Party from its origins in 1919.

William Sheridan Allen, *The Nazi Seizure of Power* (Penguin, 1989) – fascinating study of one German town.

18 Domestic policies in the Third Reich

Time chart

1933: **30 January** Hitler becomes Chancellor of Germany
1 April National boycott of Jewish shops and businesses
7 April Civil service law permits removal of Jews and other opponents
June Marriage Loan scheme is introduced for eligible racial applicants. Law to reduce unemployment is introduced
July Law for Prevention of Hereditarily Diseased Offspring is passed

1934: **September** Introduction of New Plan to control imports
October German Labour Front formed to replace trade unions

1935: **September** Nuremburg Laws prohibit marriage and sexual relations between Jews and German nationals

1936: **October** Four Year Plan announced

1938: **November** *Kristallnacht* as Jewish synagogues are burned down and Jews attacked and arrested across German

1939: Beginning of move to kill physically and mentally handicapped patients, which continues until 1941

More has been written about Hitler and about the Third Reich than about any other regime in history. The sheer volume of material and of argument about different aspects of Nazi Germany makes any study of the regime a daunting prospect. The aim of this chapter is therefore to guide you through the debates. To help you to identify the main issues we will be focusing on ten aspects of Nazi domestic policy:

- ideology
- the role of Hitler in the decision-making structure
- the extent to which the regime was based on force
- attempts to establish a *Volksgemeinschaft* ('People's Community')
- policies towards youth in the Third Reich
- the role of women
- efforts to promote racial purity

- persecution of Jews
- economic recovery
- opposition to the regime.

Ideology

Ideology is crucial. Nazi leaders had a set of beliefs and a number of strong convictions which shaped their actions and help to explain the policies they adopted once in power. Much debate has centred on *Mein Kampf*, written by Hitler during his stay in Landsberg prison. While A. J. P. Taylor dismissed it as being 'fantasies from behind bars' and therefore revealing little about Hitler's later intentions, other historians have seen it as a 'blueprint' for future aggression. A German historian, Eberhard Jäckel, has commented recently, 'Perhaps never in history did a ruler write down before he came to power what he was to do afterwards as precisely as did Adolf Hitler'. However another historian has argued that though *Mein Kampf* constitutes a 'major source for the study of Hitler', the importance of which should not be dismissed out of hand, at the same time it should not be interpreted literally as governing all Hitler's actions after 1933.

Hitler himself subsequently said of *Mein Kampf* that 'there is nothing in it I would wish to change'. There is no doubt that many of the ideas which influenced his later policies are to be found emphasised over and over again in its rambling pages. At the same time, nearly 10 years elapsed between the writing of the book and the opportunity to put some of it into action. The international situation changed in that time, and so did Germany's domestic environment. Hitler, as we saw in the last chapter, was prepared to shape his tactics to meet the prevailing situation, while holding fast to a number of deeply-held convictions. Those convictions found expression not only in *Mein Kampf* but also in his speeches, in election handouts and in the conversations he held with a variety of people. They constitute the core of Nazi ideology.

The establishment of a new national community

Hitler believed very strongly that the German nation had fallen into decline after 1918, and his first aim was to bring about a national regeneration and recreate a *Volksgemeinschaft* or people's community. Divisions of class, religion and region had weakened the German people; it was the Nazi Party's task to bridge them by inspiring in people a new, greater loyalty to the German nation and to its leader. Many Nazi supporters described this rebirth of the German people in almost mystical terms; one wrote in 1933:

> *'Our age is once more acquiring creative momentum, it is gaining depth, direction and future. The creative dynamic, the basic quality of the Germanic-Western cultural soul is awakening in the dawn of its fourth day of creation in a new type of human being . . .'*

The notion of struggle

Hitler and his fellow Nazis viewed the world as a brutal place, where people had to struggle incessantly for food, for shelter and for space. As Hitler wrote in 1928, 'It is not by the principles of humanity that man lives or is able to preserve himself above the animal world, but solely by means of the most brutal struggle'. Individuals and nations had to be prepared for this struggle; if they were not strong and prepared to fight, then they would lose out to those who were. Victory in one contest led inexorably to another battle, for as Hitler pointed out in his *Second Book* (written in 1928 but not published), 'Wherever our success may end, that will always be only the starting-point of a new fight'. Success was to be achieved by a set of domestic policies aimed at 'securing for a nation the strength, in the shape of racial quality and numbers, necessary to secure living space'.

The importance of racial purity

The quest to improve Germany's racial quality lay at the heart of Hitler's policies. He was totally convinced of the correlation between the strength of a race and its blood purity. If Germany was to be prepared to accept its destiny as the world's dominant power, the racial stock of its people had to be improved and purified. Joseph Göbbels, the party's propaganda chief, expressed this belief in 1928 when he said, 'We must have a healthy people to prevail in the world'. A year later, Hitler declared that 'if Germany was to get an increase of a million children a year and remove 7,000 to 8,000 of its weakest people, the final result might even be an increase in strength'.

As a young man, Hitler had been attracted to the notion of a hierarchy of races, with the Aryan or German people as the most creative race fighting for supremacy against lesser races such as Latins and Slavs. Below these were the yellow races and, lower still, Negroes. He grew more and more convinced that other races were conspiring to undermine the Aryan race through inter-marriage or by persuading them not to procreate. He saw it as one of his most important tasks to prevent further racial decline.

The quest for racial purity had its positive and negative aspects. On the one hand, healthy Aryans had to be persuaded to marry racially suitable partners and to produce large numbers of children. It vexed Hitler that people were prepared to take enormous pains with the breeding of live-stock, yet were not prepared to apply the same principles of careful selection to the far more important matter of racial breeding of humans. On the other hand, those deemed racially unfit had to be prevented from passing their infirmities on to another generation. Already in 1925 an internal Nazi Party memorandum outlined what sort of fate might lie in store for them:

> 'No pity is to be shown to those who occupy the lower categories of the inferior groups: cripples, epileptics, the blind, the insane, deaf and dumb, children born in sanatoria for alcoholics or in care, . . . criminals, whores, the sexually disturbed, etc. Everything done for them not only means taking resources away from more deserving causes, but counteracts the breeding selection process. Nor should we mourn the dumb, the weak, the spineless, the apathetic, those with hereditary diseases, the pathological . . . Trees which do not bear fruit should be cut down and thrown into the fire.'

KEY TERM:

Euthanasia

Putting people to death relatively painlessly, usually to prevent further suffering.

Hitler and his party colleagues were well aware that such policies would run counter to the strong religious beliefs of many Germans, but his belief that the racial stock of the German people must be strengthened led him to introduce a whole range of measures, including compulsory sterilisation and **euthanasia**, to achieve this objective.

The Jew: the eternal enemy

Sometime in his early life Hitler became a virulent anti-semite. His hatred of the Jews became stronger with every passing day and remained with him for the rest of his life. The day before he committed suicide in his Berlin bunker he pledged his successors to observe 'the scrupulous observation of the racial laws and . . . an implacable opposition against the universal poisoner of all peoples, international Jewry'. Hitler saw the Jews as constituting not a religious group but a scheming and unscrupulous race, whose members sought to weaken superior races by defiling and polluting their blood. He believed that he had a divine mission to combat the Jewish menace, claiming on more than one occasion that 'By warding off the Jew, I am fighting for the Lord's work'. He argued that 'Jewish activity produces a racial tuberculosis among nations', and that there was a Jewish virus in existence which it was his quest to eliminate. In 1942 he told colleagues that his discovery of the Jewish virus was 'one of the greatest revolutions in the world. The battle in which we are engaged today is of the same sort as the battle waged during the last century by Pasteur. How many diseases have their origin in the Jewish virus? We shall regain our health only by eliminating the Jew.' Hitler was apparently of the view that this work was of such scientific importance that he should be awarded a Nobel prize.

Hitler's ideological beliefs developed over time, and he had no pre-arranged idea of how he would put them into practice. But they lay at the heart of his plans for the development of Germany after 1933, and gave coherence to the process of decision-making in Nazi Germany. Party bosses and functionaries frequently asserted after 1933 that they were 'working towards the Führer', meaning that they were putting into practice some of his cherished notions. A set of ideological beliefs based on race shaped the domestic and foreign policies of the Third Reich and ran like a connecting thread through its rather chaotic political structures.

Hitler's role in the decision-making structure

By the middle of 1934 Hitler had completed a swift and hugely successful political revolution which swept away constitutional freedoms, political parties, trade unions and other independent bodies. A one-party state was established with himself as the unchallenged leader, or Führer. However, historians have disagreed on the extent to which in practice he operated as a dictator or authorised all the major policy decisions.

We know that Hitler hated routine work or reading documents. He refused to study official files or work to a set pattern, and while sometimes he came to rapid decisions, at other times he agonised for months. As Alan Bullock wrote in *Hitler, a Study in Tyranny*:

> 'Ministerial skill in the Third Reich consisted in making the most of a favourable hour or minute when Hitler made a decision, this often taking the form of a remark thrown out casually, which then went its way as an "Order of the Führer".'

Did Hitler's unorthodox approach to decision-making reduce his influence in the policy-making process? The German historian Hans Mommsen has described Hitler as 'unwilling to take decisions, frequently uncertain, exclusively concerned with upholding his prestige and personal authority, influenced in the strongest fashion by his current entourage, in some respects a weak dictator'. Others have claimed that the Third Reich suffered from 'leadership chaos' and that Hitler was responsible for bringing about 'the biggest confusion in government that has ever existed in a civilised state'. Some historians have described Nazi Germany as a 'polycratic' state in which Hitler's authority was only one ingredient, though an important one, in a complex structure of government. Analyses have focused on the existence of power blocs after 1933, such as Göring's Four Year Plan organisation, Himmler's SS empire and the different armed services, all competing for resources and for influence with Hitler. Some have argued that while Hitler presided over this structure, he operated as an umpire rather than as a leader, sanctioning policies rather than instigating them. Others claim that this was a political tactic which he deliberately employed in order to 'divide and rule' over his Nazi colleagues.

On the other hand, some historians are adamant that Hitler remained the undisputed leader who was the prime mover in the formulation of both domestic and foreign policy. They argue that no important policy decision could be implemented without his agreement. While there is general agreement that this is true in foreign policy, where he was 'the prime mover who made the critical decisions', there remains disagreement about the extent of its validity as far as domestic policies are concerned. A state official in 1934 gave his explanation of how the system worked:

> *'Everyone who has the opportunity to observe it knows that the Führer can hardly dictate from above everything which he intends to realise sooner or later ... Very often and in many spheres it has been the case ... that individuals have simply waited for orders and instructions ... in fact it is the duty of everybody to try to work towards the Führer along the lines he would wish. Anyone who makes mistakes will notice it soon enough ...'*

Hitler's authority was in theory absolute, but in practice he was happy to let his subordinates and state officials carry out his policies in a variety of ways, provided that they did not cut across his major strategic objectives or undermine the achievement of policy goals by incessant squabbling among themselves. Alliances were forged within the Nazi Party, and with other groups such as industrialists, financiers and the army who all made an input into the decision-making process. Policies were carried out by a range of agencies and individuals including Party functionaries, civil servants and favoured supporters such as Albert Speer. But the stamp of Hitler's overall authority was clearly on them. While Hitler frequently

KEY TERM:

Gestapo

A political police force developed by Heinrich Himmler after 1933. The **Gestapo** was used widely to control and to suppress opposition to Nazi rule and to enforce Nazi ideology.

stood aloof from detail, he could never be ignored. The power at his disposal was too strong.

To what extent was the regime based on force?

Already in the 1920s the Nazi Party had built up its armed bodyguard (the SS) and its paramilitary forces (the SA). The employment of violence and terror against targeted enemies was an integral part of its political tactics; after 1933 these were built into the structure of the Third Reich. In addition to local police forces, the SS and the SA meted out their own 'punishments', and the **Gestapo** was established to combat the regime's political opponents. Within two months of Hitler's accession to power, the Party's newspaper revealed that:

> 'the first concentration camp will be opened to accommodate 5,000 prisoners. Here, all Communist, and where necessary 'Reichsbanner' and Social Democrat functionaries who endanger state security, will be interned together as their continued stay in state prisons has proved too great a burden. Experience has shown that these people cannot be granted their freedom as they continue to agitate and create unrest when released ...'

Within a short time, many more official and 'wild' or unofficial camps had appeared, ready to deal with real or alleged threats to the security of the regime. German people remained in no doubt about what fate awaited them if they opposed the regime in any way. Existing civil law was now subordinated to the *Führerprinzip* or authority of the Führer, and from this there was no legal redress.

Although fear was an ever-present factor encouraging conformity from above, historians are increasingly drawing our attention to social processes at work within Nazi Germany which encouraged conformity from below. Enthusiastic Nazi supporters in local communities, in schools and in the workplace took the lead in showing the Nazi salute, displaying the Nazi flag and proclaiming 'Heil Hitler'. Not to follow suit was to invite suspicion, to suggest opposition to the regime and to express dissent. Most people were unwilling to expose themselves in this way, as they valued the local community and the social bonds it created. Thus they followed the lead of their Nazi neighbours and acquaintances, who, by exercising such strong social pressures, were able to achieve considerable success in mobilising wide support for the regime, at least outwardly.

The regime exploited such social processes by recruiting spies to report on the behaviour and conversations of neighbours in residences and at work. Children were encouraged by their teachers to report back on anything said by their parents which could imply hostility to the regime. The Gestapo were on hand to mete out punishment if required, which they did forcefully and sometimes indiscriminately.

Fear of the activities of the Gestapo undoubtedly ensured compliance with the policies of the regime. Yet the Gestapo remained a relatively small organisation – numbering around 30,000 out of a population of over 60 million Germans. Surviving Gestapo records indicate that a high proportion of evidence on which their agents acted came in an unsolicited way from ordinary German citizens. No fewer than 85 per cent of cases brought by the Gestapo on charges of slandering the regime were initiated as a result of denunciations made voluntarily by members of the public against their neighbours, former friends, lovers or fellow workers. In the case of transgressions against the regime's racial laws after 1935, half of the cases brought in the districts studied resulted from voluntary denunciations. Arguably, the German people were policing themselves, and handing over to the authorities any individuals who they suspected were not obeying Nazi laws. It is abundantly clear that, as well as relying on force, the Nazi regime was able to appeal to the worst side of human nature to assist it in the enforcement of order and conformity.

On the more positive side, a range of different sources from the 1930s all agree that Hitler enjoyed substantial public support from the German people. While other Nazi leaders and local party bosses were often disliked, Hitler himself was admired for his efforts in promoting an economic recovery and improving Germany's position in Europe. Party propaganda capitalised on Hitler's undoubted appeal as a charismatic leader; the strength of this image was clearly another factor in ensuring continuing support for, and compliance with, the regime.

Attempts to create a *Volksgemeinschaft*

The aim of the Nazi regime was to restructure German society in such a way that ties of class, religion and region were replaced by a new consciousness of belonging to one tightly-knit 'People's Community'. The concept was based to some extent on an idealised past society, in which individuals subordinated their individual interests to the collective good. Nazi propaganda was directed at promoting the new Germany with slogans such as *'Ein Reich, ein Volk, ein Führer'* ('One country, one people, one leader').

Various policies were implemented to strengthen people's consciousness of a new national community. Voluntary welfare schemes were promoted, such as the 'Winter help' programme – through which more affluent families collected money, food and clothing for those who had suffered as a result of mass unemployment. There was also the 'One-Pot Meal', to be eaten by families once a week, with the money saved from more elaborate dishes being donated to collectors who passed it on to the Reich. Propaganda posters referred to it as 'the meal of sacrifice for the Reich', and urged people to increase their donations as a mark of their gratitude to Hitler.

In the place of the disbanded trade unions, a new German Labour Front was set up. Within each factory, the Weimar factory committees were replaced by 'plant communities' in which workers and bosses could discuss the running of the workplace and how duties were to be allocated. Inevitably, the new structures restored authority to employers and restricted the powers of employees. However, to emphasise its concern for the welfare of the country's workforce, the regime established organisations such as 'The Beauty of Labour' to improve working conditions, and the 'Strength Through Joy' movement. This developed a range of social and sporting facilities for workers and their families, and began to pioneer cheap holiday packages both within Germany and further afield. However resentful workers might feel at the loss of their bargaining powers and at the level of their wages, evidence shows that they greatly appreciated the increase in holiday provision and the other benefits of 'Strength Through Joy'. A further initiative to emphasise how important workers were to the state was the development of the *Volkswagen* ('people's car') in the later 1930s. People were encouraged to put by a part of their wages every week to save up for a Volkswagen car. Though few actually managed to afford one, the message was clear that cars were not just for the rich but were to be available to all families. The regime also ensured that cheap radios were available in the shops. By the late 1930s Germany had one of the highest levels of private radio ownership in the world – which of course then enabled the regime to broadcast Hitler's speeches and Nazi propaganda to most homes in Germany.

While the regime was not able to eradicate deep-seated class and religious loyalties, tenaciously held particularly by older people, by many workers and Catholics, it did nonetheless win widespread support for its attempts to establish a new national community, or *Volksgemeinschaft*. This played an important part in promoting social conformity and in winning acceptance for the regime across all classes, regions and religious groups.

Policies towards youth in the Third Reich

Young people were a crucial target for the new regime. The Nazis declared in 1936 that 'the future of the German nation depends upon its youth and German youth must therefore be prepared for its future duties'. An inkling of what these duties might entail was given in a speech by Hitler the previous year to the annual Nazi Party rally at Nuremburg:

> *'What we look for from our German youth is different from what people wanted in the past. In our eyes the German youth of the future must be slim and slender, swift as the greyhound, tough as leather, and hard as Krupp's steel.'*

In the struggles which lay ahead for the German people, youth had to be prepared to play its part in fighting for German supremacy. The appropriate skills and values were to be inculcated into young people both at school and through the Hitler Youth Movement. In schools, the curricula were changed to achieve a balance between academic instruction and physical training. At least one hour a day was to be set aside for 'manly' sports like boxing which developed a 'spirit of aggression', required lightning decisions and trained the body in 'steely dexterity'. Through sports and gymnastics, boys would be prepared for military service, while girls were schooled for their role as 'a valuable link in the chain of reproduction'.

The aim of schools, according to the Minister of the Interior, Wilhelm Frick, was to 'form politically-conscious people who sacrifice and serve with every thought and deed, who are rooted in their nation, and who are totally and indivisibly anchored to the history and destiny of its state'. New areas of study were therefore introduced into the classroom, such as racial sciences. One school reported that under this subject it covered 'the concept of race, the origins of races, the European races' and 'the physical characteristics and origins of the different races in the German racial mixture'. Another gave details of how it had introduced 'cranial measuring' to help to identify racial origins. Old subjects were taught in a new way, to emphasise the importance of racial quality. For example, in elementary schools children had to calculate the following in mathematics:

> *'If a lunatic asylum cost 6 million Reichsmarks to build, and a worker's apartment on average cost 6,000 marks, how many families could be housed for the money devoted to the mentally unfit?'*

Other sums echoed the same themes; on the assumption that hereditarily unfit families had more children than healthy ones, pupils had to work out what proportions of the whole people would be unfit in 100 years or 200 years. The workbooks had suitable illustrations to reinforce the racial message (see Figure 18.1).

Alongside mathematics, Volkish poetry was studied, and English was also

Figure 18.1 *Illustration from a book,* Nation in Danger, *showing the 'menace of the subhumans'. The message is that 'criminals' were outbreeding both the classical 2.2-child 'German' family and professional couples, who tended to produce even fewer children.*

taught because it was a language of people 'racially related to us'. The study of history inevitably focused on war and on past displays of German heroism. A student later recalled:

> 'A large part of our compulsory reading in German lessons was world war literature ... these were books like Seven at Verdun ... in which, among all the horrors of modern warfare, the comradeship of the front was still triumphant and if you died you were at least awarded the Iron Cross.'

How effective all this was in inculcating new values into German youth is difficult to measure. It clearly struck a chord with many, yet others appear to have been less influenced. One man later claimed that:

> 'No one in our class ever read Mein Kampf. I myself had only used the book for quotations. In general we didn't know much about National Socialist ideology. Even anti-Semitism was taught rather marginally at school ... Nevertheless we were politically programmed: programmed to obey orders, to cultivate the soldierly "virtue" of standing to attention and saying "Yes, Sir" ...'

The schools' efforts were reinforced by activities in the Hitler Youth Movement, which expanded greatly after 1933. Whereas in the 1920s, millions of young Germans had been members of religious, political or sporting groups, they were now to be brought into one national organisation, which aimed to educate them 'physically, intellectually and morally in the spirit of National Socialism to serve the nation and the community'. There was to be an impressive admission ceremony, during which the new recruit had to swear an oath of loyalty to the Führer and was then proclaimed a 'bearer of German spirit and German honour'. While membership did not become compulsory until the late 1930s, large numbers of young people became enthusiastic members, competing in local groups to record the best sporting performance, to compile the 'most interesting travel album' or 'top collection for the Winter Relief Fund'.

An historian visiting a Catholic area of southern Germany in 1937 wrote of 'children whose Roman Catholic parents tried to keep them in the few struggling Church societies that still exist ... In every case the children wanted to join the *Hitler Jugend* [Hitler Youth]. To be outside Hitler's organisation was the worst form of punishment.' The Hitler Youth Movement was indeed very popular with both boys and girls. One youth

Figure 18.2 *Hitler Youth leaping over a camp-fire, described as 'a test of the courage of every proper youth'*

leader later recalled, 'What I liked about the Hitler Youth was the comradeship. I was full of enthusiasm when I joined . . . at the age of ten. What boy isn't fired by being presented with high ideals such as comradeship, loyalty and honour?' He fondly recounted the cub mottoes, the trips away, and evenings spent around the camp-fire (see Figure 18.2). Even the hostile SPD noted in 1934 that:

> '*Youth is still in favour of the system: the novelty, the drill, the uniform, the camp life, the fact that school and the parental home take a back seat compared to the community of young people – all that is marvellous . . . the parents experience all this too. One cannot forbid a child to do what all children are doing, cannot refuse him the uniform which the others have. One cannot ban it, that would be dangerous.*'

What was worse, from an SPD viewpoint, was that 'The children and young people then follow the instructions of the Hitler Youth and demand from their parents that they become good Nazis, that they give up Marxism, reaction and dealings with Jews'.

These youth movements opened up horizons for a whole generation, giving them opportunities to travel away at weekends, to escape from parental supervision and to participate in building a new society. At the same time, there were dissidents, those who later recalled that they had

> 'oppressive memories . . . of stolid military drill . . . endless marching . . . commands which I can still reel off in my sleep. From childhood onwards we were drilled in toughness and blind obedience. At the command "down", we had to throw ourselves with bare knees onto the gravel; when we were doing press-ups our noses were pushed into the sand.'

Not all young people were happy to undergo such experiences in preparation for the future; many found them brutalising and oppressive. There were distinct signs that as the Hitler Youth became compulsory, increasing numbers became alienated by its incessant regimentation and excessive emphasis on duty and loyalty to the Führer and to Germany.

KEY TERM:

Edelweiss

A small, white Alpine plant which was adopted as an emblem by dissident youth groups in Nazi Germany.

By the late 1930s, two distinct groups of dissidents had emerged: local 'pirate' groups in urban centres, and 'swing' groups who patronised dance halls. The local 'pirate' groups sprang up spontaneously in the late 1930s in cities in western Germany, and consisted of groups of 14–18 year olds sporting their own **edelweiss** badges and distinctive style of dress. German youth leaders acknowledged just after the start of the Second World War that 'the formation of cliques, *i.e.* groupings of young people outside the Hitler Youth, was on the increase a few years before the war, and has particularly increased . . . to such a degree that a serious risk of the political, moral and criminal breakdown of youth must be said to exist'.

A party official demanded that the police 'ensure this riff-raff is dealt with . . . The Hitler Youth are taking their lives in their hands when they go out on the streets.' A party branch complained in 1943 that:

> 'These youngsters, aged between 12 and 17, hang around into the late evening, with musical instruments and young females. Since this riff-raff is to a large extent outside the Hitler Youth and adopts a hostile attitude towards the organisation, they represent a danger to other young people . . . There is a suspicion that it is these youths who have been inscribing the walls of the pedestrian subway . . . with the slogans "Down with Hitler" . . . "Down with Nazi brutality". However often these inscriptions are removed, within a few days new ones appear on the walls again.'

The regime tried to deal with the ringleaders of such gangs by detaining them in custody or sending them to concentration camps. Some were publicly hanged. The police were successful in breaking up a number of 'pirate groups', but what they could not do was to eradicate an entire youth subculture which clearly existed by the early stages of the war, and which was increasingly sceptical of the norms of the regime and of its social values.

Members of the 'swing' movement were less of a threat in some ways. Rather than hanging about street corners and beating up members of the Hitler Youth, their passion was music, in particular US swing music. They were not directly opposed to the regime, yet the fact that they danced to 'Negro' music and indulged in unmistakable signs of decadent behaviour was a cause of enormous concern to the authorities. A report of a Hamburg 'swing' festival in 1940 attended by hundreds of young people deplored the fact that:

> 'The dance music was all English and American. Only swing dancing and jitterbugging took place . . . The dancers were an appalling sight. None of the couples danced normally . . . Sometimes two boys danced with one girl; sometimes several couples formed a circle, linking arms and jumping, slapping hands, even rubbing the backs of their heads together; and then, bent double, with the top half of the body hanging loosely down, long hair flopping in the face, they dragged themselves round practically on their knees. When the band played a rumba, the dancers went into wild ecstasy . . . Several boys could be observed dancing together, always with two cigarettes in the mouth, one in each corner.'

Far from being young, fresh-faced soldiers of the Reich, these young people revelled in hair 'grown down to the collar', and in the 'sleazy life'. One friend reminded another: 'make sure you're really casual, swinging or whistling English hits all the time, absolutely smashed and always surrounded by really amazing women'. No wonder the authorities were worried!

Yet as the 1930s went on and as the Hitler Youth became compulsory and increasingly regimented, many young people tried to opt out and develop their own form of youth culture. Many people found swing music more appealing than Nazi speeches or military drill. But for a regime which was intent on building a new society on the foundations of a committed, indoctrinated youth, any signs of deviation or of dissent were alarming. Millions of young men remained true to their Hitler Youth oaths and proved their fitness and valour in German armies all over Europe. But as we have seen, there were also many who were prepared to die rather than to submit themselves to the officially prescribed youth activities.

The role of women

Women were important to the Nazi state because of their crucial role as wives and as bearers of the next generation of healthy Germans. As Hitler emphasised in 1933, 'in my state the mother is the most important citizen'. While Nazi leaders took great pains to stress that women were not inferior to men, merely different and possessing their own natural concerns, they were definitely not fitted to take any part in politics. No woman held high office in the Nazi Party, except through the party's women's organisations, and none of the party's Reichstag delegates were women. While women had enjoyed considerable political emancipation under the Weimar regime, and had enjoyed growing educational opportunities, the Nazis aimed to reverse these processes. In 1934 Hitler declared that:

> 'The slogan "Emancipation of Women" was invented by Jewish intellectuals and its content was formed by the same spirit. In the really good times of German life the German woman had no need to emancipate herself. She possessed exactly what nature had necessarily given her to administer and preserve ... her world is her husband, her family, her children and her home ... We do not consider it correct for the woman to interfere in the world of the man ... To the one belongs the strength of feeling, the strength of the soul. To the other belongs the strength of vision, of toughness, of decision and of the willingness to act.'

A woman's duty was to marry and to bring up children. To that end the regime developed initiatives to encourage its female population. Abortions were prohibited and steps taken to restrict access to contraceptives. Financial inducements were offered in the shape of larger maternity benefits and the doubling of income tax allowances for dependent children. Generous marriage loans were introduced for couples with appropriate Aryan racial characteristics, if wives agreed to stop working after marriage. The birth of each successive child reduced the loan. However, Germany's birth rate, though it did increase after 1933, remained obstinately lower than it had been in the early 1920s. Average family size, 2.3 in the 1920s, was only 1.8 in the late 1930s. So a gold Mother's Cross was introduced in May 1939 for those with eight children, a silver cross for six and a bronze cross for four. The Hitler Youth was instructed to salute such paragons of virtue as they passed them in the streets.

Despite the best efforts of the regime, their aim to step up the birth rate failed significantly. The effect of other policies, such as promoting economic recovery and rapid rearmament, brought about a growing labour shortage which had the effect of bringing more and more women into industrial employment. Ironically, more women were working in Nazi Germany in 1939 than in 1933. But what was progressively denied to them was access to higher education and to the professions. While the regime could not turn the clock back totally, and young women managed to enjoy increasing amounts of freedom, they could only aspire to a limited role in the Third Reich. They could play no active part in national politics and every effort was made to make them feel inadequate if they were not constantly producing children. Only in one area was there a change: unmarried women were no longer stigmatised for bearing illegitimate children. As long as the children were healthy and of Aryan stock, they and their mothers were treated in exactly the same way as other more conventional families.

Efforts to promote racial purity

A key element in Nazi policy was the desire to promote Aryan supremacy and racial purity. Under the Marriage Loans scheme of June 1933, couples were disqualified from receiving a loan if 'one of the two spouses suffers from hereditary mental or physical ailments'. Increasingly, welfare benefits were only paid to 'racially fit' people. A network of local doctors, welfare officers and clergy was employed to question applicants and to ascertain fitness. After July 1933, under the Law for the Prevention of Hereditarily Diseased Offspring:

'Anyone who has a hereditary illness can be rendered sterile by a surgical operation if ... there is a strong probability that his/her offspring will suffer from serious hereditary defects ... Anyone is hereditarily ill ... who suffers from ... a) congenital feeblemindedness, b) schizophrenia, c) manic depression, d) hereditary epilepsy, e) Huntingdon's chorea, f) hereditary blindness, g) hereditary deafness, h) serious physical deformities. In addition, anyone who suffers from chronic alcoholism can be sterilised.'

The following year, the legislation was extended. Hitler specified that 'pregnancies could be terminated in the case of hereditarily ill women or women who had become pregnant by a hereditary ill partner'. Such practices brought anguish and suffering to large numbers of young women, who, for example, protested bitterly at being labelled 'feebleminded' because they had failed exams at school. Between 1934 and 1945, around 350,000 women were compulsorily sterilised or had their pregnancies terminated on racial grounds. In addition, under the Law against Dangerous Habitual Criminals, passed in late 1933, certain types of criminal, as defined by racial and biological investigation, could be detained in custody and compulsorily castrated.

Measures were extended to deal not just with criminals but with the 'workshy and the asocial'. From 1937, the streets of major German cities were to be cleared of 'persons who through minor, but repeated, infractions of the law demonstrate that they will not adapt themselves to the natural discipline of the National Socialist state, *e.g.* beggars, tramps, whores, alcoholics with contagious diseases, particularly sexually-transmitted diseases . . .'. Such undesirables were not only a menace to law and order, they also weakened Germany's racial stock. Thousands were rounded up and sent into detention or concentration camps, where their ways could be mended or they could be disposed of.

By 1940 'hereditary health guidelines' specifically excluded 'asocial persons' who 'continually come into conflict with the law, the police or the authorities' or are 'workshy and who perpetually try to burden public or private charitable foundations'. Also excluded were 'drunks' and those who were 'conspicuously dissolute in their way of life' and the 'particularly unproductive and unrestrained and who in the absence of a sense of responsibility do not conduct orderly domestic lives or raise their children to be useful racial comrades'. Such people, along with gypsies, were the target of increasing persecution, and many of them died in custody or in camps.

Homosexuals were a particular concern to the Nazis, because they were failing in their biological responsibilities to the Aryan race. They were subjected to persecution and to imprisonment if convicted, and many ended up in concentration camps. The nature of their 'offence' was spelled out by Nazi leader Himmler to an SS Officers' conference in 1937, when he pointed to the fact that Germany had lost 2 million men in the First World War and there were approximately 2 million homosexuals in Germany. Germany's 'sexual balance sheet' would therefore remain in deficit unless all men produced children, and this was a matter of life or death for the nation which overrode sexual preferences. As a result of this line of reasoning, some homosexuals were forced to undergo hormone implant operations.

Not until the late 1930s did the regime begin to remove from Germany the physically and mentally unfit. Hitler was well aware that what was deemed to be 'mercy killing' would arouse opposition particularly in religious circles. On the other hand, many thousands of people suffering from incurable illnesses and from physical and mental defects were using facilities and occupying beds in hospitals which might soon be required by German soldiers. Under cover of secrecy, therefore, the government selected a number of asylums which were to be prepared for 'mercy killing', and patients were rounded up and despatched to them in van-loads. Between 1939 and 1941, about 72,000 people were killed by monoxide gassing in six asylums. Despite attempts to conceal what was going on, relatives and friends became suspicious when patients allegedly died of appendicitis, having had their appendices removed years before, or hairpins turned up in the ashes of males. Soon the euthanasia programme became an open secret, and was vehemently and publicly attacked in a sermon in 1941 by the Catholic Archbishop of Munster, von Galen. Other clerics followed suit, and copies of von Galen's sermon were widely distributed. It has not been established how effective such protests were in ending the programme, but in August 1941 planned 'mercy killing' stopped. However, in the course of the Second World War those in charge of the mentally and physically disabled were encouraged to starve them to death or bring their lives to an end by injections.

The regime clearly had some success in its attempts to 'purify' the German race. Opposition to most of its policies was sporadic. It was only the euthanasia programme which caused a major outcry. German doctors, nurses and welfare assistants helped to identify the racially impure and unfit, and large numbers of Germans supported the campaigns to remove the workshy and asocial elements from the streets. In the relatively short period of time that the Nazis were in power, they made a determined effort to establish a strong racial state. The kinds of policies they introduced leave no room for doubt that they saw as one of their fundamental tasks the goal of increasing the purity of the German race, and that they went at least some way towards achieving it.

Persecution of the Jews

No area of Nazi policy has been the subject of more debate than the persecution of the Jews. In the light of the wartime murder of 6 million innocent victims in concentration camps throughout central and eastern Europe during the Second World War, historians are divided on the extent to which this **'holocaust'** was the logical and inevitable result of Nazi ideology. This section looks only at policies towards the Jews up to 1939. In this period the regime was mainly concerned to segregate its 500,000 Jews from the German population as a whole, and if possible to drive them out of Germany. While complete extermination may well have been a more distant goal, it was not one that Hitler believed to be

KEY TERM:

Holocaust

The name given to the programme in which 6 million European Jews were killed by the Nazis and their agents from 1941 to 1945.

practicable immediately; moreover, given his unshakeable beliefs about the importance of racial purity, he was happy in the short term to see the Jews take up residence outside Germany, thereby undermining the racial and military strength of Germany's opponents. Clearly, as the German state expanded through a series of successful struggles, Jews would be among the populations annexed, and would no doubt meet their fate at that stage. As Hitler warned in the 1930s, 'Even when we have chased the Jew from Germany, he will still remain our global enemy'.

There is no evidence that Hitler, in 1933, had a clearly worked out strategy for dealing with the Jews, though his fear and hatred of them was well-documented. Anti-Semitism had been a recurring theme in Nazi election propaganda for many years before 1933. Soon after Hitler's accession to power, Jewish stores were ransacked, Jewish judges barred from presiding over courts, and Jews who were prominent in left-wing politics were taken to 'wild' concentration camps (nearly 100 in Berlin alone) and were beaten up, tortured and sometimes murdered. Nazi teachers in schools took the lead in segregating Jewish children from other pupils, and party members all over Germany targeted Jewish businesses for attack. On 1 April 1933, to try to focus the anti-semitic activity, the Nazi leadership organised a boycott of Jewish shops and local Nazis tried to prevent non-Jewish customers from patronising them by displaying prominent posters and standing menacingly outside. The boycott was not a great success, but was quickly followed up by a Law for the Restoration of the Professional Civil Service, under which civil servants, judges and teachers who were Jewish had to retire from office unless they could demonstrate their patriotism by service in the First World War (this provision being a concession to President Hindenburg). Gradually, Jews were removed from all professions and were increasingly ostracised by former friends and acquaintances. One Jewish girl later recalled the shock she experienced in 1933 when 'people whom one regarded as friends, who were known for a long time, from one hour to the next transformed themselves'.

There were ritual burnings of so-called 'Jewish books' (see Figure 18.3) including those of Marx, Einstein and Freud. Individual Jews were the target of random violence throughout Germany. In 1935 the regime moved to eliminate the 'Jewish threat' at a racial level by forbidding sexual relations or marriage between Jews and Aryans under the Law for the Protection of German Blood and Honour. The Reich Citizenship law of 1935 decreed that Jews were not German citizens and could not therefore enjoy equal civil rights. German people were encouraged to denounce to the Gestapo those who persisted in the crimes of 'race defilement' (having sexual relations with Jews) or being a 'slave to the Jews' (showing friendship towards them).

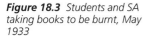

Figure 18.3 Students and SA taking books to be burnt, May 1933

From this point onwards, Hitler declared that the Jews should be removed from all professions and restricted to live in **ghettoes**, where they could wander about, in accordance with their character, 'while the German people looks on, as one looks at animals in the wild'. Many Jews took steps to leave the country, but this was by no means a simple matter. It became increasingly difficult to sell houses and businesses for a fair price. In any event, the regime did not allow them to take their money out with them. Many European countries were not enthusiastic to take in impoverished Jews, and insisted that acquaintances or relatives should find them jobs first before they could enter. Palestine was a possible destination, but the British authorities there were anxious not to upset the Arabs by sanctioning a great increase in immigration. Many older

KEY TERM:

Ghettoes

Areas of cities, often run-down and over-crowded, where Jews were made to live.

307

Jews could not believe that the discrimination against them would last. They hoped that if they stayed put and said nothing, the storm would blow over. Most paid with their lives for this tragic misjudgement.

While 120,000 Jews did escape from Germany by 1937, the *Anschluss* with Austria brought in nearly 200,000. Of the more than 50,000 Jewish businesses operating in 1933, 39,000 were still functioning in 1938. But at this point, the regime stepped up its persecution of the Jews. They were forced to sell up in a process of 'Aryanisation' which saw about 80 per cent of remaining Jewish businesses transferred at knockdown prices to German buyers. As all means of livelihood were removed, Jews were increasingly herded together in their own communities, and forced to live off whatever means they could find. Further humiliations were heaped on them: they could not sit on certain park benches, swim in public baths or go to the theatre and the cinema.

In the biggest single outburst of organised violence against them, in November 1938, 7,000 Jewish businesses were ransacked in one night, and nearly every remaining synagogue was burned down. *Kristallnacht* ('Night of broken glass') was the revenge of the regime on the hated Jews after a young Polish Jew had shot dead a minor German Embassy official in Paris in protest at the mistreatment of his parents. Twenty-six thousand Jews were rounded up and sent to concentration camps where they were tortured and terrorised for weeks to persuade them to leave Germany. Those who remained had a 'J' stamped in their passports, and had to register in the names of Sara (for women) and Israel (for men).

Jews in Austria were subjected to even greater humiliations than their German counterparts, being forced to scrub the streets and to immerse their hands in acid solutions. Their property was confiscated, and a quarter of them were forcefully evicted from the country by the end of 1938. This seemed to offer a model for the remaining Jews in Germany, and as war drew near in 1939, the Nazi leadership was working on ways to facilitate the emigration of the 160,000 or so who were left, many of them elderly and frail. However, the outbreak of war in 1939 brought new priorities to the forefront, while rendering 'internal enemies' such as the Jews even more dangerous. Already in January 1939 Hitler had prophesied to the Reichstag that 'if the international Jewish financiers in and outside Europe should succeed in plunging the nations once more into a world war, then the result will not be the Bolshevising of the earth, and thus the victory of Jewry, but the annihilation of the Jewish race in Europe'. In a brutal racial struggle for expansion against the Slavs, the Jews could expect no mercy. It was just possible that they might be rounded up and despatched to some distant settlement, but that was the best fate they could hope for.

Figure 18.4 *Anti-Jewish banner in a small village in Bavaria (southern Germany). The words on the banner read: 'Jews are not welcome here!'*

The anti-semitic policies of the Third Reich up to 1939 aroused little overt opposition. A German historian has suggested recently that there were four different categories of response by the German population to the persecution of the Jews. There was a fairly small group of devout Christians, liberal intellectuals and some businessmen who were openly critical of the regime. A somewhat larger number, who accepted the main arguments of Nazi teachings on race, were to be found mainly in rural areas (see Figure 18.4) and in the Protestant north of the country. A third category were Nazi sympathisers who found the policies of the leadership too 'moderate'. The fourth category – by far the largest and comprising most of the population – acquiesced passively in the policies, while showing considerable indifference. However, the evidence suggests that many members in this group did feel by 1939 that there was a Jewish question, that Jews were a distinct race, and on balance should be excluded from Germany. To this extent, it could be argued that the regime was successful in the main thrust of its anti-semitic policies to isolate Jews and to drive them out of Germany. The policies were not totally coherent, and kept meeting with unanticipated difficulties inside and outside Germany. Nonetheless, they succeeded in turning half a million people who in 1933 regarded themselves as German citizens, and were on the whole well integrated into German life, into refugees or racial aliens.

Economic recovery

One reason for Hitler's considerable popularity in the 1930s was the undoubted economic recovery which took place in Germany after 1933. Unemployment fell rapidly, though historians disagree about the extent to which this was due to a natural upturn in the world economy after

1933, to work-creation schemes or to a steadily growing rearmament programme. Some historians emphasise the importance of measures which had already been set in motion by the von Papen government in 1932. Others point out that Hitler, and even more so his new President of the Reichsbank Dr Hjalmar Schacht, were engaged in deficit financing and large job-creation schemes to stimulate the economy. A Law to Reduce Unemployment was introduced in June 1933, and the problems of agriculture were tackled in a number of ways. One project which had both a significant effect in reducing unemployment and important future military use was the construction of a motorway network.

Rearmament became increasingly important to internal economic recovery after 1936. Hitler was determined both to establish a powerful armaments industry and to make Germany as self-sufficient as possible. Schacht's New Plan in 1934 imposed strict controls on imports and tried to find outlets for German exports by means of bilateral trade treaties with countries in south-east Europe and South America who were willing to take German manufactures and supply her with raw materials and food in exchange.

Between 1936 and 1939, Germany experienced massive rearmament, as the Four Year Plan of 1936 aimed to put Germany on a war footing by the end of the decade. Heavy industry, iron and steel and chemicals expanded enormously. There were growing labour shortages, as military spending soared to about 23 per cent of gross national product (as against 3 per cent in 1913). By 1939 a quarter of the German workforce were working on direct orders for the armed forces. In addition, Germany was stockpiling synthetic materials and building up its supplies of aluminium for aircraft construction; by 1939 it had become the world's largest producer of aluminium, surpassing the USA. Richard Overy has calculated that a half or more of the German economy by 1939 was devoted to war or war-related products.

Rearmament placed almost intolerable strains on the German economy. Skilled labour was lacking, as was foreign exchange. Germany experienced balance of payments difficulties and, as inflationary tendencies increased, the economy threatened to overheat. Hitler was desperately concerned that standards of living and levels of consumption should not be greatly reduced, as he feared the kind of popular reaction which erupted at the end of the First World War. But the German economy could not afford to produce both guns and butter, and Hitler was adamant that rearmament should not be slowed down. He had no patience with the economists who told him that the economy would break down under the strain; he declared that 'the nation does not live for the economy' but 'the economy, economic leaders and theories . . . all owe unqualified service in this struggle for the self-assertion of our nation'.

As he approached his fiftieth birthday, Hitler was driven by the need to speed up the pace of German military expansion. Nevertheless the continuing brittleness of the economy suggested a series of short, sharp military campaigns rather than a sustained, lengthy one. As far as Hitler was concerned, the function of the economy was to serve Germany's political and military ends. He was not greatly concerned about means, but was not prepared to modify his long-term goals substantially in response to economic difficulties.

Opposition to the regime

This chapter has suggested that Hitler was extremely popular among the German people throughout the 1930s, and that considerable numbers of committed Nazis organised demonstrations of support and ensured compliance with the regime at grassroots level. Dissent was also dealt with severely, by despatch to a concentration camp, by detention in a local police cell or by an unfriendly encounter with the local Gestapo agent. While left-wing activists, Marxists and Jews were the targets of attack, the great majority of the population was courted by the regime, subjected to propaganda about a national community, and enlisted in the campaign to make Germany great once more. Opposition to Nazi policies became increasingly difficult to organise after the destruction of trade unions, the Catholic and Protestant youth groups, and all other political parties.

This offers one reply to the indignant question: 'Why was there not more opposition to the regime?' In the years immediately after 1933, most people saw no reason to express opposition. They were not greatly interested in the political process, and had been thoroughly disillusioned by their experience of democracy under the Weimar Republic. Nor did they wish to get involved with the police or the Gestapo. This does not mean that they were avid supporters of Nazi policies. What it suggests is that most people kept a low profile, got on with their lives, and in general obeyed the authorities, thankful that so many of them had work once again. In 1938, an SPD contact man in North Germany reported, 'The general mood in Germany is characterised by a widespread political indifference. The great mass of the people is completely dulled and does not want to hear anything more about politics.' People grumbled but they did not openly attack or oppose the regime.

There were brave exceptions. By 1939, there were 140,000 political prisoners in concentration camps. We have seen that church leaders spoke out in 1941 against the euthanasia programme. Throughout the 1930s Catholics organised local grassroots campaigns against Nazi attempts to remove crucifixes from Catholic schools and replace them with portraits of Hitler. A few fearless Protestant pastors were prepared to denounce the barbarities of the regime and to express their principled opposition. They suffered the inevitable consequence: imprisonment and sometimes death.

Some of Germany's traditional elites were repelled by Nazi book burnings and by attacks on great cultural figures of the past. The Mayor of Leipzig, Carl Gördeler, was outraged when he was ordered to remove the statue of the Leipzig-born Jewish composer Mendelssohn from the centre of the town. He became an outspoken opponent of the regime but, significantly, turned to his British contacts to help him in his fight against Nazi barbarity. He hoped to persuade the BBC to transmit long-wave programmes into Germany but failed to enlist much support in London.

Meanwhile, in Germany the only significant opposition before 1939 came from the highest ranks of the army, where plots were being hatched to overthrow Hitler. The army was not so much opposed to the regime in general, as to Hitler's reckless foreign policy aims which they feared might result in Germany having to fight a war on two fronts. Hitler's purge of conservative army leaders in early 1938, and his assumption of personal control over the army, increased misgivings. Some historians argue that a serious army plot against Hitler was foiled only by Hitler's bloodless victory at the Munich conference in the autumn.

In general terms, overt opposition was not great and did not trouble the regime. But what was serious was the passivity of the nation, and its apparent reluctance to contemplate war. The palpable relief of the masses that war had been averted in 1938 alarmed the authorities, and revealed that attempts to prepare the nation for the struggles ahead had not been very effective. A report of October 1938 pointed out that:

> 'There is no enthusiasm for military entanglements on account of the Sudeten German question . . . Nobody wants to contemplate a war with England and France. The education of the whole nation in the tasks required by a total war with all its burdens of various kinds is by no means adequate.'

A month later a further report revealed that 'there was great tension and concern everywhere and people expressed the wish that there should be no war . . . Political indoctrination and education, particularly to prepare people for war, is still completely inadequate.'

Thus the regime had failed to mobilise the full support of the population for its main ideological goals. People acquiesced in many of its policies, and were not prepared to oppose openly those aspects they did not approve of. But a recast German nation, suffused with new values, did not emerge. It came closest to realisation among German youth, but even here, while they followed Hitler into war in 1939, they did not do so with the enthusiasm which had been so evident in 1914.

Task: making notes

This chapter covers numerous aspects of Hitler's rule and you may need to make several sets of notes from it. Here is a technique for note-making on the issue of '*To what extent did Hitler change the lives of ordinary men, women and children in Germany?*' (Note that this includes ordinary men, women and children who were Jewish.)

1 Make photocopies of pages 294–309.

2 Use four different colours of highlighter or underlining for men, women, children and German people as a whole. Underline (or mark down the margin) passages in the text where each of your four groups is referred to.

3 Combine all the passages of the same colour – you could cut up the text.

4 Use this compilation to make notes on the position of men, women, children and citizens as a whole in Nazi Germany.

Further reading

M. Burleigh and W. Wipperman, *The Racial State: Germany 1933–45* (Cambridge University Press, 1991) – the best recent study of racial policies in the Third Reich.

Philippe Burrin, *Hitler and the Jews* (Edward Arnold, 1994) – clear and up-to-date analysis of this controversial topic.

J. Hiden and J. Farquharson, *Explaining Hitler's Germany* (Batsford, 1983) – clear discussion of how a range of domestic issues have been analysed by historians since the war.

Ian Kershaw, *Hitler* (Addison Wesley Longman, 1991) – focuses on the ways in which Hitler exercised power after 1933.

Ian Kershaw, *The Nazi Dictatorship* (Edward Arnold, 1985) – guide to the enormous range of interpretations of Nazi Germany.

J. Noakes and G. Pridham, *Nazism, 1919–45* vol. 2 'State, Economy and Society 1933–9' (University of Exeter, 1984) – wide-ranging collection of primary source material.

Richard Overy, *The Nazi Economic Recovery 1932–8* (Macmillan, 1982).

Richard Overy, *The Origins of the Second World War* chapter 4: 'Armaments and domestic politics' (Addison Wesley Longman, 1987).

Detlev Peukart, *Inside Nazi Germany* (Pelican, 1989) – invaluable study of everyday life in the Third Reich.

William Simpson, *Hitler and Germany* (Cambridge University Press, 1991).

David Welch, *The Third Reich: Politics and Propaganda* (Routledge, 1993).

19 The origins of the Second World War

Time chart

1933: February Hitler introduces a programme of rearmament
October Hitler walks out of the Disarmament Conference and announces Germany's intention of withdrawing from the League

1934: January Germany signs non-aggression pact with Poland

1935: January Germans in the Saar vote for the return of the area to Germany
March Conscription is reintroduced in Germany
June Naval treaty with Britain

1936: March German troops remilitarise Rhineland
Summer Hitler sends military aid to Franco in Spain
August Hitler drafts Four Year Plan to prepare Germany for war
November Anti-Comintern Pact signed with Japan. Rome–Berlin Axis signed between Germany and Italy

1938: March German troops march into Austria; *Anschluss* declared with Austria
October Sudeten crisis results in Munich conference, at which Sudeten lands of Czechoslovakia are handed over to Germany

1939: March German troops occupy remainder of Czechoslovakia
Lithuania agrees to transfer port of Memel to Germany
May 'Pact of steel' signed with Italy
August Germany signs pact with Russia
1 September German troops invade Poland

Hitler's war?

Since the end of the Second World War, there has been an ongoing debate about the factors which brought about a second major world conflict only 20 years after the first, and about the extent to which it could have been avoided. Was the Second World War 'Hitler's war', as Alan Bullock asserted, or was it due as much to 'the faults and failures of European statesmen' as to Hitler's ambitions, as A. J. P. Taylor alleges? Or should its origins be traced back to the unsatisfactory outcome of the First World War which left so many European problems unresolved? This chapter will examine the range of arguments which have been put forward in the past 50 years to explain the origins of the war, focusing on international instability, the nature and extent of Hitler's foreign policy goals and the role of appeasement policies.

Long-term causes of the Second World War

As Alan Sharp has commented, the First World War 'solved few of the problems which had created it'. Its length and intensity created new difficulties which could not easily be resolved in the highly unstable post-war environment. The Treaty of Versailles between the Allies and Germany was a compromise agreement which pleased none of the parties involved. Marshal Foch, who had been the military commander-in-chief of the allied armies at the end of the war, said of the settlement with great bitterness, 'This is not peace. It is an armistice for 20 years.' There were good reasons why the French, despite their hard-earned victory in the war, should feel so vulnerable and so pessimistic by the end of 1919.

1 *Withdrawal of the USA from the victorious wartime coalition*   The First World War could not have been won without the economic and military aid of the United States. However, the refusal of the American Senate to ratify the Treaty of Versailles, or to take any active part in European or League of Nations diplomacy in the 1920s, left Britain and France to police the Versailles settlement alone. It also denied eastern Europe much needed economic aid and investment capital.

2 *The Russian revolution and emergence of a Bolshevik government* in late 1917 unleashed a new ideological war across Europe and further afield, which aimed to overthrow existing governments not by external aggression but by inciting revolution from within. In addition to existing problems, therefore, governments at the end of the war had a new set of enemies to face: Bolshevik Russia and the communist supporters it could mobilise in countries across Europe.

3 *With the collapse of the Habsburg and Romanov Empires*, eastern Europe had become fragmented, divided up into a number of new, weak and unstable states. The Baltic states, Poland, Czechoslovakia, Austria and Hungary all faced serious economic problems. Nationality issues also surfaced from communities with different cultures and languages which did not necessarily share the ambitions of the national majority. The new states owed their existence to the collapse of the Russian empire on the one hand and the defeat of Germany on the other. The revival of either or both of these great powers would threaten their existence. Consequently, eastern Europe remained an insecure and very vulnerable area throughout the interwar period.

4 *The German problem* As we have seen, all German governments after 1919 were violently opposed to the Versailles settlement, and tried to evade its provisions. While the frontiers in western Europe were formally accepted in 1925 under the Treaty of Locarno, there was no similar agreement to cover Germany's eastern frontiers. Germany refused to accept the creation of the Polish corridor and the loss of Danzig and a part of Upper Silesia as permanent features of the east European territorial settlement.

5 *The Italian problem* The other major European power who was opposed to the Versailles settlement was Italy, who described it as a 'mutilated peace'. Italy felt denied legitimate territorial gains, and the hostility and nationalist agitation that erupted as a consequence contributed considerably to Mussolini's rise to power and to his restless attempts to undermine European stability.

6 *Economic instability* Throughout the 1920s, European powers experienced economic difficulties arising from the disruption which war had caused to international trade and to financial markets. While the Wall Street Crash in 1929 undoubtedly stemmed from American domestic economic policies, its impact on Europe through the Depression it triggered off was magnified as a result of economic weaknesses brought about by the war.

Many historians have drawn attention to what they see as a '20-year crisis' in Europe. They have pointed out that the First World War left Europe in a state of chronic instability which was highly likely to result in another major upheaval. This is the basis of the 'Thirty years' war thesis' which argues that the First World War brought about a complete breakdown of European order which resulted in a succession of international crises ending only with the outbreak of another world war. In the preface to the first volume of his memoirs, Winston Churchill commented that 'I must regard these volumes as a continuation of the story of the First World War which I set out in *The World Crisis* ... Together ... they will cover an account of another Thirty Years' War.' However, this view of a thirty years' conflict has been vigorously contested by other historians who agree that there was considerable instability in Europe after 1919, but do not accept that this factor contributed in a significant way to the outbreak of another war in 1939. Some point out that Europe had in fact recovered from many of the effects of the First World War by the late 1920s. Others argue that the remaining problems would not of themselves inevitably have resulted in war, and that many could have been resolved peacefully. This group of historians therefore lays most responsibility for a second conflict on Adolf Hitler. They acknowledge that his rise to power was due largely to the destabilising impact of the Depression, and that his expansionist ambitions were assisted by the fragmentation of eastern Europe. Nonetheless they argue strongly that Hitler's ambitions, because they were so extensive in scope, were bound to result in war whatever the international situation. Let us now examine the debate about the foreign policy objectives of the Third Reich.

Nazi ideology

In recent years, historians have come increasingly to echo the verdict of the Nuremburg Trial, held at the end of the Second World War, which declared that Hitler and the Nazis deliberately launched a war of aggression against Europe. Historians such as Norman Rich and Gerald Weinberg point to the fact that in writings, in speeches and in policy pronouncements throughout the 1920s and 1930s, leading Nazis identified a set of concerns relating to 'race and space' which ran like a consistent thread through their policies. These concerns centred, as we saw in the last chapter, on the importance of racial purity and of the need for a nation to be prepared to compete with its neighbours in a brutal and uncompromising struggle if it wished to expand. In *Mein Kampf*, Hitler expressed his concern that there should be 'a healthy and natural relationship between the number and growth of the population, on the one hand, and the extent and quality of its soil on the other'. He stated that 'only a sufficiently large space on this earth can ensure the independent existence of a nation'. He went on to argue that 'the aim of our political activity must be . . . the acquisition of land and soil as the objective of our foreign policy' and that 'when we speak of new land in Europe today we must principally bear in mind Russia and the border states subject to her'. These themes of racial purity and of the need for struggle to secure 'living space' or *lebensraum* in the east are echoed again and again in speeches to the faithful, in election meetings and addresses to particular interest groups and in party literature.

While there is no dispute that such themes run through Nazi speeches and writings of the 1920s and early 1930s, the argument was advanced in the 1960s that they did not materially shape Nazi foreign policy once Hitler actually became Chancellor. In his controversial book *The Origins of the Second World War*, published in 1961, A. J. P. Taylor argued that Hitler's policies after 1933 were shaped much more by the international situation and by the responses of other European leaders than by the convictions he had expressed previously. Taylor dismissed *Mein Kampf* as a long-winded and turgid book filled with half-baked ideas which Hitler wrote to while away the long months in prison. In it, France was portrayed as Germany's abiding enemy and Hitler speculated on how Italy and Britain could be won over to support Germany's campaign to overthrow the Versailles settlement. After 1933, Hitler had to temper his views to the prevailing international situation, and is best seen as a typical German statesman pursuing traditional German objectives. He was not driven by any underlying ideology or timetable for aggressive expansion in the east. Hitler was successful in overturning the Versailles settlement, but this was the fault of other European leaders who failed to fashion a coherent strategy to contain German power until it was too late. By the time Britain and France threatened to go to war, over Danzig and the Polish Corridor, who could blame Hitler for ignoring their threats which had amounted to so little in the previous years?

Taylor's book unleashed a hail of criticism. Many historians were incensed at what they saw as an attempt to 'whitewash' Hitler by suggesting that he was a typical German leader, when in fact he was anything but typical, being a ranting Austrian-German of only modest education and few social connections. Furthermore, they were not prepared to ignore *Mein Kampf*. Some historians argued that *Mein Kampf* was indeed a 'blueprint for aggression' which set out in a fair amount of detail Hitler's foreign policy aims. While there was some flexibility in implementation after 1933, when the UK went from being a desirable ally to a hated enemy and an alliance was later concluded with Russia, this did not mean that there was no underlying consistency of aim. As Alan Bullock argued, it merely showed that Hitler combined a 'consistency of aim' with 'enormous flexibility of method'. While many historians accepted Taylor's analysis that Germany was not reconciled to the Versailles settlement after 1919 and would seek to modify it, particularly in the east, they did not share his view that any interwar German leader would therefore have followed a similar set of policies to those pursued by Hitler.

In recent years, historians have concluded that ideology was fundamental to the shaping of Nazi policies after 1933. The basic ingredients of that ideology – a belief in racial purity, in the importance of balancing population, resources and soil, and the necessity of acquiring 'living space' in the east – made Nazi foreign policy so potent. They argue that the central weakness of Taylor's book is that Nazi ideology is left completely out of account, and that therefore his interpretation is fatally flawed. In *Modern Germany Reconsidered*, in 1993, the historian David Kaiser asserted that Taylor's views – that Hitler did not intend war to break out in September 1939, that he lacked a real plan for the conquest of Europe or the world, and that other governments played a crucial role in unleashing German expansion – 'are no longer regarded as valid'. Instead, the domestic and foreign policies of the Third Reich are now seen as two sides of the same coin. The domestic aim of strengthening and purifying the German race was intended to ensure the successful implementation of foreign policy. Hitler told a group of *Reichswehr* commanders just after coming to power that it was necessary for them all to work for 'the conquest and ruthless Germanisation of new living space in the east'. The German historian Jäckel is typical of the majority of historians in arguing, on the basis of many such pronouncements, that Hitler's ultimate goal was 'the establishment of a greater Germany than had ever existed before'.

The debate about continuity

A. J. P. Taylor was not alone in suggesting that Hitler's foreign policy aims were similar to those of previous German statesmen. Fritz Fischer, whose pioneering work on German ambitions in 1914 also appeared in 1961 (see chapter 8), suggested that there was a continuity of aim between German policy-makers in 1914 and Nazi leaders in the Third Reich. This was because the powerful conservative industrial and landowning classes of pre-1914 Germany remained in a strong position in the 1920s, and played a decisive role in bringing Hitler to power, seeing him as the 'right servant to carry out their aspirations'. Accordingly, both Wilhelmine Germany and the Third Reich aimed to establish power over eastern Europe, and to colonise the area for the economic and political benefit of a greater Germany.

While historians now accept that there were continuities running through the foreign policies of Wilhelmine Germany, the Weimar Republic and the Third Reich, they place more emphasis on those characteristics which made Nazi foreign policy objectives so different from preceding regimes.

The racial element

While Germany's geographical position made it inevitable that it would aspire to exert power in eastern Europe, it was only the Nazi regime which sought to establish in eastern Europe and in Russia an empire based on race, in which those of Aryan descent would rule over lesser Slav subject races. As John Hiden has pointed out, German leaders during the First World War 'followed an expansionist policy in the east primarily to help them preserve a conservative reactionary *status quo*, not a racially driven revolution of German, then European and ultimately world society!' In this sense, Hitler's aims were revolutionary. As he wrote in *Mein Kampf*:

> *'We National Socialists have intentionally drawn a line under the foreign policy of prewar Germany. We are taking up where we left off six hundred years ago. We are putting an end to the perpetual German march towards the South and West of Europe and turning our eyes towards the land in the East. We are finally putting a stop to the colonial and trade policy of the prewar period and passing over to the territorial policy of the future.'*

The change was to have far-reaching implications, as Hitler later declared, 'with the concept of race National Socialism will carry its revolution abroad and recast the world'.

Colonial and trade policy

As Hitler himself pointed out, whereas the aim of German governments before 1914 was to secure colonies overseas and to acquire markets worldwide, the objectives of the Third Reich were very different: to expand Germany's living space in eastern Europe and to try to make the country economically as self-sufficient as possible. Hitler was not greatly interested in the return of the pre-1914 German colonies; what he sought was the productive soil of the east, which could support an expansionist Germany and enable her to become one of the world's dominating powers. He believed that Germany's dependence on international trade had laid her open to the hostile influence of external enemies and in particular scheming Jewish financiers. Thus his aim was to ensure that through bilateral trade agreements and the manufacture of synthetic materials, Germany could be in full control of its economic development and therefore master of its political and military destiny.

The role of Russia

The issue of Germany's relations with Russia was a central theme of European history from the mid nineteenth century onwards. Both Bismarck after 1870 and Weimar governments in the 1920s recognised the importance of cultivating good relations with Russia, to prevent Germany from becoming encircled by a ring of hostile powers, and to give her some freedom of manoeuvre in the European diplomatic system. After 1890, Wilhelmine Germany allowed Russia to conclude a hostile alliance with France which threatened to bring Germany into conflict with Russia sooner or later, but despite this there were dynastic ties between the Kaiser and the Tsar, and the recognition of similar domestic social and political goals. Hitler's attitude to Bolshevik Russia was very different. He viewed it as an ideological enemy, a monstrous regime based on Communist doctrines of class division and led by the hated

Jews. His hostility to Russia was therefore not based on its potential strategic threat or military power but on its capacity to undermine Germany's social and political power and contaminate pure German blood. In the long run there could be no compromise with Russian Bolshevism; it had to be destroyed to make way for the establishment of an enlarged Aryan empire.

The international system

It has sometimes been suggested that Stresemann in the 1920s was pursuing aims similar to those of Hitler, centred on the removal of the shackles of Versailles and revision of frontiers in eastern Europe, which would open the door to German expansion eastwards. There is no doubt that Stresemann, like all Weimar leaders, wished to restore German power in Europe and increase its leverage in the east by securing the revision of the Versailles Treaty. Like Bismarck before him, he aimed to build up Germany's power within the existing international system, working through the League of Nations and through the conference diplomacy of Locarno. Like Bismarck, he therefore sought a pivotal, and possibly dominating, role in European diplomacy, but he did not aim to overturn the whole system. Hitler, on the other hand, saw alliances and diplomatic agreements as tactical ploys, to protect Germany from attack while it was still relatively unarmed and vulnerable. His main aim was to build up Germany's power to the point where it was in a position to challenge the existing international system and overthrow it, replacing it with a racially-based global order. Where Stresemann and Bismarck worked through diplomacy and negotiated agreement to achieve defined goals, Hitler emphasised the importance of ceaseless struggle to achieve his aims. As he wrote in 1928, 'Wherever our success may end, that will always be only the starting-point of a new fight'.

Thus Hitler's approach to international affairs was very different from that of his predecessors, or indeed from that of the foreign leaders which whom he was dealing after 1933. They sought to negotiate with him, and to restore some measure of German power, within the existing European order. His aim, as with the Weimar Republic, was to destroy that order but in the short term he was prepared to work through it to achieve his long-term goals. It was both the revolutionary nature of Hitler's ultimate goals and the accommodating flexibility of his methods which made him so different from previous German leaders and so dangerous to Europe.

Did Hitler have a foreign policy 'programme'?

Did Hitler have a foreign policy 'programme' which he followed fairly closely after 1933, or simply a 'world picture' or a number of oft-repeated convictions which he then aimed to pursue in a rather loose way? Hitler certainly saw himself as a man with a mission. As he wrote in *Mein Kampf*, '. . . just as in ordinary life a man with a fixed life-goal that he tries to achieve at all events will always be superior to those who live aimlessly, exactly likewise is it in the life of nations'. The mission was clearly to produce a master race capable of winning substantial territory in eastern Europe and of sustaining from its resources a great world empire. But did Hitler have a clear strategy for transforming the Germany of 1933 into such a superpower? Most historians now believe that he did, and that his foreign policy followed a consistent course.

Rearmament

This was Hitler's first priority. It dominated the first two years of his foreign policy. He was painfully aware that Germany's military forces were no match for those of its neighbours and rivals – France, Poland and Czechoslovakia – who between them could raise armies of over a million, to pit against Germany's puny 100,000. He told his cabinet on 8 February 1933 that rearmament was to have 'first priority' for the next four to five years, and to this end the services were mobilised for expansion. The army was encouraged to work towards an increase in strength to the size of the pre-1914 army, and sweeping plans were drawn up to bring into being a sizeable German air force within five years. In these initial stages of rearmament, the navy was to take a back seat but by the late 1930s there were also plans for the construction of a great battle fleet. While the rearmament process was under way, and Germany was still to some extent at the mercy of other powers, Hitler's diplomacy was cautious and even included a non-aggression treaty with the despised Poles in January 1934. However, as German military strength grew so did the pace and scope of Hitler's diplomatic demands.

The struggle against Versailles

The rejection of the military restrictions of the Versailles treaty marked the first stage of Hitler's 'struggle against Versailles'. Rearmament was accompanied by Hitler's dramatic departure from the League of Nations Disarmament Conference in October 1933 and from the League itself. This was followed in January 1935 by the return of the Saar industrial region to Germany, when its inhabitants voted overwhelmingly to rejoin the Reich after the allotted 15 years under League administration. In

March of 1935, Hitler introduced conscription, in flagrant defiance of the Treaty of Versailles, and in June he concluded a naval agreement with Britain, which allowed Germany to build up to 35 per cent of British tonnage in capital ships and submarines.

In March 1936, German troops remilitarised the Rhineland, in contravention of the Versailles and Locarno treaties. This was a crucial stage in Hitler's expansionist plans, because it enabled Germany to fortify its borders with France, thus helping to protect its western flank from attack while forces were mobilised in the East. Four months later, Hitler agreed to send military aid to the rebel military leader Franco on the outbreak of the Spanish Civil War (see chapter 14). By the end of the year, he had drawn close to an alliance with Italy, and had signed an anti-Comintern pact with Japan aimed against Russia. Forceful revision of Europe's eastern frontiers started in March 1938 with a union or *Anschluss* with Austria. It continued later in that year with a campaign to bring the Sudeten Germans of Czechoslovakia (who before 1914 had lived in the Habsburg Empire) into an expanded Germany, an objective finally agreed to by Italy, Britain and France at the Munich conference at the end of September. By March of the following year, German troops were invading the Czech capital Prague, and with the disappearance of the Czech republic, Hitler turned his attention to Danzig and to the Polish Corridor. It was his demand for the return of these areas, heavily populated by Germans, which Britain and France now refused to agree to, supporting the Poles in their opposition to further German expansion. Hitler's response to this opposition was to sign a pact with the Soviet Union in August of 1939 and to declare war on Poland.

Establishment of a racial empire in the East

Hitler made it clear to his army commanders on 23 May 1939 that 'It is not Danzig that is at stake. For us it is a matter of expanding our living space in the East and making food supplies secure and also solving the problem of the Baltic States . . .' At this point, however, signs of opposition from Britain and from France suggested a change in tactics, if not in ultimate strategy. In the midst of a lengthy tirade directed at the League of Nations High Commissioner in Danzig in August, Hitler declared:

> *'Everything I undertake is directed against the Russians; if the West is too stupid and blind to grasp this, then I shall be compelled to come to an agreement with the Russians, beat the West, and then after their defeat turn against the Soviet Union with all my forces. I need the Ukraine so they can't starve us out like in the last war.'*

We cannot help but be struck by the consistency between Hitler's words and his actions. Running through *Mein Kampf* and numerous subsequent speeches, addresses and private conversations was a set of racist and expansionist aims which began to be implemented after 1933 through a number of domestic and foreign policies. While the actions did not always follow the exact sequence of the words, they embodied the substance, and both pointed inexorably eastwards, towards *lebensraum* and the establishment of a racial empire on Russian and east European soil.

Many people throughout Europe predicted the course of events after 1933 with amazing accuracy. The British head of the Foreign Office, Robert Vansittart, had made a careful study of *Mein Kampf*, and after January 1933 received a stream of telegrams from the British Ambassador in Berlin describing the Nazi revolution that was gathering rapid momentum, and the atrocities that were already taking place. By August, Vansittart was warning the British Government of the moves that Hitler was likely to make in respect to eastern Europe, starting with a demand for *Anschluss* and continuing with aggressive actions aimed at the Polish Corridor and Danzig. If Hitler's objectives were so clearly spelled out in his writings and speeches, and if the likely turn of events in eastern Europe was already being accurately predicted in August 1933, why was no action taken by other powers to stop German expansion?

The 'unnecessary war'?

In volume I of his *War Memoirs*, Sir Winston Churchill called the Second World War 'the unnecessary war' and said of it that 'there never was a war more easy to prevent'. It has to be remembered, of course, that Churchill was a backbench Conservative MP during the 1930s, out of favour with the leaders of the National Government. He kept warning about the dangerous course that Nazi policies were taking, only to be ignored, as he saw it, by ignorant and complacent ministers. In his memoirs, Churchill argued that action should have been taken against Nazi Germany very early on, to prevent her from rearming and to stop her from remilitarising the Rhineland. As Germany was allowed to tear up the Treaty of Versailles without facing any reprisals, and was then able to launch an aggressive campaign of expansion in eastern Europe, those who failed to act and who instead encouraged German expansion by 'appeasement' policies should, it was suggested, bear some responsibility for the war which followed – a war which, according to Churchill, could have been prevented.

How valid is Churchill's argument? Would firm action against Hitler before 1939 have prevented war, or would it merely have brought about a military struggle at an earlier date? Why were western leaders so willing to agree to Hitler's demands up to 1939? The debate about 'appeasement policies' has been long and contentious, but in recent years historians have taken a more sympathetic view of the dilemma facing British and French leaders after 1933, and of the limited options open to them.

Appeasement

A number of factors led to the adoption of appeasement policies by Britain and France in the 1930s. In relation to the failure to prevent German rearmament and remilitarisation of the Rhineland, the most significant was the strong belief in Britain that the Treaty of Versailles had been unfair on Germany.

The discrediting of the Versailles Settlement

Throughout the 1920s, British governments had sought to revise the Treaty of Versailles in Germany's favour (see chapter 10). Though some success had been achieved – in ending the allied occupation of the Rhineland five years ahead of schedule and cancelling reparations payments – French resistance prevented more far-reaching changes. Many people in Britain believed that the continuing strong grievances of Germans against the treaty had helped Hitler to come to power, and that only the satisfaction of legitimate objections would prevent more forcible attempts to overthrow the treaty. One area of grievance was the disarmament provisions. Germany had been disarmed in 1919 as the first stage of a more general move towards European disarmament. By 1933, European disarmament had not materialised, and Germany was therefore demanding the right to rearm. On what grounds should it be refused? If Germany claimed that other powers had broken their word, and proceeded to build up its armaments, through what mechanisms could other powers prevent this? Germany walked out of the League of Nations in October 1933, allegedly in protest against the hypocrisy of other powers who preached disarmament for Germany, but refused to disarm themselves. Rather than consider reprisals against Germany, the British government was concerned to get it back into the League, and was prepared to offer concessions to this end. In relation to the build up of both the German air force and navy, Britain was more concerned to limit them by agreement than to continue the fruitless argument about the allies' failure to disarm and Germany's consequent 'right to rearm'.

Similar arguments came into play over the Rhineland. For how long was it reasonable to insist on its demilitarisation? Was it fair to prohibit a major European power from stationing troops in one part of its territory?

Most people in Britain were not prepared to support any military action designed to prevent Hitler from 'walking into his own back garden'. In any event, Britain did not have troops to spare to counter any attempt at remilitarisation; they were at full stretch in Palestine, in various parts of the British Empire and particularly in India. The British government made it clear to Hitler early in 1936 that it would not oppose a remilitarisation of the Rhineland, if it was part of a negotiated package which included a German return to the League and an air pact. With characteristic effrontery, Hitler seized the initiative and ordered German troops into the Rhineland in advance of any negotiations. While he tried to present the move as a 'token' rearmament, in a bid to play down its significance and therefore prevent a counter-attack, there were considerable numbers of reservists and of armed police stationed in the Rhineland to reinforce the front-line troops.

Britain and France were now faced with a serious dilemma. Should they sanction the invasion of French forces to oppose the remilitarisation, and face the consequences – possibly a repeat of the disastrous Ruhr occupation of 1923 – or would they accept the *fait accompli* and carry on trying to negotiate with Hitler? After some days and weeks of agonising discussions, they decided on the latter course. With hindsight, this was probably a mistaken decision. However, it is by no means certain that an armed allied response would have discredited Hitler and brought about his downfall. It might have resulted instead in an upsurge of patriotic feelings, as in 1923. And for how long were Britain and France prepared to occupy the Rhineland in the face of sustained German opposition and resistance?

Many historians have singled out the failure to prevent remilitarisation of the Rhineland in 1936 as the most decisive turning-point in the unsuccessful attempts of western powers to stop Nazi expansion short of war. But it was not seen in that light at the time. Both remilitarisation and the *Anschluss* with Austria were seen in Britain as ways of redressing legitimate German grievances over Versailles. In 1919, Wilson had preached the doctrine of self-determination, which guided many of the territorial settlements in eastern Europe. However, it had not been applied in the case of Germany. In demanding the incorporation of German-speaking peoples into the German Reich, Hitler was only asking for equality of treatment, or so it could be argued. British governments had long been unhappy about Germany's eastern frontiers, and had supported moves for peaceful revision already in the 1920s. Provided that changes were brought about peacefully, and not by war, Britain was willing to support them. It was when Germany began to occupy non-German areas such as Prague that opinion in Britain changed dramatically, and pressure built up to 'take a stand' against Hitler.

The desire to avoid another war

Another central element in appeasement policies was the determination to do everything possible to avoid another major war. Memories of the First World War remained fresh in both Britain and France. The governments of the two countries were determined to do all in their power to prevent a repetition of the situation which had brought about war in 1914. Many people in Britain blamed secret diplomacy and the 'encirclement policies' of France and Russia, aided and abetted by Britain, for precipitating war with Germany. Government leaders in the 1930s were therefore anxious to be seen to be pursuing conciliatory policies towards Germany, and to be working through the League of Nations rather than through alliances and policies of deterrence. As Britain's foreign secretary, Lord Halifax, argued soon after the *Anschluss* between Germany and Austria, 'the more closely we associated ourselves with France and Russia, the more we produced in German minds the impression that we were plotting to encircle Germany and the more difficult would it be to make any real settlement with Germany'.

A further factor in the situation was the development of air power in this period. European leaders knew that in a future war civilian populations would be infinitely more exposed to aerial bombing than in the First World War. As Stanley Baldwin told the House of Commons in 1934, 'The bomber will always get through'. Before the invention of radar systems and the development of fighter aircraft this was a frightening prospect, and spurred leaders on in their attempts to preserve the peace, even if this meant making unpalatable concessions to Hitler. As Neville Chamberlain flew to Germany en route for the Munich conference which would sanction the transfer of the Sudetenland from Czechoslovakia to Germany, he looked down on London spread out defenceless below him and vowed to do all he could to keep Europe at peace.

Fear of Communism

A very important element in interwar diplomacy was fear of the spread of Communism. Though Bolshevik Russia was not involved in fighting with her neighbours after 1920, it remained a threat to other European powers. Propaganda aimed at subverting capitalist governments and inciting workers' revolution continued to alarm governments, especially when they found radical groups in their own countries ready to respond. Hitler's attacks on German Communists won him strong support not just in Germany but across Europe. His aim to expand in eastern Europe and to wage war against Bolshevik Russia was one which many people outside Germany were happy to endorse. Faced with a choice between evils, many respectable European politicians feared Stalin and Communism

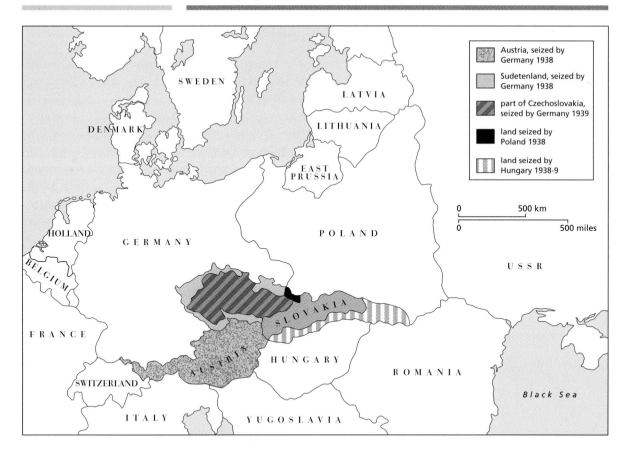

Austria, seized by
Germany 1938

Sudetenland, seized by
Germany 1938

part of Czechoslovakia,
seized by Germany 1939

land seized by
Poland 1938

land seized by
Hungary 1938-9

Figure 19.1 *Europe at the outbreak of the Second World War*

much more than they did Hitler and Nazism. Some saw Hitler as a strong buffer against Communist expansion.

Fear of Communism intensified after the outbreak of the Spanish civil war in 1936. Hitler and Mussolini publicised their support for Franco in his struggle against the Spanish republic and its Russian communist backers (see chapter 14). Strong ideological divisions polarised Europe from the mid 1930s, and they had a profound influence on the policies pursued by Britain and France. As news of Stalin's purges began to filter out of Russia, suggestions that the British and French governments should seek Russian help to counter German expansion were bound to provoke great controversy.

By the late 1930s, it was becoming clear that German eastward expansion could only be checked by concerted action on the part of British and French leaders working with Stalin. However, two decades of ideological warfare had given rise to profound suspicions between the western governments and Soviet Russia. Neither side trusted the other. On what basis could negotiations proceed? Russian troops could only get to Germany by crossing Polish territory (see Figure 19.1). The Polish government violently opposed the entry of Russian troops onto its soil, fearing that once in Poland they would never leave. Britain and France were not in any position to force the Poles to change their minds, even had they wished to do so. It is perhaps hardly surprising that Stalin felt that British and French leaders were being only half-hearted in their attempts to counter Hitler. After all, Russia had not been invited to the discussions involving the Sudeten Germans at Munich.

There are many historians who argue that only an alliance between Britain, France and Russia in the late 1930s could have prevented the outbreak of war, and that the only feasible alternative to appeasement policies was a strategy of deterrence and of alliances. As we have seen, such a strategy was avoided for most of the 1930s because it was perceived to have caused the outbreak of war in 1914. But even had it been pursued with more determination, would it have been possible for Britain and France to conclude a military agreement with Russia in 1939? The political, military and logistical difficulties were immense. There were bound to be disagreements between the parties which Hitler could exploit. And was it obvious in 1939 that Hitler was a bigger menace to Europe than Stalin? A successful war against Hitler might massively expand the mighty Soviet Russia.

It is far from clear that the conclusion of an alliance between Britain, France and Russia would have prevented war. As we have seen, Hitler knew that German expansion could only take place through a series of struggles for which its population was being carefully prepared. While it was obviously easier for Hitler to pick Germany's enemies off one by one, we know he was preparing Germany for a sustained military campaign by the late 1930s. Had Britain and France not agreed to the Munich settlement, Hitler was prepared to go to war in late 1938, and by 1939 he was regretting that he had allowed himself to be 'cheated out' of a war, as he saw it, by Chamberlain. Thus a strategy of deterrence was likely at some point or other to result in war. The issue might have been different, and the military circumstances might have been more favourable from the point of view of Britain and France. But all the evidence suggests that the two powers would still have had to fight at some stage if they wished to prevent German expansion.

Hitler – a 'moderate Nazi'

A final element in appeasement policies which needs to be considered is the view that British leaders, and in particular Neville Chamberlain – British Prime Minister from 1937 to 1940 – took of Hitler and his objectives. It may well be the case that nothing British and French leaders could have done before 1939 would have prevented Hitler from pursuing his expansionist policies. It is clear to us now that Hitler was a fanatic, driven by ideological obsessions and determined to transform Germany into an expanding racially-based state. But this was not the view which Chamberlain had of Hitler. After their first meeting, Chamberlain wrote to his sister that he had established a certain confidence with Hitler and felt that 'here was a man who could be relied upon when he had given his word'. He told the Cabinet on 17 September 1938 that Hitler's objectives were 'strictly limited', and boasted after Munich that he had secured 'peace in our time'. Despite warnings from many Germans who tried to persuade the British government that Hitler was a dangerous extremist bent on aggressive expansion at all costs, Chamberlain persisted in seeing him as a man with whom one could do business, though he conceded that 'these Dictators [Hitler and Mussolini] are men of moods'. Nonetheless, 'catch them in the right mood and they will give you anything you ask for'.

It is Chamberlain's blindness towards Hitler's real intentions, and his arrogance in believing that he could come to an agreement with the dictators, unlike his 'weaker brethren' in the Cabinet and political opponents, which is now the focus of criticism. Historians accept that it was not easy for politicians to pursue alternative policies to those of appeasement, and that such alternatives might not have prevented war in any case. But to ignore all the evidence to the contrary, and to believe that Hitler was really a 'moderate' Nazi in the grip of extremists who could be induced to behave reasonably, was a great error of judgement. Those like Churchill who had a more accurate perception of Hitler were understandably incensed by Chamberlain's blinkered approach, and not unnaturally held him partly to blame for the war which broke out in 1939.

However, some historians have emphasised the fact that Britain was not militarily prepared for war in 1937 and that Chamberlain was acutely conscious of the need for Britain to gain enough time to rearm. While Chamberlain was making concessions to Hitler in 1938, he was also stepping up the pace of rearmament in Britain to try to deter Hitler from further armed aggression and to ensure that Britain was ready for a war if it should break out. By September 1939, Britain was in a much stronger military position than she had been two years earlier. Appeasement policies had 'bought' an invaluable two-year breathing space, and Chamberlain put it to good use. The rapid build-up of air power and the development of defence systems such as radar helped Britain to withstand subsequent German air attacks. Some recent historians argue that Chamberlain should be given full credit for such policies. They have therefore viewed Chamberlain's diplomacy in a more favourable light than contemporary critics such as Churchill.

We cannot be certain of the extent to which Hitler might have been encouraged in his expansionist course by the lack of opposition he received. The view he had that Britain and France were in decline as great powers and would not therefore put up any serious resistance to his eastern expansion was reinforced, and this may have speeded up his plans. But there can be no doubt that Hitler was intent on expansion, and was prepared to fight a war or series of wars to achieve his objectives. To that end, he sought tactical alliances – with Britain, and later with Russia. He was also prepared to face opposition, and was adept at dividing his enemies and of alternately negotiating and bullying to get his way. He might have been surprised that Britain and France were finally prepared to offer Poland a guarantee against German aggression in 1939, but he was nonetheless prepared for that eventuality. After all, the evidence clearly shows that he had been busy putting Germany on a war footing since he came to power.

Conclusion: Hitler's war

Most historians now agree that the chief responsibility for unleashing war in Europe in 1939 rests on Hitler and the Nazis. They endorse the verdicts of the Nuremberg Trial and of the early studies written about Hitler that Nazi foreign policy was inherently aggressive and that, in aiming at European and ultimately world domination, it was bound to engulf Europe in war sooner or later. There still remains some disagreement about the role of Hitler *vis-à-vis* other Nazi leaders. Some historians believe that Hitler was the prime mover in the field of foreign policy, and that he was responsible for all the critical decisions, 'from launching programmes of rearmament in 1933, to a realignment of relations with Poland in 1934, to the remilitarisation of the Rhineland in 1936 and through to *Anschluss* and to Munich'. David Kaiser concludes that:

> '*It was he who decided on the alliance with the Soviets and who ordered the attacks upon Poland and France. He did so often in the teeth of opposition from his diplomats and generals and his successes increased his authority over them. His role is more apparent in foreign policy than in any other realm of Nazi government action.*'

On this line of analysis, the Second World War was most emphatically 'Hitler's war'. Other historians are not so ready to dismiss the input of fellow Nazi leaders, or the willingness of army leaders and industrialists to work in partnership with them. Taylor's contention that the outbreak of war in 1939 owed as much to 'the faults and failures of European statesmen' as it did to Hitler's ambitions has been firmly repudiated.

Clearly Hitler was able to capitalise on the economic and territorial impact of the First World War. The international environment remained highly unstable throughout the 1920s, and offered opportunities for German expansion which Hitler was quick to exploit. In this sense, the legacy of the First World War was important. To go on from this to argue that the First World War was bound to lead to another conflict, and that therefore we should see both wars as constituting a 'thirty years' war', is highly speculative. It rests on the assumption that had Hitler for some reason not been in power in Germany in the 1930s, some other German leader would have operated in the same way and followed similar policies. Put in those terms, few non-Marxist historians would accept the proposition. Individuals do possess the power to shape history, though not entirely as they would like, and the twentieth century has witnessed its fair share of powerful leaders bringing about revolutionary change. Hitler did not live to achieve the full extent of his revolutionary goals. In the end, after a long war, the opposition to his vision of a racially pure Europe was strong enough to bring about his defeat. Few would deny that it was his determination to transform the basis of European society which brought war to Europe in 1939. As Mussolini pointed out, no other European leader wanted war in 1939. In that sense, the Second World War was indeed 'Hitler's war'.

Task: interpretations of Hitler's war aims

A. J. P. Taylor's *Origins of the Second World War* was published in 1961. It caused a storm of controversy mainly because it attempted to pull the planks from under the view that the Second World War was entirely caused by Hitler, who was a wicked man who planned the evil war. In 1964 Taylor summed up the differences between himself and his opponents:

'The current versions of Hitler are, I think, two. In one view, he wanted a great war for its own sake ... he was a maniac, a nihilist, an Attila. The other view makes him more rational and, in a sense, more constructive. In this view, Hitler had a coherent, long-term plan which he pursued with unwavering persistence. For the sake of this plan he sought power. He intended to give Germany a great colonial empire in eastern Europe by defeating Soviet Russia, exterminating all the inhabitants, and then planting the vacant territory with Germans. This Reich would last a thousand years.

'Perhaps the difference between me and the believers in Hitler's constant plan for "lebensraum" is over words. By "plan" I understand something which is prepared and worked out in detail. They seem to take "plan" as a pious ... wish.'

Taylor then shows that many of Hitler's successes – becoming Chancellor and the Reichstag Fire, for example – were unplanned. He goes on:

> *'Here it seems to me is the key to the problem of whether Hitler deliberately aimed at war. He did not so much aim at war as expect it to happen, unless he could evade it by some ingenious trick ... Far from wanting war, a general war was the last thing he wanted. He wanted the fruits of total victory without total war; and thanks to the stupidity of others he nearly got them.*
>
> *'Hitler ... was fuel to an existing engine. He was in part the creation of Versailles ... Most of all he was the creation of German history and the German present. He would have counted for nothing without the support and cooperation of the German people.'*

In *Hitler's War Aims* (published in 1973) Norman Rich examines the plan Hitler put forward in *Mein Kampf*, and its timing:

> *'Whatever qualities Hitler may have attributed to himself, longevity was not among them. In a few years ... he might die. Hitler's ... awareness of his own mortality ... demanded that the conquest of "Lebensraum" should be carried out soon, at the latest within the next ten or fifteen years. Thus from the beginning time played a major role in Hitler's calculations. To remain still ... was to court disaster.'*

More recently, Richard Overy, in a chapter called 'Hitler's War Plans' in *Paths to War* (edited by R. Boyce and E. Robertson), has examined what actual war preparations were carried out, and by when:

> *'Yet many historians have argued that before 1939 German rearmament was deliberately restricted, that Germany's leaders set out to pursue short, limited wars which would make minimum demands on the civilian economy. This was partly, it is argued, from fear of political repercussions of cutting living standards and partly because of the difficulties in mobilising resources in the confused administrative jungle of the Nazi state.*
>
> *'In 1961 A. J. P. Taylor ... challenged the very idea that Hitler even planned to do more than build up limited armed strength in order to reverse the territorial clauses of the Treaty of Versailles and that he had achieved all he wanted by 1939. The evidence that Hitler wished to go*

> *further than this is now overwhelming, but whether he sought to achieve this by limited or total war is still very much in dispute. Yet as more evidence comes to light on detailed service programmes, on economic preparations under the Four Year Plan, it seems clear that the Nazi leaders intended to establish the army vision of total mobilisation.'*

1 How does Taylor deal with the arguments of 'the believers in Hitler's constant plan', as laid out in *Mein Kampf*?

2 How do you think Taylor would support his claim that Hitler was just 'the creation of Versailles . . . the creation of German history and the German present'?

3 Taylor gives two 'current versions' of Hitler's objectives. What is his own version?

4 Explain why Norman Rich thinks that the timing of war was so crucial.

5 What evidence is Richard Overy using to show that Hitler did NOT plan a 'limited war' in 1939?

6 In August 1939 Hitler told a representative of the League of Nations: 'Everything I undertake is directed against the Russians; if the West is too stupid and blind to grasp this, then I shall be compelled to come to an agreement with the Russians, beat the West and then, after their defeat, turn against the Soviet Union with all my forces.' How do you think (a) Taylor, and (b) Rich, would respond to this statement?

Further reading

Ruth Henig, *The Origins of the Second World War*, Lancaster Pamphlet (Routledge, 1985).

P. M. H. Bell, *The Origins of the Second World War in Europe* (Addison Wesley Longman, 1986) – very good review of all the arguments and debates.

Alan Bullock, *Hitler: A Study in Tyranny* (rev. ed.) Penguin, 1964) – remains a classic study of the dictator.

John Hiden, *German and Europe 1919–39* (second ed., Addison Wesley Longman, 1993) – very good introduction to interwar German foreign policy.

Gordon Martel (ed.), *Modern Germany Reconsidered* chapter 9 (Routledge, 1992).

J. Noakes and G. Pridham, *Nazism 1919–45* vol. 3 'Foreign Policy, War and Racial Extermination' (University of Exeter, 1988) – indispensable source for contemporary documents.

William Simpson, *Hitler and Germany* (Cambridge University Press, 1991) – also contains some good primary sources.

A. J. P. Taylor, *The Origins of the Second World War* (Hamish Hamilton, 1961) – key interpretation which has provoked heated debate.

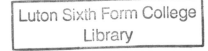

20 Europe in 1945

The two world wars punctuate the period covered by this book, profoundly influencing all the themes, countries and people we have discussed. What similarities and differences are there between them?

Some similarities are obvious. Both were 'total wars', involving civilians as well as combatants. Because both wars stretched nations' resources to the limit, the overwhelming strength of the USA was a crucial factor in determining the result. In both 1914 and 1940–41 Germany had startling initial successes but in the end could not hold out against the superior resources of their opponents.

Some apparent similarities conceal important differences. Britain, France, the USA, Russia and Belgium fought together against Germany in both wars, but in the First they were joined by Serbia, Italy and Japan, and in the Second by Czechoslovakia, Poland and the Netherlands (neutral in the First World War). Turkey and Bulgaria joined Germany and Austria-Hungary in the First World War, while Italy and Japan changed to fight in alliance with Germany in the Second. The 1914–18 war was called a world war, and indeed there was fighting outside Europe – in the Middle East, Africa and on at sea. The 1939–45 war, however, was more genuinely a world war: more of Europe saw fighting, as did north Africa and the Atlantic Ocean. But this time there was also another war over a wide expanse of another part of the globe: the Pacific War from December 1941 to August 1945.

Both wars brought tremendous casualties, but the 17 million deaths of the First World War are overshadowed by the 37.6 million (excluding the Holocaust – see page 338) of the Second. An important difference was that the proportion of civilians among those killed increased from about 15 per cent to around 35 per cent.

Clearly, the two wars were different for every country, but in the cases of Russia and Germany the differences are so great that they require comment: Hitler was initially more successful than the German High Command of the First World War, but his decision to fight on to the bitter end left his country shattered and divided. This contrasts with the German search for an armistice in autumn 1918 and underlines the significance given to it in chapter 9. As for Russia, the early disastrous defeats must have looked like history repeating itself. However, the fightback of the Second World War was in complete contrast to the sequence of events leading up to the humiliating Treaty of Brest-Litovsk of 1918.

Why did Germany do so well up to the winter of 1942–3?

The answers to this question reveal that Hitler learned the lessons of the First World War more creatively than the Allies.

 France and Britain adopted defensive strategies, relying in France's case on the Maginot Line (see page 138) and in Britain's case on the Channel and a naval blockade of Germany. Hitler, like Schlieffen, knew the dangers of a two-front war for Germany and avoided it much more successfully than the High Command in 1914. The conquest of Poland in September 1939 was carried out without the intervention of France or Britain. The Nazi–Soviet Pact kept Russia from interfering in the astounding conquest of western Europe in May–June 1940. The German invasion of the USSR in June 1941 admittedly left an undefeated Britain in the west, but Britain was not, at that time, able to inflict much damage on Germany.

Hitler did not have to face a two-front war until D-Day (June 1944), unless we count the Allied invasion of Sicily which took place in July 1943.

 German forces in western Europe in May 1940 were roughly equal in size to those of the Allies. French tanks were supposedly better than Hitler's, but Hitler had more aeroplanes. The crucial difference was that Hitler used aeroplanes, tanks (fitted with radio, unlike the French ones) and motorised infantry in rapid, coordinated thrusts: the technique called *blitzkrieg*, or lightning war.

Hitler prepared a huge army of 3 million men, 3,580 tanks and 1,830 aircraft for the invasion of Russia. Remembering the Russian defeats in 1914, the chaos which enveloped Russia for much of the interwar period and the wholesale slaughter of the upper ranks of the Red Army in the purges of 1937, it is not at all surprising that Hitler thought that 'we have only to kick the door in and the whole rotten edifice will collapse'. He understood that the huge size of the USSR made it difficult to defeat, but reasoned that if he could drive Stalin's forces out of European Russia the Communists would be forced to sue for peace. Even over the much greater distance, the German Army's *blitzkrieg* tactics were successful. Hitler's front line was 1,000 kilometres into Russia by the end of 1941.

Why was Germany defeated?

1 Hitler made some bad decisions. He had been so successful up to the end of 1942 that he believed he knew better than his generals. He often overruled their advice. There are several instances: his turning aside from an all-out drive to get to Moscow in order to capture Kiev, in late 1941; his refusal to allow von Paulus to retreat from Stalingrad, leading to the humiliating surrender of 91,000 troops and 24 generals in February 1943 – a turning-point in the war. Hitler's meddling and increasing errors of judgement undermined the morale of his generals.

2 Germany was over-extended. Like the Kaiser, Hitler was denied his need for a short war. He was obliged to come to the rescue of his ally, Mussolini, in Yugoslavia and Greece – a distraction which pushed the start of the attack on Russia dangerously late into 1941.

Once he had failed to crush Russia by the end of 1941, Hitler was committed to a war of attrition against a better-resourced enemy fighting on home territory. The extended German supply-lines, across inadequate roads in appalling winter weather, put German forces at a serious disadvantage. The demands of the Eastern Front drew resources away from North Africa so that by October 1942 Rommel had to face Montgomery at El Alamein with outnumbered forces. His defeat was another turning-point.

3 The enormous resources of the United States – in materials, money and morale – tipped the scales increasingly against the Axis powers. After Pearl Harbor (December 1941), Roosevelt could openly support the Allies: the USA provided about half of all the Allied war effort. The war cost them £84 million and they advanced another £12 million to the Allies.

4 The capacity of the USSR to resist and fight back. There are several elements to this, some of which are attributable to Stalin's regime and some of which are not:

■ The Five-Year Plans had succeeded in creating enormous industrial capacity which was turned to making armaments. Much of this was in new areas in the east, beyond the reach of the German invasion, or was moved there. By 1942 Soviet production of aeroplanes, tanks and guns was nearly double Germany's.

■ The invasion of their country united the Russian people and drove both soldiers and civilians to superhuman efforts and sacrifices. Nearly 20 million Russians died in what they call 'The Great Patriotic War'.

- Stalin panicked at first, but when he found his nerve he was able to tap into this Russian patriotism quite effectively. He even allowed a religious revival in the USSR as a source of nationalism, and his personal standing was high.

- German forces were welcomed into western USSR in 1941: Ukrainians and Byelorussians had good cause to hate Stalin. However, Hitler's vicious racism made it impossible for the German army to capitalise on these internal Russian divisions. All were, to him, 'inferior people'. They were ferociously treated and soon ready to join groups of partisans in acts of sabotage and resistance against the German invaders. As in occupied western Europe, resistance groups may not have had a direct effect, but they did tie down troops who were thus not available for front-line fighting.

The Holocaust

In March 1945 Red Army soldiers entered Auschwitz; on 4 April, US soldiers arrived at the small camp of Ohrdruf where 3,000 Jews had been murdered four days before the liberators arrived. Generals Eisenhower and Patton were with them and Lewis Weinstein, one of the US soldiers, described their reactions: 'I saw Eisenhower go to the opposite side of the road and vomit. From a distance I saw General Patton bend over, holding his head with one hand and his abdomen with the other. I suggested to General Eisenhower that cables be sent immediately to President Roosevelt, Churchill and de Gaulle, urging them to send representatives.'

There was no need: as the Allied armies moved into Germany in the last weeks of the war the full extent of the Holocaust became visible. The British saw the awful facts in their newspapers after reporters entered Belsen with British forces on 15 April 1945. It should not have been news to the world's public. Nazi persecution of the Jews in Germany before the war was well-known (see chapter 19). The 'Final Solution' began in 1941 when the expanding German Reich found itself ruling over many millions of Jews in Poland and Russia. The real figures for those killed were not known with any degree of accuracy until years later: 6 million Jews, 3 million non-Jewish Poles, 3 million Russian prisoners-of-war, a million gypsies and hundreds of thousands of homosexuals and people with disabilities.

In 1945 news of the Holocaust had two effects: firstly, the Allies were not inclined to be merciful to the Nazis and the German people; secondly, it helped to put an end to the belief that Europeans were more civilised and culturally advanced than other peoples.

'Scorched earth' tactics

Destroying everything (crops, roads, bridges, factories, farms) in the path of an enemy as they advance, usually by setting it on fire. This holds up an advance and makes the enemy's supply problems more difficult.

The devastated continent

Europe was far more devastated in 1945 than in 1918. Huge areas had been fought over, air raids had left few cities untouched, and both Germany and the USSR had used **'scorched earth' tactics** when they were retreating. Industrial production was crippled and transport systems were in ruins. The labour needed to rebuild cities and work in industry was simply not available, as millions of people tried to put their shattered lives together. The contact between mainly industrial western Europe and mainly agricultural eastern Europe was broken and there was a real danger of famine. Far from thinking about recovery, most people in Europe were struggling to keep fed, housed and warm.

The Cold War

As the Red Army moved westwards, eight states which had been independent countries before the war came under Soviet occupation: Lithuania, Latvia, Estonia, Poland, Romania, Bulgaria, Hungary and Czechoslovakia. It was clear that Stalin intended to establish pro-Soviet governments in most of the areas of eastern Europe which his armies had liberated (see Figure 20.1).

From 1870 to 1945 Europe had been at the centre of the world's events. The economic and political power generated by capitalism, and especially by industrialisation, permitted the countries of Europe to exert an influence over the lives of most of the people in the world.

In 1945 there was a real shift of emphasis. World power now lay with two 'superpowers': the USA and the USSR. Both were larger, with more people, and clearly richer, than any European country could ever be. Over the next 50 years Europe was sometimes the cockpit in which these two non-European superpowers fought out their 'Cold War'. But more often the crises occurred outside Europe: in Asia, in the Middle East, in Africa and in Central and South America.

European unity

1945 was also a dramatic turning-point in the history of the nations of western Europe. Throughout the 75 years up to 1945 dealt with in this book we have seen how, in different ways across Europe, the new forces of industry and social change clashed with old institutions and attitudes. Out of the tremendous strain produced by these processes came new ideologies and two devastating world wars.

After 1945 a new dynamic appears: European unity. For some it was a matter of security, of making Europe strong enough to resist the military power of the Soviet Union on the one hand and the economic power of the USA on the other. For others, the economic advantages of closer

339

relations between western European nations were predominant. More idealistically, there was the intention of making a further outbreak of the 'European Civil War' impossible.

We should not see these events from the suspicious point of view of successive British governments. Britain was offered the leadership of the movement to revive and unify western Europe in the late 1940s and rejected the offer: one of the most spectacular miscalculations of the postwar period. In mainland Europe from 1945 many people seriously committed themselves to greater unity – economically, militarily and politically. This commitment went beyond mundane thoughts of profit and loss. It was a matter of belief, rooted in the experience of the last 70 years, that cooperation was not only better than conflict: it was the only way to rebuild Europe.

Figure 20.1 Europe at the end of the Second World War

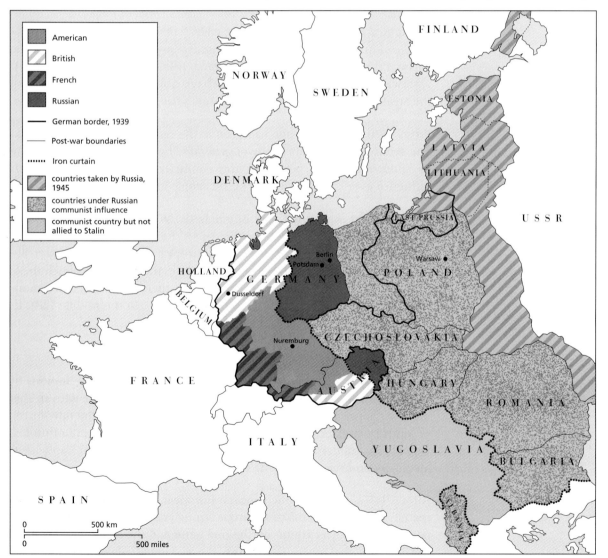

Index